OCEAN SHIPS

WITHDRAWN

BRITIS

OCEAN SHIPS

DAVID HORNSBY

LONDON

IAN ALLAN LTD

Previous page: The British Petroleum Co Ltd, *British Respect.*
British Petroleum Co Ltd

Cover: P&O Steam Navigation Co Ltd, *Royal Princess.*
Photographed by Paul Campbell, courtesy P&O Cruises Ltd

First edition published 1964
This edition published 1986

ISBN 0 7110 1502 3

Published by Ian Allan Ltd, Shepperton, Surrey;
and printed by Ian Allan Printing Ltd at their works
at Coombelands in Runnymede, England

Contents

Preface   5

Glossary   6

PART ONE
Passenger Liners   7
and Cruise Ships

PART TWO
Cargo Vessels   23
and Tankers

Addenda   259

Index   269

Preface

World shipping is continually evolving, but within many fleets the pace of change has accelerated sharply over the last few years. Despite little change in many Third World and Eastern Block fleets, less than half the vessels included in the 1982 edition remain in this new edition of *Ocean Ships*.

The excessive competition in some trades and the resulting very low cargo rates have forced many old established owners to reduce their fleets, some even to total extinction. The high cost of newbuildings and the need for specialist vessels in changing market conditions has also highlighted the trend away from direct ownership. In many fleets, the ownership 'chain' is often highly complex, involving Banks or other institutions and therefore the new fully updated fleet lists are based upon beneficial owners or managers.

The main alteration in the format of the new edition is the combining of dry cargo and tanker vessels into a single section, partly brought about by the severe contraction in many tanker fleets. The new layout allows a more balanced appraisal of the content of each fleet beneath a single heading and for the first time dry cargo deadweight tonnages are also quoted.

As with previous editions, one of the most difficult decisions has been the choice of new fleets for inclusion. Generally fleet lists are included for United Kingdom and all major Northern European owners, together with the principal national and conference service lines operating to northern Europe. Wherever possible, all vessels over 5,000 grt are listed, any major exceptions being covered by footnotes.

My grateful thanks are extended to all those friends and acquaintances who have given their time and assistance with information and photographs, but most of all to my understanding wife and family.

David Hornsby
Southampton

Glossary

The companies in each section are listed in alphabetical order under the main company name, followed by the country of origin or flag under which the majority of vessels are registered. Separately operated subsidiary fleets, but not individual owning companies, are also listed. Variants in flag or joint ownerships are generally covered by tailnotes. Funnel and hull colours are those normally used by the Companies, although these may vary when a vessel is operating on charter or a joint service.

Year	year of completion — not necessarily of launching
GRT	gross registered tonnage — volume of enclosed space — one ton equals 100cu ft
DWT	deadweight tonnes — maximum weight of cargo, fuel etc — one tonne equals 0.98 ton
LOA	length overall (metres); (- -) length between perpendiculars
Bm	overall breadth (metres)
Kts	normal service speed — one knot equals 6,080ft per hour
Eng	type of main propulsive machinery, followed by number of screws if more than one

M	diesel engine	ST	steam turbine
Me	diesel with electric drive	TE	steam turbine with electric drive
GT	gas turbine		

Type   general description of type of vessel

B	bulk carrier	LGC	liquefied gas carrier
BC	bulk/container carrier	LNG	liquified natural gas carrier
BO	bulk/oil carrier	LPG	liquified petroleum gas carrier
BV	bulk/vehicle carrier	LSC	liquid sulphur carrier
C	general cargo	O	ore carrier
CC	cellular container	OBO	ore/bulk/oil carrier
CH	chemical carrier	OS	offshore support vessel
CO	cargo/part container	OO	ore/oil carrier
CP	cargo/passenger	R	refrigerated cargo
HL	heavy-lift vessel	RO	roll-on, roll-off
HLS	heavy-lift/semi-submersible vessel	T	tanker
		TGC	tanker and LP gas carrier
LC	lighter/containers	V	vehicle carrier

Remarks: ex: previous names followed by year of change to subsequent name
pt: part of ship

Conversion table — metric to imperial

metres	1-3 feet	metres	10-33 feet	metres	100-328 feet
	2-7		20-66		150-492
	3-10		30-98		200-656
	4-13		40-131		250-820
	5-16		50-164		300-984
	6-20		60-197		350-1,148
	7-23		70-230		400-1,312
	8-26		80-262		
	9-30		90-295		

Disclaimer

The publishers, the shipping companies and the Author accept no liability for any loss or damage caused by error or inaccuracy in the information published in this edition of *Ocean Ships*.

PART ONE
Passenger Liners and Cruise Ships

Bahama Cruise Line Inc

USA

Funnel: White with orange top and stripes
Hull: White with orange upperworks

Name	Year	GRT	LOA	Bm	Kts	Eng	Former names
Veracruz 1*	1957	10,596	149	20	20	ST2	ex-Freeport 76, ex-Carnivale 75, ex-Theodor Herzl 69

* Panamanian flag
controlled by Common Bros plc

Carnival Cruise Line Inc

USA

Funnel: Red forward, blue aft, separated by white moon shape
Hull: White with red band, blue boot-topping

Carnivale*	1956	18,953	195	26	20	ST2	ex-Queen Anna Maria 75, ex-Empress of Britain 64
Festivale*	1961	26,632	232	27	23	ST2	ex-SA Vaal 77, ex-Transvaal Castle 66
Holiday*	1985	46,052	222	28	22	M2	
Mardi Gras*	1961	18,261	198	26	20	ST2	ex-Empress of Canada 72
Tropicale†	1981	22,919	206	26	21	M2	

* Panamanian flag   † Liberian flag
Celebration & *Jubilee* (45,000grt) on order

Chandris SA

Greece

Funnel: Blue with white cross, black top
Hull: White with red boot-topping

Amerikanis*	1952	12,795	176	23	19	ST2	ex-Kenya Castle 67
Britanis*	1932	18,153	192	24	18	ST2	ex-Lurline 70, ex-Matsonia 63, ex-Monterey 56
Ellinis	1932	18,564	192	24	18	ST2	ex-Lurline 63
Galileo	1963	28,084	214	29	25	ST2	ex-Galileo Galilei 84
Regina Prima*	1939	10,972	150	20	17	ST2	ex-Regina 73, ex-President Hoover 65, ex-Panama 57, ex-James Parker 46, ex-Panama 41
Romanza	1939	8,891	149	18	15	ME	ex-Aurelia 70, ex-Beaverbrae 54, ex-Huascaran 47
The Victoria*	1936	14,411	175	22	16	M2	ex-Victoria 77, ex-Dunnottar Castle 58

* Panamanian flag

China Ocean Shipping Co

China

Funnel: Yellow, red band with yellow star flanked by six wavy lines
Hull: White

Hao Long	1963	7,990	147	20	20	M2	ex-Centaur 85
Ming Hua	1962	14,424	168	20	22	M2	ex-Ancerville 73
Yao Hua	1967	10,151	152	21	21	M2	

Cie des Chargeurs Reunis

France

Nouvelle Cie de Paquebots

Funnel: White with white sea-bird on red/blue 'P'
Hull: White with red or blue boot-topping

Azur	1971	14,717	142	23	23	M2	ex-Eagle 75
Mermoz*	1957	13,804	162	20	17	M2	ex-Jean Mermoz 70
Rhapsody*	1957	24,414	196	25	19	ST2	ex-Statendam 82

* Bahamas flag

Above: Carnival Cruise Line Inc, *Tropicale.* J. Krayenbosch

Above: Chandris SA, *Romanza.* J. Krayenbosch

Below: Chandris SA, *The Victoria.* M. D. J. Lennon

Commodore Cruise Line

USA

Funnel: White with multi-coloured stripes
Hull: White with dark blue boot-topping

Name	Year	GRT	LOA	Bm	Kts	Eng	Former names
Boheme*	1968	7,056	134	21	22	M2	
Caribe I*	1953	14,533	186	24	18	M2	ex-Caribe 82, ex-Olympia 82
Venus Venturer*	1970	10,736	149	20	23	M2	ex-Scandinavian Sea 85, ex-Blenheim 82

* Panamanian flag

Costa Armatori SpA

Italy

Funnel: Yellow with narrow blue top and blue 'C'
Hull: White with blue line and blue boot-topping

Carla C	1952	19,942	183	24	22	M2	ex-Flandre 68
Costa Riviera	1962	28,137	214	29	25	ST2	ex-Guglielmo Marconi 84
Danae*	1955	10,501	162	21	19	M2	ex-Therisos Express 74, ex-Port Melbourne 72
Daphne*	1955	11,683	162	21	19	M2	ex-Akrotiri Express 74, ex-Port Sydney 72
Enrico C	1950	16,495	176	22	18	ST2	ex-Provence 65
Eugenio C	1966	30,567	217	29	27	ST2	

* Panamanian flag

CTM-Cia
Portuguesa de Transportes Maritimos

Portugal

Funnel: Orange, yellow band between two blue bands
Hull: Dark navy blue with green boot-topping

Funchal	1961	9,845	153	19	20	ST2	

Cunard Line Ltd

UK

Funnel: Red with two black rings, black top
Hull: White, light grey or charcoal grey with red boot-topping

Cunard Countess	1976	17,593	163	23	18	M2	
Cunard Princess*	1977	17,496	163	23	18	M2	ex-Cunard Conquest 76
Queen Elizabeth 2	1968	67,139	294	32	28	ST2	
Sagafjord*	1965	25,147	189	24	20	M2	
Vistafjord*	1973	24,492	191	25	20	M2	

* Bahamas flag

Cycladic Cruises

Greece

Funnel: White with blue 'K'
Hull: White with blue boot-topping

City of Mikonos	1956	4,755	112	16	15	M2	ex-San Marco 77
City of Rhodes	1966	5,276	130	17	18	M2	ex-33 Orientales 79

Peter Deilmann Reederi

FRG

Funnel: White with red 'D' outline containing insignia
Hull: White with red band

Berlin	1980	7,812	123	18	17	M2	ex-Princess Mahsuri 85, ex-Berlin 82

Above: Costa Armatori SpA, *Enrico C. M. D. J. Lennon*

Above: CTM-Cia Portuguesa de Transportes Maritimos, *Funchal. J. Krayenbosch*

Below: Cunard Line Ltd, *Sagafjord. Table Bay Underway Shipping*

VEB Deutfracht/Seereederei

GDR

Funnel: Yellow, red band bordered by narrow dark blue bands
Hull: Grey with green boot-topping

Name	Year	GRT	LOA	Bm	Kts	Eng	Former names
Volkerfreundschaft	1948	11,970	160	21	18	M2	ex-Stockholm 60
Arkona	1981	18,834	164	23	20	M2	ex-Astor 85

Epirotiki Steamship Nav Co SA

Greece

Funnel: Blue with yellow 'Byzantine' cross
Hull: Buff with blue boot-topping

Name	Year	GRT	LOA	Bm	Kts	Eng	Former names
Argonaut................................	1929	4,007	95	14	14	M2	ex-Orion, ex-Vixen 50, ex-Orion 47
Atlas......................................	1951	9,114	153	21	17	ST	ex-Ryndam 72, ex-Waterman 68, ex-Ryndam 68
Jason......................................	1965	3,719	97	16	16	M2	ex-Eros 66
Jupiter....................................	1961	6,306	127	20	16	M	ex-Alexandros 70, ex-Moledet 70
Neptune	1955	2,402	90	14	18	M	ex-Meteor 71
Orpheus	1948	4,075	114	15	15	M2	ex-Theseus 69, ex-Munster I 68, ex-Munster 68
Pegasus	1975	13,275	153	22	21	M2	ex-Sundancer 84, ex-Svea Corona 84
World Renaissance	1966	8,665	150	21	18	M2	ex-Homeric 78, ex-Renaissance 77

Soc Finanziaria Marittima (Finmare)

Italy

Funnel: White with narrow green band and red ring beneath black top
Hull: White with blue boot-topping

Name	Year	GRT	LOA	Bm	Kts	Eng
Ausonia................................	1957	11,921	159	21	21	ST2

Fearnley & Eger A/S

Norway

Funnel: White with 5-pointed yellow star above 3 narrow sloping blue stripes
Hull: White

Name	Year	GRT	LOA	Bm	Kts	Eng	Former names
North Star*............................	1966	3,095	89	14	15	M	ex-Lindmar 83, ex-Marburg 82

* Bahamas flag

Gotaas-Larsen Inc

Panama

Funnel: Blue with narrow white band beneath black top; red 'E' inside blue 5-pointed star bordered by blue ring on white flag with staff
Hull: White with blue band

Eastern Steamship Lines/Western Cruise Lines

Name	Year	GRT	LOA	Bm	Kts	Eng	Former names
Azure Seas	1955	14,673	184	24	20	ST2	ex-Calypso 80, ex-Southern Cross 73
Emerald Seas	1944	18,936	190	23	19	ST2	ex-Atlantis 72, ex-President Roosevelt 70, ex-Leilani 61, ex-Laguardia 56, ex-General W. P. Richardson 49

See also Royal Caribbean Cruise Line A/S

Hapag-Lloyd AG

FGR

Funnel: Orange with blue 'HL'
Hull: White, orange/blue band, red boot-topping

Name	Year	GRT	LOA	Bm	Kts	Eng
Europa..................................	1981	33,819	200	30	21	M2

Above: Peter Deilmann Reederei, *Berlin*. F. de Vries

Above: VEB Deutfracht/Seereederei, *Volkerfreundschaft*. M. D. J. Lennon

Below left: Epirotiki Steamship Nav Co SA, *World Renaissance*. Table Bay Underway Shipping

Below right: Hapag-Lloyd AG, *Europa*. J. Krayenbosch

Hellenic Cruises SA — 'K' Lines

Greece

Funnel: White with large blue K
Hull: White with blue band and boot-topping

Name	Year	GRT	LOA	Bm	Kts	Eng	Former names
Constellation	1962	7,952	150	20	17	M2	ex-Danaos 78, ex-Anna Nery 78
Galaxia (also Galaxy)	1957	4,858	104	16	17	M2	ex-Scottish Coast 69
Kentavros	1941	2,497	95	13	15	M2	ex-Barnegat 63
Orion	1953	5,509	127	17	18	ST2	ex-Achilieus 68

Hellenic Mediterranean

Greece

Funnel: Yellow with blue band, narrow black top
Hull: Grey witg blue band, green boot-topping

Aquarius	1972	4,591	104	14	19	M2	

Holland-America Cruises

Netherlands Antilles

Funnel: Orange with three streamlined shapes, coloured blue, white, blue
Hull: Black

Nieuw Amsterdam	1983	33,930	215	27	21	M2	
Noordam	1984	33,930	215	27	21	M2	
Rotterdam	1959	37,783	228	29	22	ST2	

Home Lines Inc

Panama

Funnel: Yellow with blue top and yellow castellated crown on blue disc
Hull: White with green boot-topping

Atlantic*	1982	19,337	205	27	23	M2	
Homeric	1986	35,000	204	29	22	M2	
Oceanic	1965	27,645	238	29	26	ST2	

* Liberian flag

Intercruise

Cyprus

Funnel: White with blue top
Hull: White with blue boot-topping

La Palma	1952	11,608	150	20	17	M2	ex-La Perla 80, ex-Delphi 77, ex-Ferdinand de Lesseps 69

Jadranska Linijsaka Plovidba (Jadrolinija)

Yugoslavia

Funnel: White with 5 pointed red star and narrow black top
Hull: White with green boot-topping

Ambasador	1958	2,637	90	13	16	M2	ex-Jedinstvo 78
Dalmacija	1964	5,634	117	17	17	M2	
Istra	1965	5,650	117	17	17	M2	

Above: Hellenic Cruises SA, *Constellation.* J. Krayenbosch

Below left: Hellenic Mediterranean, *Aquarius.* M. D. J. Lennon

Below right: Holland-America Cruises, *Noordam.* B. J. Buitendijk

Below left: Home Lines Inc, *Atlantic.* M. D. J. Lennon

Below right: Jadranska Linijsaka Plovidba, *Istra.* M. D. J. Lennon

Anders Jahre

Norway

Det. Bergenske D/S (Bergen Line)
Funnel: Yellow with white and blue houseflag
Hull: Grey with green boot-topping

Name	Year	GRT	LOA	Bm	Kts	Eng	Former names
Jupiter	1966	9,499	142	20	21	M2	also *Black Watch*
Venus	1966	9,499	142	20	21	M2	also *Black Prince*

jointly owned by Fred Olsen & Co (winter/spring)

J. Lauritzen

Denmark

Funnel: White with blue pipework
Hull: White with blue crown and wave insignia on blue band

Name	Year	GRT	LOA	Bm	Kts	Eng	Former names
Pearl of Scandinavia*	1967	12,456	153	20	22	M2	ex-Innstar 82, ex-Finnstar 81, ex-Finlandia 78

* Bahamas flag

Achille Lauro

Italy

Funnel: Blue with white star and black top
Hull: Blue with white band

Name	Year	GRT	LOA	Bm	Kts	Eng	Former names
Achille Lauro	1947	23,629	192	25	22	M2	ex-Willem Ruys 65

Mitsui-OSK Lines KK

Japan

Funnel: light red
Hull: blue

Name	Year	GRT	LOA	Bm	Kts	Eng	Former names
Nippon Maru	1962	9,745	150	20	17	M2	ex-Seven Seas 77, ex-Rosa da Fonseca 75
Shin Sakura Maru	1972	16,431	176	25	20	M	

Norwegian Caribbean Lines

Norway

Funnel: White separated by light blue band from dark blue front edge and top
Hull: White with light blue stripe and yellow 'sun' emblem, or dark blue

Name	Year	GRT	LOA	Bm	Kts	Eng	Former names
Norway	1961	70,202	316	34	17	ST2	ex-France 79
Skyward	1969	16,254	160	23	21	M2	
Southward	1971	16,607	163	23	21	M2	
Starward	1968	12,949	160	23	21	M2	
Sunward II	1971	14,110	148	22	21	M2	ex-Cunard Adventurer 77

Royal Viking Line

Funnel: White with red 'sea eagle' device, black top
Hull: White with blue band and green boot-topping

Name	Year	GRT	LOA	Bm	Kts	Eng	Former names
Royal Viking Sea	1973	28,018	205	25	18	M2	
Royal Viking Sky	1972	28,078	205	25	18	M2	
Royal Viking Star	1972	28,221	205	25	18	M2	

Ocean Cruise Lines

Greece

Funnel: Yellow with white loop device, white band beneath narrow blue top
Hull: White with blue boot-topping

Name	Year	GRT	LOA	Bm	Kts	Eng	Former names
Ocean Islander*	1956	4,563	112	16	15	M2	ex-City of Andros 84, ex-San Giorgio 76
Ocean Princess*	1967	12,218	149	21	16	M2	ex-Italia 83

* Panamanian flag

Above: Norwegian Caribbean/Royal Viking Line, *Royal Viking Sky. J. M. Kakebeeke*

Below: Ocean Cruise Lines, *Ocean Princess. M. D. J. Lennon*

17

Fred Olsen & Co
Norway

Funnel: Yellow with white and blue houseflag
Hull: Grey with green boot-topping

Name	Year	GRT	LOA	Bm	Kts	Eng	Former names
Black Prince*	1966	9,499	142	20	21	M2	also *Venus*
Black Watch*	1966	9,499	142	20	21	M2	also *Jupiter*
Braemar	1980	13,878	145	26	17	M2	ex-*Viking Song* 85

* jointly owned by Anders Jahre (summer) q.v.

P&O Steam Nav Co Ltd
UK

Funnel: Yellow (Canberra and Oriana); white funnel with blue 'Princess' insignia with flowing hair (Princesses); black funnel with two white bands (Uganda)
Hull: White

Name	Year	GRT	LOA	Bm	Kts	Eng	Former names
Canberra	1961	44,807	249	31	27	TE2	
Island Princess	1972	19,907	169	25	21	M2	ex-Island Venture 72
Oriana	1960	41,920	245	30	27	ST2	
Pacific Princess	1970	20,636	169	25	21	M2	ex-Sea Venture 75
Royal Princess	1984	44,348	231	29	22	M2	
Sea Princess	1966	27,670	210	27	21	M2	ex-Kungsholm 78
Sun Princess	1972	17,370	163	25	25	M2	ex-Spirit of London 74
Uganda	1952	16,907	165	22	16	ST2	

Polish Ocean Lines
Poland

Funnel: Yellow with red band, shield with white letters 'PLO' and trident
Hull: Black with green boot-topping

Name	Year	GRT	LOA	Bm	Kts	Eng	Former names
Stefan Batory	1952	15,044	153	21	16	ST	ex-Maasdam 68

Regency Cruises
Greece

Funnel: White with blue forward panel
Hull: White

Name	Year	GRT	LOA	Bm	Kts	Eng	Former names
Regent Sea*	1957	17,234	195	25	18	M2	ex-Samatha 84, ex-Navarino 83, ex-Gripsholm 75

*Panamanian flag

Royal Caribbean Cruise Line A/S
Norway

Funnel: White with blue crown over blue anchor
Hull: White with blue band

Name	Year	GRT	LOA	Bm	Kts	Eng	Former names
Nordic Prince	1971	23,200	194	24	20	M2	
Song of America	1982	37,584	215	32	20	M2	
Song of Norway	1970	23,005	194	24	20	M2	
Sun Viking	1972	18,559	172	24	21	M2	

jointly owned by Anders Wilhelmsen & Co, I. M. Skaugen & Co and Gotaas-Larsen Inc

Royal Cruise Line
Greece

Funnel: White, yellow crown with blue outline, two blue lines below
Hull: White

Name	Year	GRT	LOA	Bm	Kts	Eng	Former names
Golden Odyssey	1974	6,757	130	19	21	M	
Royal Odyssey	1964	17,884	181	25	20	ST2	ex-Doric 81, ex-Hanseatic 73, ex-Shalom 67

Above left: P & O Steam Nav Co Ltd, *Royal Princess. M. D. J. Lennon*   *Above right*: P & O Steam Nav Co Ltd, *Sea Princess. J. Krayenbosch*

Above: P & O Steam Nav Co Ltd, *Sun Princess. M. D. J. Lennon*

Below: Royal Cruise Line, *Royal Odyssey. J. Krayenbosch*

Sea Goddess Cruises Ltd

Norway

Funnel: White with purple emblem
Hull: White with blue boot-topping

Name	Year	GRT	LOA	Bm	Kts	Eng	Former names
Sea Goddess I	1984	4,253	105	15	17	M2	
Sea Goddess II	1985	4,260	105	15	17	M2	

'Sitmar'

Liberia

Soc Italiana Trasporti Marittimi SpA

Funnel: Yellow with blue 'V'
Hull: White

Fairsea	1956	16,627	185	24	20	ST2	ex-Fairland 71, ex-Carinthia 68
Fairsky	1984	22,120	217	28	20	ST2	
Fairstar	1957	21,619	186	24	20	ST2	ex-Oxfordshire 64
Fairwind	1957	16,667	185	24	20	ST2	ex-Sylvania 68

St Helena Shipping Ltd

UK

Funnel: Dark green with yellow crest
Hull: Dark green

St Helena	1963	3,150	100	15	14	M	ex-Northland Prince 77

Sun Line

Greece

Funnel: White, blue top with red band
Hull: Blue with red boot-topping

Stella Maris II	1960	2,682	88	14	18	M2	ex-Bremerhaven 65
Stella Oceanis	1965	3,963	105	17	17	M2	ex-Aphrodite 66
Stella Solaris	1953	10,595	166	22	20	ST2	ex-Stella V 70, ex-Cambodge 70

Sundance Cruises Corp

USA

Funnel: White with two diagonal flashes
Hull: White

Stardancer*	1982	26,747	185	27	18	M2	ex-Scandinavia 85

* Bahamas flag

C.Y. Tung Group

Hong Kong (UK)

Funnel: Yellow with red and gold flower
Hull: White or grey

Bermuda Star*	1958	14,208	188	27	21	ST2	ex-Veendam 84, ex-Monarch Star 78, ex-Veendam 76, ex-Brazil 75, ex-Veendam 74, ex-Argentine 72
Liberte*	1958	13,680	188	27	21	ST2	ex-Island Sun 85, ex-Volendam 84, ex-Monarch Sun 78, ex-Volendam 75, ex-Brasil 72
Universe†	1953	13,950	172	23	20	ST	ex-Universe Campus 76, ex-Atlantic 71, ex-Badger Mariner 57

* Panamanian flag
† Liberian flag

Above: St Helena Shipping Ltd, *St Helena. W. D. Harris*

Above left: Sun Line, *Stella Oceanis. M. D. J. Lennon*

Above right: USSR, *Estonia. M. D. J. Lennon*

Below: USSR, *Leonid Brezhnev. J. Krayenbosch*

American Hawaii Cruises Inc/USA

Funnel: White with six-petal flower, narrow blue top, narrow blue and green bands at base
Hull: White

Name	Year	GRT	LOA	Bm	Kts	Eng	Former names
Constitution	1951	20,269	208	27	22	ST2	ex-Oceanic Constitution 82, ex-Constitution 74
Independence	1950	20,220	208	27	22	ST2	ex-Oceanic Independence 82, ex-Independence 74

Ulysses SA   Greece

Funnel: White, yellow 'dolphin', blue diagonal band
Hull: White

Name	Year	GRT	LOA	Bm	Kts	Eng	Former names
Dolphin IV*	1956	8,854	153	20	19	ST2	ex-Ithaca 78, ex-Amelia de Mello 72, ex-Zion 66
Royale*	1958	15, 483	185	24	22	ST2	ex-Frederico 84

* Panamanian flag

USSR   USSR

Funnel: White or black with yellow hammer and sickle on red band
Hull: White or black

Name	Year	GRT	LOA	Bm	Kts	Eng	Former names
Aleksandr Pushkin	1965	20,502	176	24	20	M2	
Armeniya	1963	5,169	122	16	18	M2	
Ayvazoskiy	1977	7,127	121	18	19	M2	
Azerbaiydzhan	1975	13,251	157	22	21	M2	
Baikal	1962	5,230	122	16	18	M2	
Baltika	1940	7,494	136	18	16	TE2	ex-Vyacheslav Molotov 57
Bashkiria	1964	5,261	122	16	18	M2	
Belorussiya	1975	13,251	157	22	21	M2	
Dmitriy Shostakovich	1980	9,878	134	21	19	M2	
Estonia	1960	5,035	122	16	18	M2	
Fedor Shalyapin	1955	21,406	185	24	20	ST2	ex-Franconia 73, ex-Ivernia 62
Feliks Dzerjinsky	1958	5,071	122	16	18	M2	
Grigory Ordzhonikidze	1959	4,871	122	16	18	M2	
Gruziya	1975	13,251	157	22	21	M2	
Ivan Franko	1964	20,064	176	24	20	M2	
Kazakhstan	1976	13,251	157	22	21	M2	
Khabarovsk	1962	5,235	122	16	18	M2	
Latvia	1960	5,035	122	16	18	M2	
Leonid Brezhnev	1976	13,251	157	22	21	M2	ex-Kareliya 82
Leonid Sobinov	1954	21,370	185	24	20	ST2	ex-Carmania 73, ex-Saxonia 62
Lev Tolstoy	1981	9,878	134	21	19	M2	
Litva	1960	5,035	122	16	18	M2	
Maksim Gorkiy	1969	24,981	195	27	23	ST2	ex-Hanseatic 74, ex-Hamburg 73
Mikhail Kalinin	1958	5,243	122	16	18	M2	
Mikhail Lermontov	1972	20,352	176	24	20	M2	
Mikhail Suslov	1982	9,885	134	21	19	M2	ex-Vasiliv Solovyev Sedov 82
Odessa	1974	13,758	136	22	19	M2	ex-Copenhagen 75
Priamurye	1960	4,871	122	16	18	M2	
Shota Rustaveli	1968	20,499	176	24	20	M2	
Taras Shevchenko	1965	20,027	176	24	20	M2	
Turkmeniya	1961	5,127	122	16	18	M2	
Ukraina	1938	6,406	132	17	18	M2	ex-Basarabia 48

several vessels operate mainly as ferries

Vacation Line BV   Netherlands

Funnel: White with two blue rings and large arrow on deep white band.
Hull: Blue with red boot-topping

Name	Year	GRT	LOA	Bm	Kts	Eng	Former names
Vacationer	1971	2,446	77	13	12	M	ex-Nassau 82, ex-Nassau 1 80, ex-Nassau 78, ex-Kieler Forde 72, ex-Craigavon 72, ex-Kieler Forde 71

PART TWO

Cargo Vessels and Tankers

Aegis Shipping Co Ltd

Greece

Funnel: Yellow with red 'a' on broad white band bordered by narrow blue bands
Hull: Black with green boot-topping

Name	Year	GRT	DWT	LOA	Bm	Kts	Eng	Type	Former names
Aegis Athenic	1976	12,498	20,669	159	23	16	M	C	
Aegis Baltic†	1977	12,498	21,050	159	23	16	M	C	
Aegis Bravery†	1971	15,205	27,117	183	22	15	M	B	
Aegis Harvest	1972	11,225	19,017	147	23	15	M	C	
Aegis Ionic	1976	12,498	20,900	159	23	16	M	C	
Aegis Logic	1975	12,498	20,950	159	23	16	M	C	
Aegis Progress†	1971	15,204	24,417	183	22	14	M	B	
Aegis Stoic	1972	11,208	18,994	147	23	15	M	C	ex-Faith Euskalduna 72
Aegis Topic†	1974	12,498	20,950	159	23	16	M	C	
Nicholas G. Papalios	1975	29,004	53,351	207	29	15	M	B	
Nyala	1962	12,392	20,527	170	22	15	M	T	ex-Anatoli 81, ex-Lucigen 75
Sable	1957	13,458	21,672	180	23	14	M	T	ex-Cherry Bay 79, ex-Hurulu 78, ex-Johs Stove 67

†Panamanian flag

Ahlers NV

Belgium

Funnel: Yellow
Hull: Black or white with green boot-topping

Name	Year	GRT	DWT	LOA	Bm	Kts	Eng	Type	Former names
E. R. Brugge*	1979	13,384	19,775	164	23	18	M	CO	
Nedlloyd Brussel*	1979	13,251	19,863	164	23	16	M	CO	ex-E. R. Brussel 85, ex-Hodeidah Crown 84, ex-Hapag Lloyd Kiel 84, ex-E. R. Brussel 83, ex-Cast Walrus 82, ex-CP Hunter 81, ex-E. R. Brussel 80
Isla Payana†	1980	7,095	9,736	151	22	21	M	R	ex-Potomac 85
Isla Pongal†	1979	7,038	9,736	151	22	21	M	R	ex-Pocantico 85

* operated by Ernst Russ q.v.
† jointly owned with NV CMB SA q.v.

Christian F. Ahrenkiel

FRG

Funnel: Buff or buff with houseflag on blue band
Hull: Black, green or grey with red boot-topping

Name	Year	GRT	DWT	LOA	Bm	Kts	Eng	Type	Former names
Adriano	1975	28,275	50,550	216	28	15	M	BC	
Aquitania	1985	16,559	19,400	184	25	19	M	CO	ex-Euro Sun 85
Cala Atlantica*	1973	8,413	12,628	144	22	18	M	CO	ex-Rienzi 84, ex-Aqaba Crown 82, ex-Rienzi 81, ex-Bavaria Singapore 80, ex-Columbus Capricorn 79, ex-Rienzi 73
CGM Languedoc	1982	18,575	25,160	169	25	16	M	BC	ex-Campania 85, ex-City of Liverpool 84, ex-Campania 82
Cala Mediterranea*	1974	8,412	12,628	144	22	18	M	CO	ex-Tristan 84, ex-Hodeidah Crown 83, ex-Tristan 81, ex-Columbus Caribic 79, ex-Tristan 74
Candia	1984	18,756	24,140	169	26	16	M	BC	
Castor	1982	18,587	25,550	169	26	16	M	BC	
City of Liverpool	1981	18,576	25,150	169	25	16	M	BC	ex-Barrister 85, ex-Carman 81
Conscience	1983	19,005	25,150	169	25	16	M	BC	
Cranach	1983	18,850	25,150	169	26	16	M	BC	
Hanse*	1975	28,270	50,550	216	28	15	M	B	ex-Hans Sachs 82

Above: Aegis Shipping Co Ltd, *Aegis Bravery. M. D. J. Lennon*

Above: Ahlers NV, *Potomac* (now renamed *Isla Payana*). *Table Bay Underway Shipping*

Below: Christian F. Ahrenkiel, *City of Liverpool. J. Krayenbosch*

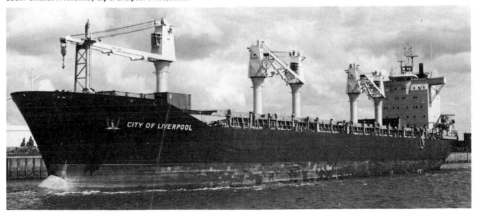

Name	Year	GRT	DWT	LOA	Bm	Kts	Eng	Type	Former names
Lanka Abhaya	1984	16,559	19,400	166	27	19	M	CC	ex-Andalusia 85
Lanka Amila	1977	10,991	13,880	145	22	19	M	CC	ex-Lanka Abhaya 83,
									ex-Usambara 82, ex-Gulf Lancer 79,
									ex-Usambara 77, ex-Eschenbach 77
Lanka Amitha	1977	10,991	13,879	145	22	19	M	CC	ex-Lanka Athula 83, ex-Urundi 81,
									ex-Gulf Ranger 78, ex-Urundi 77,
									ex-Brabant 77
Meistersinger	1973	28,260	50,549	216	28	15	M	BC	
Norasia Caria	1985	18,756	24,000	169	26	16	M	BC	ex-Caria 85
Norasia Carthago	1984	18,756	24,140	169	26	16	M	BC	ex-Carthago 84
Normannia†	1980	16,842	21,180	165	26	18	M	CO	ex-Mentor 85, ex-City of London 83,
									ex-Mentor 81
Parnassos*	1974	28,247	50,550	216	28	15	M	BC	ex-Tannhauser 82, ex-Parnassos 79,
									ex-Tannhauser 75
Rhenania	1981	80,946	89,654	287	42	20	ST	LNG	
South County‡	1976	6,096	9,115	125	19	14	M	C	ex-Roebuck 82
South Faith‡	1977	6,096	9,119	125	19	14	M	C	ex-Ravenswood 82

* Panamanian flag   ‡ Liberian flag
† Cypriot flag

Navi-Fonds Seeschiff GmbH & Co

Name	Year	GRT	DWT	LOA	Bm	Kts	Eng	Type	Former names
Fuerte Ventura	1972	74,563	139,840	282	43	15	M	B	ex-Stadt Bremen 79
TFL Franklin	1979	15,827	18,946	177	27	22	M	CC	ex-Seatrain Bennington 80

Intermare KG Kuhlschiff GmbH

Name	Year	GRT	DWT	LOA	Bm	Kts	Eng	Type	Former names
Alaska	1969	6,703	7,519	141	18	22	M	R	ex-Alaska 1 85, ex-Alaska 79,
									ex-Alaskacore 75, ex-Slevik 69
Anona*	1970	8,191	9,876	148	20	19	M	R	ex-Anonacore 74
Antarctic*	1970	6,702	7,823	141	18	22	M	R	ex-Antarcticore 75
Nectarine	1970	8,190	10,252	148	20	19	M	R	ex-Nectarinecore 75
Satsuma*	1970	8,190	9,725	148	20	19	M	R	ex-Satsumacore 75

* Panamanian flag

American President Lines Ltd   USA

Funnel: Dark blue with white eagle and stars on red band
Hull: Grey with dark grey boot-topping or black with red boot-topping

Name	Year	GRT	DWT	LOA	Bm	Kts	Eng	Type	Former names
President Cleveland	1969	15,949	22,208	184	25	21	ST	CO	ex-American Mail 78
President Eisenhower	1980	35,553	47,841	260	32	23	M	CC	ex-Neptune Jade 84
President F. D. Roosevelt	1980	35,553	47,841	260	32	23	M	CC	ex-Neptune Garnet 84
President Fillmore	1968	17,801	17,477	202	25	23	ST	CC	
President Grant	1971	26,989	37,343	250	31	22	ST	CC	ex-Golden Bear 79
President Hoover	1971	26,456	38,796	250	31	22	ST	CC	ex-Thomas E. Cuffe 79
President Jackson	1968	15,949	22,208	184	25	21	ST	CO	ex-Indian Mail 78
President Jefferson	1973	21,467	23,520	204	27	23	ST	CC	
President Johnson	1974	21,475	23,520	204	27	24	ST	CC	
President Kennedy	1964	16,542	19,286	204	23	20	ST	CC	ex-Oregon Mail 75
President Lincoln	1982	40,627	30,825	262	32	25	M	CC	
President Madison	1973	21,467	23,520	204	27	23	ST	CC	
President McKinley	1968	17,802	17,477	202	25	23	ST	CC	
President Monroe	1983	40,627	30,825	262	32	25	M	CC	
President Pierce	1973	21,475	23,520	204	27	23	ST	CC	
President Taft	1967	17,803	17,477	202	25	23	ST	CC	
President Taylor	1968	15,949	22,208	184	25	21	ST	CO	ex-Korean Mail 78
President Truman	1962	16,518	19,019	204	23	20	ST	CC	ex-Japan Mail 75
President Tyler	1972	26,990	38,796	250	31	22	ST	CC	ex-Japan Bear 79

Above: Christian F. Ahrenkiel, *Lanka Amila. F R Sherlock*

Below: American President Lines, *President Johnson. J. Krayenbosch*

Name	Year	GRT	DWT	LOA	Bm	Kts	Eng	Type	Former names
President Van Buren..............	1967	17,803	17,477	202	25	23	ST	CC	
President Washington	1982	40,627	30,825	262	32	25	M	CC	
President Wilson....................	1969	15,949	22,208	184	25	21	ST	CO	ex-Hong Hong Mail 78

Anangel Shipping Enterprises SA — Greece

Funnel: White with green 'trefilli' between two narrow red bands, narrow black top
Hull: Grey with red boot-topping

Name	Year	GRT	DWT	LOA	Bm	Kts	Eng	Type	Former names
Afovos....................................	1968	35,477	66,834	224	32	15	M	B	
Agapi	1969	10,006	15,151	142	20	14	M	C	
Alpha Challenge	1984	10,511	15,465	146	21	14	M	C	
Alpha Faith	1984	22,215	32,900	188	28	14	M	B	
Alpha Jupiter	1985	14,400	22,700	164	23	15	M	B	
Amilla	1972	13,631	22,289	164	23	15	M	B	
Anangel Apollo	1979	10,996	17,199	146	21	14	M	C	ex-Sunarawak 84, ex-Anangel Apollo 79
Anangel Ares	1980	10,996	17,154	146	21	14	M	C	ex-Al Ahad 80
Anangel Argonaut..................	1981	32,822	65,668	223	32	14	M	B	ex-Thorsdrake 82
Anagel Atlas	1984	10,511	17,000	146	21	15	M	C	
Anangel Champion	1971	9,229	15,190	141	21	14	M	C	ex-Tortugas 81, ex-Cape Rion 81, ex-Erawan 79
Anangel Diligence	1971	9,049	15,243	138	21	14	M	B	ex-Shinto Maru 76
Anangel Endeavour..............	1978	13,889	23,130	164	23	15	M	B	
Anangel Fidelity....................	1979	13,889	22,000	164	23	15	M	B	
Anangel Fortune	1974	13,633	22,670	164	23	15	M	B	
Anangel Glory	1974	13,633	22,670	164	23	15	M	B	
Anangel Happiness................	1973	13,631	22,629	164	23	15	M	B	
Anangel Harmony	1968	12,348	20,850	162	23	14	M	C	ex-Normannia 81
Anangel Honour....................	1976	13,633	22,600	164	23	15	M	B	
Anangel Hope	1974	13,633	22,670	164	23	15	M	B	
Anangel Horizon	1977	15,822	27,090	177	23	15	M	B	ex-Span Terza 82
Anangel Leader	1985	14,400	22,700	164	23	15	M	B	
Anangel Liberty	1976	13,633	22,668	164	23	15	M	B	
Anangel Luck	1968	9,118	15,623	147	21	15	M	B	ex-Nego Emperor 75, ex-Essence 73
Anangel Might	1978	13,889	23,130	164	23	15	M	B	
Anangel Peace	1974	13,631	22,631	164	23	15	M	B	
Anangel Prosperity	1976	13,633	22,314	164	23	15	M	B	
Anangel Sky........................	1979	10,933	17,199	146	21	14	M	C	ex-Suncaribe 82, ex-Anangel Sky 79
Anangel Spirit	1978	13,889	22,109	164	23	16	M	B	
Anangel Sun........................	1981	35,522	65,738	225	32	14	M	B	ex-Voreda 83
Anangel Triumph	1976	13,633	22,311	164	23	15	M	B	
Anangel Victory	1979	10,996	17,188	146	21	14	M	C	ex-Sunguajira 84, ex-Anangel Victory 79, ex-Anangel Sky 79
Anangel Wisdom	1974	13,347	22,353	164	23	15	M	B	
Anna I Angelicoussi	1971	115,925	227,492	330	49	16	ST	T	ex-Santa Rosalia 80
Annoula	1971	9,826	15,177	142	20	15	M	C	
Areti	1973	13,631	22,626	164	23	15	M	B	
Common Venture..................	1971	15,589	26,102	179	23	17	M	C	ex-Wealth Venture 74, ex-Kurushima Maru 72
Efthitis..................................	1973	10,006	15,188	143	20	13	M	C	
Elpis	1971	9,885	15,177	142	20	15	M	C	
Epimelia	1970	10,006	15,177	142	20	13	M	C	
Evimeria	1973	13,631	22,630	164	23	15	M	B	
Frangiscos C.K.	1984	22,215	37,170	188	28	14	M	B	
Fronisis................................	1971	9,882	15,139	142	20	14	M	C	
Maria Angelicoussi................	1978	10,994	16,934	143	21	15	M	B	ex-Sunmaria 84, ex-Maria Angelicoussi 79
Maria I.A.	1984	22,215	37,170	188	28	14	M	B	
Pelleas	1969	9,877	15,170	142	20	14	M	C	

Above: Anangel Shipping Enterprises SA, *Agapi. J. M. Kakebeeke*

Below: Anangel Shipping Enterprises SA, *Anangel Champion. J. M. Kakebeeke*

Name	Year	GRT	DWT	LOA	Bm	Kts	Eng	Type	Former names
Pistis	1973	13,630	22,627	164	23	15	M	B	
Unity	1971	9,508	15,141	142	20	15	M	C	

Anglo Nordic Shipping Ltd   UK

Funnel: Black with black 'AN' on broad white band with red and blue band
Hull: Black with red boot-topping

Chemical Explorer	1972	17,980	29,081	171	25	15	M	T	
Chemical Venturer	1972	17,980	29,081	171	25	15	M	T	
Nordic Louisiana	1964	18,589	26,930	189	26	16	M	LSC	ex-Naess Louisiana 73

managed by Denholm Ship Management Ltd
see also British Petroleum Co Ltd

Various Companies/Liberia

Armand Hammer*	1967	32,759	75,416	232	36	15	M	T	ex-Margaret C. Mosher 68
Eastern Enterprise†	1978	55,465	81,131	225	44	15	M	T	ex-Nordic Spirit 81
Elgin	1981	86,208	194,690	300	50	14	M	B	ex-Lake Droville 81

* managed for subsidiary of Occidental Petroleum Corp
† British flag
managed by Anglo Nordic Bulkships (Management) Ltd

Arab Maritime Petroleum Transport Co (AMPTC)

Al Berry (S)	1979	48,920	61,803	222	37	18	M2	LPG	
Al Bida (K)	1979	48,920	61,401	228	37	19	M2	LPG	
Bubiyan (K)	1975	78,655	140,763	267	44	16	M	T	ex-Thordis 75
Halul (Q)	1975	72,370	137,676	266	44	15	M	T	ex-North Monarch 75
Umm Shaif (U)	1976	65,628	137,684	266	44	15	M	T	ex-Vincenzia 76

jointly owned by Organisation of Arab Petroleum Exporting Countries (OAPEC)
(S) Saudi Arabia, (K) Kuwait, (Q) Qatar, (U) United Arab Emirates

Associated Container Transportation (Australia) Ltd   UK

Funnel: White, narrow blue top and ACT insignia in blue
Hull: Grey with red boot-topping

ACT 1	1969	24,821	28,306	217	29	22	ST	CC	
ACT 2	1969	24,821	28,308	217	29	22	ST	CC	ex-Los Angeles 84, ex-ACT 2 84
ACT 3	1971	24,216	27,953	217	29	22	ST	CC	
ACT 4	1971	24,216	27,978	217	29	22	ST	CC	
ACT 5	1972	24,212	27,978	217	29	22	ST	CC	
ACT 6	1972	25,162	28,104	217	29	22	ST	CC	
ACT 7	1977	43,992	39,712	249	32	24	M2	CC	
Dilkara	1971	13,151	20,651	199	29	21	M	RO	

a consortium formed by Blue Star Line, Ellerman Line and Port Line (Cunard) q.v.

Atlantic Container Line

Funnel: White with black top, blue 'ACL' over wavy line.
Hull: Black with ACL insignia in white

Atlantic Cartier†	1985	25,362	35,250	249	32	18	M	RO	
Atlantic Causeway*	1969	14,946	18,146	212	28	23	ST2	RO	

Above: Anglo Nordic Shipping Ltd, *Eastern Enterprise. J. Y. Freeman*

Below: Associated Container Transportation (Australia) Ltd, *ACT 7. J. Krayenbosch*

Name	Year	GRT	DWT	LOA	Bm	Kts	Eng	Type	Former names
Atlantic Companion‡	1984	25,363	36,500	249	32	18	M	RO	
Atlantic Compass‡	1984	25,348	36,500	249	32	18	M	RO	
Atlantic Concert**	1984	25,435	36,500	249	32	18	M	RO	
Atlantic Conveyor*	1985	31,850	36,000	249	32	18	M	RO	
Atlantic Saga‡	1967	14,950	22,020	223	30	21	M	RO	
Atlantic Service†	1967	15,107	18,441	223	30	21	M	RO	ex-Atlantic Span 84
Atlantic Song**	1967	14,871	20,285	223	30	20	M	RO	
Atlantic Star*	1967	14,387	20,346	223	30	21	M	RO	

* owned by Cunard Steam-Ship Co plc, British flag
† owned by Cie Generale Maritime, French flag
‡ owned by Rederi A/B Transatlantic, Swedish flag
** owned by Wallenius Rederiena, Swedish flag

Australian National Line

Australia

Funnel: Green with narrow white ring on gold band
Hull: Black with red boot-topping

Name	Year	GRT	DWT	LOA	Bm	Kts	Eng	Type	Former names
Allunga†	1971	13,217	20,601	199	29	20	M	RO	
Anro Australia	1977	16,353	22,195	213	28	16	M	RO	
Australian Emblem	1975	21,731	23,467	222	30	22	M	RO	
Australian Enterprise	1969	11,347	18,575	210	25	19	M	RO	
Australian Escort	1975	21,708	23,617	222	30	22	M	RO	ex-James Cook 76
Australian Explorer	1970	11,353	18,425	210	25	19	M	RO	ex-Matthew Flinders 75
Australian Exporter	1972	23,486	27,978	217	29	19	ST	CC	
Australian Progress	1977	74,513	139,400	283	43	15	M	B	
Australian Prospector	1976	74,513	139,346	282	43	15	M	B	
Australian Purpose	1977	64,920	122,750	268	39	15	M	B	
Australian Venture	1977	43,878	39,450	249	32	23	M2	CC	

also large Australian coastal vessels
† owned by PAD Shipping Australia Pte Ltd (jointly ANL (25%), Transatlantic Rederi A/B (50%) and Elder Smith & Co)

Bangladesh Shipping Corp

Bangladesh

Funnel: Light blue, red disc with white 'B', narrow black top
Hull: Black with red boot-topping

Name	Year	GRT	DWT	LOA	Bm	Kts	Eng	Type	Former names
Banglar Asha	1968	8,275	14,531	145	19	16	M	C	ex-Mosor 73, ex-Garciani 70
Banglar Baani	1976	9,345	15,088	141	21	15	M	C	ex-Industria 78
Banglar Gourab	1983	9,858	13,900	145	20	16	M	C	
Banglar Kakoli	1979	12,572	17,234	155	22	15	M	C	
Banglar Kallol	1980	12,573	17,223	155	22	15	M	C	
Banglar Kiron	1976	9,268	13,823	155	20	18	M	C	ex-Solidarity 85, ex-Baynunah 79, ex-Ad Dhafra 76
Banglar Mamata	1980	12,193	15,877	154	22	16	M	C	
Banglar Maya	1980	12,193	15,240	154	22	16	M	C	
Banglar Mita	1966	10,621	13,391	156	21	19	M	C	ex-Hokkaido 77
Banglar Moni	1983	8,687	12,680	150	21	17	M	CO	ex-Antje 83
Banglar Progoti	1970	7,077	9,189	131	19	17	M	C	ex-Transamerica 74
Banglar Robi	1981	8,719	12,720	150	21	17	M	C	ex-Merkur Island 82, ex-Hoegh Apapa 82, ex-Merkur Island 82
Banglar Sampad	1971	9,087	12,883	154	20	17	M	C	ex-Vishva Darshan 73
Banglar Swapna	1971	7,077	9,189	131	19	17	M	C	ex-Transcanada 73
Banglar Tarani	1962	6,706	10,435	133	18	14	M	C	ex-Gautatyr 73
Banglar Upohar	1965	8,304	14,784	146	19	16	M	C	ex-Monte Sollube 73

Above: Atlantic Container Line, *Atlantic Companion. F. R. Sherlock*

Below: Bangladesh Shipping Corp, *Banglar Robi. J. K. Byass*

Bank Line Limited

Andrew Weir & Co Ltd

Funnel: Buff with black top
Hull: Black with red boot-topping

Name	Year	GRT	DWT	LOA	Bm	Kts	Eng	Type	Former names
Clydebank	1974	11,405	15,460	162	23	18	M	C	
Crestbank	1978	12,238	18,530	161	23	16	M	C	
Dacebank	1979	12,214	18,438	162	23	16	M	C	
Forthbank	1973	11,405	15,216	162	23	18	M	C	
Ivybank	1974	11,405	15,216	161	23	18	M	C	
Meadowbank	1973	11,405	15,461	161	23	18	M	C	
Pikebank	1979	12,214	18,436	162	23	16	M	C	
Roachbank	1979	12,214	18,436	162	23	16	M	C	
Tenchbank	1979	12,214	18,500	162	23	16	M	C	
Toana Papua	1974	11,405	15,216	161	23	18	M	C	ex-Moraybank 84
Troutbank	1979	12,214	18,501	162	23	16	M	C	
Willowbank	1980	18,236	16,511	171	27	19	M	CC	

The Ben Line Steamers Ltd

UK

Wm Thomson & Co

Funnel: Yellow
Hull: Grey with green boot-topping

Name	Year	GRT	DWT	LOA	Bm	Kts	Eng	Type	Former names
Benalder	1972	58,283	49,593	283	32	22	M2	CC	
Benavon	1973	58,283	49,593	283	32	22	M2	CC	
Bencruachan	1983	78,532	150,661	274	43	14	M	B	
Benhope	1978	39,087	72,100	228	32	15	M	B	
Benvalla	1972	7,112	8,319	120	21	14	M	CC	
Celtic Link	1976	84,555	155,612	280	54	15	M	T	ex-Grey Warrior 81
City of Edinburgh*	1973	58,283	48,810	290	32	22	M2	CC	
Grey Fighter	1974	67,202	125,882	261	41	15	M	T	
Grey Hunter	1974	67,202	123,964	261	41	15	M	T	

* jointly owned by Ellerman Lines Ltd

A/S Berg & Bjorge

Norway

Funnel: Black with black 'B' silhouette on white disc
Hull: Black

Name	Year	GRT	DWT	LOA	Bm	Kts	Eng	Type	Former names
Kollbjorg	1982	31,754	54,500	207	32	15	M	BO	

Sig Bergesen dy & Co

Norway

Funnel: White with black top having diagonal light green stripe and houseflag
Hull: Light green with blue boot/topping

Name	Year	GRT	DWT	LOA	Bm	Kts	Eng	Type	Former names
Berge Adria	1972	117,409	227,557	314	50	16	M2	OO	
Berge Arrow	1978	42,701	48,821	229	32	17	M	LPG	ex-Northern Arrow 84
Berge Big	1975	140,680	285,400	348	52	15	ST	T	ex-Cyprian 82
Berge Bragd	1971	137,895	280,476	343	52	15	M	T	ex-Berge Queen 83
Berge Brioni	1973	117,409	227,558	314	50	16	M2	OO	
Berge Charlotte	1984	40,388	65,000	249	32	16	M	B	
Berge Chief	1976	140,588	289,979	345	52	15	ST	T	ex-Berge Beaumant 82, ex-Beaumont 81
Berge Duke	1973	138,009	284,002	343	52	15	M	T	
Berge Eagle	1978	42,701	48,986	229	32	17	M	LPG	ex-Northern Eagle 1 84

Above: Bank Line Ltd, *Forthbank. J. K. Byass*

Above: The Ben Line Steamers Ltd, *Benhope. J. Krayenbosch*

Below: A/S Berg & Bjorge, *Kollbjorg. J. M. Kakebeeke*

Name	Year	GRT	DWT	LOA	Bm	Kts	Eng	Type	Former names
Berge Emperor	1975	211,359	423,700	382	68	16	ST	T	
Berge Empress	1976	211,359	423,748	382	68	15	ST	T	
Berge Enterprise	1981	198,544	360,700	341	65	15	M	T	
Berge Fister	1982	20,792	31,485	158	28	15	M	LPG	
Berge Gdansk	1985	59,650	97,500	249	32	15	M	BO	
Berge Gdynia	1985	59,650	97,500	249	32	15	M	BO	
Berge Helene	1983	40,388	65,000	249	32	16	M	B	
Berge King	1970	137,895	284,919	343	52	15	M	T	
Berge Lord	1973	138,008	284,500	343	52	15	M	T	
Berge Master*	1982	66,413	143,745	264	43	15	M	B	
Berge Odel	1974	83,005	155,048	292	45	16	M	BO	ex-Lappland 76
Berge Pioneer	1980	188,728	355,020	341	65	16	M	T	
Berge Prince	1973	138,008	284,522	343	52	15	M	T	
Berge Princess	1972	138,004	284,507	343	52	15	M	T	
Berge Rachel	1984	46,600	62,296	228	36	14	M	LPG	
Berge Racine	1985	46,600	62,700	228	36	14	M	LPG	
Berge Ragnhild	1985	46,600	62,700	228	36	14	M	LPG	
Berge Saga	1979	42,654	55,173	225	34	16	M	LPG	
Berge Septimus	1974	138,008	284,512	343	52	15	M	T	
Berge Sisar	1979	42,587	55,172	225	34	16	M	LPG	
Berge Sisu	1978	42,587	55,172	225	34	16	M	LPG	
Berge Strand	1982	42,278	55,173	225	34	16	M	LPG	
Berge Sund	1981	42,278	55,500	225	34	16	M	LPG	
Bergebonde	1973	83,005	155,048	292	45	16	M	BO	ex-Atland 76
Larina†	1972	67,595	160,528	300	51	16	M	OO	
Marshall Clark†	1965	27,023	86,179	250	37	16	M	OO	
Shigeo Nagano†	1965	27,023	82,092	250	37	16	M	OO	

* Singapore flag
† Liberian flag

Bibby Bros & Co

UK

Funnel: Pink with black top
Hull: Black with red boot-topping

Name	Year	GRT	DWT	LOA	Bm	Kts	Eng	Type	Former names
Devonshire	1974	32,060	38,705	207	31	17	M	LPG	
Hampshire	1974	32,060	38,705	207	31	17	M	LPG	
Lincolnshire	1972	19,799	24,950	187	27	17	M	LPG	
Staffordshire	1977	45,311	56,188	226	34	17	M	LPG	
Wiltshire*	1968	10,036	12,320	152	21	16	M	LPG	
Yorkshire	1975	60,814	112,744	260	41	16	M	T	

* Australian flag

Billabong Ship Management A/S

Norway

Funnel: Yellow with two red stars on blue edged white panel
Hull: Grey with red boot-topping

Name	Year	GRT	DWT	LOA	Bm	Kts	Eng	Type	Former names
Star Dieppe	1977	26,477	43,000	183	31	15	M	B	ex-Star Shiraz 79, ex-Star Dieppe 77
Star Dover*	1977	23,839	42,402	183	31	15	M	B	ex-Star Esfahan 79, ex-Star Dover 77
Star Eagle	1981	24,056	39,749	180	29	15	M	BC	
Star Evviva	1982	24,056	39,718	180	29	15	M	BC	
Star Florida†	1985	25,345	40,790	183	31	14	M	B	
Star Frazer†	1985	25,345	40,840	183	31	14	M	B	
Star Fuji†	1985	25,345	40,850	183	31	14	M	B	

* Panamanian flag
† Liberian flag

Above: Sig Bergesen dy & Co, *Berge Septimus. J. Krayenbosch*

Above: Bibby Bros & Co, *Devonshire. F. R. Sherlock*

Below: Billabong Ship Management A/S, *Star Eagle. J. Krayenbosch*

Black Star Line Ltd Ghana

Funnel: Yellow with red and green bands above and below five-pointed black star, black top
Hull: Grey with green boot-topping

Name	Year	GRT	DWT	LOA	Bm	Kts	Eng	Type	Former names
Bia River	1965	7,479	10,236	139	19	16	M	C	
Keta Lagoon	1980	13,004	16,667	167	23	18	M	C	ex-Tynebank 81, ex-Keta Lagoon 80
Klorte Lagoon	1969	7,155	10,586	139	19	16	M	C	
Sissili River	1980	13,004	16,640	167	23	18	M	C	
Subin River	1969	7,155	10,586	139	19	16	M	C	
Tano River	1980	13,004	16,633	167	23	18	M	C	
Volta River	1980	13,004	16,000	167	23	18	M	C	

Blue Star Line Ltd UK

Funnel: Blue star on white disc on red funnel with black top divided by white over black bands
Hull: Black with red boot-topping or lilac grey with blue boot-topping

Name	Year	GRT	DWT	LOA	Bm	Kts	Eng	Type	Former names
Afric Star	1975	9,784	11,092	156	21	25	M	R	
Auckland Star	1985	9,900	10,300	151	22	19	M	R	
Australia Star	1978	17,082	16,114	169	25	18	M	CC	
California Star	1971	19,095	10,114	189	26	26	M	CC	
Canterbury Star	1985	9,900	10,300	151	22	19	M	R	
Columbia Star	1971	19,095	19,114	189	26	22	M	CC	
English Star	1985	9,900	10,300	151	22	19	M	R	
New Zealand Star	1979	17,082	16,114	169	25	18	M	CC	
Scottish Star	1985	10,291	11,000	151	22	19	M	R	
Southland Star	1967	11,393	13,290	168	22	21	M	CO	
Wellington Star	1967	11,393	13,686	168	22	21	M	CO	ex-New Zealand Star 77

see also Associated Container Transportation (Australia) Ltd

Booth Steamship Co Ltd

Funnel: Black with blue 'B' over red St Andrew's cross on white panel.
Hull: Black with red boot-topping

Name	Year	GRT	DWT	LOA	Bm	Kts	Eng	Type	Former names
Benedict	1979	3,636	5,200	116	17	15	M	C	
Boniface	1979	3,636	5,200	116	17	15	M	C	

Lamport & Holt Line Ltd

Funnel: Light blue with broad white band and black top
Hull: Black with white band at the Plimsoll mark

Name	Year	GRT	DWT	LOA	Bm	Kts	Eng	Type	Former names
Romney	1979	12,214	18,500	162	23	16	M	C	ex-Ruddbank 83

Bolton Maritime Management Ltd UK

Bolton Steam Shipping Co Ltd

Funnel: Black, red band with 'FB' in red on white diamond
Hull: Grey with red boot-topping

Name	Year	GRT	DWT	LOA	Bm	Kts	Eng	Type	Former names
Reynolds	1973	18,025	29,812	190	23	15	M	B	
Rubens	1976	17,966	29,685	190	23	15	M	B	

Nosira Shipping Ltd

Funnel: Black, blue diamond on white disc on red band
Hull: Grey with red boot-topping

Name	Year	GRT	DWT	LOA	Bm	Kts	Eng	Type	Former names
Nosira Lin	1981	18,040	30,900	188	23	15	M	B	
Nosira Madelaine	1982	18,039	30,900	188	23	15	M	B	
Nosira Sharon	1981	18,039	30,900	188	23	15	M	B	

Above: Black Star Line Ltd, *Tano River. J. Krayenbosch*

Above: Blue Star Line Ltd, *California Star. J. Krayenbosch*

Below: Bolton Maritime Management Ltd, *Rubens. M. D. J. Lennon*

British & Commonwealth Shipping Co Ltd UK

King Line Ltd

Funnel: Yellow with black top or black with two narrow red bands
Hull: Black with pink boot-topping

Name	Year	GRT	DWT	LOA	Bm	Kts	Eng	Type	Former names
Barnworth	1975	35,716	60,920	225	32	15	M	B	ex-Strategist 83
Bridgeworth	1983	35,749	64,310	225	32	15	M	B	
Scottish Eagle	1980	32,995	56,963	210	32	16	M	T	
Scottish Lion	1979	32,995	56,490	210	32	16	M	T	

Union-Castle Mail SS Co Ltd

Funnel: Red with black top. (Universal Reefers — Red with white 'U')
Hull: Lilac grey with brown boot-topping

Name	Year	GRT	DWT	LOA	Bm	Kts	Eng	Type	Former names
Caspian Universal	1979	9,996	10,873	155	22	22	M	R	ex-Edinburgh Universal 84, ex-Polar Honduras 81
Speedster Universal	1979	9,073	12,475	156	23	22	M	R	ex-Stirling Universal 84, ex-Hilco Speedster 81

The British Petroleum Co Ltd UK

BP Shipping Ltd

Funnel: Red with black top and large white square with BP shield
Hull: Black with red boot-topping

Name	Year	GRT	DWT	LOA	Bm	Kts	Eng	Type	Former names
BP Achiever‡	1983	65,031	127,575	261	40	13	M	T	
BP Endeavour‡	1967	13,187	19,813	171	22	14	M	T	
BP Energy‡‡	1976	18,343	31,758	171	26	14	M	T	ex-Libra 85
BP Enterprise‡	1969	13,185	19,793	171	22	14	M	T	
BP Humber‡‡	1973	15,204	24,827	170	25	15	M	T	ex-British Humber 85
BP Vigour‡‡	1975	44,572	87,271	245	39	15	M	T	ex-Prosperity Queen 85
BP Vision‡‡	1975	45,001	89,735	242	40	15	M	T	ex-Hellespoit Glory 85
British Beech	1964	12,973	21,093	171	22	14	M	T	
British Dart**	1972	15,650	25,651	171	25	15	M	T	
British Fidelity	1969	15,260	24,853	170	25	14	M	T	
British Norness†	1973	132,942	269,349	338	54	15	ST	T	
British Ranger	1976	133,035	269,881	339	54	15	ST	T	
British Reliance	1975	133,035	269,770	339	54	15	ST	T	
British Resource	1975	131,535	269,695	339	54	16	M	T	
British Respect	1974	136,601	277,747	336	55	16	ST	T	
British Tay	1973	15,650	25,650	171	25	15	M	T	
British Test**	1972	15,653	25,641	171	25	15	M	T	
British Trent	1973	15,653	25,147	171	25	15	M	T	
British Trident*	1974	133,035	275,333	339	54	15	ST	T	
British Wye**	1973	15,649	25,196	171	25	15	M	T	
Gas Enterprise	1977	43,748	53,500	231	35	20	M	LPG	ex-Razi 80

* managed by P&O Bulk Shipping Ltd q.v.
† managed by Anglo Nordic Shipping Ltd q.v.
‡ managed by Associated Steamships Pty Ltd (TNT Bulkships Ltd), Australian flag
** on charter to Irano-British Ship Service Co Ltd (formed jointly with National Iranian Tanker Co)
‡‡ Bahamas flag
Joint controllers of Stolt-Nielsens Rederi A/S q.v.

BP Thames Tanker Co Ltd

Name	Year	GRT	DWT	LOA	Bm	Kts	Eng	Type	Former names
BP Tweed‡‡	1973	15,538	25,559	171	25	15	M	T	ex-British Tweed 85
British Avon	1972	15,540	25,620	171	25	15	M	T	

40

Above: British & Commonwealth Shipping Co Ltd, *Scottish Eagle. M. D. J. Lennon*

Below: British & Commonwealth Shipping Co Ltd, *Speedster Universal. J. M. Kakebeeke*

Name	Year	GRT	DWT	LOA	Bm	Kts	Eng	Type	Former names
British Esk	1973	15,644	25,905	171	25	15	M	T	
British Forth	1973	15,540	22,551	171	25	15	M	T	
British Kennet	1973	15,538	25,531	171	25	15	M	T	
British Renown†	1974	133,035	261,011	339	54	15	ST	T	
British Resolution†	1974	133,035	270,665	339	54	15	ST	T	
British Security*	1969	15,095	24,277	170	25	14	M	T	
British Skill	1983	66,034	127,778	261	40	13	M	TT	
British Spey	1974	15,590	25,590	171	25	15	M	T	
British Spirit	1982	66,024	127,778	261	40	13	M	T	
British Success	1984	66,034	127,778	261	40	13	M	T	
British Tamar	1973	15,642	25,498	171	25	15	M	T	
British Tenacity*	1969	15,095	24,277	170	25	14	M	T	
Coltair‡	1960	10,950	16,400	160	21	15	M2	OS	ex-Forties Kiwi 82, ex-British Kiwi 76

* owned by BP Tyne Tanker Co Ltd
† owned by BP Medway Tanker Co Ltd
‡ owned by BP Oil Development Ltd
‡‡ Bahamas flag

Soc Maritime des Petroles BP et Cie/France

Funnel: Red, black top divided by red, white and green tartan band with BP shield

Name	Year	GRT	DWT	LOA	Bm	Kts	Eng	Type	Former names
Brissac	1976	117,857	239,726	334	49	15	ST	T	
Chambord	1974	131,654	269,747	338	54	15	ST	T	
Chaumont	1976	131,654	269,919	339	54	15	ST	T	
Chenonceaux	1976	131,654	269,919	339	54	15	ST	T	

Brostroms Rederi A/B   Sweden

Funnel: Black, three narrow red bands and 'AB' in white
Hull: Black or grey, with red boot-topping

Name	Year	GRT	DWT	LOA	Bm	Kts	Eng	Type	Former names
Crown Broland*	1977	18,247	31,600	171	26	16	M	T	ex-Broland 82
Silverland	1974	55,426	102,100	257	39	15	M	BO	ex-A. K. Fernstrom 77
Thuleland†	1977	21,128	31,400	186	27	15	M	B	

* managed by Denholm Ship Management Ltd, British flag
† Singapore flag

Intercontinental Transport (ICT) BV/Netherlands

Funnel: Light green, white band and disc with green I

Name	Year	GRT	DWT	LOA	Bm	Kts	Eng	Type	Former names
Incotrans Speed	1979	29,411	26,469	203	31	21	M	CC	ex-China Winds 84, ex-Incotrans Speed 83
Incotrans Spirit	1979	29,411	26,415	203	31	21	M	CC	

Th. Brovig   Norway

Funnel: Yellow with houseflag panel
Hull: Grey

Name	Year	GRT	DWT	LOA	Bm	Kts	Eng	Type	Former names
Barbara Brovig†	1982	30,687	55,363	207	32	15	M	T	
Cypress†	1974	28,640	54,256	207	29	16	M	B	ex-King Charles 83
Mandalay†	1969	49,303	107,802	278	39	15	M	T	ex-Cis Brovig 85
Ragnhild Brovig†	1981	30,687	55,406	207	32	15	M	T	
Randi Brovig	1982	30,689	55,272	207	32	15	M	T	
Valetta Trader*	1975	17,875	32,212	171	26	16	M	T	ex-Andrea Brovig 85, ex-B. T. Friendship 76

* Panamanian flag   † Liberian flag

Above: The British Petroleum Co Ltd, *British Test. M. D. J. Lennon*

Above: Brostroms Rederi A/B, *Crown Broland. J. Krayenbosch*

Below: Brostroms Rederi A/B, *Incotrans Spirit. F. de Vries*

Bugsier-Reederei und Bergungs AG FRG

Funnel: Black with broad white band
Hull: Black with red boot-topping

Name	Year	GRT	DWT	LOA	Bm	Kts	Eng	Type	Former names
Hodeidah Crown	1978	12,758	17,800	160	23	18	M	C	ex-Ostfriesland 84, ex-SA Ostfriesland 81, ex-Ostfriesland 80
Lloyd California	1979	12,754	18,045	160	23	18	M	C	ex-Elbeland 84, ex-SA Elbeland 81, ex-Elbeland 80
Lloyd Londres	1984	9,764	12,954	149	22	17	M	CC	ex-Hannoverland 85
Sudan Crown	1985	9,764	12,954	149	22	17	M	CC	ex-Royal Eagle 85, ex-Weserland 85

Burma Five Star Shipping Corp Burma

Funnel: Dark red with blue band containing five white five-pointed stars
Hull: Black with white line, red boot-topping

Name	Year	GRT	DWT	LOA	Bm	Kts	Eng	Type	Former names
Ava	1963	7,435	10,282	136	19	15	M	C	
Bassein	1963	7,435	10,282	136	19	15	M	C	
Magwe	1985	9,778	13,055	149	27	17	M	C	
Mandalay	1983	9,754	13,105	149	23	17	M	C	ex-Mahndalay 83
Maw-la-Myaing	1979	7,567	11,690	134	21	15	M	C	
Mergui	1963	7,458	10,236	138	19	15	M	C	
Myoma Ywa	1961	5,437	7,303	127	17	15	M	C	ex-Altenfels 69
Pago	1983	10,097	13,105	149	23	17	M	C	
Pinya	1963	7,423	10,172	138	19	15	M	C	
Sagaing	1985	10,097	13,100	149	23	17	M	C	
Sit-Tway	1980	7,546	11,660	134	21	15	M	C	

Burmah Oil Tanker Co Ltd UK

Funnel: Yellow with red, white and blue shield emblem
Hull: Black with red boot-topping

Name	Year	GRT	DWT	LOA	Bm	Kts	Eng	Type	Former names
Burmah Bahamas*	1980	38,975	57,708	229	32	14	M	T	
Burmah Endeavour	1977	231,629	457,841	378	68	15	ST	T	
Burmah Enterprise	1978	231,629	457,927	378	68	15	ST	T	

* on time charter from Star Field Shipping Co Ltd, Japanese flag

Cameroon Shipping Lines SA Cameroon

Funnel: Yellow with red 'C' shaped fish, green top
Hull: Grey

Name	Year	GRT	DWT	LOA	Bm	Kts	Eng	Type	Former names
Cam Bilinga	1984	12,075	16,757	152	23	15	M	CO	
Cam Bubinga	1977	9,141	13,208	150	21	17	M	C	ex-Ivory Uranus 77
Cam Doussie	1977	9,648	13,029	150	21	17	M	C	
Cam Ebene	1984	12,060	16,752	152	23	15	M	CO	
Cam Ilomba	1979	12,074	16,600	152	23	15	M	CO	
Cam Iroko	1979	12,074	16,500	152	23	15	M	CO	

Canadian Pacific Steamships Ltd UK

Funnel: Green incorporating a modern design with a triangle, a segment of a circle and part of a square
Hull: Black with 'CP Ships' in white

Name	Year	GRT	DWT	LOA	Bm	Kts	Eng	Type	Former names
Andes Trader	1971	15,680	16,963	167	26	19	M	CC	ex-CP Trader 82
Cedar Voyageur	1970	15,680	16,963	167	26	19	M	CC	ex-Louisiane 85, ex-Andes Voyageur 84, ex-CP Voyageur 82
CP Ambassador	1971	30,817	29,398	232	31	22	M	CC	ex-Dart Atlantic 81

Above: Th Brovig, *Barbara Brovig. J. Krayenbosch*

Above: Burma Five Star Shipping Corp, *Sagaing. J. Krayenbosch*

Below: Cameroon Shipping Lines SA, *Cam Iroko. J. K. Byass*

Name	Year	GRT	DWT	LOA	Bm	Kts	Eng	Type	Former names
Dart Americana	1978	15,584	18,606	177	27	19	M	CC	ex-Seapac Independence 81, ex-Seatrain Independence 81
Mississippi	1971	15,680	16,963	167	26	19	M	CC	ex-Andes Discoverer 84, ex-CP Discoverer 82

Canadian Pacific (Bermuda) Ltd

Name	Year	GRT	DWT	LOA	Bm	Kts	Eng	Type	Former names
E. W. Beatty	1973	67,914	131,260	260	42	15	M	B	
Fort Assiniboine	1980	19,982	31,764	169	27	15	M	T	
Fort Calgary	1976	21,893	35,981	184	28	15	M	B	
Fort Carleton	1978	14,088	22,174	161	23	14	M	B	
Fort Coulonge	1976	18,782	31,275	171	26	15	M	T	
Fort Dufferin	1983	35,808	63,880	225	32	14	M	B	
Fort Edmonton	1975	18,782	31,275	171	26	15	M	T	
Fort Frontenac	1983	35,808	64,000	225	32	14	M	B	
Fort Garry	1980	19,982	31,674	169	27	15	M	T	
Fort Hamilton	1978	14,088	22,174	161	23	14	M	B	
Fort Kamloops	1976	17,281	28,322	173	25	15	M	B	
Fort Kipp	1975	18,782	31,275	171	26	15	M	T	
Fort Macleod	1974	18,744	31,275	171	26	15	M	T	
Fort Nanaimo	1975	21,894	35,981	184	28	15	M	B	ex-Leda 80
Fort Nelson	1975	21,894	35,981	184	28	15	M	B	
Fort Providence	1982	36,341	64,584	224	32	14	M	B	
Fort Resolution	1982	36,284	64,413	224	32	14	M	B	
Fort Rouge	1980	19,982	31,729	170	27	15	M	T	
Fort Steele	1974	18,744	31,275	171	26	15	M	T	
Fort Toronto	1980	19,982	31,745	170	27	15	M	T	
Fort Victoria	1977	17,281	28,322	173	25	15	M	B	
Fort Yale	1977	17,280	28,322	173	25	15	M	B	
G. A. Walker	1973	18,744	31,096	171	26	15	M	T	
I. D. Sinclair	1974	133,679	254,735	338	52	15	M	T	
Port Hawkesbury	1970	133,699	257,017	338	52	15	M	T	
Port Quebec	1977	35,716	64,002	225	32	15	M	B	
Port Vancouver	1977	35,716	64,022	225	32	15	M	B	
R. A. Emerson	1973	18,744	31,096	171	26	15	M	T	
W. A. Mather	1973	18,744	31,096	171	26	15	M	T	
W. C. Van Horne	1970	33,329	58,028	227	31	15	M	B	
W. M. Neal	1974	67,915	125,107	260	42	15	M	B	

Cast (1983) Ltd

UK

Funnel: Blue with white 'C'
Hull: Black

Name	Year	GRT	DWT	LOA	Bm	Kts	Eng	Type	Former names
Cast Husky	1982	40,294	70,912	234	32	14	M	BC	
Cast Muskox	1982	40,294	70,837	234	32	14	M	BC	
Cast Otter	1982	40,294	70,870	234	32	14	M	BC	

Cenargo Navigation Ltd

UK

Funnel: Flake grey with gold three-bladed propeller, black top
Hull: Black with red boot-topping

Name	Year	GRT	DWT	LOA	Bm	Kts	Eng	Type	Former names
Merchant Pilot*	1981	15,177	25,400	185	23	15	M	B	ex-Kennington 85, ex-El Crusader 85
Merchant Pioneer	1973	12,321	18,080	161	22	14	M	C	ex-Beacon Grange 84, ex-Orduna 82
Merchant Prelude*	1980	15,313	25,400	185	23	15	M	B	ex-Battersea 85, ex-El Commodore 85
Merchant Principal*	1978	14,124	17,944	163	23	16	M	C	ex-Oropesa 84
Merchant Providence	1965	9,622	13,550	156	21	18	M	C	ex-Artico 83, ex-Tabora 74

Above: Canadian Pacific Steamships Ltd, *Fort Carleton. J. Krayenbosch*

Below: Canadian Pacific Steamship Ltd, *Fort Rouge. M. D. J. Lennon*

Central Gulf Lines Inc

Funnel: Yellow with white star on white edged red band
Hull: Black with red boot-topping

Name	Year	GRT	DWT	LOA	Bm	Kts	Eng	Type	Former names
Acadia Forest*	1969	33,231	49,835	261	32	18	M	LC	
Atlantic Forest*	1970	33,221	49,858	261	32	18	M	LC	
Bilderdykt	1972	36,974	44,799	261	32	18	M	LC	
Dawn	1963	11,309	12,932	174	23	20	ST	C	ex-African Dawn 80
Green Harbour	1974	28,488	46,892	272	30	22	ST	LC	ex-William Hooper 84, ex-Green Harbour 80
Green Island	1975	28,488	46,892	272	31	22	ST	LC	ex-George Wythe 84, ex-Green Island 80
Green Valley	1974	28,488	46,892	272	31	22	ST	LC	ex-Button Gwinnett 84, ex-Green Valley 80
Green Wave	1980	9,550	13,130	154	21	17	M	C	ex-Woermann Mira 84, ex-Sloman Mira 84
Norman Prince*	1973	18,968	32,646	182	27	17	M	B	
Norman King*	1975	44,367	90,900	242	40	15	M	T	ex-Mammoth Monarch 85, ex-Euroasia Monarch 78
Norman Queen*	1973	18,968	32,652	182	27	17	M	B	ex-Mammoth Pine 85
Rapid	1969	11,757	15,946	184	27	25	ST	RO	ex-American Rapid 84, ex-Red Jacket 82, ex-Mormacstar 70
Rover	1969	11,757	15,946	184	27	25	ST	RO	ex-American Rover 83, ex-Defiance 82, ex-Mormacsea 70

* Liberian flag
† Netherlands Antilles flag

see also Standard Oil Co (Indiana)

Ceylon Shipping Corp

Funnel: Blue with narrow orange band on broad white band
Hull: Black with red boot-topping

Name	Year	GRT	DWT	LOA	Bm	Kts	Eng	Type	Former names
Lanka Ajitha	1985	8,176	10,600	137	23	16	M	C	
Lanka Athula	1983	8,176	10,600	137	23	16	M	C	
Lanka Mahapola	1983	8,082	10,325	129	20	17	M	C	
Lanka Rani	1961	10,345	15,472	157	20	15	M	C	ex-Finnamore Valley 71
Lanka Ratna	1958	10,203	15,305	157	20	16	M	C	ex-Argo Chios 75, ex-Santa Fotini 73, ex-Argo Chios 69
Lanka Shanthi	1964	9,464	14,580	147	19	14	M	C	ex-Heering Elise 73, ex-Loucas N 70
Lanka Srimani	1982	8,438	9,700	139	22	17	M	C	
Lanka Srimathi	1982	8,438	9,700	139	22	17	M	C	

Cie des Chargeurs Reunis

Funnel: Yellow with red stars on white band
Hull: White or black with red boot-topping

Name	Year	GRT	DWT	LOA	Bm	Kts	Eng	Type	Former names
Ango*	1979	15,632	22,138	209	30	21	M	RO	
C.R. Libreville	1983	17,280	21,800	170	27	17	M	CO	
C.R. Paris	1985	37,600	41,700	235	32	21	M	CC	
C.R. Tokyo	1985	37,600	41,700	235	32	21	M	CC	
Cetra Cassiopea†	1977	40,847	74,104	244	32	15	M	B	
Cetra Corona†	1982	74,509	139,496	280	42	14	M	B	
Chevalier Paul	1976	36,505	40,420	252	31	23	ST	CC	
Chevalier Rozé	1976	36,505	40,240	252	31	23	ST	CC	
Chevalier Valbelle	1977	27,836	35,367	208	31	23	ST	CC	
Nara	1977	16,893	24,270	171	25	18	M	CO	
Narval	1968	8,554	6,599	144	20	22	M	R	
Nausicaa	1978	16,893	24,540	171	25	18	M	CO	
Orque	1969	8,559	6,595	144	20	21	M	R	
Ronsard*	1980	15,632	21,800	209	30	21	M	RO	

* jointly owned with Cie Generale Maritime (CGM) & John T. Essberger (DAL Deutsche Afrika Linien GmbH)
† managed for Consortium Europeen de Transport Maritime

Cie des Chargeurs Reunis, *Nausicaa. M. D. J. Lennon*

49

Chevron Corp

USA

Chevron USA Inc

Funnel: White, narrow black top and blue and red chevrons and 'Chevron' in black
Hull: Black

Name	Year	GRT	DWT	LOA	Bm	Kts	Eng	Type	Former names
Chevron Arizona	1977	16,941	39,836	199	29	16	GT	T	
Chevron California	1972	35,588	71,339	247	32	16	ST	T	
Chevron Colorado	1976	16,941	39,842	199	29	15	GT	T	
Chevron Louisiana	1977	16,941	39,795	199	29	15	GT	T	
Chevron Mississippi	1972	35,589	71,339	247	32	15	ST	T	
Chevron Oregon	1975	16,941	39,847	199	29	15	GT	T	
Chevron Washington	1976	16,941	39,795	199	29	15	GT	T	

Chevron Transport Corporation/Liberia

Name	Year	GRT	DWT	LOA	Bm	Kts	Eng	Type	Former names
Alden W. Clausen	1981	21,582	35,587	179	30	15	M	T	
C. W. Kitto	1974	118,218	268,345	339	54	15	ST	T	
Carla A. Hills	1981	21,582	35,596	179	30	15	M	T	
Charles Pigott	1973	118,221	268,373	339	54	15	ST	T	
Chevron Antwerp	1975	122,627	276,796	339	54	15	ST	T	
Chevron Brussels	1972	122,812	259,447	341	52	15	ST	T	
Chevron Burnaby	1974	122,627	276,775	339	54	15	ST	T	ex-Chevron Jakarta 74, ex-Chevron Bayway 74
Chevron Copenhagen	1974	118,179	268,237	339	54	15	ST	T	
Chevron Edinburgh‡	1973	118,179	268,333	339	54	15	ST	T	ex-Al-Falah 84, ex-Chevron Edinburgh 82
Chevron Feluy	1973	118,197	268,430	339	54	15	ST	T	
Chevron Frankfurt*	1967	41,923	80,137	232	37	15	ST	T	
Chevron London	1972	96,523	149,494	279	52	15	ST	T	
Chevron Nagasaki	1974	118,147	268,242	339	54	15	ST	T	
Chevron North America	1976	196,334	412,610	366	70	15	ST	T	
Chevron Pacific	1983	21,582	34,950	179	30	15	M	T	
Chevron Perth	1975	122,627	276,837	339	54	15	ST	T	
Chevron South America	1976	196,334	412,612	366	70	15	ST	T	
D. L. Bower*	1970	71,080	152,383	285	49	15	ST	T	
David Packard	1977	196,334	413,115	366	70	15	ST	T	
George H. Weyerhaeuser‡	1981	21,582	35,597	179	30	15	M	T	
George M. Keller	1972	118,316	268,247	338	54	15	ST	T	
H. J. Haynes	1970	71,080	152,404	285	49	15	ST	T	
Howard W. Bell	1972	118,342	268,314	338	54	15	ST	T	
J. R. Grey	1971	118,865	268,275	338	54	15	ST	T	
J. T. Higgins*	1970	71,080	152,404	285	49	15	ST	T	
John A. McCone	1969	71,080	149,998	285	49	15	ST	T	
Kenneth E. Hill‡	1979	43,428	80,500	250	44	16	M	T	
Kenneth T. Derr‡	1982	21,582	35,587	179	30	15	M	T	
L. W. Funkhouser	1973	118,147	268,244	339	54	15	ST	T	ex-David Packard 74
Otto N. Miller	1973	118,197	268,436	339	54	15	ST	T	
Paul L. Fahrney	1971	118,865	258,086	338	54	15	ST	T	
Ralph B. Johnson	1965	36,370	67,567	239	32	17	ST	T	
Rudolph Peterson	1972	116,624	253,554	344	52	16	ST	T	
Samuel H. Armacost‡	1982	21,582	35,607	179	30	15	M	T	
William E. Mussman	1979	41,500	79,990	250	44	16	M	T	

* owned by Gotaas-Larsen Inc, q.v.
‡ Bahamas flag

Chevron Corp. *Chevron Pacific. Table Bay Underway Shipping*

Gulf Oil Corporation/USA

Funnel: Blue grey with 'GULF' in orange disc
Hull: Blue grey with red boot-topping

Name	Year	GRT	DWT	LOA	Bm	Kts	Eng	Type	Former names
Afran Energy*	1975	47,133	98,912	253	37	16	M	T	
Afran Equator*	1977	58,336	112,745	260	41	16	M	T	ex-Geroi Kerchi 79, ex-Interoceanic II 78, ex-Robcap VI 77
Afran Horizon*	1974	60,491	123,969	259	41	15	M	T	ex-Orion Constellation 79
Afran Meteor*	1975	60,886	127,505	273	43	16	M	T	ex-Janet 80
Afran Ocean*	1974	171,310	323,094	348	53	14	M2	T	ex-Ocean Park 82
Afran Sky*	1976	77,588	154,932	280	54	16	M	T	ex-Arco Independence 82, ex-Runa 76
Afran Star*	1977	76,547	153,843	280	54	16	M	T	ex-Arco Mariner 82
Afran Stream*	1975	61,372	128,300	267	41	14	M	T	ex-Mantinia 77
Afran Sun*	1977	76,547	153,829	280	54	16	M	T	ex-Arco Discovery 82
Afran Zenith*	1972	51,083	96,716	268	39	16	M	T	ex-La Nina 79
Afran Zodiac*	1973	104,150	231,430	317	50	16	ST	T	

* Liberian flag

China Ocean Shipping Co

China

Funnel: Yellow, red band with yellow star flanked by six wavy lines
Hull: White or grey with green boot-topping

Name	Year	GRT	DWT	LOA	Bm	Kts	Eng	Type	Former names
An Da Hai	1974	16,681	26,305	167	26	15	M	B	ex-Norse Trader 77
An Dong Jiang	1979	9,324	15,160	144	20	15	M	C	ex-Bronte 83
An Fu Jiang	1979	9,324	15,160	144	20	15	M	C	ex-Browning 83
An Hua	1960	8,524	11,888	144	18	15	M	C	ex-Buku 74, ex-Sydland 72
An Ji Hai	1970	11,784	18,797	165	21	15	M	B	ex-Stove Friend 77
An Lu Jiang	1978	9,121	15,210	144	20	15	M2	C	ex-European Express 84
An Sai Jiang	1979	9,121	15,210	144	20	15	M	C	ex-African Express 84
An Shan	1981	9,530	15,721	144	21	14	M	C	
An Ting	1970	9,796	14,556	152	21	18	M	C	ex-Kunlunshan 71
Bai Yu Hai	1967	22,146	38,752	200	27	15	M	B	ex-Aegis Thunder 79, ex-Vigan 74
Bao Qing Hai	1971	45,844	85,163	239	36	15	M	D	ex-Moslane 78
Bao Ting	1965	9,817	14,073	151	21	18	M	C	ex-Datuho 72, ex-Wihuri 71
Bao Xing*	1962	9,190	12,669	153	19	15	M	C	ex-Wieniawski 77
Bi Sheng	1973	9,784	16,271	150	21	16	M	C	ex-Boleslaw Prus 82
Bing He	1985	23,542	32,700	201	28	15	M	CC	
Cang Zhau	1979	16,435	25,000	185	23	16	M	B	
Chang De	1964	9,037	12,975	148	19	15	M	C	ex-Peony 70, ex-Bonde 64
Chang Ming	1958	10,020	15,655	157	20	16	M	C	ex-Island Skipper 76
Chang Shu	1957	10,481	12,690	149	20	15	M	C	ex-Chiang Kiang 70, ex-G. D. Kennedy 67
Chang Ting	1971	9,792	14,435	152	21	18	M	C	ex-Wutaishan 72
Chang Xing	1975	9,586	15,099	145	21	16	M	C	
Chao He	1985	19,835	25,965	170	28	17	M	CC	
Chao Yang	1967	9,911	14,697	161	20	17	M	C	
Chun He	1984	19,835	25,955	170	28	17	M	CC	
Chun Lin	1973	9,706	13,427	160	22	19	M	C	
Da Chang Zhen	1963	9,554	12,826	152	20	18	M	C	ex-Wasserfels 78
Da Cheng	1973	10,715	14,522	155	22	16	M	C	
Da De	1962	9,555	12,800	152	20	18	M	C	ex-Werdenfels 73
Da Jin Chuan	1962	9,558	12,622	152	20	18	M	C	ex-Wildenfels 78
Da Long Tai	1966	9,442	12,991	152	20	19	M	C	ex-Crostafels 78
Da Ning	1962	9,555	12,622	152	20	20	M	C	ex-Wachtfels 72
Da Pu	1959	9,212	12,716	145	19	14	M	C	ex-North Sea 71, ex-Trautenfels 71
Da Qing Shan	1967	9,442	12,991	152	20	19	M	C	ex-Schonfels 78
Da Sha Ping	1972	9,995	16,003	152	21	16	M	C	ex-Tarpon Seaway 78
Da Shi Qiao	1962	9,555	12,623	152	20	18	M	C	ex-Wallenfels 78
Da Tian	1974	10,715	14,464	155	22	16	M	C	
Da Ye	1974	9,862	13,209	162	20	18	M	C	

52

China Ocean Shipping Co, *An Lu Jiang*. *J. M. Kakebeeke*

Name	Year	GRT	DWT	LOA	Bm	Kts	Eng	Type	Former names
Dai Hai	1967	19,922	28,209	176	26	14	M	B	ex-Chuetsusan Maru 77
De Du	1962	9,639	10,454	143	20	17	M	C	ex-Gaoyo 73, ex-Havtjeld 72
De Rong Hai	1969	24,599	44,233	203	29	14	M	B	ex-Aristotelis 78
De Xing*	1974	9,608	15,099	145	21	16	M	C	
Deng Long Hai	1967	41,079	77,765	251	32	15	M	B	ex-Fjordaas 79
Dong Ming	1964	10,421	15,627	157	20	15	M	C	ex-Sea Amber 73
Dun Hua	1961	8,809	12,629	142	19	14	M	C	ex-Eastfortune 70, ex-Sollen 63
Fei Cui Hai	1973	22,906	32,818	178	27	15	M	B	ex-Silverdon 78, ex-Bravenes 73
Fen He	1982	16,108	20,828	170	28	18	M	CC	
Fen Chi	1975	9,988	14,770	161	20	16	M	C	
Feng Hang	1978	9,988	14,770	161	20	16	M	C	
Feng Sheng	1978	9,974	14,800	159	20	17	M	C	
Feng Xiang	1974	10,273	15,000	161	20	15	M	C	
Feng Yan	1974	9,922	14,729	162	20	17	M	C	
Gan Jiang	1970	11,537	16,277	156	22	17	M	C	ex-Norbella 79
Guang He	1972	11,083	16,780	155	23	18	M	CO	ex-Lutz Jacob 73
Gui Hai	1964	17,198	26,261	192	24	16	M	B	ex-Adriatic Sea 76
Gui Yang	1979	9,913	14,172	161	20	17	M	C	
Hai Feng	1969	8,887	12,640	151	20	17	M	C	
Hai Men	1968	9,513	12,629	151	20	17	M	C	
Hai Zhou	1977	16,499	25,000	185	23	15	M	B	
Han Chuan	1974	10,744	15,495	157	22	18	M	C	
Hei Long Jiang	1966	9,103	12,147	155	20	19	M	C	ex-Ville de Lyon 77
Hong Men	1975	9,672	13,757	152	20	18	M	C	
Hong Qi 123	1978	12,110	18,886	162	22	16	M	B	
Hong Shou Shan	1966	10,427	13,723	157	22	19	M	C	ex-Ango 77
Hu Lin	1974	9,706	13,430	160	22	19	M	C	
Hu Po Hai	1972	21,508	38,406	193	26	15	M	B	ex-Bulk Promoter 77
Hua Chun	1962	10,915	13,249	168	22	20	M	C	ex-Yichun 77, ex-Benvalla 72
Hua Shan	1982	9,531	15,640	144	21	14	M	C	
Hua Ting	1972	9,792	14,435	152	21	18	M	C	ex-Liupanshan 73
Hua Tuo*	1983	9,228	16,000	155	23	16	M	C	
Hua Xing*	1960	9,247	12,666	153	19	15	M	C	ex-Moniuszko 82
Huai Yang	1979	9,925	14,270	161	20	17	M	C	
Huang Shan	1982	9,531	15,721	144	21	14	M	C	
Hun Jiang	1981	9,296	15,265	144	20	15	M	C	
Jia Xing*	1963	10,443	14,922	153	20	16	M	C	ex-Dlugosz 70
Jiang Chuan	1973	10,740	15,474	157	22	18	M	C	
Jiang Ting	1972	9,792	14,428	152	21	18	M	C	ex-Dahsueshan 72
Jiao Cheng	1978	10,302	16,251	148	22	15	M	C	ex-Amalia 80
Jiao Zhou Hai	1979	29,562	57,727	223	32	16	M	B	ex-Koyo Venture 80
Jin Cheng	1975	11,423	15,745	148	23	15	M	C	ex-Star Alcyone 79, ex-Aristomachos 76
Jin Cheng Jiang	1971	10,199	14,866	146	22	16	M	C	ex-Leersum 77
Jin Hai	1969	21,820	37,289	194	26	15	M	C	ex-Ringstad 77
Jin Jiang	1972	9,774	16,270	150	21	16	M	C	ex-Aquitania 81, ex-Ilse Schulte 77
Jin Shan Hai	1983	20,582	34,971	176	28	14	M	B	
Jin Tian Hai	1972	50,342	92,832	250	35	16	M	B	ex-Sardinia Weipa 78
Jin Zhou Hai	1970	18,246	30,759	197	23	15	M	B	ex-Doric Arrow 80
Jin Zhou	1973	16,465	23,000	186	23	15	M	B	
Jing Hai	1968	12,404	20,026	159	22	14	M	B	ex-Baynes 73
Ju Hai	1966	26,489	47,602	216	29	16	M	B	ex-Drake Sea 76, ex-Vardass 74
Jun Liang Cheng	1970	9,966	16,350	150	21	16	M	C	ex-Arabonne 77
Kang Hai	1965	18,088	30,309	183	24	15	M	B	ex-Benvorlich 76, ex-Ribena 73
Kang Su Hai	1975	36,232	64,444	224	32	14	M	B	ex-Vesteroy 80
Kuang Hai	1965	21,937	35,562	193	26	14	M	B	ex-Roald Jarl 74
Kun Ming	1963	10,421	15,627	157	20	15	M	C	ex-Sea Coral 73
Le Ting	1966	9,891	14,116	151	21	18	M	C	ex-Wisa 71
Lei Zhou Hai	1982	36,318	64,170	225	32	15	M	B	
Li Ming	1963	10,893	13,056	162	21	16	M	C	ex-London Tradesman 64
Li Yang	1973	10,341	14,065	162	21	18	M	C	

China Ocean Shipping Co, *Fen He. F. R. Sherlock*

Name	Year	GRT	DWT	LOA	Bm	Kts	Eng	Type	Former names
Lian Yun Shan	1967	10,427	13,799	157	22	19	M	C	ex-Dupleix 77
Liao Hai	1961	15,719	26,740	177	23	15	M	B	ex-Mosdale 74
Liao Yang	1974	9,856	14,225	162	20	18	M	C	
Ling Quan He	1983	7,691	10,974	134	21	15	M	CO	ex-Papua 85
Liu Lin Hai	1971	22,489	38,406	193	26	15	M	B	ex-Belmor 77, ex-Bibo 75, ex-Aristokratis 74
Long Hua	1959	8,814	14,189	145	19	14	M	C	
Long Lin	1974	9,706	13,433	160	22	19	M	C	
Lu Ban*	1981	14,125	15,607	155	23	16	M	C	
Lu Cheng	1966	10,527	13,500	156	21	18	M	C	ex-SA Tugelaland 78, ex-Tugelaland 74, ex-Concordia Land 73, ex-Tugelaland 72
Lu Feng	1970	9,105	12,701	151	20	19	M	C	
Lu Shan	1982	9,531	15,607	144	21	14	M	C	
Luan He	1978	18,572	25,550	169	26	15	M	BC	ex-Victoria Bay 83, ex-Columbia 81, ex-Arabian Strength 79, ex-Columbia 78
Luo Fu Shan	1968	29,419	55,120	218	30	14	M	B	ex-King Alfred 83
Luo He	1983	19,915	26,015	170	28	17	M	CC	
Luo Shan Hai	1968	41,088	76,545	251	32	16	M	B	ex-Thara 78
Mei Jiang	1976	8,792	14,241	141	20	15	M	C	ex-Ormos 78
Mi Yun Hai	1967	19,672	38,378	193	28	15	M	B	ex-Pelopidas 81, ex-Irish Elm 79
Ming Xi Hai	1967	30,724	61,849	226	32	16	M	B	ex-Struma 78, ex-Oron 69
Nan Jiang	1978	8,746	15,240	141	20	15	M	C	ex-Sea Lion 82
Nan Ping	1964	9,107	12,483	156	20	18	M	C	ex-Flores Sea 74, ex-Don Antonio 72
Nan Ping Shan	1978	9,567	15,780	144	21	14	M	C	ex-Aegis Sailor 81
Nei Jiang	1972	9,784	16,299	150	21	16	M	C	ex-Andalusia 81, ex-Elizabetha Schulte 77
Ning Hai	1981	16,473	25,667	185	23	14	M	B	
Ping Ding Shan	1972	9,412	14,445	140	21	16	M	C	ex-Klaus Schoke 81, ex-Nyanga 79, ex-Klaus Schoke 77, ex-Verena Wiards 72
Ping Jiang	1978	9,119	15,301	141	21	15	M	C	ex-Funing 82
Qi Lian Shan	1977	10,108	16,475	143	22	14	M	B	ex-Canadian Express 80, ex-Duck Yang Rose 77
Qi Men	1973	9,651	13,340	152	20	17	M	C	
Qian Shan	1973	9,698	16,270	150	21	16	M	C	ex-Charlotte Kogel 82
Qing He	1982	16,108	20,828	170	28	17	M	CC	
Qing He Cheng	1963	11,537	11,629	166	23	20	M	C	ex-Glenfalloch 77
Qing Jiang	1978	9,327	15,290	141	21	15	M	C	ex-Cluden 82
Qing Shui	1964	9,337	11,278	159	21	17	M	C	ex-Nara 72
Quan Zhou Hai	1982	36,318	64,170	225	32	15	M	B	
Qiu He	1984	19,732	25,808	171	29	15	M	CC	
Rong Jiang	1978	9,117	15,434	141	21	15	M	C	ex-Morviken 82
Sha He	1983	19,915	26,025	171	28	17	M	CC	
Shan Yin	1961	9,575	13,560	156	21	17	M	C	ex-Indian Ocean 74, ex-Tanganyika 71
Shao Xing	1978	10,326	13,720	162	21	17	M	C	
Shen Zhou	1978	16,500	25,000	185	23	15	M	B	
Shi Tang Hai	1973	35,545	74,212	244	32	15	M	B	ex-Dimitris A. Lemos 81
Song Lin	1973	9,713	13,698	160	22	19	M	C	
Tai Bai Shan	1978	9,463	15,780	144	21	14	M	C	ex-Aegis Captain 80
Tai Xing	1960	10,443	14,922	158	20	16	M	C	ex-Beniowski 71, ex-Argo Altis 60
Tai Zhou Hai	1982	36,319	64,230	225	32	15	M	B	
Tang He	1983	16,100	20,830	170	28	18	M	CC	
Tao Lin	1974	9,706	13,433	160	22	19	M	C	
Tian Men	1974	9,672	13,869	152	20	18	M	C	
Tian Tai Shan	1970	11,256	16,449	156	22	17	M	C	ex-Ocean Prosper 79
Tong Cheng	1977	11,364	18,862	148	23	15	M	C	ex-Aristonidas 78
Tong Chuan	1974	10,744	15,480	157	22	18	M	C	

China Ocean Shipping Co, *Tuo He. J. Krayenbosch*

Name	Year	GRT	DWT	LOA	Bm	Kts	Eng	Type	Former names
Tong Hai	1981	16,473	25,667	185	23	15	M	B	
Tu Men Jiang	1964	9,125	12,320	155	20	19	M	C	ex-Ville de Bordeaux 77
Tuo He	1978	18,571	25,550	169	26	15	M	BC	ex-California 83, ex-Arabian Endeavour 81
Wang Jiang	1974	10,591	16,166	151	21	14	M	C	ex-Chinsha Career 82, ex-Tahiti Maru 80
Wang Ting	1970	9,792	14,556	152	21	18	M	C	ex-Taihanshan 71
Wei Hei	1979	18,588	25,550	169	26	15	M	BC	ex-Nedlloyd Caledonia 83, ex-Caledonia 81
Wen Deng Hai	1968	41,089	76,645	251	32	16	M	B	ex-Essi Kristine 78
Wen Zhou Hai	1982	33,539	64,120	225	32	15	M	B	
Wu Jiang	1977	9,422	15,200	143	20	13	M	C	ex-Sea Eagle 80
Wu Tai Shan	1967	10,427	13,799	157	22	19	M	C	ex-Forbin 77
Xi Feng Kou	1980	12,321	14,019	177	27	18	M	RO	
Xia Hai	1975	20,340	35,060	182	26	14	M	B	ex-Ocean Brave 82
Xia Men	1975	9,672	13,706	152	20	18	M	C	
Xiang Cheng	1976	11,418	18,813	148	23	15	M	C	ex-Star Procyon 79, ex-Aristeidis 77
Xiang He	1983	24,043	31,000	200	28	17	M	CC	
Xin Feng	1970	9,105	12,396	151	20	18	M	C	
Xing Cheng	1973	9,348	12,930	150	22	17	M	C	ex-Golden Harvest 78, ex-Union Aotearoa 78
Xing He	1985	19,237	25,925	170	28	15	M	CC	
Xing Hua	1960	8,929	12,909	148	19	15	M	C	ex-Changpaishan 70, ex-Saldura 67
Ya Lu Jiang	1970	9,951	14,738	163	23	15	M	C	ex-Iberia 77
Yan Shan	1976	11,275	16,214	148	22	15	M	C	ex-Aloha 80
Yan Ting	1973	9,792	14,552	152	21	18	M	C	
Yang Ming Shan	1965	25,123	44,670	206	27	15	M	B	ex-Goldan Alliance 82, ex-Atherstone 78
Yi Men	1978	9,014	13,780	153	20	18	M	C	
Yong Chun	1963	10,870	13,183	168	22	20	M	C	ex-Benarmin 72
Yong Ding	1964	8,871	13,209	148	19	16	M	C	ex-Patrice 77, ex-Patricia 76, ex-Salambria 73
Yong Feng Hai	1967	15,355	25,456	177	23	13	M	B	ex-Costas Frangos 78
Yong Jiang	1978	10,014	16,269	150	21	16	M	C	
Yong Ning	1967	8,689	11,760	153	19	16	M	C	
Yong Xing	1977	9,801	16,219	150	21	16	M	C	
You Hao	1959	8,405	11,512	154	19	14	M	C	ex-Etha Rickmers 64
Yu Jiang	1969	9,640	12,853	140	22	16	M	C	ex-Birkaland 79
Yu Lin	1972	9,758	13,519	160	22	19	M	C	
Yu Men	1966	9,491	12,492	151	20	16	M	C	
Yuan Jiang	1981	9,294	15,200	144	20	15	M	C	
Yun Cheng	1977	11,364	18,856	148	23	16	M	C	ex-Aristodikos 79
Yun Tai Shan	1971	11,274	16,441	156	22	17	M	C	ex-Ocean Progress 80
Zhang Heng	1982	14,199	16,078	155	23	16	M	C	
Zhang Jia Kou	1980	12,321	13,996	180	27	18	M	RO	
Zhao Yang Hai	1977	17,960	30,917	197	23	15	M	B	ex-Mericunda 78
Zhen Jiang	1966	10,834	15,713	158	21	15	M	C	
Zheng Rong Hai	1966	21,896	38,904	200	27	15	M	B	ex-Amax MacGregor 79, ex-Thorbjorg 75
Zhi Hai	1968	15,353	25,933	177	23	17	M	B	ex-Aurora II 76
Zhong Shan	1969	12,979	20,349	160	23	15	M	C	ex-Marina del Cantone 82, ex-Zelzate 79
Zhu Hai	1964	15,237	24,334	178	23	15	M	B	ex-Ceram Sea 73, ex-Victoria 1 72, ex-Victoria 68
Zi Jin Shan	1978	9,463	15,751	144	21	14	M	C	ex-Aegis Pilot 80

* Chinese-Polish Joint Stock Co (Chinsko-Polskie Towarzystwo Okretowe SA)

the above list comprises less than 50% of the current fleet, but gives a typical cross section of the main types.

Above: China Ocean Shipping Co, *Ya Lu Jiang. J. K. Byass*

Below: China Ocean Shipping Co, *Yu Men. M. D. J. Lennon*

Cho Yang Shipping Co Ltd

South Korea

Funnel: Red with white 'P', black top
Hull: Black or dark blue with red boot-topping

Name	Year	GRT	DWT	LOA	Bm	Kts	Eng	Type	Former names
Coral	1965	10,272	17,171	152	20	13	M	B	ex-Belita 74
Duchess*	1976	13,085	24,144	164	24	14	M	B	
Goldean Pioneer†	1970	67,530	121,550	261	42	15	M	B	ex-Fukukawa Maru 84
Korean Chance	1980	29,362	34,274	213	32	23	M	CC	
Korean Loader*	1972	12,047	13,440	173	24	21	M	CC	ex-Seatrain Lexington 80, ex-Plutos 77
Korean Peace	1979	16,899	26,811	170	26	16	M	B	
Korean Pigeon	1979	16,899	26,811	170	26	16	M	B	
Korean Pioneer	1983	21,686	36,757	186	28	14	M	B	
Ocean Pearl*	1983	35,744	61,748	225	32	14	M	B	
Ocean Trader*	1984	35,744	61,748	225	32	14	M	B	
Southern Pacific*	1983	18,596	31,431	183	24	14	M	B	
Southern Progress*	1983	18,596	31,427	183	24	16	M	B	
Testarosa*	1970	66,903	115,721	261	41	14	M	B	ex-Goldean Mariner 85, ex-Jade Transporter 84, ex-Chikugo Maru 83

* Panamanian flag   † Philippine flag

H. Clarkson & Co Ltd

UK

Funnel: Red with white 'C' on white cross, black top separated by white band
Hull: White

Name	Year	GRT	DWT	LOA	Bm	Kts	Eng	Type	Former names
Jade Bounty	1978	5,480	6,596	119	19	17	M	RO	ex-Fremantle Express 85, ex-Jade Bounty 84, ex-Strider Gallant 78
Santa Marta	1978	5,480	6,596	119	19	17	M	RO	ex- Sapphire Bounty 85, ex-Adelaide Express 85, ex-Sapphire Bounty 84, ex-Nedlloyd Bounty 81, ex-Sapphire Bounty 80, ex-Strider Hero 78

NV CMB SA

Belgium

Funnel: Yellow with blue 'CMB'
Hull: Grey with red boot-topping or orange-brown with black boot-topping

Name	Year	GRT	DWT	LOA	Bm	Kts	Eng	Type	Former names
CMB Europe	1970	30,826	29,283	232	31	21	M	CC	ex-Dart Europe 84
Dart Continent	1979	15,683	18,643	177	27	22	M	CC	ex-Seapac Yorktown 81, ex-Seatrain Yorktown 81
Fabiolaville	1972	13,303	15,350	161	23	20	M	C	
Isla Plaza†	1980	7,096	9,728	151	22	21	M	R	ex-Pocahontas 85
Legia	1977	46,326	83,981	254	34	16	M	T	ex-E. R Legia 85
Maeterlinck	1984	32,696	38,981	207	32	20	M	CC	
Magritte	1983	38,235	75,724	242	32	14	M	B	
Mercator†	1976	35,493	39,590	252	31	24	ST	CC	
Methania	1978	78,511	67,879	280	42	19	ST	LNG	
Mineral Antwerpen†	1981	75,728	140,121	265	43	13	M	B	
Mineral Hoboken	1978	40,067	75,200	244	32	15	M	B	
Mineral Luxembourg	1977	40,067	75,203	244	32	15	M	B	
Mineral Marchienne	1973	36,330	66,350	235	32	16	M	B	
Mineral Samitri	1978	40,067	75,200	244	32	15	M	B	

Above: Cho Yang Shipping Co Ltd, *Korean Chance.* J. Krayenbosch

Below: H. Clarkson & Co Ltd, *Sapphire Bounty* (now renamed *Santa Marta*). J. Krayenbosch

Name	Year	GRT	DWT	LOA	Bm	Kts	Eng	Type	Former names
Montenaken	1969	11,519	16,562	161	23	20	M	C	
Montsalva	1973	11,748	16,500	161	23	18	M	C	
Ortelius*	1978	52,444	50,313	259	32	22	M2	CC	
Plantin	1981	20,849	25,070	186	28	20	M	CC	
Quellin	1977	14,967	20,597	164	26	17	M	CO	
Rhein Express........................	1984	32,696	38,200	207	32	20	M	CC	ex-Verhaeren 84
Vesalius†	1983	68,769	135,160	249	45	13	M	OBO	
Van Dyck	1977	14,967	20,663	164	26	17	M	CO	

* jointly owned by DAL Deutsche Afrika-Linien GmbH q.v.
† jointly owned by Ahlers NV q.v.

Bocimar NV
Funnel: Green with green 'B' on yellow band

Name	Year	GRT	DWT	LOA	Bm	Kts	Eng	Type	Former names
Eeklo*	1978	38,460	75,724	242	32	16	M	B	
Ensor	1982	68,769	135,160	249	45	13	M	OBO	
Permeke	1982	70,827	135,169	249	45	13	M	OBO	
Petrogas II*	1983	34,497	46,316	216	32	18	M	LPG	ex-Eupen 84
Temse*	1979	38,460	75,720	242	32	16	M	B	
Tielrode*	1983	18,128	36,060	155	27	16	M	LPG	ex-Petrogas II 83

Petrobulk Carriers NV
Funnel: Red-bown with logo on cream band
Hull: Red-brown with cream 'PETROBULK', dark red boot-topping

Name	Year	GRT	DWT	LOA	Bm	Kts	Eng	Type	Former names
Jahre Lion	1985	26,134	44,584	172	32	14	M	T	
Jahre Tiger	1985	26,113	46,100	172	32	14	M	T	
Naess Leopard	1985	26,134	45,372	172	32	14	M	T	
Naess Panther......................	1985	26,134	45,372	172	32	14	M	T	

* owned by NV Boelwerf SA

Common Bros (Management) Ltd   UK
Funnel: Black, blue edged white band with blue leaf logo within blue pennant outline
Hull: Black with red boot-topping

Name	Year	GRT	DWT	LOA	Bm	Kts	Eng	Type	Former names
David Gas†	1969	18,013	21,380	185	26	17	M	LPG	ex-Danian Gas 83, ex-Reliance Gas 77, ex-Amy Multina 77, ex-Phillips Arkansas 71
Sheldon Gas†	1967	13,334	14,982	177	24	16	M	LPG	ex-Isfonn 83
Simon Gas†	1968	6,463	8,205	124	20	16	M	LPG	ex-Permian Gas 83, ex-Global Gas 77, ex-Cap d'Antibes 75
Spring Delight	1984	12,783	9,891	152	24	18	M	R	

† Liberian flag

Conoco Inc.   USA
Funnel: Red with white 'globe' device
Hull: Black with red boot-topping

Name	Year	GRT	DWT	LOA	Bm	Kts	Eng	Type	Former names
Venture Europe*	1975	122,394	276,050	341	54	15	ST	T	ex-Conoco Europe 78
Venture Independence*	1976	117,646	274,774	337	55	16	ST	T	ex-Conoco Independence 78

* Liberian flag

Above: NV CMB SA, *Maeterlinck.* J. Krayenbosch

Below: NV CMB SA, *Van Dyck.* J. K. Byass

CTM-Cia Portuguesa de Transportes Maritimos

Portugal

Funnel: Orange, yellow band between two blue bands
Hull: Dark blue with green boot-topping

Name	Year	GRT	DWT	LOA	Bm	Kts	Eng	Type	Former names
Bailundo	1969	11,586	16,097	158	12	15	M	C	ex-Artemonas 69
Bernardino Correa	1972	11,612	12,241	161	23	20	M	C	ex-Daphne 72
Carvalho Araujo	1972	11,327	12,291	161	23	20	M	C	ex-Itaquera 72
Congo	1961	9,543	11,520	158	19	18	M	C	ex-Nurnberg 71
H. Capelo	1965	10,946	12,500	166	21	18	M	C	ex-Moerdyk 73
Leiria*	1976	9,215	14,800	141	21	15	M	C	ex-Santa Ursula 82
Lobito	1959	5,981	9,974	145	18	15	M	C	
Malange	1971	12,203	14,813	172	22	18	M	C	
Muxima	1962	9,550	11,520	158	19	17	M	C	ex-Wolfsburg 71
Pereira d'Eca	1972	11,230	12,029	161	23	20	M	C	ex-Juno 72
Porto	1968	9,220	12,814	172	22	17	M	C	
Rio Cuanza	1971	19,660	32,671	202	24	17	M	B	
Rio Zambeze	1971	19,767	32,671	199	24	15	M	B	
Rocadas	1971	11,876	16,700	170	22	19	M	C	ex-Tropico 71
Serpa Pinto	1970	11,879	16,700	170	22	18	M	C	ex-Tropicalia 71

* Liberian flag

The Cunard Steam-Ship Co plc

UK

Funnel: Red with two black rings, black top; Yellow with red 'M' in blue bordered white diamond, black top
Hull: Grey with red boot-topping; black with red boot-topping (tankers)

Name	Year	GRT	DWT	LOA	Bm	Kts	Eng	Type	Former names
Carinthia	1973	9,749	10,972	156	21	20	M	R	ex-Cantaloupe 76
Carmania	1972	9,742	10,974	156	21	22	M	R	ex-Orange 76
Lucerna	1975	23,736	39,865	183	32	15	M	T	
Lumiere	1972	14,925	24,951	170	25	15	M	T	
Luminetta	1972	14,925	24,951	170	25	15	M	T	
Samaria	1973	12,059	12,374	175	23	23	M	R	ex-Chrysantama 76
Saxonia	1972	12,029	12,376	175	23	23	M	R	ex-Gladiola 76
Scythia	1972	12,059	12,376	175	23	23	M	R	ex-Iris Queen 76
Servia	1972	12,059	12,182	175	23	23	M	R	ex-Orchidea 76

see also Atlantic Container Line Ltd and Associated Container Transportation (Australia) Ltd

A/S Thor Dahl

Norway

Funnel: Grey with 'C' shaped blue fish on broad white band between two narrow red bands. Red stars fore and aft on white band
Hull: Grey with red boot-topping

Name	Year	GRT	DWT	LOA	Bm	Kts	Eng	Type	Former names
Thor 1	1978	14,795	20,075	165	23	17	M	C	
Thorsaga	1973	139,681	284,299	343	52	15	M	T	
Thorscape	1977	14,794	20,075	165	23	20	M	C	
Thorseggen*	1983	14,578	18,567	166	25	15	M	B	
Thorsholm	1973	139,680	284,299	343	52	15	M	T	

* British flag

Dammers & Van der Heide

Netherlands

Funnel: White with black 'V' between two blue bands
Hull: White with blue boot-topping

Name	Year	GRT	DWT	LOA	Bm	Kts	Eng	Type	Former names
Christina	1980	8,041	10,550	155	23	22	M	R	
Freezer Leopard	1978	7,546	7,674	141	20	20	M	R	ex-Freezer Ace 85

Above: CTM-Cia Portuguesa de Transportes Maritimos, *Bernardino Correa. J. K. Byass*

Above: The Cunard Steam-Ship Co plc, *Carmania. J. Krayenbosch*

Below: Dammers & Van der Heide, *Lanai. F. de Vries*

Name	Year	GRT	DWT	LOA	Bm	Kts	Eng	Type	Former names
Honolulu	1979	8,041	10,598	155	23	22	M	R	
Lanai	1980	8,041	10,598	155	23	22	M	R	
Peggy Dow	1985	11,335	10,550	155	23	23	M	R	
Rio Frio	1980	8,041	10,550	155	23	22	M	R	
Spring Bear	1984	12,739	9,472	152	24	19	M	R	ex-Spring Dream 85
Spring Bob	1984	12,105	10,098	151	24	19	M	R	ex-Spring Blossom 85
Spring Panda	1984	12,187	10,140	151	24	19	M	R	ex-Spring Ballard 85, ex-Spring Blossom 84
Tineke	1984	11,335	10,550	155	23	23	M	R	

J & J Denholm Ltd

UK

Funnel: Various
Hull: Black or grey with red boot-topping

Name	Year	GRT	DWT	LOA	Bm	Kts	Eng	Type	Former names
Australia	1974	22,294	21,103	209	27	23	M2	CC	ex-Malmos Monsoon 84
Broompark	1982	18,189	30,670	188	23	15	M	B	
Ga Chau	1977	18,622	29,554	170	27	15	M	B	ex-Wellpark 85
Lamma Forest	1977	18,604	29,560	170	27	15	M	B	ex-Clarkspey 81, ex-Star Bay 81, ex-Clarkspey 78
Lantau Trader	1979	17,414	28,873	180	23	15	M	B	ex-Graiglwyd 79
Malayan Reefer	1978	7,598	7,676	141	20	20	M	R	ex-Freezer Queen 85
Mexican Reefer	1979	7,599	7,603	141	20	20	M	R	ex-Freezer Prince 85
Pacific Express*	1971	48,321	103,480	257	39	15	M	OBO	ex-Navios Commodore 84, ex-Atlantic Bounty 82, ex-Dalsland 79, ex-Eric K. Fernstrom 78

* Liberian flag

VEB Deutfracht/Seereederei

GDR

Funnel: Yellow, red band bordered by narrow dark blue bands
Hull: Grey with green boot-topping

Name	Year	GRT	DWT	LOA	Bm	Kts	Eng	Type	Former names
Aken	1978	5,993	7,293	122	18	15	M	C	
Albin Kobis	1965	7,712	10,400	142	19	15	M	C	
Altenburg	1967	8,501	10,080	150	20	17	M	C	
Anton Saefkow	1965	7,723	10,400	142	19	15	M	C	
Arnstadt	1985	6,520	7,960	(113)	20	14	M	CC	
Aue	1959	15,827	23,815	182	23	14	M	OBO	ex-Virtaia 69
Bergen	1978	5,972	7,923	122	18	15	M	C	
Berlin-Hauptstadt der DDR	1980	10,225	13,655	157	22	18	M	CO	
Bernburg	1967	8,501	10,080	150	20	17	M	C	
Bernhard Bastlein	1965	7,723	10,400	142	18	15	M	C	
Blankenburg	1967	8,501	10,149	150	20	17	M	C	
Blankensee	1978	5,650	7,309	121	18	16	M	C	
Boizenburg	1967	8,501	10,080	150	20	17	M	C	
Burg	1974	5,999	7,923	122	18	15	M	C	ex-Joboy 77
Bussewitz	1983	14,377	13,935	152	23	12	M	LPG	
Colditz	1980	23,060	38,250	201	28	15	M	B	
Cottbus	1979	10,225	13,600	157	22	18	M	C	
Crimmitschau	1979	9,232	12,685	150	21	17	M	C	
Cunewalde	1976	5,744	7,496	121	18	16	M	C	
Dresden	1976	10,047	15,094	157	22	19	M	C	ex-Hawk 79
Edgar Andre	1962	7,704	10,300	142	19	15	M	C	
Eichsfeld	1967	6,110	7,499	136	18	17	M	C	
Eichwalde	1976	5,744	7,486	121	18	16	M	C	
Eilenburg	1967	8,501	10,080	150	20	17	M	C	
Eisenhuttenstadt	1960	23,357	38,242	200	27	15	M	O	ex-Mertainen 70
Erfurt	1980	10,229	13,600	157	22	18	M	C	
Ernst Moritz Arndt	1973	6,653	9,075	141	18	23	M	R	ex-King Edmund 77, ex-Bristol Clipper 77

Above: Dammers & Van der Heide, *Spring Panda. J. Krayenbosch*

Below: J & J Denholm Ltd, *Broompark. J. M. Kakebeeke*

Name	Year	GRT	DWT	LOA	Bm	Kts	Eng	Type	Former names
Ernst Schneller	1963	7,704	10,301	142	19	15	M	C	
Espenhain	1962	8,136	11,780	152	19	15	M	O	
Ferdinand Freiligrath	1967	5,587	6,600	153	19	22	M	R	ex-Parma II 74, ex-Parma 73
Fichtelberg	1975	5,055	7,597	138	21	18	M2	RO	ex-Tor Caledonia 75
Flaming	1967	6,110	7,499	136	18	17	M	C	
Fleesensee	1978	5,651	7,309	121	18	16	M	C	
Fliegerkosmonaut der DDR Sigmund Jahn	1979	9,231	12,685	150	21	17	M	C	
Frankfurt/Oder	1979	10,230	13,600	157	22	19	M	C	
Franz Stenzer	1965	5,955	8,128	131	18	17	M	C	ex-Lloyd Helsinki 75, ex-Transatlantic 72
Frederic Joliot Curie	1970	5,711	6,950	129	17	17	M	C	
Freital	1977	5,993	7,922	122	18	15	M	C	
Freyburg	1969	8,600	10,150	150	20	17	M	C	
Friedrich Engels	1972	11,023	13,100	166	23	21	M	C	
Fritz Reuter	1964	4,571	6,149	139	18	19	M	R	ex-Pacific Express 73
Furstenberg	1971	5,711	6,950	130	17	17	M	C	
Furstenwalde	1976	5,744	7,496	121	18	16	M	C	
Georg Handke	1965	9,576	13,500	156	21	18	M	C	ex-Talana 75
Georg Schumann	1966	7,723	10,400	142	19	15	M	C	
Georg Weerth	1967	5,565	6,600	153	19	22	M	R	ex-Padua 74
Gerhart Hauptmann	1974	6,650	7,076	141	18	23	M	R	ex-King Egbert 78, ex-Liverpool Clipper 76
Geringswalde	1977	5,744	7,486	121	18	16	M	C	
Glauchau	1980	9,224	12,685	157	22	18	M	C	
Gleichberg	1982	4,691	6,704	138	21	18	M2	RO	
Gorlitz	1974	22,798	38,249	200	28	15	M	B	
Gotha	1971	24,649	43,444	203	29	16	M	B	ex-Budapest 84
Groditz	1972	22,798	38,249	200	28	15	M	B	
Halberstadt	1985	6,520	7,960	(113)	20	14	M	CC	
Halle	1976	10,047	15,694	157	22	19	M	C	ex-Phenix 79
Heinrich Heine	1975	6,641	9,146	141	18	22	M	R	
Heinz Kapelle	1965	7,723	10,476	142	19	15	M	C	
Hettstedt	1976	5,960	7,922	122	18	15	M	C	ex-Jobebe 77
Jena	1978	15,979	23,200	177	23	15	M	BC	
Johanngeorgenstadt	1985	6,520	7,960	(113)	20	14	M	CC	
John Brinckman	1964	6,313	6,249	139	18	19	M	R	ex-Belnippon 73
John Schehr	1966	7,723	10,400	142	19	15	M	C	
Karl Marx	1971	11,023	13,100	166	23	21	M	C	
Karl Marx Stadt	1977	10,050	15,094	157	22	18	M	C	ex-Crop 81, ex-Condor 80
Kolpinsee	1979	5,664	7,309	121	18	16	M	C	
Kothen	1978	5,992	7,888	122	18	16	M	C	
Leipzig	1980	10,149	13,600	157	22	18	M	C	
Liebenwalde	1977	5,744	7,496	121	18	16	M	C	
Lieselotte Herrmann	1965	7,723	10,400	140	18	14	M	C	
Lubbenau	1961	8,229	11,830	152	19	15	M	O	
Luckenwalde	1976	5,744	7,496	121	18	16	M	C	
Magdeburg	1970	8,529	10,149	150	20	17	M	C	
Mansfeld	1962	8,228	11,830	152	19	15	M	O	
Mathias Thesen	1966	7,723	10,400	142	19	15	M	C	
Max Reichpietsch	1966	7,712	10,400	142	19	15	M	C	
Meissen	1979	15,979	23,200	177	23	17	M	BC	
Meyenburg	1968	8,501	10,080	150	20	17	M	C	
Mittenwalde	1977	5,744	7,496	121	18	16	M	C	
Muggelsee	1979	5,664	7,309	121	18	16	M	C	
Muhlhausen Thomas-Muntzer Stadt	1976	11,127	12,350	150	22	19	M	C	ex-Muhlhausen 80
Naumburg	1967	8,501	10,080	151	20	17	M	C	
Neubrandenburg	1970	8,529	10,130	150	20	17	M	C	
Nienburg	1969	8,584	10,080	150	20	17	M	C	
Nordhausen	1976	11,127	12,349	150	22	19	M	C	

Below: VEB Deutfracht/Seereederei, *F. Freilirath. J. Krayenbosch*

Above: VEB Deutfracht/Seereederei, *Luckenwalde. M. D. J. Lennon*

Name	Year	GRT	DWT	LOA	Bm	Kts	Eng	Type	Former names
Oranienburg	1968	8,501	10,080	150	20	17	M	C	
Pasewalk	1979	9,231	12,685	150	21	18	M	C	
Potsdam	1978	10,224	13,600	157	22	19	M	C	
Premnitz	1981	23,060	38,250	200	28	16	M	B	
Prignitz	1967	6,110	7,499	136	18	17	M	C	
Pritzwalk	1978	9,231	12,685	150	21	18	M	C	
Quedlinburg	1967	8,501	10,080	150	20	17	M	C	
Rabenau	1979	4,841	6,780	130	17	16	M	C	
Radebeul	1984	13,557	17,330	158	23	13	M	CO	
Rhinsee	1980	5,651	7,309	120	18	16	M	CO	
Ronneburg	1968	8,501	10,080	150	20	17	M	C	
Rostock	1967	8,501	10,080	150	20	17	M	C	
Rudolf Breitscheid	1964	7,723	10,419	142	19	15	M	C	
Rudolf Diesel	1975	5,735	7,434	121	18	16	M	C	
Rudolstadt	1985	6,520	7,950	(113)	20	14	M	CC	
Sangerhausen	1977	11,127	12,350	150	22	19	M	C	
Schonwalde	1977	5,744	7,486	121	18	16	M	C	
Schwarzburg	1968	8,501	10,080	150	20	18	M	C	
Schwedt	1975	33,134	59,650	212	32	17	M	T	ex-Jane Maersk 84
Schwerin	1979	10,224	13,600	157	22	18	M	C	
Schwielowsee	1979	5,744	7,486	121	18	16	M	C	
Senftenberg	1962	8,228	11,704	152	19	15	M	O	
Sondershausen	1977	11,127	12,350	150	22	19	M	C	
Sonneberg	1969	5,715	6,950	129	17	16	M	C	
Stollberg	1970	5,711	6,950	129	17	17	M	C	
Suhl	1976	10,047	15,094	157	22	19	M	C	ex-Merlin 1 79
Thale	1960	14,489	22,564	172	22	14	M	B	ex-H. L. Lorentzen 64
Theodor Fontane	1966	4,979	4,875	135	18	21	M	R	
Theodor Korner	1975	6,641	9,146	141	18	22	M	R	
Theodor Storm	1966	4,950	4,875	135	18	21	M	R	
Trattendorf	1962	8,136	11,869	152	19	15	M	O	
Trentsee	1980	5,664	7,309	121	18	16	M	C	
Vockerode	1963	8,136	11,773	152	19	15	M	O	
Weimar	1977	15,979	23,199	177	27	15	M	BC	
Werbellinsee	1979	5,644	7,309	121	18	16	M	C	
Werner Seelenbinder	1964	7,704	10,300	142	19	15	M	C	
Wilhelm Florin	1964	7,704	10,300	142	19	15	M	C	
Wismar	1969	5,715	6,950	129	17	16	M	C	
Wittenberg	1969	5,711	6,950	129	17	17	M	C	
Zwickau	1958	15,611	23,319	182	23	14	M	OBO	ex-Vitafors 69

H. Ditlev Simonsen & Co — Norway

Funnel: Yellow with swallow-tail houseflag and narrow black top
Hull: Grey with red boot-topping

Name	Year	GRT	DWT	LOA	Bm	Kts	Eng	Type	Former names
A.M. Carrier*	1982	19,867	40,490	176	32	15	M	T	ex-Mosor Carrier 85
A.M. Trader*	1983	22,054	40,520	176	32	15	M	T	ex-Moser Trader 83
Biscaya‡	1973	55,219	103,332	257	39	15	M	BO	ex-Viscaya 85
Stolt Ventura*	1978	17,091	29,500	171	30	15	M	T	ex-Ventura 85
Stolt Vincita*	1977	17,092	29,034	171	30	15	M	T	ex-Vincita 85
Taibit†	1963	12,665	19,508	170	22	15	M	T	ex-Vibit 85
Vanja	1978	178,446	357,599	363	60	15	ST	T	
Velma	1977	178,445	357,632	363	60	15	ST	T	
Vigan†	1973	36,269	64,435	224	32	14	M	B	ex-Vikara 85

* Liberian flag   † owned by O. Ditlev-Simonsen Jnr, Panamanian flag   ‡ British flag

Team Ship Ltd/UK

Funnel: Orange with white 'ST'
Hull: Orange with red boot-topping

Name	Year	GRT	DWT	LOA	Bm	Kts	Eng	Type	Former names
London Team	1974	56,273	104,850	256	39	15	M	BO	
Scandia Team	1974	56,008	105,550	256	39	15	M	BO	

Above: VEB Deutfracht/Seereederei, *Radebeul.* J. M. Kakebeeke

Above: H. Ditlev-Simonsen & Co, *Stolt Vincita.* J. Krayenbosch

Below: Peter Dohle Schiffahrts KG, *Ville du Sahara.* J. M. Kakebeeke

Peter Dohle Schiffahrts KG

FGR

Funnel: Black, black 'PD' on white diamond on broad red band bordered by narrow white bands
Hull: Black or grey, green boot-topping

Name	Year	GRT	DWT	LOA	Bm	Kts	Eng	Type	Former names
Actuaria*	1983	8,516	12,300	148	22	15	M	CC	
Arkona	1985	18,200	22,600	165	27	19	M	CC	
Carolina	1978	9,311	12,710	151	21	17	M	CO	ex-Auvergne 84, ex-Carolina 83, ex-Tielbank 81, ex-Carolina 79
Charlotta	1978	9,311	12,710	151	21	17	M	CO	ex-Testbank 81, ex-Charlotta 79
Norlandia	1983	4,998	4,250	106	18	12	M2	RO	ex-Barber Norlandia 85, ex-Norlandia 84
Vesna	1982	9,084	11,812	147	23	16	M	CC	ex-Katjana 85, ex-Contship Asia 83, ex-Katjana 82
Vida	1981	7,897	11,847	133	21	16	M	CC	ex-Amaranta 85
Ville du Ponant III*	1983	8,516	13,126	148	22	15	M	CC	ex-Arabella 85
Ville du Sahara	1984	12,691	17,253	151	25	19	M	CC	ex-Altonia 84
Zim Brisbane	1983	9,829	14,355	148	23	14	M	CC	ex-Apollonia 83

* Singapore flag

The East Asiatic Co Ltd

Denmark

A/S Det Ostasiatiske Kompagni

Funnel: Yellow, with 'EAC' in blue
Hull: Black with white line and red boot-topping

Name	Year	GRT	DWT	LOA	Bm	Kts	Eng	Type	Former names
Boringia	1978	20,295	19,974	202	26	22	M	CC	
Falstria	1971	20,325	20,215	202	26	21	M	CC	
Fionia	1977	20,295	19,974	202	26	22	M	CC	
FP Carrier*	1976	24,014	38,816	182	29	16	M	B	ex-Patula 82
FP Clipper*	1985	22,890	41,200	(178)	29	14	M	B	
FP Conveyor*	1975	23,996	38,860	182	29	16	M	B	ex-Ponderosa 82
Jutlandia	1973	54,035	40,824	289	32	26	M3	CC	
Malacca	1976	35,904	63,980	225	32	15	M	B	
Meonia	1972	20,325	20,215	202	26	22	M	CC	
Mixteco	1978	16,150	23,771	159	25	16	M	CO	ex-Samoa 83
Morelia	1976	35,904	63,980	225	32	15	M	B	
Panama	1977	20,943	33,401	171	26	15	M	T	
Paranagua	1977	20,943	33,401	171	26	15	M	T	
Pasadena†	1976	20,511	33,715	171	26	15	M	T	
Patagonia†	1976	20,550	33,715	171	26	15	M	T	ex-Piraeus Sea 76
Pattaya	1981	20,933	33,420	171	26	15	M	T	
Selandia	1973	54,035	40,824	289	32	26	M3	CC	

* owned by Forest Product Carriers (International) Ltd, Bahamas flag
† Bahamas flag

Ellerman City Liners

UK

Funnel: Buff, black top and white dividing band
Hull: Grey with red boot-topping

Name	Year	GRT	DWT	LOA	Bm	Kts	Eng	Type	Former names
ACT 8*	1978	53,790	47,209	259	32	21	M2	CC	ex-City of Durban 85, ex-Portland Bay 84, ex-City of Durban 83
City of York	1976	10,801	16,213	150	21	16	M	C	

* owned jointly with Charente Steamship Co Ltd (Harrison Line)
See also Associated Transportation (Australia) Ltd and Ben Line Steamers Ltd

Above: The East Asiatic Co Ltd, *Selandia. J. M. Kakebeeke*

Below: Ellerman City Liners, *ACT 8. J. Krayenbosch*

Empresa de Nav Alianca SA

Brazil

Funnel: Bands of yellow, red and white below black top; two yellow linked circles with black A
Hull: Blue with red boot-topping

Name	Year	GRT	DWT	LOA	Bm	Kts	Eng	Type	Former names
Alcyon	1980	17,893	26,131	173	27	15	M	B	ex-Paulina 80
Alessandra	1983	8,680	14,279	141	20	15	M	C	
Almaris	1981	17,893	26,151	173	27	15	M	B	
Alnave	1982	17,893	26,151	173	27	15	M	B	
Ana Luisa	1981	8,680	14,328	141	20	15	M	B	
Bianca	1981	8,680	14,328	141	21	15	M	C	
Copacabana	1984	20,995	27,000	179	31	18	M	CC	
Daniela	1981	26,512	38,687	201	27	15	M	B	
Flamengo	1985	21,000	27,000	179	31	18	M	CC	
Lily	1984	26,512	38,847	201	27	15	M	B	ex-Arpoador 85
Maringa	1971	10,417	12,487	161	23	20	M	C	
Monte Alto	1979	8,680	14,328	135	21	15	M	C	
Monte Cristo	1979	8,680	15,022	135	21	15	M	C	
Monte Pascoal	1979	8,680	15,022	135	21	15	M	C	
Olinda	1972	10,417	12,487	161	23	20	M	C	
Rafaela	1980	26,512	38,822	201	27	15	M	B	
Renata	1983	8,680	14,279	141	20	15	M	C	

Empresa Lineas Maritimas Argentinas SA

Argentina

Funnel: Black with wide white band and two narrow blue bands and blue flag incorporating an anchor and St Andrew's cross
Hull: Black or grey, red boot-topping

Name	Year	GRT	DWT	LOA	Bm	Kts	Eng	Type	Former names
Almirante Stewart	1967	6,531	8,278	148	20	17	ST	C	
Almirante Storni	1978	9,236	14,930	141	20	15	M	C	
Catamarca II	1976	10,229	15,513	150	21	16	M	C	
Chaco	1978	12,762	20,704	159	23	15	M	C	
Chubut	1977	12,762	20,717	159	23	16	M	C	
Cordoba	1977	10,113	15,895	141	21	15	M	C	
Corrientes II	1977	12,762	20,717	159	23	15	M	C	
Dr Atilio Malvagni	1980	9,236	14,930	140	20	16	M	C	
Entre Rios II	1977	12,762	20,805	159	23	16	M	C	
Formosa	1978	12,762	20,717	159	23	15	M	C	
General Manuel Belgrano	1980	9,236	14,930	141	20	15	M	C	ex-General Belgrano 81
Glacier Ameghino	1981	9,013	10,452	146	21	20	M	R	
Glacier Perito Moreno	1981	9,013	10,450	146	21	20	M	R	
Glacier Viedma	1982	9,013	10,450	146	21	20	M	R	
Jujuy II	1977	9,236	14,930	141	20	15	M	R	
La Pampa	1978	10,076	15,644	145	21	16	M	C	
La Rioja	1976	10,231	15,486	150	21	16	M	C	
Lago Lacar	1962	8,486	10,457	157	20	15	M	C	
Libertador General Jose de San Martin	1979	9,236	14,930	140	20	15	M	C	
Mendoza	1977	10,232	15,515	150	21	16	M	C	
Misiones II	1979	12,762	20,717	159	23	15	M	C	
Neuquen II	1979	9,230	14,930	141	20	15	M	C	
Presidente Ramon S. Castillo	1980	9,236	14,930	140	20	15	M	C	
Rio Abaucan	1973	8,558	10,232	151	22	18	M	C	
Rio Calchaqui	1972	10,409	11,500	153	21	17	M	C	
Rio Calingasta	1973	8,558	10,232	151	22	18	M	C	
Rio Cincel	1973	9,059	10,070	148	20	18	M	C	

Above: Empresa de Nav Alianca SA, *Flamengo. J. Krayenbosch*

Above: Empresa de Nav Alianca SA, *Monte Cristo. J. K. Byass*

Below: Empresa Lineas Maritimas Argentinas SA, *Glacier Perito Moreno. J. Krayenbosch*

Name	Year	GRT	DWT	LOA	Bm	Kts	Eng	Type	Former names
Rio Corrientes	1963	8,482	10,476	157	20	15	M	C	
Rio de la Plata	1971	10,409	11,500	153	21	15	M	C	
Rio Deseado	1974	9,059	10,070	148	20	18	M	C	
Rio Esquel	1976	9,059	10,070	148	20	18	M	C	
Rio Gualeguay	1976	9,059	10,070	148	20	18	M	C	
Rio Iguazu	1975	9,059	10,070	148	20	18	M	C	
Rio Limay	1974	9,059	10,070	148	20	18	M	C	
Rio Los Sauces	1973	8,558	10,232	151	22	18	M	C	
Rio Marapa	1972	8,558	10,232	151	22	18	M	C	
Rio Negro II	1977	12,762	20,717	159	23	16	M	C	
Rio Neuquen	1974	8,558	10,232	151	22	18	M	C	
Rio Olivia	1977	9,059	10,070	148	20	18	M	C	
Rio Parana	1971	10,409	11,500	153	21	17	M	C	
Rio Pilcomayo	1973	8,558	10,232	151	22	18	M	C	
Rio Salado	1966	5,904	7,854	150	19	19	M	C	
Rio Teuco	1973	9,059	10,070	148	20	18	M	C	
Salta	1976	9,236	14,980	141	20	15	M	R	
San Juan	1976	10,232	15,489	150	21	16	M	C	
San Luis	1977	10,232	15,001	150	21	16	M	C	
Santa Cruz II	1977	12,762	20,717	159	23	16	M	C	
Santa Fe II	1976	12,762	20,704	159	23	16	M	C	
Santiago del Estero	1977	10,232	15,413	150	21	16	M	C	
Tierra Del Fuego II	1977	12,762	20,717	159	23	16	M	C	
Tucuman	1978	9,236	14,930	141	20	15	M	R	

John T. Essberger   FRG
DAL Deutsche Afrika Linien Gmbh

Funnel: Buff, narrow red band on black-edged broad white band, black top
Hull: Grey with red boot-topping

Name	Year	GRT	DWT	LOA	Bm	Kts	Eng	Type	Former names
Acquila Trader‡	1975	114,468	260,849	338	52	14	ST	T	ex-Marietta 84
Auriga‡	1976	194,992	431,232	378	69	15	ST	T	ex-Robinson 85, ex-Golar Patricia 79
Corona Star‡	1976	114,553	232,750	317	50	16	ST	T	ex-Okeanos 84
Elbia†	1978	7,030	14,100	135	22	14	M	B	
Helvetia†	1980	15,291	25,400	185	23	15	M	B	
Invicta†	1983	9,948	16,430	145	22	15	M	B	
Juventia†	1982	15,176	24,482	185	23	14	M	B	
Maringa†	1977	12,761	20,409	162	23	16	M	CO	ex-Tagama 84, ex-Talana 78, ex-Transkei 77
Padang‡	1971	12,123	19,469	156	23	15	M	B	ex-Sanaga 84, ex-Woermann Sanaga 76
Sarnia†	1974	11,229	19,427	156	23	15	M	B	ex-Selinda 84, ex-Senegal 76, ex-Woermann Senegal 76
Sunda Sea†	1972	12,111	19,435	156	23	15	M	B	ex-Hudson Deep 84, ex-Woermann Sassandra 80
Tagama*	1982	11,918	17,400	158	23	17	M	CO	ex-Woermann Wahehe 85, ex-Wahehe 84
Transvaal	1978	52,811	49,730	259	32	23	M2	CC	
Ubena	1983	20,345	28,422	174	28	18	M	CC	
Usaramo	1982	20,345	28,149	174	28	18	M	CC	
Victoria Bay	1983	20,345	28,422	174	28	18	M	CC	ex-Usambara 84
Volans‡	1975	164,758	362,118	363	60	15	ST	T	ex-London Trader 85, ex-Sea Stratus 78
Woermann Wadai†	1984	11,918	17,400	158	23	17	M	CO	ex-Wadai 84
Woermann Wakamba	1977	13,734	19,259	162	23	16	M	CO	ex-Tabora 85
Zambesi†	1973	12,109	19,426	156	23	15	M	B	ex-Maritime Transporter 78, ex-Woermann Sambesi 76

* Togo flag
† Panamian flag
‡ Liberian flag

Above: John T. Essberger, *Usaramo. J. Krayenbosch*

Below: John T. Essberger, *Woermann Wadai. J. Krayenbosch*

The Ethiopian Shipping Lines

Ethiopa

Funnel: Green with yellow lion on brown eight-spoke wheel beneath deep red top
Hull: Grey with red boot-topping

Name	Year	GRT	DWT	LOA	Bm	Kts	Eng	Type	Former names
Abbay Wonz	1984	10,830	10,420	137	23	16	M	C	ex-Mengistu H. M. 84
Abyot	1985	10,881	10,500	137	23	16	M	C	
Andinet	1985	11,691	14,000	(126)	23	14	M	C	
Lion of Ethiopia	1966	5,182	6,655	121	17	15	M	C	ex-Lion of Judah 75
Queen of Sheeba	1966	5,182	6,655	121	17	15	M	C	
Ras Dedgen	1961	6,615	9,513	139	18	15	M	C	ex-Barbergate 75, ex-Ferngate 73

Evergreen Marine Corp (Taiwan) Ltd

Taiwan

Funnel: Black with green eight-pointed star on broad white band
Hull: Black with red boot-topping

Name	Year	GRT	DWT	LOA	Bm	Kts	Eng	Type	Former names
Ever Better*	1984	7,017	9,688	121	21	15	M	CC	
Ever Breeze*	1984	7,017	9,692	121	21	15	M	CC	
Ever Bridge*	1984	7,017	9,680	121	21	15	M	CC	
Ever Garden	1984	37,203	43,401	231	32	20	M	CC	
Ever Gather	1984	37,023	43,401	231	32	20	M	CC	
Ever Genius	1984	37,023	43,401	231	32	20	M	CC	
Ever Gentle	1984	37,023	43,401	231	32	20	M	CC	
Ever Gentry	1984	37,023	43,401	231	32	20	M	CC	
Ever Giant*	1984	37,023	43,198	231	32	20	M	CC	
Ever Gifted	1984	37,023	43,401	231	32	20	M	CC	
Ever Gleamy	1985	37,000	43,000	231	32	20	M	CC	
Ever Globe*	1984	37,042	43,285	231	32	20	M	CC	
Ever Glory*	1984	37,042	43,310	231	32	20	M	CC	
Ever Going*	1983	37,042	43,198	231	32	20	M	CC	
Ever Golden	1985	37,023	42,700	231	32	20	M	CC	
Ever Goods*	1985	40,300	32,800	231	32	20	M	CC	
Ever Govern	1985	36,500	42,700	231	32	20	M	CC	
Ever Grace*	1984	37,023	43,198	231	32	20	M	CC	
Ever Grade*	1984	37,042	43,198	231	32	20	M	CC	
Ever Grand*	1984	37,042	42,700	231	32	20	M	CC	
Ever Greet*	1984	37,042	43,293	231	32	20	M	CC	
Ever Growth	1984	37,042	42,700	231	32	20	M	CC	
Ever Guard*	1983	37,042	43,198	231	32	20	M	CC	
Ever Guide*	1983	37,042	43,137	231	32	20	M	CC	
Ever Laurel	1980	24,804	28,904	203	30	21	M	CC	ex-Ever Large 85
Ever Level	1980	24,804	28,896	203	30	21	M	CC	ex-Ever Light 83
Ever Linking*	1983	24,802	28,916	203	30	18	M	CC	
Ever Living	1980	24,804	28,902	203	30	21	M	CC	ex-Ever Lucky 83
Ever Loading*	1983	24,802	28,849	203	30	18	M	CC	
Ever Lyric	1979	24,804	28,900	203	30	21	M	CC	ex-Ever Loyal 83
Ever Oasis*	1982	14,743	29,290	183	24	15	M	CC	
Ever Obtain*	1983	17,343	30,254	183	24	15	M	CC	
Ever Ocean*	1982	18,518	27,071	183	24	15	M	CC	
Ever Onward*	1982	15,993	31,194	183	24	15	M	CC	
Ever Order*	1982	18,518	27,071	183	24	15	M	CC	
Ever Orient*	1982	17,343	30,254	183	24	15	M	CC	
Ever Shine*	1976	12,413	15,764	174	24	20	M	CC	
Ever Spring*	1975	12,413	15,752	174	24	20	M	CC	
Ever Summit*	1975	12,413	15,752	174	24	20	M	CC	
Ever Superb*	1976	12,413	15,752	174	24	20	M	CC	
Ever Trust*	1972	12,529	15,276	152	22	16	M	C	ex-Ever Safety 80
Ever Valor*	1978	14,949	20,186	187	25	19	M	CC	
Ever Value*	1978	14,949	20,158	187	25	19	M	CC	
Ever Vigor	1979	16,358	20,025	187	25	23	M	CC	
Ever Vital	1979	16,358	20,151	187	25	23	M	CC	

Above: The Ethiopian Shipping Lines, *Lion of Ethiopia. J. M. Kakebeeke*

Below: Evergreen Marine Corp (Taiwan) Ltd, *Ever Globe. F. R. Sherlock*

Uniglory Marine Corp

Name	Year	GRT	DWT	LOA	Bm	Kts	Eng	Type	Former names
Uni-Forever	1979	12,869	18,813	162	23	15	M	CC	ex-Ever Forever 84, ex-Green Forever 83
Uni-Fortune	1978	13,396	18,828	162	23	15	M	CC	ex-Ever Fortune 84, ex-Green Fortune 83
Uni-Forward	1978	12,901	18,821	162	23	15	M	CC	ex-Ever Forward 84, ex-Green Forward 83
Uni-Handsome*	1976	11,317	17,821	155	23	16	M	CC	ex-Ever Handsome 85
Uni-Humanity*	1975	11,289	17,806	155	23	15	M	CC	ex-Ever Humanity 85
Uni-Master*	1977	11,401	16,859	163	23	15	M	CC	ex-Accord 84, ex-Galleon Amethyst 82, ex-Ever Master 79
Uni-Mercy*	1976	11,652	16,822	163	23	15	M	CC	ex-Action 84, ex-Galleon Sapphire 82, ex-Ever Mercy 80
Uni-Modest*	1976	11,401	16,862	163	23	15	M	CC	ex-Access 84, ex-Galleon Topaz 82, ex-Ever Modest 80
Uni-Moral*	1976	11,507	16,802	163	23	15	M	CC	ex-Achieve 84, ex-Galleon Opal 84, ex-Galleon Onyx 81, ex-Ever Moral 80
Uni-Pioneer	1973	7,806	11,875	145	19	16	M	CC	ex-Ever Pioneer 85
Uni-Promoter	1973	7,806	11,857	145	19	16	M	CC	ex-Ever Promoter 85

* Panamanian flag
70% owned associated Company

Exxon Corp   USA

Funnel: Black with red letters 'EXXON' over wide blue stripe on white band
Hull: Black

Name	Year	GRT	DWT	LOA	Bm	Kts	Eng	Type	Former names
Exxon Baltimore	1960	23,299	52,759	226	31	16	ST	T	ex-Esso Baltimore 73
Exxon Baton Rouge	1970	34,266	76,813	247	38	17	ST	T	ex-Esso Boston 73
Exxon Baytown	1984	25,180	43,000	194	32	16	M	T	
Exxon Benicia	1979	75,272	175,547	276	53	15	ST	T	
Exxon Boston	1960	23,299	52,800	226	31	17	ST	T	ex-Esso Boston 73
Exxon Charleston	1983	27,798	40,802	194	32	16	M	T	
Exxon Galveston	1970	12,769	27,726	171	29	12	M2	T	ex-Exxon Sunshine State 78, ex-Enco Sunshine State 73 (tug), ex-Exxon Port Everglades 78, ex-Enco Port Everglades 73 (barge)
Exxon Gettysburg	1957	23,665	41,528	218	28	16	ST	T	ex-Esso Gettysburg 73
Exxon Houston	1964	31,697	72,688	244	36	17	ST	T	ex-Esso Houston 73
Exxon Jamestown	1957	19,734	41,528	218	28	16	ST	T	ex-Esso Jamestown 73
Exxon Lexington	1958	19,734	41,566	218	28	16	ST	T	ex-Esso Lexington 73
Exxon New Orleans	1965	32,035	72,655	244	36	17	ST	T	ex-Esso New Orleans 73
Exxon North Slope	1979	75,272	175,305	276	53	14	ST	T	
Exxon Philadelphia	1970	34,266	77,382	247	38	17	ST	T	ex-Esso Philadelphia 73
Exxon Princeton	1982	22,025	43,648	201	27	15	M	T	ex-Eileen Ingram 84
Exxon San Francisco	1970	34,266	76,813	247	38	17	ST	T	ex-Esso San Francisco 73
Exxon Washington	1957	19,734	41,590	218	28	16	ST	T	ex-Esso Washington 73
Exxon Wilmington	1984	25,150	43,000	194	32	16	M	T	
Exxon Yorktown	1983	22,025	43,643	201	27	15	M	T	ex-Hunter Armistead 84

Esso Petroleum Co Ltd/UK

Funnel: Black with red 'Esso' inside blue ring on broad white band
Hull: Black or grey with red boot-topping

Name	Year	GRT	DWT	LOA	Bm	Kts	Eng	Type	Former names
Esso Aberdeen	1967	58,273	112,834	277	42	17	ST	T	ex-Imperial Ottawa 78
Esso Clyde	1972	12,317	20,449	167	23	16	M	T	
Esso Demetia	1973	125,293	258,979	341	52	16	ST	T	
Esso Fawley	1967	11,064	18,377	163	22	16	M	T	

Above: Evergreen Marine Corp (Taiwan) Ltd, *Ever Loading* J. M. Kakebeeke

Below: Exxon Corp, *Esso Hafnia.* J. Krayenbosch

Name	Year	GRT	DWT	LOA	Bm	Kts	Eng	Type	Former names
Esso Forth...............	1967	40,675	76,209	247	38	15	M	T	ex-Esso Antwerp 83
Esso Humber	1969	12,824	21,457	170	24	14	M	T	ex-Esso Penang 78
Esso Mersey	1972	12,323	20,187	167	23	15	M	T	
Esso Milford Haven	1967	10,902	18,089	163	22	16	M	T	
Esso Severn	1975	12,316	20,449	167	23	16	M	T	
Esso Tees...............	1970	12,683	21,116	170	24	15	M	T	ex-Esso Bataan 83
Esso Warwickshire	1962	48,049	86,115	263	34	17	ST	T	

Esso Italiana SpA/Italy

Name	Year	GRT	DWT	LOA	Bm	Kts	Eng	Type	Former names
Esso Genova...........	1973	13,679	22,349	161	24	15	M	T	ex-Esso Brisbane 81
Esso Venezia	1969	13,073	21,413	170	24	15	M	T	ex-Esso Chittagong 81

Esso Eastern Marine Ltd/Australia

Name	Year	GRT	DWT	LOA	Bm	Kts	Eng	Type	Former names
Esso Gippsland	1972	15,579	24,489	172	24	14	M	T	

managed by Associated Steamships Pte Ltd (TNT Bulkships Ltd)

Esso Soc Anon Francaise/France

Name	Year	GRT	DWT	LOA	Bm	Kts	Eng	Type	Former names
Esso Languedoc...........	1973	126,186	256,726	348	52	15	ST	T	
Esso Normandie	1974	137,578	273,999	349	52	16	ST	T	
Esso Parentis	1973	13,544	22,698	161	24	15	M	T	ex-Esso Guam 82
Esso Picardie	1976	137,578	278,734	349	52	15	ST	T	
Esso Port Jerome........	1972	13,544	22,726	161	24	15	M	T	ex-Esso Kumamoto 80

Esso Tankers Inc/Liberia

Name	Year	GRT	DWT	LOA	Bm	Kts	Eng	Type	Former names
Esso Africa*	1975	137,166	274,467	349	52	15	ST	T	
Esso Albany............	1973	12,806	23,694	161	24	15	M	T	
Esso Atlantic*	1977	259,532	516,893	400	71	15	ST	T	
Esso Bangkok†	1968	12,994	22,755	170	24	15	M	T	
Esso Bombay†	1968	12,994	22,755	170	24	15	M	T	
Esso Bayonne	1974	17,211	29,634	170	26	16	M	T	
Esso Bayway	1978	27,439	50,915	197	37	16	M	T	
Esso Bilbao*	1975	146,309	283,271	342	53	16	ST	T	
Esso Caribbean......	1976	208,060	395,156	378	68	15	ST	T	ex-Andros Petros 77
Esso Castellon†	1968	39,085	77,514	247	38	16	M	T	
Esso Coral Gables..........	1975	19,568	38,691	192	27	15	M	T	
Esso Fuji†	1973	55,897	66,173	246	40	15	M	LPG	
Esso Geneva*	1975	150,622	307,233	340	56	15	ST	T	ex-Esso Al-Duriyah 84, ex-Al-Duriyah 83, ex-Esso Geneva 77
Esso Hawaii*	1975	146,309	283,274	342	53	16	ST	T	
Esso Honolulu*	1974	146,309	283,397	343	53	16	ST	T	
Esso Indonesia	1974	114,797	261,230	338	52	15	ST	T	
Esso Japan	1976	192,679	406,640	362	70	15	ST	T	
Esso Kagoshima	1974	114,797	261,158	338	52	16	ST	T	
Esso Kaohsiung*	1983	57,858	88,649	245	40	15	M	T	
Esso Kawasaki*	1974	150,622	307,431	340	56	15	ST	T	
Esso Le Havre†	1976	173,086	387,936	373	64	15	ST	T	
Esso Madrid*	1976	188,634	388,119	374	64	16	ST	T	
Esso Mediterranean	1976	202,798	395,367	378	68	15	ST	T	ex-Homeric 77
Esso Melbourne.........	1974	17,211	29,591	171	26	16	M	T	
Esso Mexico†	1982	45,799	87,170	245	40	15	M	T	
Esso Nassau*	1982	57,858	88,429	245	40	15	M	T	ex-Esso Puerto Rico 82
Esso Okinawa.........	1973	114,797	260,910	338	52	15	ST	T	
Esso Osaka*	1973	146,312	283,154	343	53	16	ST	T	
Esso Pacific...........	1977	234,627	516,423	400	71	15	ST	T	
Esso Palm Beach†	1978	27,439	50,801	197	37	16	M	T	

Above: Exxon Corp, *Esso Forth.* J. Krayenbosch

Below: Exxon Corp, *Esso Osaka.* M. D. J. Lennon

Name	Year	GRT	DWT	LOA	Bm	Kts	Eng	Type	Former names
Esso Portland	1978	27,439	50,888	197	37	16	M	T	
Esso Shimizu	1973	17,218	29,634	170	26	16	M	T	
Esso Tampa	1975	19,568	38,711	192	27	15	M	T	
Esso Westernport*	1977	63,495	67,840	240	32	15	M	LPG	
Esso Zurich†	1965	37,336	67,681	244	35	16	M	T	

* owned by Esso International Shipping (Bahamas) Co Ltd, Bahamas flag
† Panamanian flag

Esso Tankschiff Reederei GmbH/FGR

Name	Year	GRT	DWT	LOA	Bm	Kts	Eng	Type	Former names
Esso Deutschland	1976	203,869	421,684	377	69	16	ST	T	
Esso Hamburg	1974	126,192	256,740	348	52	15	ST	T	

Esso Tankvaart Nederlandse Antillen NV/Netherlands Antilles

Name	Year	GRT	DWT	LOA	Bm	Kts	Eng	Type	Former names
Esso Saba	1974	126,192	256,740	348	52	15	ST	T	

A/S Norske Esso/Norway

Name	Year	GRT	DWT	LOA	Bm	Kts	Eng	Type	Former names
Esso Slagen	1968	11,059	18,797	163	22	16	M	T	

Esso Tankers (S) Pte Ltd/Singapore

Name	Year	GRT	DWT	LOA	Bm	Kts	Eng	Type	Former names
Esso Orient	1974	50,853	99,900	272	39	15	M	TGC	ex-Svea Marina 78
Esso Port Dickson	1968	12,994	21,456	170	24	15	M	T	
Esso Yokohama	1969	12,994	21,445	170	24	15	M	T	

Dansk Esso A/S/Denmark

Funnel: Yellow with narrow black top and 'Esso' sign on broad white band
Hull: Grey with red boot-topping

Name	Year	GRT	DWT	LOA	Bm	Kts	Eng	Type	Former names
Esso Callunda	1974	13,503	22,691	161	24	15	M	T	
Esso Danica	1975	21,961	38,720	191	27	14	M	T	
Esso Hafnia	1974	13,503	23,211	161	24	15	M	T	

Farrell Lines Inc

USA

Funnel: Yellow, with red, white and blue houseflag, narrow black top
Hull: Black, red boot-topping and white dividing line

Name	Year	GRT	DWT	LOA	Bm	Kts	Eng	Type	Former names
American Resolute	1979	17,902	16,205	186	24	20	ST	CC	ex-Resolute 82
Argonaut	1979	17,902	16,401	186	24	20	ST	CC	
Export Challenger	1963	11,000	12,726	150	22	19	ST	CO	
Export Champion	1963	11,000	12,726	150	22	19	ST	CO	
Export Freedom	1972	17,904	16,605	186	24	21	ST	CC	
Export Patriot	1973	17,904	16,605	186	24	21	ST	CC	

Fearnley & Eger A/S

Norway

Funnel: Black with blue Maltese Cross on white panel on red band
Hull: Grey or red with red boot-topping

Name	Year	GRT	DWT	LOA	Bm	Kts	Eng	Type	Former names
Ferncarrier	1975	39,039	52,092	225	41	14	M	HLS	ex-Kollbris 82
Ferncourt*	1985	22,000	39,600	176	32	15	M	T	
Ferncraig*	1985	22,000	39,600	176	32	15	M	T	
Ferncroft	1982	3,204	5,600	130	19	11	M	RO	
Ferngolf*	1980	9,830	10,729	165	28	18	M	V	ex-Ocean Golf 84
Fernpassat*	1981	15,670	10,678	165	28	18	M	V	ex-Ocean Passat 84

Above: Farrel Lines Inc., *American Resolute*. F. R. Sherlock

Below: Fearnley & Eger A/S, *Ferncarrier*. M. D. J. Lennon

Name	Year	GRT	DWT	LOA	Bm	Kts	Eng	Type	Former names
Fernteam	1975	66,118	123,043	257	39	15	M	BO	ex-Gothia Team 81, ex-Angelic Harmony 78
Manhattan Prince†	1974	48,041	87,061	246	38	15	M	T	
Mirafiori*	1974	140,563	290,271	348	52	15	ST	T	ex-Ocean Trader 84, ex-Vespasian 82
Nahoda Biru†	1971	20,715	28,876	179	26	16	M	BV	ex-Blue Master 84

* Liberian flag   † Singapore flag

NV Stoomvaart-Maats 'Oostzee'/Netherlands

Funnel: Yellow with red bordered black band, black top
Hull: Black or grey with red boot-topping

Name	Year	GRT	DWT	LOA	Bm	Kts	Eng	Type	Former names
Bulk H	1982	35,561	62,343	225	32	14	M	B	ex-Hilversum 85
Bulk I	1982	35,561	62,343	225	32	14	M	B	ex-Ittersum 85
Norman Amstel*	1983	35,911	64,000	224	32	14	M	B	
Norman Maas	1983	35,911	64,210	224	32	14	M	B	

* Singapore flag

Fednav Ltd   Canada

Funnel: White, red design incorporating part of maple leaf, interlinked 'F' and 'C', broad black top
Hull: Red with dark red boot-topping

Name	Year	GRT	DWT	LOA	Bm	Kts	Eng	Type	Former names
Atlantic Superior	1982	24,638	38,510	223	23	15	M	B	
Federal Lakes*	1973	16,382	20,544	208	23	19	M2	RO	ex-Avon Forest 85

* US flag

Belcan SA/Belgium

Name	Year	GRT	DWT	LOA	Bm	Kts	Eng	Type	Former names
Amazon	1981	74,729	140,832	267	43	14	M	B	
Federal Danube	1980	21,661	35,630	216	23	14	M	B	
Federal Hudson	1978	18,758	28,660	177	23	15	M	BC	ex-Rocroi 79
Federal Hunter	1984	75,733	140,194	265	43	14	M	B	
Federal Huron	1978	18,461	28,660	177	23	15	M	BC	ex-Fontenov 79
Federal Maas	1981	22,285	35,630	216	23	14	M	B	
Federal Ottawa	1980	21,661	35,630	216	23	14	M	B	
Federal Skeena	1983	75,733	140,194	289	43	14	M	B	
Federal Thames	1981	21,661	35,630	216	23	14	M	M	
Orinoco	1982	74,729	140,832	267	43	14	M	B	

managed by UBEM SA

Federal Pacific (Liberia) Ltd/Liberia

Name	Year	GRT	DWT	LOA	Bm	Kts	Eng	Type	Former names
Federal Calumet	1977	20,182	35,927	222	23	14	M	B	
Federal Elbe	1981	18,237	28,645	177	23	15	M	B	
Federal Fraser	1977	22,377	40,110	184	28	15	M	B	
Federal Rhine	1977	20,182	35,910	222	23	14	M	B	
Federal Saguenay	1978	16,986	30,353	189	23	15	M	B	
Federal Schelde	1977	21,484	35,922	222	23	14	M	B	
Federal St Laurent	1978	16,986	30,350	189	23	15	M	B	

Soc Finanziaria Marittima (FINMARE)   Italy

'Italia' Soc per Azioni di Nav

Funnel: White with red top and separate narrow green band
Hull: Black with white line or white with green line

Name	Year	GRT	DWT	LOA	Bm	Kts	Eng	Type	Former names
Acadia	1971	13,130	18,909	175	23	20	M	CC	ex-Atlantica Genova 76, ex-Gruenfels 71
Americana	1975	22,245	23,838	208	31	23	ST	CC	

Above: Fednav Ltd, *Federal Hudson*. J. K. Byass

Below: Soc Finanziaria Maritima, *Serena*. J. Krayenbosch

Name	Year	GRT	DWT	LOA	Bm	Kts	Eng	Type	Former names
D'Albertis	1978	19,501	17,239	186	27	23	M	RO	
Da Mosto	1979	19,500	17,240	186	27	23	M	RO	
Italica	1975	22,245	24,220	210	31	23	ST	CC	
Pancaldo	1979	19,500	17,241	186	27	23	M	RO	

Lloyd Triestino SpA di Nav

Funnel: Yellow with blue top and narrow blue band
Hull: White with blue line and boot-topping or black

Name	Year	GRT	DWT	LOA	Bm	Kts	Eng	Type	Former names
Adria	1981	7,431	6,820	148	23	20	M2	RO	
Africa	1977	27,835	25,332	208	31	23	ST	CC	
Apulia	1981	6,977	5,408	148	23	20	M2	RO	
Europa	1978	27,839	23,942	208	31	23	ST	CC	
Julia	1981	6,225	6,496	146	23	20	M2	RO	
Lloydiana	1972	28,688	34,044	226	31	25	ST	CC	
Mediterranea	1973	26,794	26,093	208	31	23	ST	CC	ex-Nipponica 73
Nipponica	1972	26,784	26,093	208	31	23	ST	CC	ex-Perla 73
Serena	1978	10,804	12,825	160	22	22	M	C	
Torre del Greco	1982	7,431	6,812	148	23	20	M2	RO	
Trieste	1978	10,804	12,825	160	22	22	M	C	

O/Y Finnlines Ltd   Finland

Funnel: Black with black 'F' in white oval interrupting blue band between two white bands
Hull: Grey or black with green boot-topping

Name	Year	GRT	DWT	LOA	Bm	Kts	Eng	Type	Former names
Finn Falcon*	1984	21,625	32,813	195	25	14	M	B	ex-Finnfalcon 85
Finn Whale*	1985	21,625	32,800	195	25	14	M	B	ex-Finnwhale 85
Finn Timber*	1974	15,646	23,698	177	23	15	M	B	ex-Finntimber 85
Finnarctis	1979	12,385	14,906	155	21	16	M	C	
Finnbeaver	1975	19,906	34,995	196	24	15	M	B	ex-Passad 78, ex-Matai 78
Finneagle	1978	9,075	14,763	183	24	18	M	RO	ex-Foss Eagle 85, ex-Abuja Express 83, ex-Emirates Express 81
Finnfighter†	1978	12,390	14,931	159	21	16	M	C	ex-Kaipola 79
Finnfury	1975	19,906	34,995	196	24	15	M	B	ex-Monsun 78, ex-Forano 78
Finnhawk	1980	13,341	18,451	194	27	19	M2	RO	
Finnmerchant†	1982	8,426	13,025	155	25	18	M	RO	
Finnoak	1971	5,690	7,316	118	18	14	M	C	ex-Kaipola 75
Finnoceanis	1978	12,407	14,874	159	21	14	M	C	ex-Walki 80
Finnpine†	1972	6,616	8,123	129	19	17	M	C	
Finnpolaris	1981	12,385	14,906	155	21	16	M	C	
Finnnrose	1980	13,375	18,541	194	27	19	M2	RO	
Finntrader	1985	18,000	31,000	185	28	15	M	B	
Koiteli	1972	5,689	7,214	118	18	14	M	C	
Kotkaniemi	1968	12,052	18,289	158	22	14	M	B	
Lotila	1977	12,410	14,829	159	21	16	M	C	
Pokkinen	1980	12,385	14,883	159	21	16	M	C	
Puhos	1977	16,994	30,017	189	23	15	M	B	
Rautaruukki	1976	7,439	10,890	143	21	15	M	B	
Tuira	1972	5,690	7,214	118	18	15	M	C	
Varjakka	1979	12,385	14,938	159	21	16	M	C	

* British flag   † owned by Neste O/Y

Finska Angfartygs A/B (EFFOA)   Finland

Funnel: Black with two white bands
Hull: Grey, green or white with red or blue boot-topping

Name	Year	GRT	DWT	LOA	Bm	Kts	Eng	Type	Former names
Aldebaran	1977	12,887	16,560	164	23	15	M	BC	ex-Khalij Enterprise 78, ex-Aldebaran 77
Antares	1977	12,904	16,560	164	23	15	M	BC	ex-Chase One 79, ex-Antares 78

Above: OY Finnlines Ltd, Finnhawk. C. R. Sherlock

Below: Finska Ang. A/B, Aldebaran. J. Krayenbosch

Name	Year	GRT	DWT	LOA	Bm	Kts	Eng	Type	Former names
Arcturus	1982	8,425	13,030	155	25	18	M	RO	
Ariel	1970	7,571	9,529	147	19	17	M	C	
Astrea	1978	13,044	16,560	164	23	15	M	BC	
Atalaya	1978	13,069	16,559	164	23	15	M	BC	ex-Chase Two 79, ex-Atalaya 78
Canopus	1977	4,817	6,565	142	19	18	M2	RO	ex-Finnforest 82, ex-Rolita 79
Castor	1972	6,616	8,253	129	19	17	M	C	ex-Finntrader 82
Clio	1972	5,690	7,329	118	18	14	M	C	ex-Finnkraft 82, ex-Valkeakoski 77
Hektos*	1978	9,350	12,200	165	26	19	M2	RO	ex-Timmerland 84
Hesperus*	1979	9,350	12,007	165	26	19	M2	RO	ex-Vasaland 83
Oihonna	1984	20,203	12,870	155	25	20	M	RO	
Pallas	1971	7,890	10,160	147	20	17	M	C	
Patria	1978	14,233	17,435	156	23	17	M	C	
Pollux	1977	14,116	17,161	155	23	15	M	C	
Rhea	1971	7,890	10,160	147	20	17	M	C	
Salla	1979	12,390	14,863	159	21	15	M	B	ex-Walki Paper 79
Taurus	1983	24,464	37,425	183	30	15	M	BC	
Tellus	1984	24,869	37,425	183	30	15	M	BC	

* managed for Oy Partek Ab

James Fisher & Sons plc

UK

Funnel: Buff with black 'F' on white band below black top
Hull: Black with red boot-topping

Name	Year	GRT	DWT	LOA	Bm	Kts	Eng	Type
Sir John Fisher*	1982	37,811	67,368	228	32	14	M	B
Thamesfield*	1977	30,427	50,300	213	30	16	M	B

* managed by Hunting Stag Management Ltd

Albright & Wilson Ltd

Funnel: Green with white 'AW' logo

Name	Year	GRT	DWT	LOA	Bm	Kts	Eng	Type
Albright Explorer	1968	6,870	10,689	126	18	14	M	CH
Albright Pioneer	1968	6,789	10,469	126	18	14	M	CH

Flota Mercante Grancolombiana SA

Colombia

Funnel: White, yellow ship's wheel intertwined with brown rope, black centre with 'Flota Mercante Grancolombia' and colour map of western hemisphere
Hull: Black with red boot-topping

Name	Year	GRT	DWT	LOA	Bm	Kts	Eng	Type	Former names
Almirante Jose Padilla	1984	12,286	17,300	159	25	15	M	CO	
Arturo Gomez J.	1983	12,287	17,300	159	25	16	M	CO	
Cartagena de Indias	1982	12,287	16,012	159	25	16	M	CO	
Ciudad de Armenia	1978	11,942	12,132	182	27	17	M	CO	
Ciudad de Barrancabermeja	1975	24,136	39,860	183	32	15	M	T	ex-Lucellum 78
Ciudad de Bogota	1964	11,655	12,450	166	21	16	M	C	
Ciudad de Bucaramanga	1965	11,687	12,352	166	21	16	M	C	
Ciudad de Buenaventura	1966	11,687	12,362	166	21	16	M	C	
Ciudad de Cucuta	1966	11,855	12,362	166	21	16	M	C	
Ciudad de Manizales	1971	10,301	12,149	168	24	16	M	C	
Ciudad de Medellin	1971	10,301	12,148	168	24	16	M	C	
Ciudad de Neiva	1977	11,699	12,880	181	27	17	M	C	
Ciudad de Pasto	1978	11,955	16,000	175	27	17	M	CO	
Ciudad de Popayan	1976	11,699	15,000	181	27	17	M	C	
Ciudad de Santa Marta	1977	11,693	15,000	181	27	17	M	C	
Golfo de Chiriqui†	1977	11,945	16,167	181	27	17	M	CO	ex-Ciudad de Quito 84
Republica de Colombia	1983	12,287	16,010	159	25	16	M	CO	
Rio Magdalena	1968	11,189	12,362	166	21	19	M	C	
San Andres y Providencia	1983	12,286	15,969	159	25	16	M	CO	
Simon Bolivar	1984	12,286	17,300	159	25	16	M	CO	

† Panamanian flag

Above: Finska Ang. A/B, *Arcturus. J. K. Byass*

Below: Flota Mercante Grancolombiana SA, *Cartagena de Indias. F. R. Sherlock*

Furness Withy & Co Ltd

Houlder Bros & Co Ltd

Funnel: Black with white Maltese Cross on broad red band (or blue with white 'S' logo*)
Hull: Black with red boot-topping

Name	Year	GRT	DWT	LOA	Bm	Kts	Eng	Type	Former names
Abbey*	1979	63,301	118,750	264	41	16	M	B	ex-Andwi 79
British Steel*	1984	90,831	173,028	287	47	14	M	B	
Cavendish†	1971	26,802	29,528	194	29	17	M	LPG	
Clerk-Maxwell	1966	8,298	9,067	141	19	15	M	LPG	
Faraday	1971	19,754	25,150	187	27	15	M	LPG	
Lord Kelvin	1978	21,374	28,400	192	26	19	M	LPG	
Oswestry Grange	1964	5,440	8,076	113	16	15	M	B	ex-Chelwood 74

† jointly owned by Gazocean SA

Hadley Shipping Co Ltd (Warwick & Esplen Ltd)

Funnel: Yellow with black top and black 'HSC' in white diamond
Hull: Black with red boot-topping

Name	Year	GRT	DWT	LOA	Bm	Kts	Eng	Type	Former names
Clymene	1976	5,999	7,923	122	18	15	M	C	ex-Barbizon 79, ex-Oyapok 78, ex-Jocare 77
Corato	1983	15,175	24,492	185	23	15	M	B	

Pacific Steam Navigation Co Ltd/Shaw Savill & Albion Co Ltd

Funnel: Buff with black top (SS&A) or yellow (PSN)
Hull: Light grey with red boot-topping or black with green boot-topping

Name	Year	GRT	DWT	LOA	Bm	Kts	Eng	Type	Former names
Andes	1984	32,152	37,042	203	32	15	M	CC	
Dunedin	1980	18,140	16,378	176	27	19	M	CC	
Oroya	1978	14,124	17,944	163	23	16	M	C	

See also C. Y. Tung Group

Geest Industries Ltd

Funnel: White with red 'G' on outlined yellow diamond between two narrow blue bands
Hull: White with green boot-topping

Name	Year	GRT	DWT	LOA	Bm	Kts	Eng	Type	Former names
Geestbay	1981	7,729	9,970	159	21	19	M	R	
Geestland	1972	5,871	7,630	149	19	21	M	R	
Geestport	1981	7,729	9,970	159	21	19	M	R	
Geeststar	1973	5,871	7,654	149	19	21	M	R	

Cie Generale Maritime

Funnel: White with red and blue insignia, black top
Hull: Black or white with red boot-topping

Name	Year	GRT	DWT	LOA	Bm	Kts	Eng	Type	Former names
Anjou	1978	16,505	23,648	173	23	17	M	CO	ex-Ville de Brest 83
Caraibe	1978	27,366	23,058	204	31	21	M	CC	
Cavelier de la Salle	1977	23,909	38,962	188	28	15	M	B	
CGM Bretagne	1977	6,417	8,511	129	19	16	M	C	ex-Impala 85
CGM Var	1977	16,649	20,760	163	26	18	M	CO	ex-Mansart 85, ex-Hapag Lloyd Trier 82, ex-Mansart 81
CGM Velay	1977	16,649	20,760	163	26	18	M	CO	ex-Haussmann 85
Champlain	1974	68,596	121,934	261	41	15	M	OBO	
Dumont d'Urville	1977	23,909	38,923	188	28	15	M	B	
Eiffel	1977	16,649	20,754	163	27	18	M	CO	

Below: Cie Generale Maritime, *Caraibe.* J. K. Byass

Name	Year	GRT	DWT	LOA	Bm	Kts	Eng	Type	Former names
Fort Desaix†	1981	30,401	28,955	215	31	21	M	CC	
Fort Fleur d'Epee	1980	32,670	30,998	210	32	22	M2	CC	
Fort Royal	1979	32,670	30,998	210	32	22	M2	CC	
Fort Saint Charles†	1980	30,401	28,955	215	31	21	M	CC	
Gauguin	1977	13,928	19,669	164	27	19	M	RO	
Kangourou	1971	26,437	29,810	228	30	21	ST	CC	
Korrigan	1973	57,249	48,850	289	32	22	M2	CC	
La Fayette	1978	27,305	22,842	204	31	22	M	CC	
Licorne Atlantique	1973	131,619	264,596	336	54	15	ST	OO	
Licorne Oceane**	1975	137,854	286,000	339	54	15	ST	T	
Licorne Pacifique	1975	132,810	269,007	347	52	15	ST	T	
Maripasoula	1977	6,417	8,542	129	19	17	M	C	ex-Atlanta II 82, ex-Atlanta 79
Monet	1978	13,928	19,669	164	27	19	M	RO	
Monge	1977	43,738	54,158	231	35	20	M	LPG	
Montcalm	1977	64,971	123,125	268	39	15	M	B	
Pascal	1976	13,218	19,044	153	23	16	M	LPG	
Pointe la Rose	1974	6,561	8,600	155	21	20	M	RO	
Pointe Madame	1973	6,561	8,600	155	21	20	M	RO	
Pointe Sans Souci	1973	6,561	8,600	155	21	20	M	RO	
Renoir	1978	13,928	19,669	164	27	19	M	RO	
Rodin	1975	13,979	21,700	207	30	22	M	RO	
Rostand	1976	13,979	21,653	207	30	22	M	RO	
Rousseau	1976	13,979	21,643	207	30	22	M	RO	
Sibelius*	1972	3,990	5,618	138	20	19	M	RO	
Soufflot	1977	17,715	20,747	163	26	18	M	CO	
Tellier‡	1973	27,426	21,301	197	29	18	ST	LNG	
Utrillo	1978	13,928	19,669	164	27	19	M	RO	
Zambeze	1971	13,208	17,666	167	24	19	M	C	
Zeebrugge	1971	13,208	17,666	167	24	19	M	C	

* owned by Cie Generale Trans-Baltique (jointly by Wallenius Rederierna q.v.)
† owned by Cie Nav Atlantique

** Liberian flag   ‡ jointly owned by Gaz de France
see also Atlantic Container Line

Cie de Nav D'Orbigny

Name	Year	GRT	DWT	LOA	Bm	Kts	Eng	Type	Former names
Ro-Ro Genova*	1980	8,957	10,208	170	25	18	M	RO	ex-Qatar Express 81, ex-Ro-Ro Genova 80
Ro-Ro Manhatten*	1980	8,957	10,208	170	25	18	M	RO	
Toulon	1972	13,208	17,680	167	24	19	M	C	ex-Zelande 83, ex-Zanzibar 72

* owned by Soc Dunkerquoise d'Armement

Horn-Linie/FRG
Funnel: Grey with white H on blue above red bands
Hull: White

Name	Year	GRT	DWT	LOA	Bm	Kts	Eng	Type	Former names
Hornbay*	1970	8,064	6,629	144	20	20	M	R	ex-Fort Sainte Marie 81
Horncap*	1968	8,064	6,625	144	20	20	M	R	ex-Aquilon 81
Hornfels	1985	4,453	6,000	106	18	15	M	C	

* Liberian flag

Globtik Management Ltd   UK
Funnel: Black with white 'T' on blue disc
Hull: Black with GLOBTIK TANKERS, red boot-topping

Name	Year	GRT	DWT	LOA	Bm	Kts	Eng	Type	Former names
Brazil Glory**	1981	54,094	88,389	247	40	15	M	T	
Brazil Pride**	1983	54,095	96,296	247	40	15	M	T	
Globtik Britain**	1980	55,326	86,648	244	42	14	M	T	
Globtik London*	1973	213,894	483,933	379	62	14	ST	T	
Globtik Tokyo*	1973	213,866	483,662	379	62	15	ST	T	
Narnian Sea**	1979	54,055	88,868	247	40	14	M	T	

* Liberian flag   ** Bahamas flag

Cie Generale Maritime, *Licorne Atlantique. J. K. Byass*

95

Gorthons Rederier

Sweden

Funnel: Yellow with curled device on blue disc
Hull: Grey

Name	Year	GRT	DWT	LOA	Bm	Kts	Eng	Type	Former names
Ada Gorthon	1984	13,525	9,995	156	22	15	M	RO	
Alida Gorthon	1977	10,574	14,299	141	22	15	M	B	
Ingrid Gorthon	1977	10,538	14,299	141	22	15	M	B	
Joh. Gorthon	1977	4,506	8,350	142	21	15	M	RO	
Lovisa Gorthon	1979	4,094	6,421	120	21	14	M	RO	
Margit Gorthon	1977	10,538	14,298	141	22	15	M	B	
Maria Gorthon	1984	13,496	9,995	156	22	15	M	RO	
Ragna Gorthon	1979	4,116	6,422	120	21	14	M	RO	
Stig Gorthon	1979	4,095	6,381	120	21	14	M	RO	
Tilia Gorthon	1975	7,284	9,662	129	20	15	M	B	

Gotaas-Larsen Inc A/S

Liberia

Funnel: Blue, white flag with blue five-pointed star within blue ring
Hull: Charcoal grey with red or green boot-topping

Name	Year	GRT	DWT	LOA	Bm	Kts	Eng	Type	Former names
Gimi	1976	84,855	72,480	294	42	19	ST	LGC	
Golar Freeze	1977	85,159	66,200	288	43	20	ST	LGC	
Golar Frost*	1980	42,587	55,200	225	34	16	M	LPG	
Golar Kansai	1972	98,905	219,287	316	48	16	ST	T	
Golar Kanto	1974	98,905	219,175	327	48	16	ST	T	
Golar Petrosea	1976	19,608	32,574	171	26	15	M	T	
Golar Petrosun	1978	19,608	31,645	171	26	17	M	T	
Golar Petrotrade	1975	19,118	31,499	171	26	15	M	T	
Golar Robin	1973	98,905	219,387	316	48	16	ST	T	
Golar Spirit	1981	93,815	80,239	289	45	19	ST	LGC	
Hilli	1975	84,855	72,479	293	42	19	ST	LGC	ex-Golar Glacier 75
Honan Ruby	1970	99,011	215,780	327	48	16	ST	T	ex-Golar Nichu 80
Khannur	1977	84,855	73,074	293	42	19	ST	LGC	

* Norwegian flag
see also Chevron Corp.

Great Eastern Shipping Co Ltd

India

Funnel: Yellow, with 'AHB' on red and green houseflag, narrow black top
Hull: Grey or black with red boot-topping

Name	Year	GRT	DWT	LOA	Bm	Kts	Eng	Type	Former names
Jag Deesh	1976	13,392	21,402	162	23	15	M	C	
Jag Dharma	1976	13,392	21,420	162	23	15	M	C	
Jag Dhir	1976	13,392	21,379	162	23	15	M	C	
Jag Doot	1975	13,392	21,293	162	23	15	M	C	
Jag Jiwan	1968	13,766	22,105	160	23	13	M	B	ex-Anne Mildred Brovig 73
Jag Jyoti	1968	11,096	17,893	160	21	16	M	T	ex-Anco Jyoti 77, ex-Jag Jyoti 74, ex-Anco Knight 72, ex-Athel Knight 70
Jag Krishi	1968	11,661	20,359	156	23	14	M	B	ex-Sonid 85, ex-Rachel 80
Jag Laadki	1972	66,724	101,500	257	39	13	M	OBO	ex-Athel Laadki 77, ex-Jag Laadki 74
Jag Laxmi	1976	66,724	122,146	257	39	15	M	OBO	
Jag Leela	1976	66,724	122,146	256	39	15	M	OBO	
Jag Manek	1967	13,755	23,710	160	23	15	M	B	ex-Andrea Brovig 73
Jag Palak	1985	20,500	25,300	170	26	15	M	T	
Jag Pari	1982	20,991	29,139	171	27	14	M	T	
Jag Prabhat	1985	20,500	25,300	170	26	15	M	T	
Jag Pragati	1985	20,500	25,300	170	26	15	M	T	
Jag Prakash	1974	15,849	25,073	171	25	15	M	T	
Jag Preeti	1981	21,206	29,139	171	27	14	M	T	
Jag Priya	1975	20,416	32872	171	26	14	M	T	

Gorthons Rederier, *Margit Gorthon*. J. Krayenbosch

Name	Year	GRT	DWT	LOA	Bm	Kts	Eng	Type	Former names
Jag Rakshak	1969	9,443	14,966	138	20	13	M	C	ex-Mahakiran 83, ex-Jag Ravi 80, ex-Green Walrus 71
Jag Shakti	1972	15,498	26,646	183	22	15	M	B	ex-Cunard Caravel 74
Jag Shanti	1972	15,498	26,646	183	22	15	M	B	ex-Cunard Campaigner 74

Christian Haaland

Norway

Funnel: White with black 'H' and top
Hull: Black with white band

Name	Year	GRT	DWT	LOA	Bm	Kts	Eng	Type	Former names
Concordia Fjord	1983	15,709	24,470	159	24	17	M	LPG	
Concordia Star	1977	16,821	17,230	171	25	18	M	C	ex-Hoegh Star 84, ex-Costa Atlantica 83, ex-Concordia Star 82
Concordia Sun	1979	16,816	18,080	171	25	17	M	C	ex-Hoegh Sun 84, ex-Costa Mediterranea 83, ex-Concordia Sun 82
Nyhammer	1975	40,397	48,772	231	32	18	M	LPG	
Nyhavn	1968	12,974	15,230	163	23	18	M	LPG	
Nyholt	1975	17,923	31,501	171	26	16	M	T	
Nyhorn	1975	17,922	31,501	171	26	16	M	T	

Hapag-Lloyd AG

FRG

Funnel: Yellow with black, white and red bands at top
Hull: Black with red boot-topping

Name	Year	GRT	DWT	LOA	Bm	Kts	Eng	Type	Former names
Alemania Express	1978	27,939	23,103	204	31	21	M	CC	
America Express	1978	27,939	23,103	204	31	22	M	CC	
Bavaria	1966	10,896	12,429	165	22	21	M	C	
Biscay*	1972	14,211	21,876	165	23	15	M	CC	ex-Fulda Express 84, ex-Frankenfels 80, ex-Aristandros 74
Borussia	1965	10,897	12,429	165	22	21	M	C	
Bremen Express	1972	57,495	47,838	287	32	23	ST	CC	
Caribia Express	1976	27,936	23,047	204	31	22	M	CC	
CGM Lorraine	1970	16,736	21,307	181	28	21	M	CC	ex-Leverkusen Express 85, ex-Leverkusen 78
Dusseldorf Express	1977	32,928	32,477	222	32	21	M	CC	
Erlangen Express	1970	16,736	21,185	181	29	21	M	CC	ex-Incotrans Progress 82, ex-Erlangen Express 81, ex-Erlangen 79
Frankfurt Express	1981	58,384	51,480	288	32	23	M2	CC	
Hamburg Express	1972	58,000	49,532	288	32	23	ST	CC	
Hammonia	1965	10,900	12,430	164	22	20	M	C	
Hongkong Express	1972	57,496	47,838	287	32	23	ST	CC	
Humboldt Express	1984	32,444	34,307	200	32	16	M	CC	
Incotrans Pacific	1971	16,736	21,307	181	29	21	M	C	ex-Hoechst Express 84, ex-Incotrans Promise 83, ex-Hoechst Express 81, ex-Hoechst 79
Isar Express*	1973	14,211	21,885	171	23	16	M	CC	ex-Ibn Al Suwaidi 82, ex-Frauenfels 80, ex-Aristipos 74
Isla de la Plata†	1984	32,444	34,000	200	32	16	M	CC	ex-Cordillera Express 84
Koln Express	1978	32,959	32,484	210	32	22	M	CC	
Leeward*	1972	14,211	21,834	169	23	16	M	CC	ex-Lizard 85, ex-Neckar Express 84, ex-Freienfels 80, ex-Aristarchos 74
Ludwigshafen Express	1970	16,736	21,305	181	28	21	M	CC	ex-Ludwigshafen 79
Melbourne Express	1970	25,558	31,610	218	29	22	ST	CC	
Nurnberg Express	1978	39,500	40,900	241	32	22	M	CC	

Above: Hapag-Lloyd AG, *Isar Express. F. R. Sherlock*

Below: Hapag-Lloyd AG, *Isla de la Plata. J. Krayenbosch*

Name	Year	GRT	DWT	LOA	Bm	Kts	Eng	Type	Former names
Passero†	1971	13,017	18,909	175	23	20	M	CC	ex-Ruhr Express 85, ex-Geyerfels 80, ex-Seatrain Bremen 80, ex-Geyerfels 79, ex-Seatrain Valley Forge 78, ex-Atlantic Livorno 77, ex-Geyerfels 71
Sierra Express	1977	27,939	23,051	204	31	21	M	CC	ex-Cordillera Express 83
Stuttgart Express	1977	38,930	40,900	241	32	22	M	CC	
Sydney Express	1970	27,407	33,333	226	31	22	ST	CC	
Tokio Express	1973	57,994	47,700	273	32	23	ST	CC	ex-Scandutch Edo 85, ex-Tokio Express 84
Windward*	1974	14,212	21,885	169	23	16	M	CC	ex-Werra 84, ex-Werra Express 84, ex-Freudenfels 80, ex-Aristotelis 76

* owned by Hansa Bulk Pte Ltd, Singapore flag
† Panamanian flag

Kosmos Bulkschiffahrt GmbH
Funnel: Orange, broad white band with blue swallowtail pennant
Hull: Black, red boot-topping

Name	Year	GRT	DWT	LOA	Bm	Kts	Eng	Type	Former names
Berlin*	1975	176,008	392,798	370	64	16	ST	T	ex-Ioannis Colocotronis 76

* Liberian flag

T & J Harrison Ltd   UK
The Charente Steamship Co Ltd
Funnel: Black with red band between two white bands
Hull: Black with red boot-topping

Name	Year	GRT	DWT	LOA	Bm	Kts	Eng	Type	Former names
Author	1980	28,031	22,858	203	31	22	M	CC	ex-Benarmin 82, ex-Author 81
CGM Provence	1977	27,867	23,491	204	31	21	M	CC	ex-Adviser 85, ex-Asia Winds 84, ex-Adviser 83
Pisces Pioneer	1984	21,309	35,310	178	30	15	M	B	
Pisces Planter	1984	21,309	35,310	178	30	15	M	B	
Wanderer	1973	16,317	27,570	174	23	15	M	B	
Warrior	1974	16,317	27,571	174	23	15	M	B	
Wayfarer	1973	16,317	27,571	174	23	15	M	B	

See also Ellerman-Harrison Container Line and Associated Container Transportation (Australia) Ltd

Harrisons (Clyde) Ltd   UK
Funnel: Red with black top
Hull: Blue with red boot-topping

Name	Year	GRT	DWT	LOA	Bm	Kts	Eng	Type	Former names
Valdivia	1981	35,522	65,785	225	32	14	M	B	

see also Fednav Ltd

Cardigan Shipping Co Ltd
Funnel: Black with red/yellow houseflag
Hull: Black with red boot-topping

Name	Year	GRT	DWT	LOA	Bm	Kts	Eng	Type	Former names
Norse Falcon*	1981	42,235	88,725	229	43	14	M	T	

* Bahamas flag

Above: Hapag-Lloyd AG, *Sydney Express. J. K. Byass*

Below: T & J Harrison Ltd, *Author. J. Krayenbosch*

A/S Havtor Management

Norway

Funnel: Grey with white 'M' over two red bands
Hull: Light grey with red boot-topping

Name	Year	GRT	DWT	LOA	Bm	Kts	Eng	Type	Former names
Athene	1974	125,910	260,150	341	52	16	ST	T	
Celsius	1979	13,984	17,157	151	25	16	M	LPG	
Centum	1978	28,941	38,534	206	31	17	M	LPG	
Century	1974	27,142	22,036	182	29	—	M	LGC	ex-Lucian 80
Havfalk	1977	23,489	40,299	182	29	14	M	B	
Havist†	1970	11,188	16,790	147	22	17	M	LPG	
Havjo	1978	23,489	40,300	183	29	15	M	B	
Havkatt‡	1972	16,012	27,273	163	26	15	M	B	
Havlyn	1982	8,311	11,772	128	21	16	M	LPG	
Havorn	1977	23,463	40,300	183	29	14	M	B	
Havtroll‡	1973	16,137	26,703	163	26	15	M	B	
Igloo Finn*	1981	8,263	11,665	128	21	16	M	LPG	
Igloo Moss	1985	10,075	13,200	136	22	16	M	LPG	
Igloo Norse*	1982	8,878	11,665	128	21	16	M	LPG	
Igloo Polar*	1982	8,878	12,426	128	21	16	M	LPG	

* jointly owned by Neste o/y, Finnish flag
† Panamanian flag
‡ Liberian flag

Headlam & Son

UK

Rowland & Marwood's SS Co Ltd

Funnel: Black with blue cross on broad white band
Hull: Grey with red boot-topping

Name	Year	GRT	DWT	LOA	Bm	Kts	Eng	Type	Former names
Egton	1962	9,958	15,069	155	20	14	M	C	

Per Henriksen

Denmark

Funnel: Bright red with light grey edged blue-grey shield containing winged anchor, black top
Hull: Blue-grey with light grey 'MERCANDIA', bright red boot-topping

Name	Year	GRT	DWT	LOA	Bm	Kts	Eng	Type	Former names
Cumana	1984	15,375	9,250	160	21	16	M	RO	ex-Mercandian Gigant 85
Diplomat	1983	7,955	7,225	132	20	15	M	RO	ex-Mercanadian Diplomat 85
Mercandian Admiral II	1983	7,955	7,200	132	20	15	M	RO	
Mercandian Ambassador II	1983	7,955	7,200	132	20	15	M	RO	ex-Ambassador II 85, ex-Mercandian Ambassador II 84
Mercandian Duke	1984	7,955	7,200	132	19	15	M	RO	
Mercandian Governor	1982	3,041	7,225	132	20	15	M	RO	ex-Governor 85, ex-Mercandian Governor 84
Mercandian Ocean	1985	13,575	9,250	160	21	16	M	RO	
Mercandian President	1982	3,041	7,230	132	19	15	M	RO	ex-President 1 84, ex-Mercandian President 84
Mercandian Prince II	1984	7,955	7,200	131	19	15	M	RO	
Mercandian Queen II	1984	7,955	7,200	132	19	15	M	RO	
Mercandian Senator	1983	7,955	7,200	132	20	15	M	RO	
Valencia	1985	15,375	9,250	160	21	16	M	RO	ex-Mercandian Globe 85

Sigurd Herlofson & Co A/S

Norway

Funnel: Yellow with red 'H' on white diamond on broad blue band
Hull: Grey with red boot-topping

Name	Year	GRT	DWT	LOA	Bm	Kts	Eng	Type	Former names
Obo Baron*	1970	55,032	103,230	257	39	15	M	BO	ex-Varenna 83
Obo Empress*	1971	55,062	103,332	247	39	15	M	BO	ex-Vanessa 83

Above: A/S Havtor Management, *Igloo Finn. Table Bay Underway Shipping*

Below: Sigurd Herlofson & Co A/S, *Obo Empress. J. M. Kakebeeke*

Name	Year	GRT	DWT	LOA	Bm	Kts	Eng	Type	Former names
Obo King	1974	65,305	117,999	266	40	16	M	OBO	ex-Victoria Venture 81, ex-Snestad 78
Obo Princess	1976	66,118	127,050	257	39	15	M	OBO	ex-Britannia Team 81, ex-Angelic Blessing 78
Obo Queen*	1971	54,761	103,230	258	39	16	M	BO	

* Bahamas flag

Leif Hoegh & Co A/S   Norway

Funnel: White with blue top and houseflag interrupting white band
Hull: Grey with red boot-topping

Name	Year	GRT	DWT	LOA	Bm	Kts	Eng	Type	Former names
Ambia Fair*	1981	40,134	78,733	243	32	14	M	OBO	
Ambia Finjo*	1981	40,131	78,733	243	32	14	M	OBO	
Hoegh Banniere	1980	16,744	24,223	187	32	17	M	RO	
Hoegh Cairn	1979	22,734	31,555	183	27	19	M	CO	
Hoegh Cape	1977	18,994	27,817	171	26	17	M	CO	ex-Tsu 85, ex-Barber Tsu 84, ex-Tsu 91, ex-Thalatta 77
Hoegh Clipper	1979	22,734	31,555	183	27	18	M	CO	
Hoegh Dene	1984	30,150	41,600	198	32	16	M	CO	
Hoegh Drake	1984	30,150	41,600	198	32	16	M	CO	
Hoegh Duke†	1984	30,061	41,949	198	32	16	M	CO	
Hoegh Dyke	1984	30,150	41,400	198	32	16	M	CO	
Hoegh Falcon	1981	45,760	82,460	247	32	15	M	OBO	
Hoegh Favour	1981	45,760	82,460	247	32	15	M	OBO	
Hoegh Foam	1981	44,834	78,571	243	32	14	M	OBO	
Hoegh Fortuna	1982	44,834	78,531	243	32	14	M	OBO	
Hoegh Forum	1983	44,833	78,585	243	32	14	M	OBO	
Hoegh Fountain	1982	44,834	78,488	243	32	14	M	OBO	
Hoegh Fulmar	1983	44,833	78,585	243	32	14	M	OBO	
Hoegh Gandria	1977	95,683	70,498	288	44	20	ST	LGC	
Hoegh Hill	1971	128,980	249,259	326	52	15	ST	OBO	
Hoegh Hood	1973	128,954	249,259	326	52	15	ST	OBO	
Hoegh Mallard	1977	29,212	45,063	201	31	15	M	BC	
Hoegh Marlin	1977	29,212	45,063	201	31	15	M	BC	
Hoegh Mascot	1977	29,212	45,063	201	31	15	M	BC	
Hoegh Minerva	1979	29,214	44,016	201	31	15	M	BC	
Hoegh Miranda	1979	29,214	44,016	201	31	15	M	BC	
Hoegh Skean	1971	31,918	38,930	207	31	17	M	LPG	ex-Hoegh Multina 77
Hoegh Sword	1979	45,769	48,224	229	32	17	M	LPG	
Hual Tracer*	1981	12,783	12,961	180	29	18	M	V	
Hual Trader	1982	23,597	32,772	213	32	17	M	V	ex-Hoegh Trader 82
Hual Transporter	1982	23,597	32,695	213	32	17	M	V	
Hual Trapper*	1981	12,783	12,961	180	29	18	M	V	
Hual Traveller	1983	14,660	14,600	180	29	18	M	V	
Hual Trotter	1983	14,659	14,600	180	29	18	M	V	
Marathon*	1984	27,100	37,400	192	31	15	M	T	
Norman Lady‡	1973	76,416	53,624	250	40	18	ST	LGC	
Target*	1974	7,274	10,750	188	23	18	M	V	ex-Hoegh Target 82, ex-Dyvi Adriatic 75
Trigger*	1976	6,923	9,835	188	23	18	M	V	ex-Hoegh Trigger 84

* Liberian flag   † British flag
‡ jointly owned by Buries Markes Ltd (SA Louis-Dreyfus & Cie), Liberian flag

Soc Navale de l'Ouest/France

Funnel: White with 'SCADOA' on black band
Hull: Grey with red boot-topping

Name	Year	GRT	DWT	LOA	Bm	Kts	Eng	Type	Former names
Saint Roch	1980	16,744	24,260	187	32	18	M	RO	ex-Hoegh Belle 81
Saint Roland*	1979	18,289	27,980	188	33	17	M	RO	ex-Bullaren 84, ex-Tarifa 83, ex-Vindafjord 81, ex-Bullaren 81
Saint Romain	1981	16,744	24,223	187	32	17	M	RO	ex-Hoegh Biscay 84

* owned by Cie Navale Transatlantique

Above: Leif Hoegh & Co A/S, *Hoegh Drake. J. Krayenbosch*

Above: Leif Hoegh & Co A/S, *Hual Trader. M. D. J. Lennon*

Below: Leif Hoegh & Co Soc Navale de l'Ouest, *Saint Romain. J. Krayenbosch*

India Steamship Co Ltd

India

Funnel: Black with yellow star on broad red band
Hull: Black with red boot-topping

Name	Year	GRT	DWT	LOA	Bm	Kts	Eng	Type	Former names
Indian Courier	1977	3,498	6,421	119	19	18	M	CC	ex-Strider Diamond 81, ex-Saudi Crown 80
Indian Endurance	1975	10,016	14,093	154	20	17	M	C	
Indian Explorer	1976	10,011	14,086	154	20	17	M	C	
Indian Faith	1971	8,976	15,119	142	20	16	M	C	ex-Titika Halcoussi 75
Indian Fame	1972	8,978	15,126	143	20	16	M	C	ex-Pericles Halcoussis 75
Indian Fortune	1972	8,978	15,154	143	20	16	M	C	ex-Leonis Halcoussis 76
Indian Fraternity	1972	9,824	15,188	143	20	14	M	C	ex-Sea Gull 77
Indian Freedom	1971	8,976	15,123	142	20	16	M	C	ex-Dimos Halcoussis 76
Indian Glory	1978	13,482	21,344	150	21	17	M	C	
Indian Goodwill	1978	14,267	20,571	162	23	15	M	C	
Indian Grace	1978	13,482	21,283	150	21	17	M	C	
Indian Prestige	1971	12,035	18,842	148	23	15	M	C	ex-Aristagoras 74
Indian Progress	1971	12,035	18,854	148	23	15	M	C	ex-Aristodimos 74
Indian Prosperity	1971	12,035	17,964	148	23	15	M	C	ex-Ioanna 75
Indian Security	1958	9,300	12,264	155	20	17	M	C	
Indian Trust	1960	9,417	12,238	155	20	17	M	C	
Indian Valour	1971	9,629	15,550	145	21	16	M	C	
Indian Venture	1972	9,629	15,550	145	21	16	M	C	

Irish Shipping Ltd

Eire

Funnel: Yellow with green band between two narrow white bands
Hull: Grey with white line, green boot-topping

Name	Year	GRT	DWT	LOA	Bm	Kts	Eng	Type	Former names
Irish Spruce	1983	39,773	69,700	226	32	14	M	B	

Islamic Rep of Iran Shipping Lines

Iran

Funnel: Red, broad white band with green ship device, green top
Hull: Grey with green boot-topping

Name	Year	GRT	DWT	LOA	Bm	Kts	Eng	Type	Former names
Iran Abad	1971	12,015	16,630	161	23	19	M	C	ex-Arya Taj 80
Iran Adalat	1977	14,433	19,212	167	25	18	M	C	ex-Arya Sepehr 80
Iran Adi	1983	22,027	37,537	186	28	15	M	B	ex-World Fraternity 84
Iran Afzal	1983	22,027	37,564	186	28	15	M	B	ex-Manila Faith 84, ex-Primelock 83
Iran Akhavan	1984	20,576	34,853	198	24	15	M	B	ex-Philippine Success 84
Iran Amanat	1983	20,576	34,858	198	24	15	M	B	ex-Manila Pride 84
Iran Ashrafi	1985	25,768	40,000	190	30	14	M	B	
Iran Azadi	1979	20,672	35,839	180	28	15	M	B	ex-Oinoussian Friendship 81
Iran Bahonar	1983	21,959	40,325	176	32	14	M	T	ex-Cleon 83
Iran Bayan	1974	10,205	16,265	150	21	16	M	C	ex-Arya Sepand 80, ex-Aristonimos 75
Iran Beheshti	1979	22,048	39,026	205	26	15	M	T	ex-Selma 82
Iran Besat	1968	10,171	13,823	161	21	20	M	C	ex-Arya Pake 80, ex-Marie Delmas 73
Iran Borhan	1975	10,205	16,265	150	21	16	M	C	ex-Arya Gohar 80
Iran Chamran	1985	25,768	43,369	190	30	14	M	B	
Iran Dahr†	1971	12,257	19,833	155	23	14	M	BV	ex-Asia Morality 83
Iran Dastghayb	1984	25,768	43,369	190	30	14	M	B	
Iran Deyanat	1983	25,939	44,127	200	29	15	M	B	ex-Odinlock 84
Iran Ehsan	1975	10,205	16,265	150	21	16	M	C	ex-Arya Akhtar 80, ex-Aristaios 75
Iran Ejtehad	1967	12,294	13,516	172	24	21	M	C	ex-Gulf Osprey 83, ex-Phrontis 82, ex-Pembrokeshire 72
Iran Ekram	1974	8,408	11,795	145	19	15	M	C	ex-Arya Rokh 80
Iran Elham	1974	8,407	11,765	145	19	15	M	C	ex-Arya Kish 80

Above: India Steamship Co Ltd, *Indian Grace. M. D. J. Lennon*

Below. Islamic Rep. of Iran Shipping Lines, *Iran Eslami. J. Y. Freeman*

Name	Year	GRT	DWT	LOA	Bm	Kts	Eng	Type	Former names
Iran Emdad†	1968	10,268	18,820	155	23	15	M	B	ex-Manila Enterprise 84, ex-Asia Botan 81
Iran Enghelab†	1978	20,674	35,840	180	28	15	M	B	ex-Oinoussian Destiny 81
Iran Entekhab	1978	20,691	35,896	180	28	15	M	B	ex-Oinoussian Prestige 81
Iran Ershad	1972	12,015	16,630	161	23	19	M	C	ex-Arya Tab 80
Iran Eshraghi	1985	25,768	43,300	190	30	14	M	B	
Iran Eslami	1972	20,735	35,578	180	28	15	M	B	ex-Oinoussian Superiority 81, ex-Shuko Maru 76
Iran Esteghial	1978	20,691	35,839	180	28	15	M	B	ex-Oinoussian Virtue 81
Iran Fakori	1971	16,737	27,359	170	26	14	M	B	ex-United Cove 83, ex-United Wave 81, ex-Eastern Wave 80
Iran Fallahi	1972	17,716	33,657	186	27	16	M	B	ex-Eastern Lilac 84
Iran Fateh	1968	9,372	16,894	148	22	14	M	B	ex-Manila Mariner 84, ex-Cloverlock 80, ex-Regent Botan 80, ex-Sendan Maru 70
Iran Ghafari	1985	25,678	43,369	190	30	14	M	B	
Iran Ghazi	1985	25,768	43,300	190	30	14	M	B	
Iran Gheyam†	1975	8,408	11,792	145	19	15	M	C	ex-Arya Rooz 80
Iran Gheyamat	1978	14,433	19,212	167	25	18	M	C	ex-Arya Shams 80
Iran Hojjat†	1964	11,019	16,205	155	21	14	M	C	ex-Arya Far 80, ex-Arya Pey 73, ex-Vinstra 69
Iran Jahad	1971	12,015	16,630	161	23	19	M	C	ex-Arya Pas 80
Iran Jamal	1985	25,768	43,300	190	30	14	M	B	
Iran Javad	1968	11,425	18,529	185	23	15	M	B	ex-Asia Rindo 84
Iran Jenant†	1975	10,205	16,265	150	21	16	M	C	ex-Arya Neda 80, ex-Aristolaos 75
Iran Jomhuri	1978	20,672	35,830	180	28	15	M	B	ex-Oinoussian Leadership 81
Iran Kalam	1975	9,206	12,140	153	19	18	M	C	ex-Arya Seem 80
Iran Kashani	1984	25,768	43,369	190	30	14	M	B	
Iran Madani	1985	25,768	43,369	190	30	14	M	B	
Iran Meead	1970	12,015	16,580	161	23	19	M	C	ex-Arya Gam 80
Iran Meelad	1971	12,015	16,630	161	23	19	M	C	ex-Arya Nur 80
Iran Meezan	1975	10,206	16,266	150	21	16	M	C	ex-Arya Sooroosh 80
Iran Meysam	1972	12,576	22,452	163	24	14	M	B	ex-Manila Progress 85, ex-Asia Gem 82
Iran Modares	1977	19,244	33,667	182	27	15	M	B	ex-Gentle River 83, ex-Treana 78
Iran Mofateh	1985	25,768	43,300	190	30	14	M	B	
Iran Motaharai	1979	19,799	35,110	198	24	14	M	B	ex-Marcoplata 83, ex-Cardona 79
Iran Nabuvat	1977	14,433	19,212	167	25	18	M	C	ex-Arya Shahab 80
Iran Nahad	1970	12,057	16,580	161	23	19	M	C	ex-Arya Naz 80
Iran Namjoo	1968	11,425	18,529	155	23	15	M	B	ex-Asia Momo 83
Iran Nasr	1971	10,438	19,847	155	23	14	M	BV	ex-Asia Flamingo 83
Iran Nehzat	1968	10,171	13,823	161	21	17	M	C	ex-Arya Omid 80, ex-Helene Delmas 73
Iran Rajai	1983	21,959	40,367	176	32	14	M	T	ex-Ferncraig 83
Iran Reshadat†	1966	10,450	12,587	166	23	30	M	C	ex-Bergen Maru 83
Iran Sabr	1971	12,258	19,845	155	23	14	M	BV	ex-Asia Loyalty 83
Iran Sadr	1985	25,768	43,300	190	30	14	M	B	
Iran Salam	1975	9,206	12,140	153	18	18	M	C	ex-Arya Zar 80
Iran Sadoughi	1985	25,768	40,000	190	30	14	M	B	
Iran Sarbaz	1984	20,576	34,859	198	24	15	M	B	
Iran Seeyam	1974	9,206	12,140	153	19	18	M	C	ex-Arya Sun 80
Iran Sepah	1976	19,702	34,388	186	26	14	M	B	ex-Ocean Cosmos 84
Iran Shahadat†	1969	10,171	13,823	161	20	17	M	C	ex-Arya Shad 80, ex-Irma Delmas 73
Iran Shahamat	1972	12,367	19,796	155	23	16	M	B	ex-Apennines Maru 83
Iran Shariat	1983	23,486	44,127	200	29	15	M	B	ex-Thorlock 84
Iran Shariati	1985	25,768	43,300	190	30	14	M	B	
Iran Shojaat	1971	12,367	19,795	155	23	15	M	B	ex-Alps Maru 83
Iran Sokan	1975	10,205	16,265	150	21	16	M	C	ex-Arya Navid 80
Iran Takhti	1978	16,150	23,720	159	25	16	M	CO	ex-Sargodha 84
Iran Taleghani	1985	25,768	43,300	190	30	14	M	B	

Islamic Rep. of Iran Shipping Lines, *Iran Bayan.* *J. M. Kokebeeke*

Name	Year	GRT	DWT	LOA	Bm	Kts	Eng	Type	Former names
Iran Teyfouri	1979	16,150	23,720	159	25	16	M	CO	ex-Simba 84
Iran Torab	1971	17,629	29,569	171	26	15	M	B	ex-Asia Hunter 84
Iran Vahdat	1977	14,434	19,212	167	25	18	M	C	ex-Arya Keyhan 80
Iran Vojdan	1975	10,205	16,265	150	21	16	M	C	ex-Arya Kay 80, ex-Aristonidas 75

† vessel damaged in Iran-Iraq hostilities

Soc Ivoirienne de Transport Maritime   Ivory Coast

Funnel: Green, white band with elephant outline over 'SITRAM', orange top
Hull: White, with green boot-topping

Name	Year	GRT	DWT	LOA	Bm	Kts	Eng	Type	Former names
Agboville	1978	12,991	16,465	156	24	15	M	CO	
Bondoukou	1978	11,771	16,000	157	23	18	M	C	
Bonoua	1978	11,771	16,000	158	23	18	M	C	
Bouake	1978	11,771	16,000	157	23	18	M	C	
Jacqueville	1978	13,538	16,746	156	24	15	M	CO	
Ono	1969	8,553	6,625	144	20	20	M	R	ex-Favorita 83
Yakasse	1978	13,530	16,891	156	24	15	M	CO	
Yamoussoukro	1977	13,531	16,746	156	24	15	M	CO	
Yopougon	1977	13,022	16,909	156	24	15	M	CO	

Ernst Jacob   FRG

Funnel: Black, white diagonal cross on broad blue band with blue 'J' on white centre diamond
Hull: Grey with red boot-topping or white with blue boot-topping

Name	Year	GRT	DWT	LOA	Bm	Kts	Eng	Type	Former names
Blumenthal	1984	9,417	11,806	146	21	22	M	R	ex-Helene Jacob 84
Bremerhaven	1984	9,417	11,806	146	21	22	M	R	ex-Walter Jacob 84
Brigitte Jacob	1980	24,575	43,190	176	32	15	M	T	
Dirk Jacob	1976	19,497	33,788	171	26	15	M	T	
Erika Jacob	1975	19,486	33,400	171	26	17	M	T	ex-Protan Maas 75
Fjord Bridge*	1972	28,151	50,901	205	30	15	M	B	ex-Babette Jacob 82
Fjord Land*	1976	28,079	50,825	205	30	15	M	B	ex-Lutz Jacob 84
Fjord Mariner*	1975	28,147	50,826	206	30	15	M	B	ex-Margot Jacob 83
Fjord Ranger*	1973	28,160	50,947	206	30	15	M	B	ex-Rolf Jacob 82
Fjord Trader*	1974	28,218	50,550	216	28	15	M	B	ex-Tom Jacob 83
Fjord Wind*	1974	28,255	50,531	216	28	15	M	B	ex-Wera Jacob 82
Gertrud Jacob	1976	19,490	33,790	171	26	17	M	B	
Tanja Jacob	1980	24,575	43,190	176	32	15	M	B	

* Panamanian flag

Anders Jahre   Norway

Funnel: Black with white and blue houseflag on broad red band, or yellow with houseflag, and narrow black top
Hull: Grey with green boot-topping

Name	Year	GRT	DWT	LOA	Bm	Kts	Eng	Type	Former names
Freeport Chief*	1980	30,875	68,039	229	32	15	M	T	
Jacinth	1981	39,148	68,817	224	32	15	M	T	
Jaguar	1981	40,446	58,327	228	32	14	M	T	
Jalinga†	1979	30,814	54,990	207	32	15	M	T	ex-Viking Gull 85
Jamunda†	1980	30,814	54,990	207	32	14	M	T	ex-Viking Snipe 85
Janega*	1971	23,891	41,262	192	30	15	M	B	
Janus	1982	40,482	67,208	226	32	14	M	T	
Japana*	1976	35,676	60,920	225	32	15	M	BV	ex-Pioneer Japan 83, ex-Japana 80, ex-Eastern City 79
Jarabella†	1979	30,814	54,990	207	32	15	M	T	ex-Viking Tern 85
Jaraconda†	1985	22,000	38,220	180	31	14	M	B	
Jarama	1981	42,105	77,673	244	32	15	M	BC	
Jarena	1982	77,704	128,000	265	49	14	M	T	

Above: Soc Ivoirienne de Transport Maritime, *Agboville. J. K. Byass*

Above: Ernst Jacob, *Bremerhaven. J. Krayenbosch*

Below: Ernst Jacob, *Tanja Jacob. J. Y. Freeman*

111

Name	Year	GRT	DWT	LOA	Bm	Kts	Eng	Type	Former names
Jarilla†	1985	22,091	38,220	180	31	14	M	B	ex-Southern Virgo 85
Jarmada	1976	188,098	390,364	374	64	16	ST	T	
Jarmina	1981	42,105	77,673	244	32	15	M	BO	
Viking Chief*	1980	30,876	68,027	229	32	15	M	T	

* Liberian flag
† Panamanian flag

A/S Kristian Jebsens Rederi

Norway

Funnel: Light blue, broad white band with blue wavy line
Hull: Dark grey with red boot-topping

Name	Year	GRT	DWT	LOA	Bm	Kts	Eng	Type	Former names
Beaver†	1977	19,169	34,537	180	28	15	M	B	ex-Bessnes 84
Bedouin Birknes**	1974	18,695	35,224	177	28	15	M	B	
Bedouin Brunes**	1977	19,158	34,488	180	28	15	M	B	
Edco***	1980	22,605	38,300	194	26	15	M	B	
Falknes	1983	7,944	12,078	129	20	13	M	B	
Finnsnes**	1978	8,098	12,358	135	21	14	M	B	
Fjellnes†	1982	7,367	12,334	129	20	14	M	B	
Fjordnes‡	1983	7,363	12,319	129	20	14	M	B	
Frines**	1978	8,098	12,358	135	21	14	M	B	
General Aguinaldo*	1982	29,759	61,315	223	32	14	M	B	ex-Limelock 82
General Capinpin*	1972	12,982	21,916	156	23	14	M	B	ex-Swiftnes 82
General Cruz	1983	36,209	63,800	225	32	14	M	B	ex-Rangelock 85
General Hizon*	1984	27,798	47,893	189	32	14	M	B	ex-Langnes 84
General Lim*	1970	4,570	7,491	123	17	13	M	B	ex-Fjellnes 80, ex-Jennes 77, ex-Midigirl 76, ex-Jennes 74
General Santos*	1984	27,798	47,879	189	32	14	M	B	ex-Locknes 84
Jebsen Napier*	1985	19,510	28,936	175	28	14	M	B	
Lindnes†	1984	27,798	47,882	189	32	14	M	B	
Tertnes	1985	6,259	7,100	(112)	21	14	M	B	
Tinnes	1983	6,792	10,110	118	21	14	M	B	
Torgnes	1985	6,400	8,700	113	20	14	M	B	
Tornes	1984	6,389	8,600	113	20	14	M	B	
Trollnes	1985	4,500	8,500	113	20	14	M	B	

* owned by Aboitiz Jebsen Bulk Transport Corp, Philippine flag
** owned by Jameel-Jebsen Carriers Ltd, Liberian flag
*** jointly owned by Misr Edco Shipping Co Ltd, Egyptian flag
† Panamanian   ‡ Liberian flag   †† Singapore flag

Jebsens (UK) Ltd/UK

Name	Year	GRT	DWT	LOA	Bm	Kts	Eng	Type	Former names
Binsnes	1981	16,421	26,354	175	26	15	M	B	ex-Lord Curzon 83, ex-Lord Jellicoe 81
Bolnes	1981	16,421	26,354	175	26	15	M	B	ex-Lord Byron 83
Farnes‡	1979	8,116	12,274	135	21	14	M	B	
Firmnes‡	1979	8,116	12,274	135	21	14	M	B	ex-Inchcape 77
Fossnes‡	1982	7,363	12,078	129	20	14	M	B	
General Segundo*	1976	18,815	34,541	180	28	15	ST	B	ex-Baynes 82
General Tinio*	1976	18,353	35,208	177	28	15	M	B	ex-New Zealand Alliance 84, ex-Eastern Alliance 82, ex-Bolnes 81
Jebsen Tauranga	1985	19,510	28,936	175	28	14	M	B	
Jebsen Timaru	1985	19,800	28,936	175	28	14	M	B	
Lakenes	1984	25,956	45,090	183	31	14	M	B	
Loftnes	1984	25,956	45,090	183	31	14	M	B	
Telnes	1982	6,794	10,110	118	21	14	M	B	

‡ Liberian flag   * Philippine flag

Above: Anders Jahre, *Jarilla.* J. Krayenbosch

Below: A/S Kristian Jebsens Rederi, *Bergnes.* M. D. J. Lennon

Reederei J. Jost/FGR

Name	Year	GRT	DWT	LOA	Bm	Kts	Eng	Type	Former names
Bergnes†	1977	20,473	34,503	180	28	15	M	B	
Brooknes†	1977	20,164	35,138	177	28	15	M	B	

† Panamanian flag

Johnson Line A/B   Sweden

Funnel: Black with blue 'J' on yellow five-pointed star on broad blue band between two narrow yellow bands
Hull: Grey or orange with red boot-topping

Annie Johnson	1969	15,932	14,936	174	26	21	M2	CO	
Axel Johnson	1969	15,932	14,936	174	26	21	M2	CC	
Bahia Blanca	1964	10,351	12,355	173	19	18	M2	CO	
Bo Johnson	1984	31,446	34,680	201	32	18	M	CC	
Johnson Chemspan*	1982	18,697	33,532	183	30	15	M2	T	
Johnson Chemstar	1980	22,246	37,532	175	32	15	M2	T	
Johnson Chemstream*	1983	17,180	17,465	149	22	16	M	T	
Johnson Chemsun	1980	22,246	37,532	175	32	15	M2	T	
Margaret Johnson	1970	15,769	14,936	174	26	21	M2	CC	
Nordic Stream	1979	8,708	14,484	183	24	18	M	RO	ex-Qatar Express 82, ex-Finneagle 81
Rosa Blanca	1985	33,047	17,930	185	23	17	M	RO	
San Francisco	1970	15,769	14,936	174	26	21	M2	CO	

* Singapore flag
tankers operated as a joint fleet with J. O. Odfjell as 'Odfjell Johnson Chemical Tankers'

Jugolinija   Yugoslavia

Funnel: Blue, white band with red star, black top
Hull: Black or grey with green boot-topping

August Cesarec	1967	6,042	8,950	151	20	17	M	C	
Bakar	1969	6,239	8,713	152	20	18	M	C	
Baltik	1974	8,955	13,945	153	20	19	M	C	
Baska	1961	6,662	7,053	136	18	17	M	C	
Bosna	1969	9,501	14,018	155	21	18	M	C	ex-Pleiades 69
Bribir	1979	5,597	7,478	148	22	17	M	RO	
Buzet	1979	8,711	12,430	146	23	17	M	CO	ex-Holstenclipper 82, ex-Seaway Clipper 80, ex-Holstenclipper 79
Crikvenica	1972	9,688	14,956	147	21	15	M	C	
Dobra	1969	9,411	15,124	145	21	14	M	C	ex-Betelgeuse 83
Dragonja*	1982	16,664	24,500	193	23	16	M	C	ex-Konkar Triton 85
Drava	1974	14,712	25,200	178	23	14	M	B	
Drvar	1975	8,955	13,950	153	20	17	M	C	
Gacka*	1982	16,399	24,113	193	23	16	M	C	ex-Konkar Triaina 85
Goran Kovacic	1967	6,174	8,900	150	20	17	M	C	
Grobnik	1963	6,879	6,741	136	19	17	M	C	
Hreljin	1977	8,084	11,031	154	22	18	M	CC	
Hrvatska	1969	9,501	14,038	155	20	16	M	C	ex-Cassiopeia 69
Jadran Express	1978	13,423	19,455	164	26	17	M	CC	
Jesenice	1960	9,453	13,630	155	21	18	M	C	
Kastav	1968	6,239	8,713	152	20	18	M	C	
Korana	1969	9,372	15,124	145	21	14	M	C	ex-Bellatrix 83
Kostrena	1963	9,435	13,658	155	21	18	M	C	
Kraljevica	1968	6,276	8,713	152	20	18	M	C	
Kranjcevic	1966	6,174	8,878	151	20	18	M	C	
Krasica	1979	16,150	23,721	159	25	16	M	CO	ex-Sinaloa 85
Krk	1977	9,699	13,694	155	21	18	M	C	

Above: Johnson Line A/B, *Johnson Chemstream. J. Krayenbosch*

Above: Johnson Line A/B, *Nordic Stream. J. K. Byass*

Below: Jugolinija, *Dobra. J. M. Kakebeeke*

Name	Year	GRT	DWT	LOA	Bm	Kts	Eng	Type	Former names
Kumrovec	1967	6,174	8,920	150	20	17	M	C	
Kupa	1973	18,662	30,830	197	23	15	M	B	ex-Adriatik 83
Ledenice	1979	5,597	7,478	144	22	17	M	RO	
Lika	1979	16,150	23,720	159	25	16	M	CO	ex-Siena 85, ex-Tarasco 85, ex-Siena 83
Losinj	1972	9,746	15,170	148	21	15	M	C	
Moscenice	1976	9,699	13,870	157	22	18	M	C	
Motovun	1977	9,699	13,914	157	22	18	M	C	
Mreznica	1969	9,412	14,885	145	21	14	M	C	ex-Denebola 83
Nehaj	1967	9,470	10,972	155	21	18	M	C	
Nikola Tesla	1957	8,581	12,980	146	18	14	M	C	
Novi Vinodolski	1961	6,662	6,912	136	18	17	M	C	
Opatija	1973	9,746	15,142	149	21	16	M	C	
Pag	1969	8,502	10,550	148	20	18	M	C	ex-Logatec 69
Pazin	1969	6,239	8,713	152	20	18	M	C	
Rab	1972	9,688	14,956	147	21	16	M	C	
Rijeka	1981	13,551	16,728	160	24	16	M	C	
Rjecina	1969	9,372	15,124	145	21	14	M	C	ex-Arcturus 83
Sava	1973	18,603	30,832	197	23	15	M	B	
Senj	1972	9,715	15,322	147	21	14	M	C	
Slovenija	1980	9,700	14,600	157	22	18	M	C	
Susak	1977	8,084	11,031	154	22	18	M	CC	
Topusko	1975	8,955	13,945	153	20	18	M	C	
Treci Maj	1957	8,766	12,280	146	18	13	M	C	
Trepca	1958	8,766	12,889	146	18	13	M	C	
Triglav	1981	11,274	15,642	152	23	16	M	C	ex-Bhava Bhuti 81
Trsat	1966	9,470	13,930	155	21	18	M	C	
Tuhobic	1983	13,328	16,648	160	24	16	M	C	
Velebit	1981	11,279	15,709	153	23	16	M	C	ex-Bhasa 81
Vojvodina	1981	9,480	14,600	157	22	18	M	C	
Volosko	1972	9,715	15,322	147	21	15	M	C	
Zagreb	1982	13,551	16,728	160	24	16	M	C	

* Panamanian flag

Jugoslavenska Oceanska Plovidba

Funnel: White with red five-pointed star and red top
Hull: Black with red boot-topping

Name	Year	GRT	DWT	LOA	Bm	Kts	Eng	Type	Former names
Admiral Zmajevik	1965	8,569	12,787	154	20	16	M	C	
Banat	1963	9,013	13,020	152	19	15	M	C	
Budva	1972	17,891	28,215	181	25	15	M	B	ex-Pacific Endeavour 72
Durmitor	1982	12,375	17,400	153	23	16	M	C	
Herceg Novi	1981	9,698	14,719	157	22	17	M	C	
Kapetan Martinovic	1964	8,569	12,808	154	20	16	M	C	
Kordun	1978	38,551	72,050	228	32	15	M	B	
Kosmaj	1977	38,551	72,050	228	32	15	M	B	
Kotor	1965	23,072	39,674	200	28	15	M	B	
Kozara	1965	23,072	39,674	200	28	15	M	B	
Krusevac	1966	23,072	39,674	200	28	15	M	B	
Kumanovo	1966	23,072	39,674	200	28	15	M	B	
Lovcen	1982	12,375	17,400	158	23	17	M	CO	
Metohija	1963	9,208	13,025	152	19	15	M	C	
Moslavina	1961	9,013	13,031	152	19	15	M	C	
Orjen	1977	38,551	72,150	228	32	15	M	B	
Prvi Februar	1968	17,233	28,906	187	23	15	M	B	
Risan	1981	9,698	14,719	157	22	17	M	C	
Slavonija	1959	6,314	10,298	146	18	13	M	C	
Sumadija	1961	9,013	13,466	152	19	15	M	C	
Sutjeska	1976	38,551	72,149	228	32	15	M	B	
Tivat	1981	9,698	14,719	157	22	17	M	C	

Jugoslavenska Oceanska Plovidba, *Lovćen*. *J. M. Kakebeeke*

Name	Year	GRT	DWT	LOA	Bm	Kts	Eng	Type	Former names
Trinaesti Juli	1968	17,233	28,906	187	23	15	M	B	
Zeta	1958	8,742	11,624	146	18	13	M	C	

Atlantska Plovidba

Funnel: Yellow with red seven-pointed star, narrow black top
Hull: Grey with green boot-topping

Name	Year	GRT	DWT	LOA	Bm	Kts	Eng	Type	Former names
Banija	1966	16,906	28,000	187	23	15	M	B	
Banja Luka..........................	1968	16,018	26,193	190	23	15	M	B	
Baranja	1967	16,019	26,400	190	23	15	M	B	
Bosanka..............................	1967	16,955	28,025	187	23	15	M	B	
Cast Caribou	1982	35,338	70,947	234	32	14	M	BC	
Cast Polarbear	1982	35,338	70,947	234	32	14	M	BC	
Cvijeta Zuzoric	1974	15,398	27,020	183	22	17	M	B	
Dubrovnik	1971	14,714	24,437	165	23	13	M	B	ex-Magdalena del Mar 71
Getaldic..............................	1969	9,907	16,158	145	21	15	M	C	
Gundulic.............................	1969	9,907	16,158	144	21	15	M	C	
Hercegovina.........................	1977	18,426	30,880	197	23	15	M	B	
Ivo Vojnovic	1973	9,868	16,050	145	21	15	M	C	
Jadran................................	1976	38,551	72,149	228	32	15	M	B	
Konavle..............................	1984	40,260	71,242	236	32	14	M	BC	
Kragujevac..........................	1963	10,483	16,247	166	21	16	M	C	
Mavro Vetranic	1973	9,868	16,051	145	21	15	M	C	
Mljet.................................	1983	17,818	29,643	190	23	14	M	B	
Peljesac..............................	1983	40,248	70,200	236	32	14	M	B	
Plitvice	1964	10,483	16,234	166	21	16	M	C	
Ruder Boskovic	1974	15,398	27,020	183	22	17	M	B	

Istarska Plovidba

Funnel: Grey, blue and red bands on broad white band interrupted by white diamond with blue 'ip'
Hull: Black with red boot-topping

Name	Year	GRT	DWT	LOA	Bm	Kts	Eng	Type	Former names
Franina...............................	1982	9,263	14,711	149	19	14	M	C	ex-Antonio Maura 82
Istranka	1979	11,155	15,884	153	23	15	M	C	
Jurina	1981	9,397	14,731	149	19	14	M	C	ex-Elena Perez 81
Porer	1983	13,382	16,648	160	24	16	M	C	
Ucka..................................	1979	11,154	15,980	153	23	15	M	C	

M. A. Karageorgis SA   Greece

Funnel: Black, broad white band with white 'MK' on blue diamond
Hull: Black with red boot-topping

Name	Year	GRT	DWT	LOA	Bm	Kts	Eng	Type	Former names
Aristagelos..........................	1978	9,960	16,270	150	21	16	M	C	
Aristogenis..........................	1980	9,960	16,270	150	21	16	M	C	
Messiniaki Anagennisis	1970	17,485	30,228	171	26	16	M	T	
Messiniaki Doxa	1970	17,485	30,228	171	26	16	M	T	ex-Messiniaki Bergen 81, ex-Messiniaki Drys 70

Kawasaki Kisen KK   Japan

Funnel: Grey, deep red top with white 'K'
Hull: Grey with red boot-topping

Name	Year	GRT	DWT	LOA	Bm	Kts	Eng	Type	Former names
Akikawa Maru	1980	41,139	60,945	205	37	15	M	T	
Alps Highway*	1982	9,609	9,074	155	28	17	M	V	
Atlantic Highway	1976	13,366	11,290	192	24	20	M	V	
Australian Highway*	1981	9,579	9,147	155	28	17	M	V	
Bay Bridge†	1985	35,000	34,700	(210)	32	20	M	CC	
Century Highway No 1	1984	22,968	15,237	186	32	18	M	V	
Century Highway No 2	1985	44,500	11,000	186	32	18	M	V	

Atlantska Plovidba, *Cast Caribou*. J. M. Kakebeeke

119

Name	Year	GRT	DWT	LOA	Bm	Kts	Eng	Type	Former names
Chikumagawa Maru	1982	37,039	57,959	210	32	14	M	T	
Chishirokawa Maru	1983	113,514	224,666	315	50	12	M	B	
Clean River	1983	43,413	51,894	215	34	15	M	LNG	
Columbia Highway*	1970	15,503	12,831	188	23	18	M	V	ex-Toyota Maru No 11 84
Eastern Alliance*	1983	38,089	60,962	220	35	14	M	T	
European Highway*	1973	13,458	15,164	197	28	20	M	V	
Fujisan Maru*	1980	56,151	91,442	242	42	15	M	T	
Global Highway*	1982	19,700	15,148	200	32	18	M	V	
Goho Maru*	1979	35,592	51,817	208	32	15	M	T	
Golden Gate Bridge	1985	34,334	34,700	(210)	32	20	M	CC	
Great Marine†	1976	28,059	59,489	207	32	15	M	T	ex-Grace Marine 84
Jupiter No 1	1976	23,938	37,517	196	28	15	M	BV	
Kazukawa Maru	1970	20,520	20,658	211	25	19	M	CC	ex-Golden Arrow 80
Kiho Maru*	1979	58,154	90,842	250	41	15	M	T	
Kinokawa Maru	1981	26,166	35,709	175	30	13	M	T	
Laurel Wreath	1975	76,873	138,705	287	45	15	M	OO	
Lions Gate Bridge	1973	29,861	26,880	219	31	22	M	CC	
Macassar Maru*	1970	9,356	13,607	150	22	16	M	C	
Melbourne Highway†	1983	43,259	16,483	183	32	18	M	V	
Mizukawa Maru	1982	74,160	133,592	270	43	13	M	B	
Nippon Highway*	1980	17,589	17,702	199	30	17	M	V	
Nisshu Maru*	1984	25,777	42,972	186	30	13	M	B	
Ocean Highway*	1980	16,245	14,201	186	32	18	M	V	
Oriental Road	1969	9,271	14,299	182	25	21	M	RO	ex-Australian Searoader 85
Orion Highway	1984	44,576	14,384	179	32	19	M	V	
Pacific Highway	1977	13,533	11,277	192	24	20	M	V	
Pacific Road*	1971	23,640	19,759	188	28	14	M	V	ex-Toyota Maru No 17 82
Queen's Way Bridge	1972	30,136	30,465	226	31	22	M	CC	ex-Silver Arrow 73
Richmond Bridge	1983	31,403	32,150	218	32	22	M	CC	
River Princess	1975	33,896	114,645	261	40	15	M	O	
Sachikawa Maru	1979	62,396	112,905	239	42	14	M	B	ex-Sachikawa 82
Sacramento Highway	1970	15,502	12,857	188	23	18	M	V	ex-Toyota Maru No 10 84
Sally Ocean†	1977	12,963	20,799	161	25	15	M	C	ex-Sally 77
Scandinavian Highway*	1978	20,400	19,142	197	32	18	M	V	
Seven Ocean‡	1977	13,288	24,928	157	26	14	M	B	
Seven Seas Bridge	1975	39,152	35,331	265	32	25	M2	CC	
Shinanogawa Maru	1976	124,768	241,936	324	54	16	ST	T	
Shuho Maru*	1974	135,880	258,000	337	55	16	ST	T	
Shoho Maru No 2*	1976	88,886	173,864	295	45	16	M	T	
Shokawa Maru*	1968	20,255	20,118	210	26	22	M	CC	ex-Kashu Maru 81
Shun-El Maru*	1983	15,163	23,404	159	25	14	M	C	
Sirius Highway†	1984	44,576	14,332	179	32	18	M	V	
Sun Kobe††	1981	26,191	38,695	183	29	14	M	B	ex-La Estancia 83
Sun Maya††	1979	25,776	38,696	183	29	15	M	B	ex-Charles L.D. 83
Sun River*	1974	43,781	51,868	224	33	16	M	LPG	
Titan	1976	38,826	72,399	234	32	15	M	B	
Tohoku Maru	1971	34,843	42,105	197	30	13	M	B	
Tokyo Highway	1984	45,700	11,400	(180)	32	18	M	V	
Toyoshima Maru*	1981	34,832	64,471	225	32	15	M	B	
Toyota Maru No 15*	1971	14,479	13,119	225	24	19	M	V	
Toyota Maru No 16*	1971	23,607	13,894	188	28	15	M	BV	
Transworld Bridge	1980	35,598	43,070	246	32	23	M	CC	
Ujigawa Maru	1975	113,622	231,487	319	53	16	ST	T	ex-Lotus 84
Vermilion Highway*	1981	17,565	17,596	199	30	18	M	V	
Verrazano Bridge	1973	39,153	35,582	265	32	26	M2	CC	
Violet Ocean†	1977	9,733	16,866	147	23	16	M	B	ex-Gloria Peak 84
Western Highway*	1977	9,832	9,880	161	25	18	M	V	
Yamatogawa††	1980	30,914	60,695	210	36	14	M	T	
Yonekawa Maru	1972	16,418	12,682	175	25	14	M	BV	

* jointly owned with other Japanese companies

† Panamanian flag   †† Sri Lanka flag   ‡ Philippine flag   ‡‡ Liberian flag

Torvald Klaveness & Co A/S — Norway

Funnel: Yellow with blue 'K' on white disc and blue edged narrow white band
Hull: Grey or orange with red boot-topping

Name	Year	GRT	DWT	LOA	Bm	Kts	Eng	Type	Former names
Anniversary Thistle‡	1982	35,976	63,560	225	32	14	M	B	
Bajka*	1972	16,021	27,269	163	26	15	M	B	
Bakar*	1972	16,012	27,376	163	26	15	M	B	
Balao	1973	16,137	27,146	163	26	15	M	B	
Banta*	1971	16,012	27,259	163	26	15	M	B	
Bardu	1979	21,630	33,660	177	27	15	M	B	
Barry	1979	21,630	33,595	177	27	15	M	B	
Barwa*	1973	16,137	27,146	163	26	15	M	B	
Bauchi	1980	21,630	33,595	177	27	15	M	B	
Baumare*	1981	33,343	64,120	225	32	15	M	B	
Bavang	1978	21,630	33,608	177	27	15	M	B	
Bissaruni**	1980	9,634	13,359	122	23	14	M2	BO	
Manaka†	1978	14,088	22,174	161	23	14	M	B	ex-Fort Walsh 84
Probo Bani	1985	20,000	37,000	183	32	14	M	OBO	
Susan B*	1981	33,343	63,990	225	32	15	M	B	

* Liberian flag   ** British flag   † Bahamas flag   ‡ jointly owned by Jardine Shipping Ltd, Hong Kong (British flag)

Korea Shipping Corp Ltd — South Korea

Funnel: Black, broad white band with three red rings interrupted by red circle
Hull: Grey or black with red boot-topping

Name	Year	GRT	DWT	LOA	Bm	Kts	Eng	Type	Former names
Haisbon*	1976	12,633	19,190	158	22	15	M	B	ex-Sea Champion 84, ex-Akitsushima Maru 79
Jesbon	1971	9,491	13,612	156	21	18	M	C	ex-Nichiwa Maru 79
Jinsbon	1972	9,494	13,618	156	21	16	M	C	ex-Nichiiku Maru 79
Kim Hae	1965	34,953	56,883	223	32	15	M	O	ex-Yashiokawa Maru 72
Korea Pacific	1968	28,198	48,053	211	30	15	M	B	
Korea Rainbow	1968	28,493	47,965	211	30	15	M	B	
Korean Jacejin	1979	26,489	25,418	208	31	23	ST2	CC	
Korean Jacewon	1979	26,489	25,444	208	31	23	ST2	CC	
Korean Wonis Jin	1971	25,827	25,447	208	31	23	ST	CC	ex-Korean Commander 80, ex-Taeping 77
Korean Wonis One	1972	23,930	26,979	235	26	21	M	CC	ex-Korean Leader 80, ex-Oriental Chevalier 75
Korean Wonis Seven	1981	27,050	29,361	208	31	23	M	CC	
Korean Wonis Sun	1975	25,683	25,975	213	31	23	ST	CC	ex-Korean Jupiter 80, ex-Oriental Financier 78
Leadbon*	1974	9,134	16,181	140	21	14	M	C	ex-Saleve 80, ex-Diamond Trader 80, ex-Daioh Maru 78
Linngsbon	1972	16,328	26,181	175	25	15	M	BV	ex-Pacific Royal 81, ex-Ryusei Maru 75
Monisbon	1971	9,377	13,615	156	21	16	M	C	ex-Pacific 82, ex-Nichibu Maru 79
Mostbon	1973	10,053	16,143	140	21	13	M	C	ex-Cape Erimo 80
Nasbon*	1982	13,454	23,638	161	23	15	M	B	
One West No 7	1960	9,262	11,752	156	20	18	M	C	ex-Korean Runner 78, ex-Crystal Laurel 77, ex-Seta Maru 71
One West No 8	1964	8,145	12,100	153	19	15	M	C	ex-Korean Winner 78, ex-Manchester City 71
One West No 9	1957	9,642	13,757	149	20	14	M	C	ex-Sae Jong 79, ex-Longta 65, ex-Yinni 64
Sonisbon	1970	9,127	12,964	150	21	16	M	C	ex-Atlantic 82, ex-Naruto Maru 79
Swibon	1982	14,456	25,057	158	26	15	M	B	
West Daori	1973	63,898	118,435	260	40	16	M	B	ex-Polyviking 81
West Jinoriwon*	1972	24,615	41,872	194	29	14	M	B	ex-Inveralmond 80
West Junori	1972	56,933	108,198	261	41	14	M	B	ex-Barbro 81
West Mannori	1982	34,654	61,502	224	32	14	M	B	

Kawasaki Kisen KK, *Transworld Bridge. F. R. Sherlock*

Name	Year	GRT	DWT	LOA	Bm	Kts	Eng	Type	Former names
West Sunori*	1968	19,229	28,900	181	29	14	M	B	ex-J. V. Clyne 79
West Wonori*	1974	71,043	138,588	297	41	16	ST	OBO	ex-Ocean Dolphin 80,
									ex-Ernesto Fassio 78
Westbon	1969	13,074	21,315	159	23	14	M	B	ex-Baugnes 80
Westin	1974	87,117	160,180	299	44	15	M	OBO	ex-Recife 83
Westin Won	1984	34,654	61,502	224	32	14	M	B	ex-West Ballori 84
Wonsbon	1975	13,346	21,528	162	23	15	M	C	ex-Valene 81, ex-Atlantic Albatross 79

* Panamanian flag

Kuwait Oil Tanker Co SAK   Kuwait

Funnel: Red with white and gold Arabic characters on wide white band, two narrow white bands, black top
Hull: Black with red boot-topping

Name	Year	GRT	DWT	LOA	Bm	Kts	Eng	Type	Former names
Al-Faiha	1977	136,614	267,908	340	53	15	ST	T	
Al-Funtas	1983	160,010	294,739	336	60	14	M	T	
Al-Maqwa	1973	21,123	35,338	201	27	16	M	T	ex-Khanaqin 84
Al-Rawdatain	1976	66,807	63,726	281	42	20	ST	LNG	ex-El Paso Sonatrach 84
Al-Rekkah	1977	210,068	407,822	366	70	15	ST	T	
Bahrah	1979	18,012	30,509	171	26	16	M	T	
Gas Al Ahmadi	1979	43,604	46,723	230	35	16	M	LPG	
Gas Al Burgan	1979	43,604	46,723	230	35	21	M	LPG	
Gas Al Kuwait	1977	43,604	46,723	231	35	16	M	LPG	ex-Gas Al-Kuwait 1 78
Gas Al Minagish	1980	43,604	46,723	231	35	16	M	LPG	
Kazimah	1982	160,010	294,739	336	60	14	M	T	
Ras Al Barshah	1982	17,559	27,401	171	25	15	M	T	
Ras Al Jlay'Ah	1982	17,559	27,401	171	25	15	M	T	
Ras Al Zour	1982	17,559	27,401	171	25	15	M	T	
Rehab	1975	11,114	18,522	146	22	13	M	T	ex-Mighty 78
Umm Al Aish	1981	55,453	81,283	232	44	16	M	T	
Umm Al Jathathel	1983	47,170	65,602	241	32	15	M	T	
Umm Al Maradem	1981	55,454	79,999	232	44	16	M	T	
Umm Al Negah	1972	113,780	253,994	348	52	16	ST	T	ex-Porchester Sky 85,
									ex-Kudat sea 84, ex-Irene Lemos 84
Umm Al Roos	1982	47,169	65,602	241	32	15	M	T	
Umm Casbah	1981	55,620	79,999	238	43	15	M	T	
Umm Matrabh	1981	55,621	81,282	238	43	15	M	T	
Umm Ruwaisat	1982	47,170	66,652	241	32	15	M	T	

F. Laeisz Schiffahrts GmbH & Co   FRG

Funnel: Yellow
Hull: Black

Name	Year	GRT	DWT	LOA	Bm	Kts	Eng	Type	Former names
Irene Greenwood‡	1982	13,482	22,035	177	23	15	M	BC	ex-Stephan Reeckmann 83
Maersk Clementine	1972	13,294	13,439	173	24	21	M	CC	ex-Pluvius 85,
									ex-Incotrans Promise 85,
									ex-Pluvius 84, ex-Hellenic Prince 83,
									ex-Pluvius 81,
									ex-Seatrain Princeton 80,
									ex-Pluvius 77
Norasia Dagmar†	1982	13,483	23,323	177	23	15	M	BC	ex-Dagmar Reeckmann 83
Pharos	1983	45,051	75,466	244	32	15	M	OBO	
Planeta	1978	9,154	12,800	145	22	18	M	CC	ex-Incotrans Progress 85,
									ex-Planeta 84
Plata	1978	9,162	12,800	145	22	18	M	CC	ex-TFL Plata 81, ex-Plata 81,
									ex-Seaway Express 80
Protektor*	1967	43,218	80,184	253	35	15	M	B	ex-Ursula Schulte 78
Puritan	1983	13,998	9,728	148	26	17	M	CC	

see also under Ahlers NV
* Panamanian flag   † Liberian flag   ‡ Australian flag

J. Lauritzen A/S, *Belgian Reefer*. J. Krayenbosch

J. Lauritzen A/S

Denmark

Funnel: Red, ivory band with white 'J' above and 'L' below
Hull: Red with vessel's name in large white letters amidships

Name	Year	GRT	DWT	LOA	Bm	Kts	Eng	Type	Former names
African Reefer†	1985	12,411	14,572	145	24	18	M	R	
American Reefer‡	1985	12,411	14,400	145	24	18	M	R	
Anita Dan†	1976	19,451	37,523	196	27	15	M	B	ex-Asian Adventuress 81, ex-Aldgate 79, ex-Scapdale 79
Asian Reefer†	1978	8,890	12,299	144	24	21	M	R	
Australian Reefer†	1984	12,411	14,400	145	24	18	M	R	
Balkan Reefer†	1978	8,938	12,299	144	24	21	M	R	
Belgian Reefer†	1974	8,729	12,100	146	22	21	M	R	ex-Blumenthal 81
Brazilian Reefer†	1975	8,413	11,300	143	22	21	M	R	ex-Bremerhaven 81
Canadian Reefer	1979	8,849	12,570	144	24	21	M	R	
Ecuadorian Reefer	1980	8,849	12,300	144	24	22	M	R	
Jonna Dan*	1975	34,745	71,703	230	32	16	M	B	ex-Silver Trident 80, ex-Norse Falcon 76
Nivi Ittuk	1973	4,999	7,620	135	18	17	M	C	ex-Bamse Dan 82
Samoan Reefer	1973	5,915	8,941	145	21	22	M	R	
Tunisian Reefer	1974	5,915	8,941	144	21	22	M	R	

* Liberian flag†   Bahamas flag   ‡ Singapore flag

DFDS A/S (Det Forenede Dampskibs — Selskab A/S)

Funnel: Black with broad red band, white Maltese Cross on blue disc
Hull: Grey with red boot-topping

Name	Year	GRT	DWT	LOA	Bm	Kts	Eng	Type	Former names
Dana Futura	1975	5,991	6,528	144	23	22	M2	RO	ex-Drosselfels 77, ex-Damman Express 76, ex-Dana Futura 76
Dana Hafnia	1976	5,991	6,605	144	24	22	M2	RO	ex-Drachenfels 77, ex-Dana Gloria 76

Achille Lauro

Italy

Funnel: Blue with white star and black top
Hull: White or black

Name	Year	GRT	DWT	LOA	Bm	Kts	Eng	Type	Former names
Caprolo	1970	12,379	13,209	162	23	22	M	CO	
Cervo	1971	12,379	12,896	162	23	22	M	CO	
Gazzella	1970	12,379	12,863	163	23	20	M	CO	
Gioacchino Lauro	1972	11,373	15,714	155	23	18	M	C	ex-Turkis 72
Palizzi	1956	8,947	12,661	146	19	14	M	C	ex-Lubeck 69
Raffaele Cafiero	1962	24,434	39,969	211	29	17	M	T	
Tigre	1970	12,279	12,863	163	23	20	M	CO	
Volere	1976	126,468	254,891	349	52	16	M	T	

C. M. Lemos & Co

Greece

Funnel: Yellow with houseflag, black top
Hull: Black or grey

Name	Year	GRT	DWT	LOA	Bm	Kts	Eng	Type	Former names
Ethnic	1975	125,947	274,629	337	55	16	ST	T	
Patriotic	1976	125,947	269,500	337	55	16	ST	T	
Tactic	1974	105,422	237,085	320	53	16	ST	T	

J. Lauritzen A/S, *Jonna Dan.* F. R. Sherlock

Leonhardt & Blumberg Reederei

FGR

Funnel: Black with red '×' and black '+' combined on broad white band
Hull: Black

Name	Year	GRT	DWT	LOA	Bm	Kts	Eng	Type	Former names
Adolf Leonhardt‡	1964	18,617	37,677	202	26	15	M	B	
Anja Leonhardt††	1977	12,264	21,515	161	23	13	M	B	ex-Bright Ever 80, ex-Hakuho 79
Anna Leonhardt†	1975	3,895	6,551	103	17	14	M	C	ex-Gloria Ace 81, ex-Blue Uranus 77
Barbara Leonhardt**	1968	5,484	6,850	124	18	18	M	C	ex-Wille II 79, ex-Columbus Tahiti 79, ex-Meta Reith 77
Beata Leonhardt†	1973	4,447	7,292	110	18	18	M	C	ex-May Carp 81, ex-Lancing Ace 73
Hans Leonhardt*	1976	6,603	11,679	129	20	16	M	C	
Heide Leonhardt††	1969	9,406	15,251	140	21	16	M	C	ex-Finn Heide 70
Ingrid Leonhardt**	1976	7,134	11,679	129	21	15	M	C	
Iris Leonhardt†	1970	3,909	5,867	109	16	13	M	C	ex-Kiti Samut 80, ex-Ocean Naga 70
Karl Leonhardt†	1974	3,943	6,551	106	16	12	M	C	ex-Makiy 82, ex-Pasania 76
Klaus Leonhardt††	1969	9,407	16,907	140	21	16	M	C	
Luise Leonhardt**	1971	10,890	16,950	155	23	18	M	C	ex-Maersk Pinto 81, ex-Maersk Mango 78, ex-Luise Leonhardt 75
Marita Leonhardt**	1969	9,406	15,210	140	21	16	M	C	ex-Altenfels 70, ex-Marita Leonhardt 69
Otto Leonhardt††	1967	23,414	40,441	202	29	16	M	B	
Renate Leonhardt†	1975	6,445	9,100	134	18	14	M	B	ex-Ibn Zaidoun 80
Ursula Leonhardt†	1974	3,941	6,557	106	16	12	M	C	ex-Satsuky 82, ex-Juno I 76
Walter Leonhardt**	1966	26,555	44,015	227	27	15	M	B	ex-Bornheim 83

* Panamanian flag ** Cypriot flag † Singapore flag ‡ Liberian flag †† Vanuatu flag

Livanos Group

Greece

Funnel: Black with broad white band outlined blue and red 'L'
Hull: Grey with red boot-topping

Name	Year	GRT	DWT	LOA	Bm	Kts	Eng	Type	Former names
Aliakmon	1968	16,229	29,139	181	23	15	M	B	
Amazon Pioneer*	1973	18,798	32,250	188	27	15	M	T	ex-Esso Montreal 83
Amazon Prosperity*	1972	18,782	32,250	188	27	15	M	T	ex-Esso Saint John 83
Archangelos	1984	24,984	42,964	193	30	16	M	B	
Atlantic Emperor*	1974	128,398	292,641	347	52	15	ST	T	
Atlantic Hawk	1969	16,229	29,171	181	23	15	M	B	
Atlantic Helmsman	1969	16,229	29,165	181	23	15	M	B	
Atlantic Heritage	1969	16,229	29,168	181	23	15	M	B	
Atlantic Hero	1969	16,229	29,156	181	23	15	M	B	
Atlantic Horizon	1969	16,229	29,163	181	23	15	M	B	
Atlantic Marquess	1968	40,962	88,272	256	39	16	M	T	
Atlantic Seaman	1976	15,608	27,405	177	23	15	M	B	ex-Kiyo 84
Chios	1982	22,333	40,632	178	30	14	M	T	
Evros*	1984	24,310	39,990	178	30	15	M	T	
Ioannis Zafirakis	1968	16,227	29,118	181	23	15	M	B	
Marina	1980	48,167	97,839	244	41	14	M	T	
Meandros	1982	23,333	40,632	178	30	14	M	T	
Prosperity	1974	124,556	267,801	344	52	16	ST	T	ex-Atlantic Baron 77
Stavros G. L.	1976	163,810	357,130	363	60	15	ST	T	
Strymon	1969	16,229	29,159	181	23	15	M	B	
Theofano Livanos	1983	22,172	42,320	193	30	16	M	B	
Tina	1976	163,810	357,130	363	60	15	ST	T	

* Liberian flag

Leonhardt & Blumberg Reederei, *Ursula Leonhardt*. J. M. Kazebeke

Cia de Nav Lloyd Brasileiro (Lloydbras) Brazil

Funnel: White, red diagonal top and bottom quarters, 'L' and 'B' on white quarters, narrow black top
Hull: Black with red boot-topping

Name	Year	GRT	DWT	LOA	Bm	Kts	Eng	Type	Former names
Autoestrada	1981	9,858	6,680	134	21	18	M2	RO	
Autovia	1981	9,858	6,680	134	21	18	M2	RO	
Calandrini	1979	10,218	11,999	161	23	20	M	C	
Cantuaria	1979	10,218	11,808	161	23	21	M	C	
Itabera	1972	10,417	12,676	161	23	20	M	C	
Itagiba	1972	10,416	12,938	161	23	20	M	C	
Itaimbe	1970	10,417	12,915	161	23	20	M	C	
Itaite	1971	11,793	13,963	177	23	20	M	CO	
Itanage	1969	11,793	13,963	177	23	20	M	CO	
Itapage	1971	11,793	13,963	177	23	20	M	CO	
Itape	1971	11,793	13,963	177	23	20	M	CO	
Itapuca	1971	10,846	12,222	161	23	20	M	C	
Itapui	1971	10,846	12,222	161	23	20	M	C	
Itapura	1972	10,846	12,222	161	23	20	M	C	
Itaquatia	1971	11,793	13,963	177	23	20	M	CO	
Itassuce	1972	10,846	12,222	161	23	20	M	C	
Lloyd Alegrete	1981	11,372	14,650	160	21	17	M	C	
Lloyd Altamira	1975	6,922	8,690	142	20	18	M	C	
Lloyd Argentina	1981	9,112	14,347	141	21	15	M	C	
Lloyd Atlantico	1985	24,700	24,440	188	30	18	M	CC	
Lloyd Bage	1973	5,378	7,850	140	18	21	M	R	ex-Bage 73
Lloyd Bahia	1982	11,373	14,236	160	21	17	M	C	
Lloyd Cuiaba	1975	6,922	12,193	142	19	18	M	C	
Lloyd Genova	1977	9,112	15,088	141	20	15	M	C	
Lloyd Hamburgo	1974	9,111	14,688	141	20	15	M	C	
Lloyd Houston	1982	9,112	14,347	141	21	15	M	C	
Lloyd Liverpool	1974	9,111	14,682	141	20	15	M	C	
Lloyd Mandu	1979	11,373	14,236	160	21	17	M	C	
Lloyd Marselha	1977	9,112	15,088	141	20	15	M	C	
Lloyd Mexico	1981	9,112	15,036	141	21	15	M	C	
Lloyd Pacifico	1984	22,783	29,265	188	32	18	M	CC	
Lloyd Santarem	1975	6,922	12,193	142	20	18	M	C	
Lloyd Santos	1973	6,739	7,850	140	18	21	M	R	ex-Araraquara 73
Lloyd Tupiara	1980	11,373	14,236	160	21	17	M	C	
Lloyd Venezuela	1983	9,112	14,347	141	21	15	M	C	
Lloydbras	1973	9,112	14,992	141	20	15	M	C	
Rio Branco	1980	21,733	38,097	194	28	16	M	B	
Rio Grande	1980	21,733	38,097	194	28	16	M	B	
Rio Negro	1978	21,733	37,798	194	28	16	M	B	
Rio Purus	1985	25,000	39,000	183	29	14	M	B	
Rio Tefe	1985	25,000	50,000	200	32	15	M	B	
Rio Trombetas	1983	33,684	63,130	200	32	15	M	B	ex-Genesio Pires 85
Rio Verde	1977	21,733	38,403	194	28	16	M	B	

London & Overseas Freighters Ltd UK

Funnel: Yellow with red star on white over blue band
Hull: Black, with red boot-topping

Name	Year	GRT	DWT	LOA	Bm	Kts	Eng	Type
London Spirit	1982	39,280	62,094	219	32	15	M	T
London Victory	1982	36,865	62,153	219	32	15	M	T
Overseas Argonaut	1975	74,336	140,905	270	43	16	M	T

Above: Cia de Nav Lloyd Brasileiro, *Lloyd Bage. J. M. Kakebeeke*

Below: Cia de Nav Lloyd Brasileiro, *Lloyd Tupiara. J. K. Byass*

Oivind Lorentzen A/S — Norway

Funnel: White, broad green band with green 'L' on yellow diamond
Hull: Orange with 'NOSAC', red boot-topping

Name	Year	GRT	DWT	LOA	Bm	Kts	Eng	Type	Former names
Nosac Barbro†	1982	20,300	17,863	194	32	19	M	V	ex-Nopal Barbro 84
Nosac Branco*	1971	13,826	12,395	191	23	19	M	V	ex-Nopal Branco 84, ex-Amalia 73
Nosac Express	1985	48,357	15,000	195	32	19	M	V	
Nosac Mascot†	1978	17,647	17,406	195	32	19	M	V	ex-Nopal Mascot 84
Nosac Sel*	1976	7,494	10,379	188	23	20	M2	V	ex-Nopal Sel 84
Nosac Tasco‡	1985	48,393	15,000	195	32	19	M	V	
Nosac Verde*	1972	13,826	10,398	191	23	19	M	V	ex-Nopal Verde 84, ex-Joana 73

* Liberian flag † owned by Gerner Mathiesen Rederi A/S ‡ owned by Wilh Wilhelmsen — joint owner of 'NOSAC'

SA Louis Dreyfus & Cie — France

Funnel: Black with blue 'LD & C' on white band between two narrow red bands
Hull: Black

Name	Year	GRT	DWT	LOA	Bm	Kts	Eng	Type	Former names
Alain LD	1985	27,800	39,500	(188)	29	14	M	B	
Cetra Sagitta†	1983	74,512	131,650	280	42	14	M	B	
Charles LD	1985	25,000	39,500	(188)	29	14	M	B	
Dominique LD	1974	16,023	27,244	175	23	15	M	B	ex-Roseline 83
Edouard LD	1977	78,212	67,460	281	42	20	ST	LNG	
Francois LD	1984	26,139	39,273	183	29	14	M	B	
Gerald LD	1974	25,223	39,008	182	29	15	M	B	
La Richardais	1976	16,988	30,244	189	23	15	M	B	ex-Philippe LD 85, ex-Peter 81
Monique LD	1985	26,139	39,273	183	29	14	M	B	
Pierre LD	1980	26,325	38,715	183	29	15	M	B	
Sophie B	1977	4,576	7,020	111	19	13	M	C	ex-Havstril 83, ex-Kings River 79

† managed for Consortium European de Transport Maritime

Buries Markes Ltd/UK

Funnel: Black with blue 'BM' on white band between two narrow red bands
Hull: Black with white line and red boot-topping

Name	Year	GRT	DWT	LOA	Bm	Kts	Eng	Type	Former names
Brierfield	1981	26,942	38,695	175	29	14	M	B	ex-La Sierra 83
Chelsfield	1984	27,818	39,500	(188)	29	14	M	B	
Harefield	1984	27,818	41,646	(188)	29	14	M	B	
La Chacra	1982	41,880	77,300	230	32	13	M	B	
La Pampa	1982	41,934	77,300	230	32	14	M	B	
Mela*	1976	16,407	30,242	189	23	15	M	B	ex-Pamela 83
Petersfield	1985	27,818	39,500	(188)	29	14	M	B	ex-Peter LD 85
Westfield	1985	25,000	39,500	(188)	29	14	M	B	

* Panamanian flag
see also Leif Hoegh & Co

Lykes Bros Steamship Co Inc — USA

Funnel: Black with white 'L' on blue diamond on broad white band. Some ships have the 'L' and diamond on the sides of the bridge
Hull: Black with red boot-topping

Name	Year	GRT	DWT	LOA	Bm	Kts	Eng	Type	Former names
Adabelle Lykes	1969	16,757	15,635	201	25	19	M	CC	ex-Mosel Express 84
Almeria Lykes	1972	21,667	39,026	267	32	19	ST	LC	
Ashley Lykes	1963	11,892	14,515	181	21	18	ST	CO	

Above: Oivind Lorentzen Gerner Mathiesen Rederi, *Nopal Barbro* (now renamed *Nosac Barbro*). *M. D. J. Lennon*

Below: SA Louis Dreyfus & Cie/Buries Markes Ltd, *Chelsfield*. *M. D. J. Lennon*

Name	Year	GRT	DWT	LOA	Bm	Kts	Eng	Type	Former names
Brinton Lykes	1962	11,891	14,515	181	21	18	ST	CO	
Charles Lykes	1976	23,382	20,275	209	31	21	ST	RO	ex-Nevada 79
Charlotte Lykes	1968	16,757	19,650	201	25	19	M	CC	ex-Weser Express 84
Doctor Lykes	1972	21,667	39,026	267	32	19	ST	LC	
Elizabeth Lykes	1966	10,955	14,897	165	23	20	ST	C	
Genevieve Lykes	1967	10,723	14,897	165	23	20	ST	C	
James Lykes	1960	11,891	14,530	181	21	17	ST	CO	
Jean Lykes	1961	11,891	14,489	181	21	17	ST	CO	
John Lykes	1960	11,891	14,530	181	21	17	ST	CO	
Joseph Lykes	1960	11,891	14,515	181	21	17	ST	CO	
Leslie Lykes	1962	11,892	14,759	181	21	18	ST	CO	
Letitia Lykes	1968	10,723	14,897	165	23	20	ST	C	
Louise Lykes	1965	10,955	14,897	165	23	20	ST	C	
Mallory Lykes	1966	10,718	14,897	165	23	20	ST	C	
Margaret Lykes	1968	17,823	15,400	201	25	19	M	CC	ex-Elbe Express 84
Marjorie Lykes	1962	11,891	14,530	181	21	18	ST	CO	
Nancy Lykes	1961	11,891	14,530	181	21	17	ST	CO	
Ruth Lykes	1965	10,954	14,897	165	23	20	ST	C	
Sheldon Lykes	1969	17,834	15,770	201	25	19	M	CC	ex-Alster Express 84
Shirley Lykes	1962	11,891	14,526	181	21	18	ST	CO	
Solon Turman	1961	11,891	14,759	181	21	18	ST	CO	
Stella Lykes	1966	10,723	14,897	165	23	20	ST	C	
Thompson Lykes	1960	11,891	14,530	181	21	17	ST	CO	
Tillie Lykes	1973	21,667	39,026	267	32	19	ST	LC	
Tyson Lykes	1975	23,382	20,275	209	31	23	ST	RO	ex-Maine 79
Velma Lykes	1967	10,723	14,897	165	23	20	ST	C	
Zoella Lykes	1960	11,892	14,530	181	21	17	ST	CO	

Lyle Shipping plc

UK

Funnel: Buff with black top
Hull: Grey with red boot-topping

Name	Year	GRT	DWT	LOA	Bm	Kts	Eng	Type	Former names
Cape Arnhem	1980	16,024	26,066	173	27	15	M	B	
Cape Finisterre	1982	16,024	26,003	176	27	15	M	B	
Cape Hawke	1971	14,710	24,091	163	23	15	M	B	
Cape Otway	1977	20,819	32,505	170	27	15	M	B	
Cape Race†	1971	14,885	23,310	165	23	15	M	B	
Port Royal	1981	16,024	26,060	173	27	15	M	B	ex-Cape Trafalgar 84
Sea Taian	1984	24,750	41,815	193	31	16	M	B	ex-Cape Breton 84
Taichu	1984	24,750	42,239	193	31	16	M	B	ex-Cape Wrath 84

H. Hogarth & Sons Ltd

Name	Year	GRT	DWT	LOA	Bm	Kts	Eng	Type	Former names
Baron Belhaven†	1971	14,885	23,310	165	23	15	M	B	
Baron Kinnaird	1981	16,024	26,066	173	27	15	M	B	
Baron Murray	1977	20,819	32,490	179	27	15	M	B	

† managed for Aluminium Co of Canada Ltd (ALCAN)

'Malaysian International Shipping Corp

Malaysia

Funnel: Blue, broad red band divided by white band with yellow star
Hull: Grey with green boot-topping or black with red boot-topping

Name	Year	GRT	DWT	LOA	Bm	Kts	Eng	Type	Former names
Bunga Angsana	1972	11,254	13,560	156	22	17	M	CC	
Bunga Chempaka	1972	20,759	34,201	186	26	14	M	B	
Bunga Kantan	1981	18,151	31,960	183	28	15	M	B	
Bunga Kemboja	1973	44,484	78,875	246	38	16	M	T	ex-Yukon Maru 83, ex-Toh Yo Maru 76

Above: Lykes Bros Steamship Co Ltd, *Ruth Lykes. J. Krayenbosch*

Below: Lyle Shipping plc/H. Hogarth & Sons Ltd, *Baron Kinnaird. J. K. Byass*

Name	Year	GRT	DWT	LOA	Bm	Kts	Eng	Type	Former names
Bunga Kenanga	1982	18,151	31,960	183	28	15	M	B	
Bunga Kesidang	1982	30,098	65,690	225	32	14	M	B	
Bunga Kesumba	1975	18,959	29,956	170	25	15	M	T	
Bunga Mawar	1973	81,231	169,623	295	47	15	M	OBO	
Bunga Melati	1973	10,812	13,240	153	22	23	M	CC	
Bunga Melawis	1973	32,321	32,718	196	29	14	M	B	
Bunga Melor	1971	14,658	18,992	188	25	19	M	CC	
Bunga Orkid	1971	10,730	12,384	153	22	23	M	CC	
Bunga Permai	1979	43,470	49,227	267	32	26	M2	CC	
Bunga Raya	1970	14,658	18,992	188	25	19	M	CC	
Bunga Selasih	1975	18,959	29,956	170	25	15	M	T	
Bunga Sepang	1975	18,959	29,956	170	25	15	M	T	
Bunga Seroja	1972	10,812	13,240	153	22	19	M	CC	
Bunga Srigading	1982	30,098	65,921	225	32	14	M	B	
Bunga Sripagi	1976	22,297	41,683	184	28	17	M	B	
Bunga Suria	1979	43,470	49,149	267	32	26	M2	CC	
Bunga Tanjong	1971	10,727	12,341	153	22	23	M	C	
Bunga Tembusu	1972	32,348	32,725	196	29	14	M	B	
Bunga Teratai	1972	11,214	13,613	156	22	17	M	CC	
Rimba Balau	1976	13,993	24,479	171	23	15	M	B	
Rimba Keruing	1976	13,993	24,130	171	23	14	M	B	
Rimba Meranti	1976	15,532	27,849	177	25	12	M	B	
Rimba Merbau	1977	20,567	37,522	186	28	17	M	B	
Rimba Ramin	1976	15,532	27,409	177	25	12	M	B	
Rimba Sepetir	1977	20,567	37,535	186	28	15	M	B	
Tenega Dua	1979	68,086	72,083	282	42	20	ST	LNG	
Tenega Empat	1981	68,086	72,083	282	42	20	ST	LNG	
Tenega Lima	1981	68,085	72,083	282	42	20	ST	LNG	
Tenega Satu	1979	68,085	72,083	282	42	20	ST	LNG	
Tenega Tiga	1981	68,086	72,083	282	42	20	ST	LNG	

Armement L. Martin SA — France

Funnel: Yellow, pale blue broad band with white disc
Hull: White with red boot-topping

Name	Year	GRT	DWT	LOA	Bm	Kts	Eng	Type	Former names
Mungo	1975	11,740	15,610	159	23	18	M	CO	ex-Calvados 83

Mavroleon Bros Ltd — Greece

Funnel: Yellow with red 'M' on white over blue bands
Hull: Black with white line

Name	Year	GRT	DWT	LOA	Bm	Kts	Eng	Type	Former names
Kasos	1976	15,111	26,246	183	23	15	M	B	ex-Camilla M 79
Vasilis	1979	16,432	28,869	181	23	15	M	B	ex-Golden Swan 79
Violetta	1981	15,819	29,002	180	23	16	M	B	
Vitina	1975	15,111	26,702	183	23	15	M	B	ex-Anna M 79

Mediterranean Shipping Co SA — Switzerland

Funnel: Yellow with 'MSC' on black disc, narrow black band below black top
Hull: Black with red boot-topping

Name	Year	GRT	DWT	LOA	Bm	Kts	Eng	Type	Former names
Alexa II	1967	9,154	13,656	156	21	17	M	C	ex-Al Kadisiah 81
Alexandra	1971	6,645	8,723	145	22	22	M	CC	ex-Ivor 84, ex-Atlantic Prowess 83, ex-Cathy 81, ex-New England Hunter 80, ex-Fiery Cross Isle 73
Aniello	1972	10,778	15,967	155	23	17	M	C	ex-Jogoo 80, ex-Turmalin 78

Above: Malaysian International Shipping Corp, *Bunga Kesumba. J. K. Byass*

Below: Malaysian International Shipping Corp, *Rimba Keruing. J. Krayenbosch*

Name	Year	GRT	DWT	LOA	Bm	Kts	Eng	Type	Former names
Chiara S	1963	14,841	26,068	192	24	15	M	BC	ex-Nai Carolina 82, ex-Carolina Lolli-Ghetti 74, ex-Lerici Seconda 69
Diego	1963	7,833	13,603	173	21	18	M	C	ex-Danaos 83, ex-Concordia Danaos 81, ex-Danaos 80, ex-Capria 77
Emilia S	1970	10,686	14,329	153	23	20	M	C	ex-Sternenfels 80
Francesca	1971	10,607	14,436	153	23	20	M	C	ex-Stockenfels 80
Giovanna S	1966	17,257	28,393	186	24	15	M	B	ex-Nemesis 84, ex-Fidelio 81, ex-Citadel 76
Leila*	1969	13,543	22,240	161	23	15	M	BC	ex-Temple Arch 78
Michele	1965	17,254	28,501	192	24	15	M	BC	ex-Manuela Prima 84
Rafaela	1963	11,091	20,276	162	22	15	M	BC	ex-Gungnir V 82, ex-Sunray 79, ex-Tonto 64
Regina D	1971	15,769	14,936	174	26	23	M2	CO	ex-Antonia Johnson 85
Rosa S	1969	9,192	13,656	156	21	17	M	C	ex-Al Odailiah 81
Simona 1	1963	15,006	28,767	192	24	15	M	BC	ex-Simonetta 81
Valeria	1970	10,618	14,436	153	23	20	M	C	ex-Lone Star 81, ex-Steinfels 80

all Panamanian flag except * Cypriot flag

Andrea Merzario SpA

Italy

Funnel: Yellow with blue square logo of plane, rails, road and waves.
Hull: Yellow with blue boot-topping.

Name	Year	GRT	DWT	LOA	Bm	Kts	Eng	Type
Andrea Merzario	1980	25,382	38,000	226	32	19	M	RO
Comandante Revello	1981	25,400	38,000	226	32	19	M	RO
Merzario Arabia*	1978	12,389	10,651	164	24	16	M2	RO
Merzario Arcadia	1979	8,904	9,450	133	20	14	M	RO
Merzario Britannia	1985	19,730	25,000	193	27	16	M	RO
Merzario Fenicia	1979	9,399	10,270	141	20	14	M	RO
Merzario Italia	1984	21,500	21,600	193	27	16	M	RO
Merzario Persia*	1978	13,478	13,900	173	22	16	M	RO

* Liberian flag

Mitsui-OSK Lines KK

Japan

Funnel: Light red
Hull: Grey or bright blue with red or green boot-topping

Name	Year	GRT	DWT	LOA	Bm	Kts	Eng	Type	
Africa Maru	1979	15,967	18,865	166	26	16	M	CO	
Alaska Maru	1973	29,342	29,000	238	30	22	M	CC	
Alkuds	1975	72,368	139,394	271	44	15	M	T	
Alpine Rose†	1969	33,500	42,124	198	30	13	M	B	ex-Tonami Maru 81
Altai Maru	1979	15,976	23,284	166	26	16	M	CO	
Amagisan Maru*	1976	74,302	135,830	273	44	15	M	O	
Amazon Maru*	1974	8,256	12,349	144	21	17	M	C	
America Maru	1982	31,855	32,207	223	32	22	M	CC	
Andes Maru	1978	14,792	21,200	161	25	15	M	C	
Arimasan Maru*	1974	75,352	135,748	273	44	15	M	O	
Asia Maru	1971	24,278	24,131	212	30	22	M	CC	
Astra Peak	1976	13,585	20,425	161	24	17	M	C	
Atlantic Maru	1979	15,964	18,600	166	26	16	M	CO	
Atlantic Patriot‡	1971	62,918	111,410	260	40	15	M	B	ex-Hosho Maru 84
Atlas Maru	1978	15,118	20,763	161	25	15	M	C	
Australia Maru	1969	24,044	23,312	213	29	22	M	CC	
Aurora Ace*	1984	33,548	17,090	190	32	18	M	V	

Above: Mediterranean Shipping Co SA, *Leila. F. R. Sherlock*

Below: Mediterranean Shipping Co SA, *Valeria. Table Bay Underway Shipping*

Name	Year	GRT	DWT	LOA	Bm	Kts	Eng	Type	Former names
Canadian Ace†	1971	11,538	7,216	162	23	18	M	RO	ex-Canada Maru 80
Canberra Maru*	1979	32,163	29,888	216	32	22	M	CC	
Celchem Catalyst††	1982	24,562	42,312	178	32	14	M	T	
Century Hope**	1984	36,843	69,171	223	32	15	M	B	
Century Progress**	1984	36,843	69,201	223	32	15	M	B	
Chidorisan Maru*	1972	88,884	164,644	292	45	15	M	O	
Chihirosan Maru*	1973	63,218	110,906	260	40	15	M	B	
Chikumasan Maru*	1972	86,460	160,533	289	44	15	M	O	
Clover Ace*	1982	17,418	18,217	186	30	18	M	V	
Co-op Sunshine	1983	50,105	53,372	220	38	16	M	LPG	
Crystal Ace†	1983	8,920	10,538	161	27	16	M	V	
Eastern Lily†	1979	11,002	18,244	146	23	14	M	B	
Elbe Maru	1972	51,623	35,228	269	32	27	M3	CC	
Fairwinds†	1974	8,915	15,142	143	20	13	M	C	ex-Oakland 85
Full Moon†	1977	11,757	19,157	148	23	13	M	B	ex-Kenkon Maru 83, ex-Banff 77
Gas Rising Sun††	1978	41,097	55,173	223	34	15	M	LPG	
Glorious Ace*	1981	16,888	17,743	190	32	18	M	V	
Godwit*	1976	31,670	29,194	222	32	24	M	CC	
Golden Ace†	1978	14,407	18,426	119	30	18	M	V	
Green Saikai	1983	11,155	18,433	148	23	14	M	B	
Harriet Maru*	1982	92,332	177,754	300	48	14	M	B	
Himalaya Maru*	1979	15,729	23,220	167	26	16	M	CO	
Ibaraki Maru	1972	63,139	11,064	260	40	15	M	B	
Izumisan Maru**	1970	38,872	38,838	215	32	16	M	T	
Katorisan Maru*	1976	120,957	237,569	324	53	16	ST	T	
Kohjusan Maru*	1973	87,305	167,698	295	47	15	M	O	
Kohzan Maru	1983	24,715	35,653	175	30	14	M	T	
Kokisan Maru*	1984	75,905	145,967	273	43	15	M	B	
Kunimisan Maru*	1972	63,087	11,524	259	40	15	M	O	
Kurotakisun Maru*	1982	42,236	69,995	228	36	14	M	B	
Lumber State†	1970	10,815	17,302	154	22	14	M	C	ex-Kenan Maru 83
Meisho Maru*	1973	88,885	173,511	295	45	15	M	T	ex-Shoho Maru 81
Meitai Maru*	1974	123,940	234,230	324	54	16	M	T	
Menina Daniela†	1984	14,031	23,400	(150)	24	14	M	B	
Mercury Ace	1985	26,700	14,500	(166)	29	17	M	V	
Mifunesan Maru*	1971	65,404	123,553	270	42	14	M	O	
Mitsui Maru*	1970	37,310	61,260	229	32	15	M	B	
Mitsui Maru No 2*	1972	37,313	61,147	229	32	15	M	B	
Mont Blanc Maru	1974	29,955	28,849	217	31	23	M	CC	
Muse†	1984	24,712	40,970	183	31	14	M	B	
Neptune Ace	1985	36,209	14,200	(166)	29	17	M	V	
New Jersey Maru	1973	37,799	33,024	263	32	25	M2	CC	
New Progress†	1985	23,602	40,000	186	30	15	M	B	
New Promotion†	1985	26,200	42,000	186	30	15	M	B	
New York Maru	1972	38,826	33,287	263	32	25	M2	CC	
Ocean Cavalier†	1973	10,626	11,447	175	26	18	M	RO	ex-Regent Cedar 84
Oceania Maru*	1976	74,636	137,240	267	44	17	M	O	
Ohminesan Maru	1974	124,027	234,157	324	54	15	M	T	
Orange Ace†	1977	12,304	13,732	176	32	19	M	V	
Orchid Ace	19??	11,916	12,507	176	27	17	M	V	
Orient Maru	1968	16,404	14,745	187	25	22	M	CC	ex-America Maru 82
Oriental Pine†	1978	12,324	13,713	176	32	18	M	V	
Osaka Ace†	1984	26,758	11,554	158	28	17	M	V	
Oscar Maru	1981	31,382	33,185	211	32	18	M	CC	
Panama Maru*	1981	17,140	22,597	170	27	17	M	CC	
Patricia VI†	1977	20,652	33,051	185	26	15	M	B	ex-Brave Eagle 84
Port Latta Maru*	1968	50,817	93,355	249	39	15	M	O	
Rainbow Ace*	1983	15,300	16,461	190	32	19	M	V	
Rhine Maru	1972	51,040	35,543	261	32	22	M2	CC	
Rokkahsan Maru*	1970	46,434	82,617	240	36	15	M	B	

Andrea Mersario SpA, *Merzario Persia*. F. R. Sherlock

Name	Year	GRT	DWT	LOA	Bm	Kts	Eng	Type	Former names
Silver Ace	1976	27,880	21,831	181	28	15	M	BV	ex-Sea Corridor 79
Southern Cross Trader†	1971	104,253	227,401	324	54	15	M	T	ex-Gohryusan Maru 83
Sunny Wisteria†	1985	23,076	37,000	(190)	28	14	M	B	
Suzukasan Maru	1978	14,132	13,689	176	32	19	M	V	
Tagasan Maru	1980	54,986	81,229	243	42	15	M	T	
Taikai Maru*	1971	31,951	28,848	196	30	15	M	B	
Takatorisan Maru*	1976	66,989	123,314	259	41	15	M	T	
Tama Maru	1972	6,998	9,222	175	25	18	M	V	
Tenryusan Maru	1980	55,123	89,039	243	42	15	M	T	
Thames Maru	1977	58,683	42,000	290	32	22	M2	CC	
Tokurasan Maru	1974	44,821	80,680	246	38	15	M	T	ex-Pacific Rainbow 79
Tokyo Maru	1983	32,152	32,312	222	32	22	M	CC	
Trade Winds†	1974	8,915	15,147	143	20	13	M	C	ex-Long Beach 84
Tsukubasan Maru	1985	25,982	42,959	186	30	14	M	B	
Wendy†	1983	17,098	26,360	166	28	15	M	BC	ex-C.C. Los Angeles 84

* jointly owned with other Japanese companies
† Panamanian flag
†† Liberian flag
‡ Taiwan flag
** British flag

Mobil Oil Corporation   USA

Funnel: Black with 'MOBIL' in blue with letter 'O' in red on white panel, except *Al Haramain*, and *Saudi Glory* which have black funnels with white/green design
Hull: Black or dark grey with white bulwark line and red boot-topping

	Year	GRT	DWT	LOA	Bm	Kts	Eng	Type	Former names
Mobil Arctic	1972	57,834	131,087	283	40	17	ST	T	
Mobil Meridian	1961	28,218	49,981	224	31	16	ST	T	ex-Stanvac Meridian 61

Mobil Tankships (UK) Ltd/UK

	Year	GRT	DWT	LOA	Bm	Kts	Eng	Type	Former names
Sachem	1972	18,245	29,905	172	26	15	M	T	
Satucket	1971	18,245	30,397	172	26	15	M	T	

Matco Tankships Ltd/UK

	Year	GRT	DWT	LOA	Bm	Kts	Eng	Type	Former names
Matco Avon	1964	43,691	78,943	267	32	16	ST	T	ex-Mobil Valiant 75
Matco Clyde	1982	54,171	81,944	243	42	15	M	T	
Matco Thames	1976	51,472	89,390	247	40	16	M	T	

jointly owned with British Enterprise Oil Ltd, Texas Eastern (UK) Ltd and Amerada Hess Exploration Ltd

Mobil Shipping & Transportation Co Ltd/Liberia

	Year	GRT	DWT	LOA	Bm	Kts	Eng	Type	Former names
Al Haramain†	1975	125,394	281,595	341	54	13	M	T	ex-Mobil Supplier 75
Alkisma Alarabia*	1972	143,962	264,591	336	54	16	M	OO	ex-Lauderdale 82
Al Nisr Al Arabi††	1976	131,608	284,091	340	54	15	M	T	ex-Mobil Eagle 85
Alsama Alarabia*	1974	160,423	315,695	335	56	15	ST	T	ex-Arabian Sky 81, ex-Limatula 81
Arabian Sea*	1975	160,435	315,695	335	56	15	ST	T	ex-Linga 81
Mobil Acme	1971	63,129	138,496	274	44	15	M	T	ex-Sankoqueen 79
Mobil Aladdin	1974	74,134	140,804	270	43	16	M	T	ex-Aramis 82, ex-Hoegh Lance 79, ex-Sydhav 79
Mobil Astral	1974	60,946	127,505	273	42	16	M	T	ex-Pacific Star 80
Mobil Challenge	1983	22,587	39,731	174	32	15	M	T	
Mobil Courage	1983	22,587	39,776	174	32	15	M	T	
Mobil Endeavour	1982	21,909	33,187	171	30	15	M	T	
Mobil Endurance	1982	19,580	33,235	171	30	15	M	T	

Mobil Oil Corp. *Mobil Endurance. J. K. Byass*

143

Name	Year	GRT	DWT	LOA	Bm	Kts	Eng	Type	Former names
Mobil Engineer.........................	1973	18,843	32,590	171	26	15	M	T	
Mobil Enterprise.....................	1983	19,580	38,452	171	30	15	M	T	
Mobil Falcon	1975	125,394	277,000	341	54	15	M	T	
Mobil Hawk	1976	131,573	285,452	340	54	15	M	T	
Mobil Navigator	1973	18,843	32,590	171	26	15	M	T	
Mobil Swift.............................	1973	119,969	272,494	332	56	15	M	T	ex-Takakurasan Maru 78
Mobil Valiant	1982	41,135	81,282	243	42	15	M	T	
Mobil Vanguard	1982	41,135	81,283	243	42	15	M	T	
Saudi Glory†.........................	1974	122,297	276,368	341	54	13	M	T	ex-Mobil Mariner 75
Yanbu Pride*........................	1971	107,570	214,992	326	48	16	ST	T	ex-Mobil Pride 81
Yanbu Progress*	1971	107,603	215,002	326	48	16	ST	T	ex-Mobil Progress 81

* jointly owned by Arabian International Maritime Co, Saudi Arabian flag
† jointly owned by Saudi Maritime Co Ltd; (††Saudi Arabian flag)

Mobil Overseas Shipping Co/Liberia

Name	Year	GRT	DWT	LOA	Bm	Kts	Eng	Type	Former names
Conastoga*	1972	17,506	29,967	172	26	15	M	T	
Corsicana*	1973	17,505	29,960	172	26	15	M	T	
Mobil Brilliant*	1970	54,134	113,256	257	40	15	M	T	ex-Toko Maru 76
Mobil Kestrel*........................	1971	104,361	227,756	324	54	16	M	T	ex-Mitsuminesan Maru 77
Mobil Marketer.......................	1974	18,258	31,102	170	26	15	M	T	
Mobil Petrel	1973	133,560	280,428	340	54	15	ST	T	ex-Yanbu Star 85, ex-Al Bilad 83, ex-Mobil Magnolia 83
Mobil Producer.......................	1974	18,258	31,102	170	26	15	M	T	

* Bahamas flag

Mobil Oil Francaise/France

Name	Year	GRT	DWT	LOA	Bm	Kts	Eng	Type	Former names
Athos.....................................	1974	140,745	276,234	341	54	16	M	T	
D'Artagnan	1974	140,745	275,225	341	54	16	M	T	

Mobil Oil Australia Ltd

Name	Year	GRT	DWT	LOA	Bm	Kts	Eng	Type	Former names
Mobil Australis......................	1972	16,890	27,069	171	25	15	M	T	
Mobil Flinders	1982	93,939	149,235	290	48	14	M	T	

Petroleum Transport International (Pte) Ltd/South Africa

Name	Year	GRT	DWT	LOA	Bm	Kts	Eng	Type	Former names
Mobil Refiner........................	1975	18,939	31,102	170	26	16	M	T	

A. P. Moller   Denmark

Funnel: Black with seven-pointed white star on broad blue band
Hull: Light blue with red boot-topping

Name	Year	GRT	DWT	LOA	Bm	Kts	Eng	Type	Former names
A. P. Moller	1984	28,010	50,600	183	32	15	M	T	
Adrian Maersk	1975	40,600	30,760	225	31	24	M	RO	
Albert Maersk	1975	40,640	30,461	225	31	24	M	RO	
Alva Maersk	1976	34,382	36,462	223	31	26	M	CC	
Anders Maersk	1976	33,401	35,108	239	31	26	M	CC	pt ex-Arthur Maersk 83
Anna Maersk..........................	1975	33,401	35,108	239	31	26	M	CC	pt ex-Anders Maersk 84
Arild Maersk	1976	34,382	36,462	223	31	26	M	CC	
Arnold Maersk	1975	40,549	31,560	223	31	26	M	RO	
Arthur Maersk	1976	33,401	35,108	239	31	26	M	CC	
Axel Maersk	1976	33,401	35,108	239	31	26	M	CC	pt ex-Anna Maersk 84

Above: Mobil Oil Corp, *Mobil Producer.* J. K. Byass

Below: A. P. Moller, *Svendborg Maersk.* J. Krayenbosch

Name	Year	GRT	DWT	LOA	Bm	Kts	Eng	Type	Former names
Cecilie Maersk	1967	21,609	24,617	197	30	22	M	CC	
Challenger	1974	38,540	32,153	261	32	26	M2	CC	ex-Dragor Maersk 85, ex-Seatrain Charleston 80, ex-Svendborg Maersk 79
Charlotte Maersk	1968	21,623	24,937	197	30	22	M	CC	
Chastine Maersk	1968	21,609	25,007	197	30	22	M	CC	
Christian Maersk	1968	21,609	24,937	197	30	22	M	CC	
Clifford Maersk	1969	21,609	25,130	197	30	22	M	CC	
Cornelia Maersk	1967	21,609	24,617	197	30	22	M	CC	
Dagmar Maersk	1984	51,838	69,999	236	40	15	M	T	
Dirch Maersk	1982	51,838	99,800	236	40	15	M	T	
Dorthe Maersk	1983	51,838	99,800	236	40	15	M	T	
Elisabeth Maersk	1980	13,706	21,050	182	27	18	M	RO	
Emma Maersk	1985	28,010	50,600	183	32	15	M	T	
Evelyn Maersk	1985	28,010	50,600	183	32	15	M	T	
Gerd Maersk	1977	19,042	32,395	171	26	15	M	T	ex-Messiniaki Anatoli 79
Gjertrud Maersk	1974	19,922	32,056	171	26	15	M	T	
Gudrun Maersk	1973	19,922	32,056	171	26	15	M	T	
Henriette Maersk.................	1982	8,750	13,845	128	20	14	M	T	
Herta Maersk	1982	8,952	13,845	128	20	14	M	T	
Hulda Maersk	1982	8,750	13,845	128	20	14	M	T	
Inge Maersk.........................	1972	9,177	11,835	139	21	17	M	LPG	
Jakob Maersk	1976	33,081	59,650	212	32	17	M	T	
Jeppeson Maersk..................	1976	33,081	59,650	212	32	17	M	T	
Jesper Maersk.......................	1978	33,072	59,649	212	32	17	M	T	
Karama Maersk	1977	167,728	337,733	370	56	15	ST	T	
Karen Maersk	1977	167,728	337,816	370	56	16	ST	T	
Karoline Maersk	1976	167,207	339,308	370	56	15	ST	T	
Kate Maersk	1976	167,207	339,206	370	56	15	ST	T	
Katrine Maersk	1974	167,204	339,104	370	56	15	ST	T	
Kirsten Maersk......................	1975	167,207	339,303	370	56	15	ST	T	
Kristine Maersk.....................	1974	167,204	336,107	370	56	15	ST	T	
Lars Maersk	1984	43,431	53,400	270	32	24	M	CC	
Laura Maersk.......................	1980	43,233	53,000	270	32	23	M	CC	
Laust Maersk	1984	40,366	48,600	256	32	24	M	CC	
Leda Maersk	1982	43,233	53,000	270	32	24	M	CC	
Leise Maersk........................	1980	43,233	53,000	270	32	23	M	CC	
Lexa Maersk	1981	43,233	53,000	270	32	23	M	CC	
Lica Maersk..........................	1981	30,694	34,240	212	32	24	M	CC	
Louis Maersk........................	1984	43,431	42,800	270	32	24	M	CC	
Luna Maersk	1982	36,988	44,221	241	32	24	M	CC	
Maersk Neptun†	1975	33,240	60,920	220	32	15	M	B	ex-Caledonia 79
Maersk Triton†	1977	33,240	90,920	225	32	15	M	B	ex-Calabria 79
Maersk Wave†	1980	9,354	7,300	153	26	21	M	V	
Maersk Wind†	1981	9,354	7,300	153	26	21	M	V	
Nele Maersk	1979	39,280	69,900	247	32	16	M	T	
Nelly Maersk........................	1978	39,280	69,903	247	32	16	M	T	
Nicolai Maersk......................	1979	39,332	69,900	247	32	16	M	T	
Nicoline Maersk....................	1978	39,280	69,903	247	32	16	M	T	
Niels Maersk	1978	39,220	69,900	247	32	16	M	T	
Nora Maersk	1977	39,220	69,900	247	32	16	M	T	
Olga Maersk	1984	14,139	18,270	153	25	17	M	LPG	
Oluf Maersk	1984	14,139	18,270	153	25	17	M	LPG	
Paula Maersk	1982	29,660	47,803	183	32	15	M	T	
Peter Maersk	1981	29,660	39,536	183	32	15	M	T	
Prima Maersk.......................	1982	29,660	47,803	183	32	15	M	T	
Regina Maersk......................	1983	36,988	43,600	241	32	24	M	CC	
Sally Maersk	1981	14,062	18,270	153	25	17	M	LPG	
Sine Maersk	1976	9,377	11,000	139	21	18	M	LPG	
Sofie Maersk........................	1977	9,342	11,830	139	21	17	M	LPG	

Above: A. P. Moller/The Maersk Co Ltd, *Maersk Ascension*. M. D. J. Lennon

Below: A. P. Moller/The Maersk Co Ltd, *Maersk Sembawang*. J. Y. Freeman

Name	Year	GRT	DWT	LOA	Bm	Kts	Eng	Type	Former names
Stream Balabac†	1973	20,532	33,042	185	26	14	M	BV	ex-Stream Dolphin 85
Stream Bantayan†	1972	20,539	33,024	185	26	14	M	BV	ex-Stream Bollard 85
Stream Busuanga†	1973	20,539	33,115	185	26	14	M	BV	ex-Stream Hawser 85
Stream Biliran†	1973	20,532	33,051	185	26	14	M	BV	ex-Stream Rudder 85
Susan Maersk	1981	14,062	18,270	153	25	17	M	LPG	
Svend Maersk	1982	14,062	18,270	153	25	17	M	LPG	
Svendborg Maersk	1981	14,062	18,270	153	25	17	M	LPG	
TFL Adams	1968	21,609	25,078	197	30	22	M	CC	ex-Clara Maersk 84

† Liberian flag

The Maersk Co Ltd/UK

Name	Year	GRT	DWT	LOA	Bm	Kts	Eng	Type	Former names
Maersk Angus	1968	53,334	102,316	268	39	17	ST	T	ex-Evelyn Maersk 79
Maersk Ascension	1976	33,093	59,850	212	32	17	M	T	ex-Jessie Maersk 83
Maersk Buchan	1968	53,334	102,316	268	39	17	ST	T	ex-Elisabeth Maersk 79
Maersk Harrier	1982	8,959	13,605	128	20	14	M	T	ex-Hans Maersk 84
Maersk Mango*	1978	7,588	11,008	129	23	16	M	CC	
Maersk Sebarok*	1981	30,738	62,728	225	32	17	M	B	
Maersk Seletar*	1981	30,738	62,728	225	32	17	M	B	
Maersk Sembawang	1984	31,580	63,170	225	32	17	M	B	
Maersk Sentosa*	1981	30,741	63,777	225	32	15	M	B	
Maersk Serangoon*	1983	31,581	63,170	225	32	17	M	B	
Maersk Tempo*	1978	7,588	11,007	129	23	16	M	CC	

* owned by The Maersk Co (Singapore) Pte, Singapore flag

A/S J. Ludwig Mowinckels Rederi — Norway

Funnel: Yellow with black top separated by red, white and blue bands
Hull: Grey with red boot-topping

Name	Year	GRT	DWT	LOA	Bm	Kts	Eng	Type	Former names
Egda*	1974	24,591	38,631	182	29	14	M	B	
Fjord Thistle*	1974	19,208	29,719	172	26	14	M	B	
Folga	1982	24,999	38,806	182	29	16	M	B	
Fosna	1976	77,351	138,350	267	44	15	M	T	
Grena*	1974	24,997	39,249	182	29	14	M	B	
Heina	1984	27,962	43,022	188	29	13	M	B	
Horda	1981	24,999	38,787	182	29	16	M	B	
Lista	1984	27,962	39,500	188	29	13	M	B	
Molda	1979	24,999	38,008	182	29	14	M	B	
Team Borga	1973	18,651	32,717	171	26	16	M	T	ex-Borga 82, ex-Team Vesta 79
Team Frosta	1981	22,980	41,985	184	30	14	M	T	ex-Frosta 82
Team Troma	1982	22,980	42,010	184	30	14	M	T	ex-Troma 82
Vinga	1975	77,351	138,344	267	44	15	M	T	

* jointly owned by Jardine Matheson & Co Ltd, British flag

Cia Nacional de Navegacao Sarl — Portugal

Funnel: Black with wide blue band bordered with narrow white bands
Hull: Grey with green boot-topping, or black

Name	Year	GRT	DWT	LOA	Bm	Kts	Eng	Type	Former names
Alcoutim	1968	10,518	14,209	148	21	19	M	C	ex-Castorp 72
Amarante	1969	10,548	14,438	148	21	19	M	C	ex-Lubeck 72
Cabo Bojador	1962	4,156	5,543	108	16	15	M	C	ex-Haukefjell 71
Cabo Verde	1962	3,875	5,646	108	16	15	M	C	ex-Sirefjell 71
Cap Ferrato*	1974	7,148	9,735	145	18	21	M	R	ex-Frigoantartico 84
Cap Frio*	1974	7,148	9,735	145	18	21	M	R	ex-Frigoartico 82
Cassinga	1971	19,510	32,208	202	24	15	M	B	
Cunene	1969	11,557	16,573	158	21	16	M	C	
Manica	1961	9,248	11,281	157	19	18	M	C	ex-Kulmerland 71

Above: A/S J. Ludwig Mowinckels Rederi, *Folga. J. Krayenbosch*

Below: Cia Nacional de Navegacao Sarl, *Nacional Sagres. M. D. J. Lennon*

Name	Year	GRT	DWT	LOA	Bm	Kts	Eng	Type	Former names
Nacala	1966	9,059	10,927	149	20	18	M	C	ex-Hunan 68
Nacional Aveiro	1971	12,880	21,496	149	23	15	M	B	ex-Llaranes 81
Nacional Braganca	1974	30,371	53,349	207	29	14	M	B	ex-Garthnewydd 81
Nacional Faro	1985	23,000	38,300	201	26	16	M	B	
Nacional Figueira	1985	23,000	38,300	201	26	16	M	B	
Nacional Funchal	1985	23,000	38,300	201	26	16	M	B	
Nacional Monchique*	1967	27,223	54,486	229	29	15	M	B	ex-Brussels 80, ex-Brussel 78
Nacional Sagres*	1977	9,012	14,797	141	21	15	M	C	ex-Aracaju 83
Nacional Setubal*	1976	9,012	14,800	141	21	15	M	C	ex-Santa Isabella 82
Nacional Sines	1971	30,406	53,450	211	31	15	M	B	ex-Manuel Yllera 81
Quelimane	1963	8,719	12,965	148	19	15	M	C	ex-Evina 68

* Panamanian flag

Cie Nationale de Navigation (ELF)

France

Funnel: Black with houseflag incorporating the letters 'CNN'
Hull: Grey

Name	Year	GRT	DWT	LOA	Bm	Kts	Eng	Type	Former names
Floreal	1983	51,870	56,174	250	36	17	M	LPG	
Thermidor	1976	130,798	262,166	343	52	16	ST	T	ex-Opportunity 79, ex-Tyne Pride 76
Vendemiaire	1977	52,151	92,034	257	38	16	M	T	ex-Capo Berta 77

Soc Navale Chargeurs Delmas Vieljeux

France

Funnel: Blue with white ships wheel having five red stars in central square
Hull: Black

Name	Year	GRT	DWT	LOA	Bm	Kts	Eng	Type	Former names
Adeline Delmas	1985	18,000	33,000	176	30	14	M	B	
Andre Delmas	1976	14,555	21,839	156	25	15	M	B	
Cantal	1974	11,740	15,814	159	23	18	M	CO	
Creuse	1973	11,740	15,814	159	23	18	M	CO	
Etienne Denis†	1984	30,667	31,983	189	32	18	M	CC	
Frank Delmas	1975	16,431	27,213	167	25	17	M	B	
Helene Delmas	1978	20,394	24,946	189	27	20	M	CC	
Lucie Delmas	1978	20,394	24,946	189	27	20	M	CC	
Lucien Delmas	1976	14,555	21,842	156	25	15	M	B	
Marie Delmas	1978	20,394	29,946	189	27	20	M	CC	
Maris Otter*	1976	12,440	16,217	159	23	18	M	CO	ex-Rochefort 83
Maris Sportsman*	1976	12,440	16,217	159	23	18	M	CO	ex-Ile de France I 83, ex-Royan 82
Michel Delmas	1976	17,079	26,643	173	25	15	M	B	
Nathalie Delmas	1982	20,424	26,287	177	28	18	M	CC	
Patricia Delmas	1982	20,652	26,287	177	28	18	M	CC	
Renee Delmas	1982	20,424	26,287	177	28	18	M	CC	
Rosandra‡	1978	20,594	24,946	189	27	20	M	CC	ex-Irma Delmas 85
Suzanne Delmas	1982	20,424	26,287	177	28	18	M	CC	
Therese Delmas	1983	30,750	32,100	189	32	18	M	CC	
Veronique Delmas	1984	30,667	32,100	189	32	18	M	CC	
Yolande Delmas	1984	30,700	30,000	189	32	18	M	CC	

* Panamanian flag
† jointly owned by Cie de Navigation Denis Freres SA
‡ Italian flag

Cie Navale Worms

France

Societe Francaise de Transports Maritimes

Funnel: Black with broad red band
Hull: Black

Name	Year	GRT	DWT	LOA	Bm	Kts	Eng	Type	Former names
Armagnac	1977	16,505	23,916	173	23	17	M	C	ex-Ville de Rouen 83
Artois	1977	16,505	24,300	173	23	17	M	C	ex-Ville de Reims 83

Above: Soc Navale Chargeurs Delmas Vieljeux, *Nathalie Delmas. F. R. Sherlock*

Below: Cie Navale Worms, *Ville d'Anvers. F. R. Sherlock*

Name	Year	GRT	DWT	LOA	Bm	Kts	Eng	Type	Former names
Elbe Ore†	1972	86,339	160,565	299	44	16	M	OBO	ex-Bretagne 76
Ile de la Reunion	1977	13,928	19,358	163	27	19	M	RO	ex-Degas 83
Ile Maurice	1977	13,928	19,669	163	27	19	M	RO	ex-Cezanne 83
Ville d'Anvers	1977	21,111	25,400	199	25	17	M	CC	
Ville de Bordeaux	1978	21,541	21,081	201	25	17	M	C	ex-Hapag Lloyd Kiel 82, ex-Ville de Bordeaux 81, ex-Seatrain West Point 79, ex-Ville de Bordeaux 78
Ville de Dunkerque	1978	8,670	12,993	170	25	18	M	RO	ex-Foss Dunkerque 81, ex-Ville de Dunkerque 79
Ville de Genes	1972	12,602	16,265	171	24	20	M	C	
Ville de Marseille	1974	12,609	16,570	171	24	20	M	C	
Ville de Nantes	1975	12,609	16,570	171	24	19	M	C	
Ville de Strasbourg	1975	12,609	16,836	171	24	19	M	C	
Ville du Havre	1978	8,670	12,993	170	25	18	M	RO	ex-Foss Havre 81, ex-Ville du Havre 78

managed by Navale et Commerciale Havraise Peninsulaire
† Liberian flag

Soc Nantaise de Chargeurs de L'Ouest

Funnel: Black, band of red and blue vertical strips bordered by white rings
Hull: Black

Name	Year	GRT	DWT	LOA	Bm	Kts	Eng	Type	Former names
Penavel	1977	23,626	38,931	185	26	14	M	B	
Penbreizh	1982	22,476	44,363	200	29	14	M	B	ex-Tamarin 82
Penchateau*	1976	64,967	123,126	268	39	15	M	B	
Pengall	1982	74,150	138,480	280	47	17	M	B	
Penthievre	1975	93,831	168,937	295	47	15	M	OO	ex-Champagne 83

* jointly owned by Total Cie Francaise de Nav

Soc Francaise de Transports Petroliers

Funnel: Black
Hull: Grey with red boot-topping

Name	Year	GRT	DWT	LOA	Bm	Kts	Eng	Type	Former names
Camargue	1976	69,016	136,099	281	41	16	M	T	
Obernai	1970	79,746	142,806	289	44	16	M	T	
Poitou	1976	69,016	135,500	280	41	16	M	T	
Sologne	1977	69,016	135,500	280	41	16	M	T	
Stolt Energie	1974	15,163	25,200	165	25	15	M	T	ex-Anco Energie 83, ex-Post Energie 78
Stolt Entente	1975	15,163	25,200	165	25	15	M	T	ex-Anco Entente 83, ex-Post Entente 78
Touraine	1975	50,197	92,100	251	36	16	M	T	ex-Changi Star 80, ex-St Raphael 77, ex-Adamant 77

Nedlloyd Lijnen BV

Netherlands

Funnel: Black with broad orange band
Hull: Black or grey with red boot-topping

Name	Year	GRT	DWT	LOA	Bm	Kts	Eng	Type	Former names
Hapag Lloyd Brasil	1971	6,547	12,403	140	21	16	M	C	ex-Niger 85, ex-Nedlloyd Niger 84
Nedlloyd Bahrain	1978	13,176	22,500	173	27	17	M	CO	
Nedlloyd Baltimore	1978	13,176	22,500	173	27	17	M	CO	
Nedlloyd Bangkok	1978	13,176	22,500	173	27	17	M	CO	
Nedlloyd Barcelona	1979	13,176	22,500	173	27	17	M	CO	
Nedlloyd Clarence	1983	33,405	38,235	210	32	18	M	CC	
Nedlloyd Clement	1983	33,405	37,897	210	32	18	M	CC	
Nedlloyd Colombo	1982	32,114	32,841	211	32	19	M	CC	

Above: Cie Navale Worms, *Penchateau. J. K. Byass*

Below: Nedlloyd Lijnen BV, *Nedlloyd Marseilles. F. de Vries*

Name	Year	GRT	DWT	LOA	Bm	Kts	Eng	Type	Former names
Nedlloyd Dejima	1973	58,613	46,989	287	32	25	M2	CC	
Nedlloyd Delft	1973	58,613	46,989	287	32	25	M2	CC	
Nedlloyd Hoorn	1978	52,553	48,439	259	32	21	M2	CC	
Nedlloyd Houtman	1977	52,562	49,262	259	32	23	M2	CC	ex-Largs Bay 82, ex-Nedlloyd Houtman 80
Nedlloyd Katwijk	1971	11,497	16,828	163	23	17	M	C	
Nedlloyd Kembla	1971	11,497	17,098	163	23	17	M	C	
Nedlloyd Kimberley	1971	11,852	16,921	163	23	20	M	C	ex-Rushmore 71
Nedlloyd Kingston	1971	11,852	16,921	163	23	20	M	C	
Nedlloyd Kyoto	1970	11,852	16,967	163	23	20	M	C	ex-Rainier 71
Nedlloyd Leuve	1966	10,804	13,154	162	24	20	M	CO	ex-Leuve Lloyd 77
Nedlloyd Linge	1967	10,804	13,191	162	24	20	M	CO	ex-Neder Linge 77
Nedlloyd Loire	1967	10,804	13,652	162	24	20	M	CO	ex-Loire Lloyd 77
Nedlloyd Madras	1978	14,123	21,376	187	23	17	M	C	ex-Amstelstad 80, ex-Marindus Quebec 79
Nedlloyd Manila	1978	13,484	21,376	187	23	17	M	C	ex-Manila 84, ex-Nedlloyd Manila 84, ex-Manila 83, ex-Nedlloyd Manila 83, ex-Amstelsluis 80, ex-Marindus Trios Rivieres 79
Nedlloyd Marseilles	1978	13,484	21,376	187	23	17	M	C	ex-Amstelslot 80, ex-Marindus Rimouski 79
Nedlloyd Moji	1977	15,464	16,186	158	25	15	M	C	ex-Trans Nova 80, ex-Nortrans Egero 79
Nedlloyd Nagasaki	1972	12,123	15,600	165	24	20	M	C	ex-Straat Nagasaki 78
Nedlloyd Nagoya	1971	12,123	15,937	165	24	20	M	C	ex-Straat Nagoya 78
Nedlloyd Napier...................	1972	12,123	15,937	165	24	20	M	C	ex-Straat Napier 77
Nedlloyd Nassau	1972	12,123	15,937	165	24	20	M	C	ex-Straat Nassau 77
Nedlloyd Oranjestad..............	1971	7,256	11,650	169	24	21	M	C	ex-Oranjestad 82, ex-Rotterdam 81, ex-Trident Rotterdam 79
Nedlloyd Rochester................	1979	19,072	22,520	197	32	19	M	RO	
Nedlloyd Rosario	1979	21,145	29,098	212	32	19	M	RO	
Nedlloyd Rotterdam	1979	19,072	22,564	197	32	20	M	RO	
Nedlloyd Rouen	1978	21,145	29,218	212	32	19	M	RO	
Nedlloyd San Juan	1975	15,807	21,642	171	26	21	M	CO	ex-McKinney Maersk 85
Nedlloyd Santos	1975	15,809	21,300	171	26	21	M	CO	ex-Margrethe Maersk 85
Nedlloyd Seoul	1975	15,801	22,727	171	26	20	M	CO	ex-Mathilde Maersk 85
Nedlloyd Singapore	1974	15,807	29,730	171	31	18	M	CO	ex-Marchen Maersk 85
Nedlloyd van Diemen	1984	23,790	29,730	183	31	18	M	CC	
Nedlloyd van Neck................	1983	23,930	29,730	183	31	17	M	CC	
Nedlloyd van Noort...............	1984	23,790	29,930	183	31	17	M	CC	
Nedlloyd Willemstad	1970	7,256	11,580	169	24	21	M	C	ex-Willemstad 82, ex-Amsterdam 85, ex-Trident Amsterdam 79
Nile	1972	9,453	12,403	140	21	16	M	C	ex-Nedlloyd Nile 84
Safocean Mildura	1967	12,622	15,390	187	24	21	M	C	ex-Nedlloyd Lek 80, ex-Neder Lek 77
Tasman	1971	27,614	33,350	226	31	21	ST	CC	ex-Nedlloyd Tasman 84, ex-Able Tasman 78

Nedlloyd Bulk BV

Name	Year	GRT	DWT	LOA	Bm	Kts	Eng	Type	Former names
Amsteldiep............................	1970	12,592	20,015	160	22	14	M	B	ex-Putten 77
Amsteldreef	1970	12,592	20,015	160	22	14	M	B	ex-Voorne 77
Amstelmeer	1975	34,026	54,431	221	32	16	M	B	ex-Politechnika Gdanska 75
Amstelmolen.........................	1976	34,023	54,440	221	32	16	M	B	
Amstelvaart	1980	22,973	37,991	201	28	16	M	B	
Amstelvliet............................	1981	22,973	37,991	201	28	16	M	B	
Amstelvroon..........................	1981	22,973	37,991	201	28	16	M	B	
Amstelwal	1981	70,665	132,700	270	42	15	M	B	ex-Niels Onstad 85
Antilla Bay	1973	33,288	39,931	216	32	17	M	LPG	
Gastor†	1976	68,247	61,000	275	42	19	ST	LNG	
Maaskade*............................	1975	18,911	32,214	171	26	15	M	T	
Maaskant*	1975	18,911	32,235	171	26	15	M	T	

Above: Nedlloyd Lijnen BV, *Nedlloyd van Neck. F. de Vries*

Below: Nedlloyd Lijnen BV, *Maasslot. J. M. Kakebeeke*

Name	Year	GRT	DWT	LOA	Bm	Kts	Eng	Type	Former names
Maaskerk*	1975	18,911	32,235	171	26	15	M	T	
Maaskroon*	1976	18,911	32,234	171	26	15	M	T	
Maasslot	1982	24,794	38,039	172	32	15	M	T	
Maassluis	1982	24,794	38,039	172	32	15	M	T	
Maasstad	1983	24,794	38,039	172	32	15	M	T	
Maasstroom	1983	24,794	38,039	172	32	15	M	T	

* owned by Nedlloyd Bulk (Belgie) NV, Belgian flag
† Panamanian flag

Koninklijke Nederlandsche Stoomboot-Maatschappij BV

Funnel: Black with two white bands widely separated
Hull: Black or grey, red boot-topping

Name	Year	GRT	DWT	LOA	Bm	Kts	Eng	Type	Former names
Baarn	1972	9,954	16,250	150	21	16	M	C	ex-Araluck 76, ex-Appian 72
Breda	1972	9,954	15,927	150	21	16	M	C	ex-Gordian 76
Nedlloyd Alkmaar	1971	10,239	17,011	191	24	22	M	C	ex-Alkmaar 82, ex-Lloyd Auckland 81, ex-Alkmaar 80, ex-Pearlstone 72
Nedlloyd Amersfoort	1970	10,239	17,061	191	24	22	M	C	ex-Amersfoot 82, ex-Lodestone 72
Nedlloyd Hollandia	1977	27,770	23,678	204	31	21	M	CC	ex-Hollandia 82
Zeelandia	1980	28,362	24,007	206	31	20	M	CC	ex-Java Winds 85, ex-Nedlloyd Zeelandia 83, ex-Benattow 82, ex-Zeelandia 80

NV Koninklijke Hollandsche Lloyd

Name	Year	GRT	DWT	LOA	Bm	Kts	Eng	Type	Former names
Flevoland	1973	9,799	13,945	153	20	18	M	C	ex-Nedlloyd Flevoland 83, ex-Flevoland 82, ex-Jomara 73
Nedlloyd Gooiland	1969	4,846	8,475	148	19	15	M	C	ex-Gooiland 82
Salland	1974	9,800	13,945	153	20	18	M	C	ex-Nedlloyd Salland 83, ex-Salland 82

Mammoet Shipping BV

Funnel: Yellow
Hull: Yellow with blue lettering 'Mammoet' and mammoth design, red or green boot-topping

Name	Year	GRT	DWT	LOA	Bm	Kts	Eng	Type	Former names
Happy Buccaneer	1984	16,341	9,170	146	28	15	M2	HL	
Happy Mammoth	1967	3,539	7,357	130	21	12	M2	HL	ex-Docklift 2 81
Waalekerk	1968	10,710	13,282	167	23	20	M	C	ex-Nedlloyd Waalekerk 84, ex-Waalekerk 78
Westerkerk	1967	10,710	13,282	167	23	20	M	C	ex-Nedlloyd Westerkerk 84, ex-Westerkerk 78
Willemskerk	1967	10,710	13,282	167	23	20	M	C	ex-Nedlloyd Willemskerk 84, ex-Willemskerk 77
Wissekerk	1967	10,710	13,503	167	23	20	M	C	ex-Nedlloyd Wissekerk 84, ex-Wissekerk 77

Asia Australia Express Ltd/Hong Kong

Funnel: Black with chequered band
Hull: Grey

Name	Year	GRT	DWT	LOA	Bm	Kts	Eng	Type	Former names
Asian Jade	1978	21,121	24,383	186	28	19	M	CC	
Asian Pearl	1978	21,122	24,354	186	28	19	M	CC	

jointly controlled by Nedlloyd Group, Overseas Containers Ltd and China Navigation Co Ltd (managed by Mercury Shipping Co Ltd)

Above: Nedlloyd Lijnen BV/K.N.S.M. *Nedlloyd Amersfoort.* F. R. Sherlock

Below: Nedlloyd Lijnen BV/Mammoet Shipping BV, *Waalekerk.* B. J. Buitendijk

Neptune Orient Lines Ltd

Singapore

Funnel: Blue with red trident on wide white band, narrow black top
Hull: Grey with red boot-topping

Name	Year	GRT	DWT	LOA	Bm	Kts	Eng	Type	Former names
Anro Temasek	1977	16,063	22,319	213	24	20	M	RO	
Neptune Agate	1962	6,718	9,364	126	20	15	M	C	ex-Cygnus 70
Neptune Aldebaran	1984	32,341	66,822	223	32	14	M	B	
Neptune Altair	1983	32,340	66,764	225	32	14	M	B	
Neptune Amber	1980	30,323	38,492	231	32	23	M	CC	
Neptune Aries	1974	16,445	26,909	171	25	15	M	T	
Neptune Beryl	1984	11,208	18,461	161	25	17	M	CC	
Neptune Canopus	1983	30,703	64,711	225	32	18	M	B	
Neptune Coral	1977	31,076	30,934	222	32	23	M	CC	
Neptune Crystal	1980	30,323	38,551	231	32	23	M	CC	
Neptune Cyprine	1972	8,823	12,107	143	20	14	M	C	
Neptune Diamond	1979	30,323	38,492	231	32	23	M	CC	
Neptune Emerald†	1973	20,234	25,369	225	27	19	M	CC	
Neptune Iolite	1977	8,879	15,048	143	20	13	M	C	
Neptune Iris	1977	8,879	15,059	143	20	13	M	C	
Neptune Jasper	1984	11,208	18,461	161	25	17	M	CC	
Neptune Kiku	1973	8,823	15,057	142	20	13	M	C	
Neptune Leo	1977	51,502	96,499	243	40	15	M	T	
Neptune Orion	1974	16,444	29,908	171	25	15	M	T	
Neptune Pavo	1981	39,995	86,417	244	42	14	M	T	
Neptune Pearl	1976	31,076	30,934	222	32	23	M	CC	
Neptune Pegasus	1981	39,995	86,408	244	42	15	M	T	
Neptune Peridot	1977	8,921	15,030	143	20	13	M	C	
Neptune Ruby	1972	8,846	15,108	143	20	13	M	C	
Neptune Sapphire†	1973	20,243	25,369	225	27	19	M	CC	
Neptune Sardonyx	1978	8,920	14,967	143	20	13	M	C	
Neptune Schedar	1984	19,670	37,636	187	28	13	M	B	
Neptune Seginus	1984	19,670	32,850	188	28	13	M	B	
Neptune Sheratan	1983	19,663	32,850	187	28	13	M	B	
Neptune Sirius	1982	19,663	37,659	187	28	13	M	B	
Neptune Spinel	1978	8,788	14,967	143	20	13	M	C	
Neptune Tourmaline	1977	8,879	15,059	143	20	14	M	C	
Neptune Turquoise	1976	8.879	15,069	143	20	14	M	C	

† owned by Jurong Shipyard Ltd

New Zealand Line

New Zealand

Funnel: Red, brown top over broad blue band bordered by narrow white bands.
Hull: Black

Name	Year	GRT	DWT	LOA	Bm	Kts	Eng	Type	Former names
New Zealand Caribbean†	1980	19,613	18,250	169	28	18	M	CC	
New Zealand Mariner	1977	10,991	13,879	145	22	19	M	CC	ex-Ulanga 85, ex-Gulf Clipper 78, ex-Ulanga 77
New Zealand Pacific	1978	42,276	38,642	249	32	23	M2	CC	
New Zealand Trader	1980	6,165	8,477	118	18	15	M	CC	ex-Atlantic 83

† British flag

Niarchos Group

Greece

Funnel: Black with white 'N' interrupting red over white over blue bands
Hull: Black with red boot-topping

Name	Year	GRT	DWT	LOA	Bm	Kts	Eng	Type
Northern Naiad*	1967	22,817	45,796	190	29	15	M	B
World Achilles II	1975	19,451	37,389	196	27	15	M	B

Above: Neptune Orient Lines Ltd, *Neptune Cyprine*. M. D. J. Lennon

Below: New Zealand Line, *New Zealand Caribbean*. J. Y. Freeman

Name	Year	GRT	DWT	LOA	Bm	Kts	Eng	Type	Former names
World Aegeus	1979	19,264	37,428	196	27	15	M	B	
World Agamemnon	1976	19,264	37,451	196	27	15	M	B	
World Ajax	1975	19,451	37,419	196	27	15	M	B	
World Amphion	1979	19,267	37,428	196	27	15	M	B	
World Apollo	1972	19,426	37,530	196	27	15	M	B	
World Ares	1974	19,264	37,623	196	27	15	M	B	
World Aretus	1977	19,265	37,472	196	27	15	M	B	
World Argonaut	1976	19,264	37,451	196	27	15	M	B	
World Argus	1973	19,451	37,580	193	27	15	M	B	
World Duality*	1970	56,799	114,144	264	38	15	M	BO	
World Duet*	1971	56,800	114,092	264	38	15	M	BO	
World Kinship*	1981	40,651	88,557	247	40	15	M	T	
World Kudos*	1981	40,651	88,460	247	40	15	M	T	
World Marine	1973	19,451	37,637	196	27	15	M	B	
World Nature*	1967	23,347	44,496	195	28	14	M	B	
World Nautilus*	1967	23,347	44,420	195	28	14	M	B	ex-World Happiness 67
World Navigator	1967	22,817	45,805	190	29	15	M	B	
World Negotiator*	1968	22,782	45,453	190	29	15	M	B	
World News*	1968	22,798	45,547	190	29	15	M	B	
World Nobility	1967	22,817	45,821	190	29	15	M	B	
World Nomad*	1968	22,798	45,557	190	29	15	M	B	
World Process	1984	17,199	29,990	171	26	15	M	T	
World Produce	1984	17,199	29,990	171	26	15	M	T	
World Prologue	1985	17,199	29,990	171	26	15	M	T	
World Prophet	1985	18,300	29,990	171	26	15	M	T	
World Protector	1974	18,204	31,161	171	26	15	M	T	ex-World Prospector 74
World Recovery*	1973	125,972	234,753	328	49	15	ST	OBO	ex-Havkong 76
World Resolve*	1972	114,709	249,261	334	49	15	ST	T	ex-Ferncourt 76
World Scholar*	1979	126,238	268,112	344	52	14	M	T	
World Score*	1978	126,261	267,401	345	55	15	M	T	ex-Cartsdyke Glen 77
World Umpire*	1983	28,268	47,623	196	32	15	M	B	
World Utility*	1983	28,268	47,828	196	32	15	M	B	

* Liberian flag

Van Nievelt, Goudriaan & Co BV   Netherlands

Funnel: Yellow with white star on broad blue band
Hull: Black with yellow line and red boot-topping or grey

Name	Year	GRT	DWT	LOA	Bm	Kts	Eng	Type
Aldabi	1977	10,444	14,467	143	21	16	M	C
Alhena	1977	10,444	14,678	143	21	16	M	C
Alnati	1977	10,444	14,678	143	21	16	M	C
Alphacca	1978	10,444	14,746	143	21	16	M	C

Nigerian National Shipping Line Ltd   Nigeria

Funnel: Green with black top, black band and white 'N'
Hull: Pale green with darker green boot-topping

Name	Year	GRT	DWT	LOA	Bm	Kts	Eng	Type
River Aboine	1979	10,985	11,810	147	23	16	M	C
River Adada	1979	13,164	16,487	175	23	18	M	C
River Andoni	1979	10,985	11,557	147	23	16	M	C
River Asab	1979	10,985	11,672	147	23	16	M	C
River Guma	1980	10,985	11,801	147	23	16	M	C
River Gurara	1980	13,194	16,329	175	23	18	M	C
River Hadejia	1974	9,388	11,618	146	22	17	M	C
River Ikpan	1980	13,362	16,620	147	23	16	M	C
River Jimini	1979	10,985	11,664	147	23	16	M	C
River Kerewa	1979	10,985	11,620	147	23	16	M	C
River Mada	1979	10,984	11,620	147	23	16	M	C

Above: Niarchos Group, *World Amphion* J. Krayenbosch

Below: Van Nievelt. Goudriaan & Co BV. *Alhena. B. J. Buitendijk*

Name	Year	GRT	DWT	LOA	Bm	Kts	Eng	Type	Former names
River Maje	1980	13,197	16,489	175	23	18	M	C	
River Majidun	1979	13,161	16,333	175	23	18	M	C	
River Ngada	1980	13,362	16,000	147	23	16	M	C	
River Ogbese	1980	13,197	16,479	175	23	18	M	C	
River Oji	1979	13,165	16,487	175	23	18	M	C	
River Oli	1979	13,164	16,487	175	23	18	M	C	
River Oshun	1980	13,197	16,487	175	23	18	M	C	
River Osse	1979	10,985	11,620	147	23	16	M	C	
River Rima	1979	10,985	11,620	147	23	16	M	C	

Nippon Yusen Kaisha

Japan

Funnel: Black with broad white band containing two red bands
Hull: Black with white line and red boot-topping

Name	Year	GRT	DWT	LOA	Bm	Kts	Eng	Type	Former names
Amagi Maru*	1983	18,307	13,702	190	29	17	M	V	
Arion††	1975	18,714	28,881	179	25	14	M	V	ex-Toyota No 21 85
Asama Maru*	1978	8,372	9,321	150	21	20	M	R	
Astral Mariner†	1985	16,800	27,500	167	23	14	M	B	
Astral Neptune†	1985	16,800	27,500	167	23	14	M	B	
Astral Ocean†	1985	16,800	27,500	167	23	14	M	B	
Atlantic Concord†	1984	17,999	29,135	175	27	14	M	B	
Banshu Maru*	1983	104,121	67,055	283	45	19	ST	LNG	
Bishu Maru*	1983	100,295	70,546	282	44	19	ST	LNG	
Century Leader No 1	1984	45,422	11,961	180	32	18	M	V	
Century Leader No 2	1985	21,100	14,300	(170)	32	19	M	V	
Chiaki Maru*	1971	62,250	115,534	260	38	14	M	B	
Chikubu Maru*	1976	65,798	119,513	255	40	15	M	B	
Chikuho Maru	1975	63,287	111,229	260	40	15	M	B	
Chikura Maru	1970	39,936	71,694	242	32	14	M	B	
Chita Maru*	1971	63,172	111,499	260	40	15	M	B	
Dewa Maru*	1984	102,376	67,055	283	45	19	ST	LNG	
Echigo Maru*	1983	102,390	67,219	283	45	19	ST	LNG	
Fuji Maru	1984	47,751	15,000	190	32	18	M	V	
Fujikawa Maru*	1975	116,768	234,478	320	53	16	ST	T	
Fushimi Maru	1970	10,986	12,620	158	22	18	M	C	
Fuso Maru	1970	10,986	12,611	158	22	18	M	C	
Futami Maru	1971	10,976	12,517	159	22	18	M	C	
Gulf Glory†	1984	17,214	29,125	171	27	13	M	B	
Gulf Harvest†	1984	17,214	28,540	171	27	13	M	B	
Gulf Ideal†	1984	17,214	28,540	171	27	13	M	B	
Hachinohe Maru*	1972	40,571	54,187	230	34	13	M	B	
Hakata Maru	1974	30,920	27,203	219	31	22	M	CC	
Hakone Maru*	1983	35,309	29,733	212	32	21	M	CC	
Hakuba Maru	1979	36,723	29,701	216	32	21	M	CC	
Hakusan Maru*	1973	23,602	22,934	209	30	22	M	CC	
Hayakawa Maru	1982	31,549	32,953	211	32	18	M	CC	
Heiwa Maru*	1973	116,136	237,677	322	52	15	ST	T	ex-Showa Maru 75
Hermes Ace	1976	9,913	14,833	159	22	17	M	CC	ex-Seatrain Italy 81, ex-Sovreign Express 77
Hikawa Maru*	1974	24,770	23,513	214	31	23	M	CC	
Hira Maru*	1978	24,794	24,344	215	31	24	M	CC	
Hotaka Maru*	1970	21,057	20,400	196	27	22	M	CC	
Hyogo Maru*	1973	9,054	14,059	182	25	21	M	RO	
Hyuga Maru*	1984	35,084	30,124	(194)	32	22	M	CC	
Jindai Maru*	1973	8,755	8,796	137	20	16	M	V	
Jinei Maru	1976	17,821	15,437	197	28	20	M	V	ex-Polar Bear 78
Jingu Maru	1978	18,450	15,896	189	30	18	M	V	
Jinmei Maru	1978	19,799	16,307	225	32	18	M	V	

Above: Nigerian National Shipping Line Ltd, *River Oshun*. *J. Krayenbosch*

Below: Nippon Yusen Kaisha, *Futami Maru*. *J. Krayenbosch*

Name	Year	GRT	DWT	LOA	Bm	Kts	Eng	Type	Former names
Jinryn Maru	1971	36,480	37,402	224	32	14	M	V	ex-Fuji Maru 84, ex-Zenkoren Maru No 7 80
Jinsen Maru	1970	20,323	19,265	172	25	14	M	V	ex-Shin Honshu Maru 78
Jinto Maru*	1981	17,381	17,376	199	30	17	M	V	
Jinyo Maru*	1982	9,816	10,449	161	27	16	M	V	
Jinyu Maru*	1975	16,109	16,343	225	32	23	M	V	
Kaga Maru	1966	14,131	14,459	187	23	20	M	CC	
Kai Maru	1966	14,136	14,901	187	23	20	M	C	
Kamakura Maru	1971	51,070	34,437	261	32	24	M2	CC	
Kasuga Maru	1976	58,440	43,050	289	32	26	M2	CC	
Kasugai Maru	1970	34,948	42,212	197	30	13	M	B	
Kenyo Maru*	1981	50,169	81,283	232	44	16	M	T	
Kiho Maru	1976	89,262	169,521	295	47	15	M	OBO	ex-Cosmic Jupiter 85
Kii Maru	1966	14,127	14,657	187	23	20	M	C	
Kiso Maru	1972	38,540	31,724	261	32	25	M2	CC	
Kitano Maru	1972	51,269	34,474	261	32	24	M2	CC	
Kotowaka Maru*	1984	97,788	70,833	281	44	19	ST	LNG	
Kurama Maru	1972	59,407	43,476	290	32	22	M2	CC	
Kurobe Maru	1972	37,845	32,343	260	32	24	M2	CC	
Kyoei Maru*	1971	110,037	216,119	316	50	16	ST	T	
Lantana†	1982	15,578	21,124	166	27	15	M	CO	
Maizuru Maru	1973	34,836	60,187	225	32	15	M	B	
Mino Maru	1982	21,815	35,941	190	28	14	M	B	
Musashi Maru	1968	24,682	23,698	194	29	14	M	V	
Mutsu Maru	1969	24,720	24,513	194	29	14	M	V	
Nada III‡	1978	9,796	10,890	165	28	18	M	V	ex-Kyo Jin 83
Nada V†	1984	43,101	15,129	186	32	18	M	V	
Nelson Maru*	1971	17,434	24,077	165	25	15	M	B	
New League†	1985	26,951	46,000	(180)	32	14	M	B	
Nichigoh Maru*	1980	36,912	32,023	217	32	21	M	CC	
Nichirin Maru*	1970	29,545	45,132	208	32	14	M	O	
Ocean Hawk†	1981	10,420	17,727	147	23	13	M	B	ex-Harukawa Maru 84
Ohtsu Maru	1969	58,262	107,019	260	38	14	M	O	
Ondo Maru	1982	59,789	105,577	245	42	14	M	B	
Onga Maru	1985	104,000	170,400	(290)	50	14	M	B	
Onoe Maru No 2*	1978	65,655	117,961	262	40	15	M	B	
Oriental Phoenix†	1985	27,200	8,050	158	28	17	M	V	
Orion Diamond	1982	19,280	15,396	214	32	18	M	V	
Owari Maru	1969	58,800	106,458	259	42	15	M	O	
Pacific Aries†	1985	27,267	11,678	158	28	17	M	V	
Pacific Trader	1978	21,806	22,536	198	29	22	M	CC	
Papyrus Maru	1972	19,523	26,060	176	24	14	M	B	
Sagami Maru	1980	35,099	61,981	224	32	15	M	B	ex-Argos Peace 83
Saikai Maru	1980	44,580	40,407	228	36	14	M	B	
Sanyo Maru	1984	50,905	82,600	(219)	43	14	M	B	
Sapporo Maru	1984	48,844	80,984	240	38	14	M	B	
Senshu Maru*	1984	102,330	69,594	283	45	19	ST	LNG	
Setsuyo Maru	1985	88,921	170,808	(280)	46	13	M	B	
Shinano Maru	1981	77,052	138,237	270	43	14	M	B	
Shin-Ohgishma Maru	1981	98,511	194,109	300	50	16	M	B	
Shiraishi Maru	1982	75,295	145,177	273	43	13	M	B	
Shiromine Maru	1982	52,982	92,067	247	42	14	M	B	
Shirtae Maru	1981	76,747	140,152	270	43	14	M	B	
Snimos Ace*	1983	14,209	21,858	162	38	13	M2	RO	
Snimos King*	1984	14,211	21,000	162	38	13	M2	RO	
Sovereign Accord	1976	9,913	14,883	159	22	17	M	CC	
Sun Hope‡	1979	15,670	10,850	165	28	18	M	V	
Taiei Maru*	1973	117,184	233,378	317	50	16	ST	T	
Tajima Maru	1980	53,404	81,281	235	42	15	M	T	
Takasaka Maru	1975	116,470	235,048	320	53	16	ST	T	

Above: Nippon Yusen Kaisha, *Kasuga Maru. F. R. Sherlock*

Below: Nippon Yusen Kaisha, *Wakatake Maru. J. Krayenbosch*

Name	Year	GRT	DWT	LOA	Bm	Kts	Eng	Type	Former names
Takayama Maru*	1973	117,178	233,396	317	50	15	ST	T	
Tamba Maru	1979	53,400	81,280	248	42	15	M	T	
Tango Maru	1979	53,400	81,281	248	42	15	M	T	
Tenryu Maru	1982	49,369	53,171	228	37	16	M	LPG	
Tokitsu Maru	1976	129,508	261,546	332	55	16	ST	T	
Tokiwa Maru*	1973	116,140	237,455	322	53	15	ST	T	
Tottori Maru*	1972	116,143	237,380	322	53	16	ST	T	
Toyota Maru No 18*	1971	17,716	11,111	192	24	20	M	V	
Toyota Maru No 19	1971	22,567	17,297	194	26	14	M	V	
Toyota Maru No 20*	1972	23,575	37,349	196	27	14	M	V	
Tsushima Maru	1974	87,516	157,674	289	44	15	M	OO	ex-Golden Wisteria 79
Vesta	1976	13,664	20,520	168	23	16	M	C	
Wakaba Maru	1985	101,800	68,000	283	45	19	ST	LNG	
Wakagiku Maru*	1978	15,492	24,268	163	25	16	M	C	
Wakakusa Maru*	1968	7,657	11,263	139	19	15	M	C	
Wakamizu Maru	1978	14,478	22,120	163	24	16	M	C	
Wakanami Maru	1978	14,479	22,107	163	24	16	M	C	
Wakatake Maru	1978	15,490	24,383	163	25	16	M	C	
Wakaume Maru	1970	9,916	13,859	156	22	17	M	C	
Yujin‡	1981	18,302	10,480	165	28	19	M	V	ex-Yujin Maru 85

* jointly owned with other Japanese companies
† Panamanian flag
†† Singapore flag
‡ Liberian flag

Ocean Transport & Trading plc

UK

Blue Funnel Bulkships Ltd

Funnel: Blue with black top
Hull: Black with pink boot-topping

Name	Year	GRT	DWT	LOA	Bm	Kts	Eng	Type	Former names
Clytoneus	1976	32,576	56,078	210	32	16	M	T	
Nestor	1977	78,915	78,400	275	42	19	ST	LGC	

China Mutual SN Co Ltd

Name	Year	GRT	DWT	LOA	Bm	Kts	Eng	Type	Former names
Barber Hector	1984	27,991	43,986	262	32	21	M	RO	
Barber Perseus	1979	21,747	32,435	228	32	22	M	RO	
Barber Priam	1979	21,747	32,435	228	32	22	M	RO	
Lloyd Sao Francisco	1977	16,031	21,287	165	26	18	M	CO	ex-Memnon 84, ex-Barber Memnon 84, ex-Memnon 81
Maron	1980	16,482	21,310	165	26	18	M	CO	
Melampus	1977	16,030	21,618	165	26	18	M	CO	
Menelaus	1977	16,031	21,241	165	26	18	M	CO	ex-Barber Menelaus 84, ex-Menelaus 80
Menestheus	1977	16,031	21,081	165	26	18	M	CO	ex-Lloyd Parana 85, ex-Barber Menestheus 84, ex-Menestheus 80
Myrmidon	1980	16,482	21,215	165	26	18	M	CO	ex-Cape Town Carrier 85, ex-Myrmidon 84

Elder Dempster Lines Ltd

Funnel: Yellow
Hull: Black with red boot-topping

Name	Year	GRT	DWT	LOA	Bm	Kts	Eng	Type	Former names
Bello Folawiyo	1979	9,240	11,587	145	22	17	M	CO	ex-Sekondi 85
Sapele	1980	9,240	11,587	145	22	17	M	CO	
Sokoto	1979	9,145	11,644	145	22	17	M	CO	ex-Bello Folawiyo 84, ex-Sokoto 83

see also Overseas Containers Ltd

Above: Ocean Transport & Trading plc, *Barber Priam. J. Krayenbosch*

Below: Ocean Transport & Trading plc, *Maron. J. Krayenbosch*

J. O. Odfjell A/S

Funnel: Blue with interlinked white 'JOO'
Hull: Orange with blue 'J O TANKERS', red boot-topping

Name	Year	GRT	DWT	LOA	Bm	Kts	Eng	Type	Former names
Betula*..............................	1970	6,549	10,033	121	19	15	M	T	ex-Jo Rogn 83, ex-Bow Rogn 80
Jo Birk................................	1982	21,568	39,016	175	32	16	M	T	
Jo Clipper...........................	1981	18,706	33,695	183	30	15	M	T	ex-Polux 81
Jo Cypress†	1983	11,712	17,465	149	22	16	M	T	
Jo Lind*.............................	1969	6,344	9,995	121	19	15	M	T	ex-Bow Lind 80
Jo Lonn†.............................	1982	21,568	39,273	175	32	16	M	T	
Jo Oak†...............................	1983	21,568	40,271	175	32	16	M	T	

* Liberian flag
† Dutch flag
Fleet operated jointly with Johnson Line q.v.

A/S Rederiet Odfjell

Funnel: Yellow with white/red/blue linked rings, black top
Hull: Orange with blue 'O.W.L. TANKERS', red boot-topping

Name	Year	GRT	DWT	LOA	Bm	Kts	Eng	Type
Bow Cedar	1969	12,868	21,723	171	22	16	M	T
Bow Fagus	1975	17,919	31,501	171	25	17	M	T
Bow Fighter	1982	19,313	34,982	174	32	15	M	T
Bow Flower..........................	1975	17,919	31,501	171	25	17	M	T
Bow Fortune	1975	17,060	27,954	171	25	17	M	T
Bow Hunter*........................	1983	13,331	23,002	158	23	15	M	T
Bow Pioneer*.......................	1982	14,834	23,077	158	23	15	M	T
Bow Saphir..........................	1982	11,450	15,200	161	23	15	M	T
Bow Sea...............................	1978	17,057	28,084	171	25	17	M	T
Bow Sky	1977	17,056	28,060	171	25	17	M	T
Bow Spring..........................	1976	17,056	27,954	171	25	17	M	T
Bow Star	1976	17,056	28,085	171	25	17	M	T
Bow Sun	1977	17,056	28,021	171	25	17	M	T

vessels operated as joint fleet with Westfal-Larsen & Co A/S
* Panamanian flag

Rudolf A. Oetker

Hamburg-Sudamerikanische Dampfschiffahrts-ges

Funnel: White with red top
Hull: Red or white with red boot-topping

Name	Year	GRT	DWT	LOA	Bm	Kts	Eng	Type	Former names
Avon.....................................	1977	12,157	15,000	162	22	18	M	CC	ex-Monte Sarmiento 83, ex-Columbus Tasmania 80, ex-Santa Rosa 79
Bahia	1985	21,000	37,640	193	28	15	M	B	
Columbus America	1971	19,146	22,002	194	29	22	ST	CC	
Columbus Australia...............	1971	19,146	22,002	194	29	22	ST	CC	
Columbus Louisiana..............	1979	19,194	20,100	168	28	19	M	CC	
Columbus New Zealand.........	1971	19,146	22,002	194	29	22	ST	CC	
Columbus Queensland	1979	21,871	24,320	184	28	19	M	CC	
Columbus Victoria................	1976	14,160	15,789	161	26	19	M	CC	
Columbus Virginia	1977	14,173	15,719	161	26	19	M	CC	
Columbus Wellington	1977	14,173	15,789	161	26	19	M	CC	
Danisa†................................	1981	26,937	46,570	183	32	14	M	T	ex-St Petri 85
Monte Cervantes...................	1982	21,863	23,520	185	28	17	M	CC	
Monte Rosa..........................	1981	21,871	24,300	185	28	17	M	CC	
Monte Sarmiento	1979	21,871	24,320	185	28	18	M	CC	ex-Columbus Canterbury 83

Above: J. O. Odfjell A/S, *Jo Cypress. J. Krayenbosch*

Below: A/S Rederiet Odfjell, *Bow Flower. F. R. Sherlock*

Name	Year	GRT	DWT	LOA	Bm	Kts	Eng	Type	Former names
Olinda	1985	21,000	37,640	193	28	15	M	B	
Saxon Star	1975	12,188	15,500	162	22	18	M	CC	ex-Columbus California 83, ex-Monte Olivia 82, ex-Columbus Taranaki 80, ex-Santa Rita 79
St Michaelis	1981	26,937	45,574	183	32	14	M	T	
St Nikolai	1982	26,937	45,574	183	32	14	M	T	
Tamaitai Samoa*	1970	10,549	14,399	153	23	20	M	C	ex-Santa Monica 84, ex-Torm Africa 83, ex-Deneb 81, ex-Gutenfels 80, ex-Atlantica New York 73, ex-Gutenfels 71
Tausala Samoa*	1970	10,543	14,389	153	23	20	M	C	ex-Santa Clara 84, ex-Torm America 83, ex-Goldenfels 81, ex-Atlantica Montreal 75, ex-Goldenfels 72

* jointly owned by Government of West Samoa, Western Samoan flag
† Panamanian flag

Egon Oldendorff

FGR

Funnel: Grey, blue band with 'EO', 'H' or 'R' in white
Hull: Grey with red boot-topping

Name	Year	GRT	DWT	LOA	Bm	Kts	Eng	Type	Former names
Alybella*	1971	4,810	7,405	117	17	15	M	C	ex-Gebe Oldendorff 84, ex-Terespolis 73, ex-Glebe Oldendorff 71
Baltic Mermaid†	1984	35,319	64,145	225	32	14	M	B	
Bernhard Oldendorff†	1967	27,456	54,140	214	31	15	M	B	
Bold Challenger	1965	19,342	37,750	202	26	15	M	B	ex-Regina Oldendorff 83
Caroline Oldendorff†	1969	9,097	15,315	139	21	15	M	C	ex-Breda 73, ex-Caroline Oldendorff 72
Dora Oldendorff*	1974	40,967	73,974	244	32	15	M	B	
Dorthe Oldendorff*	1971	9,079	15,017	141	20	15	M	C	
Eckert Oldendorff†	1970	35,227	67,925	253	32	15	M	B	
Elisabeth Oldendorff†	1969	9,097	15,315	140	21	15	M	C	ex-Baarn 75, ex-Elisabeth Oldendorff 72
Fair Spirit	1974	8,952	14,971	141	20	15	M	C	ex-Eibe Oldendorff 81
Future Hope	1979	9,187	15,060	144	20	15	M	C	
Gerdt Oldendorff†	1973	9,608	16,300	150	21	16	M	C	
Globe Trader	1980	9,187	15,060	144	20	15	M	C	
Good Faith	1979	9,187	15,060	144	20	15	M	C	
Gretke Oldendorff†	1973	9,599	16,300	150	21	16	M	C	
Happy Chance*	1974	9,067	14,971	141	20	15	M	C	ex-Hinrich Oldendorff 81
Hille Oldendorff*	1972	9,077	15,017	141	21	15	M	C	
Hugo Oldendorff†	1968	9,786	16,300	149	21	16	M	C	
Imme Oldendorff*	1972	9,077	15,017	141	20	15	M	C	
Ludolf Oldendorff*	1974	40,967	74,024	244	32	15	M	B	
Maria Oldendorff†	1969	9,104	15,315	140	21	15	M	C	ex-Barneveld 75, ex-Maria Oldendorff 72
Marine Ranger	1984	33,886	64,000	225	32	15	M	B	
Nautic Pioneer	1967	19,447	38,100	202	26	16	M	B	ex-Tete Oldendorff 83
Noble Supporter	1967	19,484	38,074	202	26	16	M	B	ex-Rixta Oldendorff 83
Ocean Traveller*	1974	40,967	74,027	244	32	15	M	B	ex-Birte Oldendorff 81
Sea Scout	1981	33,343	63,990	225	32	15	M	B	ex-Karen T 82
Splendid Fortune*	1974	9,070	14,970	141	20	15	M	C	ex-Catharina Oldendorff 81
United Venture*	1975	40,967	74,013	244	32	15	M	B	ex-Helga Oldendorff 81
Western Glory	1965	19,367	38,230	202	26	15	M	B	ex-Dietrich Oldendorff 83

all Liberian flag, except Singapore flag* or Panamanian flag†

Above: Rudolf A. Oetker/H.S.D.G., *Monte Rosa. J. K. Byass*

Above: Rudolf A. Oetker/H.S.D.G., *Saxon Star. J. M. Kakebeeke*

Below: Egon Oldendorff, *Dorthe Oldendorff. J. K. Byass*

Fred Olsen & Co

Norway

Funnel: Yellow with white and blue houseflag
Hull: Grey with green boot-topping

Name	Year	GRT	DWT	LOA	Bm	Kts	Eng	Type	Former names
Balduin	1976	5,171	10,320	168	21	18	M2	RO	
Bayard	1975	5,171	10,302	168	21	18	M2	RO	
Bohemund	1975	5,171	10,320	168	21	18	M2	RO	
Star Lanao*	1968	16,533	27,890	172	26	16	M	B	ex-Star Clipper 81
Star Sulu*	1973	19,147	29,709	172	26	15	M	B	ex-Star Ching 83, ex-Star Boxford 82

* Philippine flag

Olympic Maritime SA

Greece

Funnel: Orange, large white disc with blue/yellow pennant and five interlocking coloured rings above and below
Hull: White or black with red boot-topping

Name	Year	GRT	DWT	LOA	Bm	Kts	Eng	Type	Former names
Alexander S. Onassis*	1977	126,588	277,553	343	52	16	ST	T	
Aristotle S. Onassis*	1976	125,465	273,900	337	55	16	ST	T	ex-Universe Frontier 77
Artemis Garofalidis†	1977	57,211	112,745	260	41	16	M	T	ex-Geroi Novorossiyska 79, ex-Interoceanic 1 77
Ceekay	1975	15,208	26,923	183	22	15	M	B	ex-Skyros 83, ex-Swedish Wasa 79
Costas Konialidis	1981	29,694	58,370	223	32	15	M	B	ex-Eva Venture 81
Olympic Armour II†	1975	138,037	268,450	346	52	15	ST	T	ex-Lotor 80, ex-Lotorium 80
Olympic Aspiration*	1972	106,123	222,968	330	48	15	ST	T	
Olympic Avenger*	1972	106,123	222,968	330	48	15	ST	T	
Olympic Banner*	1972	128,561	268,889	345	52	15	ST	T	
Olympic Bond*	1972	126,027	269,244	331	51	15	ST	T	
Olympic Breeze*	1976	126,990	273,844	337	55	15	ST	T	
Olympic Brilliance*	1973	128,561	269,057	345	52	15	ST	T	
Olympic Dignity†	1985	17,879	29,640	182	23	14	M	B	
Olympic Dream	1974	18,204	31,086	171	26	15	M	T	ex-World Prospect 75
Olympic Harmony*	1973	15,498	27,071	183	22	15	M	B	ex-Cunard Cavalier 78
Olympic History	1972	15,498	27,071	183	22	15	M	B	ex-Cunard Carronade 78
Olympic Hope	1973	15,478	26,958	183	22	15	M	B	ex-Graigaur 78, ex-Torre del Oro 75
Olympic Leader†	1977	14,722	27,560	183	23	15	M	B	ex-London Voyager 83, ex-Welsh Voyager 82
Olympic Liberty†	1977	14,644	27,450	183	23	14	M	B	ex-London Earl 83
Olympic Melody	1984	17,879	29,640	182	23	14	M	B	
Olympic Merit†	1985	17,879	29,611	182	23	14	M	B	
Olympic Miracle†	1984	17,879	29,670	182	23	14	M	B	
Olympic Peace*	1969	15,688	27,440	176	23	15	M	B	
Olympic Phoenix†	1977	14,638	27,451	183	23	15	M	B	ex-London Baron 83
Olympic Progress	1969	15,688	27,451	176	23	15	M	B	
Olympic Promise†	1977	14,644	27,540	183	23	15	M	B	ex-London Viscount 83
Olympic Rainbow	1975	47,344	96,651	243	40	15	M	T	ex-Oceanic Erin 80
Olympic Splendour	1976	57,211	112,744	260	41	15	M	T	ex-Geroi Sevastopolya 79, ex-Kyra Lynn 76
Olympic Star*	1978	51,647	107,245	245	39	14	M	T	ex-Khan Krun 79
Olympic Sun II*	1975	40,559	82,056	244	34	16	M	T	ex-Lissa 78
Patricia R†	1984	17,879	29,693	182	23	14	M	B	

* Liberian flag
† Panamanian flag

Overseas Containers Ltd

Funnel: Green with 'OCL' insignia in white
Hull: Mid-brunswick green with blue boot-topping

Name	Year	GRT	DWT	LOA	Bm	Kts	Eng	Type	Former names
Botany Bay	1969	27,835	29,262	227	31	21	M	CC	
Cardigan Bay	1972	58,497	47,442	290	32	23	M2	CC	
Discovery Bay	1969	26,757	29,288	227	31	21	M	CC	
Encounter Bay	1969	27,835	29,260	227	31	21	M	CC	
Flinders Bay	1969	26,756	29,262	227	31	21	ST	CC	
Kowloon Bay	1972	58,497	47,442	290	32	23	M2	CC	
Liverpool Bay	1972	58,497	47,442	290	32	23	M2	CC	
Mairangi Bay	1978	43,995	38,757	249	32	23	M2	CC	
Moreton Bay	1969	26,757	29,288	227	31	21	M	CC	
Mosel Express	1978	15,503	21,207	178	26	18	M	CC	ex-Orient Winds 84, ex-Falmouth Bay 84, ex-Seatrain Trenton 81, ex-Marestar 78
Osaka Bay	1973	58,497	47,442	290	32	23	M2	CC	
Providence Bay	1983	34,003	34,477	216	32	17	M	CC	
Remuera Bay	1973	41,814	32,713	252	32	24	M	CC	ex-Remuera 77
Resolution Bay	1977	43,995	38,757	249	32	23	M2	CC	
Tokyo Bay	1972	58,497	47,200	290	32	23	M2	CC	
Tolaga Bay	1977	53,784	47,197	259	32	23	M2	CC	ex-Table Bay 82, ex-Barcelona 81, ex-Table Bay 79
Tor Bay	1982	34,004	34,589	216	32	17	M	CC	

container consortium formed by British & Commonwealth Group, Ocean Transport & Trading plc and Peninsular & Oriental SN Co Ltd

Australia Japan Container Line Ltd

Funnel: Black, broad white band with boomerang/ring insignia
Hull: White

Name	Year	GRT	DWT	LOA	Bm	Kts	Eng	Type	Former names
Arafura	1970	25,247	23,016	211	30	23	M	CC	
Ariake	1976	37,487	34,345	238	32	26	M2	CC	ex-Ariake I 77
Main Express	1978	15,788	21,178	178	26	18	M	CC	ex-Strathconon 85, ex-Seatrain Valley Forge 80, ex-Marejet 78

jointly owned by A/B Helsingborg and Australian West Pacific Line

see also under Nedlloyd Group and John Swire & Sons Ltd

P&O Steam Nav Co Ltd

Funnel: Blue, with 'P&O' outlined in white
Hull: Black or white with red boot-topping

Name	Year	GRT	DWT	LOA	Bm	Kts	Eng	Type	Former names
Aurora	1975	81,175	154,489	291	43	15	M	B	
Galconda	1978	34,893	43,386	220	29	17	M	LPG	
Galpara	1978	34,893	43,388	220	29	17	M	LPG	
Gambada	1973	21,357	23,869	178	26	16	M	LPG	
Gambhira	1969	10,977	11,470	153	21	16	M	LPG	ex-Butavanal 73, ex-Butanueve 71
Gandara	1976	15,611	17,651	161	24	17	M	LPG	
Garala	1979	34,893	43,386	220	29	16	M	LPG	
Garbeta	1975	15,481	18,165	166	23	16	M	LPG	
Garinda	1977	34,895	41,683	220	29	16	M	LPG	
Gazana	1971	21,357	23,869	178	26	16	M	LPG	
Jedforest	1972	83,714	154,900	292	45	16	M	BO	
Kildare	1972	83,714	155,450	292	45	16	M	BO	
Newforest	1972	83,985	155,759	292	45	16	M	OBO	ex-Lake Tahoe 83, ex-Koll 76

Above: Overseas Containers Ltd, *Providence Bay. F. R. Sherlock*

Above: P & O Steam Nav Co Ltd, *Vendee. J. Krayenbosch*

Below: P & O Steam Nav Co Ltd, *Pollenger. M. D. J. Lennon*

175

Name	Year	GRT	DWT	LOA	Bm	Kts	Eng	Type	Former names
Pollenger	1974	76,496	49,982	261	40	19	ST	LNG	ex-LNG Challenger 79
Vendee	1971	6,088	8,365	132	19	18	M	R	ex-Zaida 75
Vosges	1972	6,088	8,026	132	19	18	M	R	ex-Zira 75

see also Overseas Containers Ltd
joint owners of Anglo Nordic Shipping Ltd q.v.
LPG carriers jointly owned by Overseas Shipholding Group Inc

Pakistan National Shipping Corp   Pakistan

Funnel: Black, white ship's wheel on broad blue band bordered by narrow yellow bands
Hull: Black or grey with red boot-topping

Name	Year	GRT	DWT	LOA	Bm	Kts	Eng	Type	Former names
Ayubia	1981	11,941	17,715	152	23	15	M	CO	
Aziz Bhatti	1966	9,406	13,309	152	20	15	M	C	
Bagh-E-Dacca	1966	8,967	12,843	155	20	17	M	C	
Bolan	1980	12,479	18,153	153	23	17	M	CO	
Chitral	1980	12,479	18,145	153	23	17	M	CO	
Hinglaj	1972	10,684	15,929	150	21	15	M	C	ex-Universal Venture 77
Hunza	1972	10,684	15,920	150	21	14	M	C	ex-Fortune Venture 77
Hyderabad	1980	12,437	18,257	153	23	17	M	CO	
Johar	1976	43,430	89,937	247	40	15	M	T	ex-Cys Fortune 82
Kaghan	1981	11,941	17,764	152	23	15	M	CO	
Kaptai	1967	10,216	13,120	154	20	18	M	C	
Khairpur	1981	12,010	15,100	155	23	17	M	CO	
Lalazar	1974	9,026	13,540	155	20	17	M	C	
Makran	1979	16,241	15,630	159	25	16	M	CO	
Malakand	1980	12,478	18,224	153	23	17	M	CO	
Moenjodaro	1968	8,917	12,569	154	20	16	M	C	
Multan	1980	12,437	18,257	153	23	17	M	CO	
Murree	1981	11,941	18,050	152	23	15	M	CO	
Nawabshan	1981	12,010	15,100	155	23	17	M	CO	
Ocean Envoy	1972	9,126	14,910	141	20	15	M	C	
Ohrmazd	1968	11,046	13,399	157	21	19	M	CP	
Rangamati	1968	8,909	13,069	154	20	18	M	C	
Sarfaraz Rafiqi	1966	9,406	13,368	152	20	18	M	C	ex-Sarfraz Rafiqi 66
Sargodha	1980	12,438	18,242	153	23	17	M	CO	
Shalamar	1970	8,942	13,066	155	20	18	M	C	
Shams	1960	8,929	11,300	143	20	17	M2	C	
Sibi	1981	12,010	15,100	155	23	17	M	CO	
Sunderbans	1968	8,917	12,569	155	20	18	M	C	
Tarbela	1968	9,739	13,544	154	20	18	M	C	
Taxila	1968	8,910	12,489	154	20	18	M	C	
Warsak	1968	9,739	13,554	154	20	18	M	C	

Palm Line Ltd   UK

Funnel: Green with black top and green palm tree on white disc and band
Hull: Dark grey with red boot-topping

Name	Year	GRT	DWT	LOA	Bm	Kts	Eng	Type	Former names
Badagry Palm	1979	12,279	16,525	155	23	16	M	CO	
Lloyd Australia	1982	15,575	18,864	177	25	18	M	CO	ex-Lokoja Palm 84, ex-Wameru 83, ex-Lokoja Palm 83
Lloyd Rio	1981	15,575	18,864	177	25	18	M	CO	ex-Lagos Palm 84
Lloyd Texas	1979	11,223	15,000	150	23	17	M	CO	ex-Bamenda Palm 84
Matadi Palm	1970	8,870	14,001	148	21	16	M	T	

Above: Pakistan National Shipping Corp, *Sibi. J. Krayenbosch*

Below: Palm Line Ltd, *Lloyd Australia. J. Y. Freeman*

Petrofina SA

Belgium

Funnel: Black with Fina Shield over red over white bands
Hull: Grey, red boot-topping

Name	Year	GRT	DWT	LOA	Bm	Kts	Eng	Type	Former names
Fina America	1978	43,850	84,701	231	44	16	M	T	ex-Nordic Faith 83
Fina Belgica	1983	44,342	84,671	247	42	15	M	T	ex-Eagle 83, ex-World Eagle 83

Societe Maritime Fina/France

Name	Year	GRT	DWT	LOA	Bm	Kts	Eng	Type	Former names
Fina Italie	1975	60,504	117,992	259	42	14	M	T	
Fina Norvege	1964	38,704	64,858	249	32	16	M	T	

Phillips Petroleum Company

USA

Funnel: Black, blue band with 'PHILLIPS 66' on shield
Hull: Black

Name	Year	GRT	DWT	LOA	Bm	Kts	Eng	Type	Former names
Arctic Tokyo‡	1969	44,088	32,878	243	34	18	ST	LNG	
Phillips America*	1976	123,165	276,643	339	54	15	ST	T	
Phillips Arkansas*	1980	26,974	54,031	209	32	16	M	T	
Phillips Enterprise*	1973	113,999	232,918	325	48	16	ST	T	ex-Kollbjorg 79
Phillips Mexico*	1979	26,973	54,057	208	32	15	M	T	
Phillips Oklahoma*	1979	26,973	54,046	208	32	15	M	T	
Phillips Venezuela*	1979	26,973	54,049	208	32	15	M	T	
Philmac Venturer†	1982	20,952	39,931	204	27	15	M	T	
Polar Alaska‡	1969	44,088	32,878	243	34	18	ST	LNG	

* owned by Philtankers Inc, Liberian flag
† Panamanian flag
‡ jointly owned by Marathon Oil Co, Liberian flag

Polish Government

Poland

Polskie Towarzystwo Okretowe (Polish Shipping Association)

Funnel: Yellow with red band, shield with white letters 'PLO' and trident
Hull: Black or grey with red or green boot-topping

Name	Year	GRT	DWT	LOA	Bm	Kts	Eng	Type	Former names
Adam Asnyk*	1974	9,632	15,099	144	21	16	M	C	
Adam Mickiewicz	1979	17,553	17,235	190	25	25	M	CO	
Aleksander Zawadzki	1966	8,681	11,855	153	19	16	M	C	
Artur Grottger**	1980	13,024	17,063	168	24	22	M	C	
Boleslaw Chrobry	1967	8,427	9,895	145	19	16	M	C	
Boleslaw Krzywousty	1970	8,146	11,627	145	19	17	M	C	
Boleslaw Ruminski**	1980	13,012	17,070	168	24	22	M	C	
Boleslaw Smialy	1967	8,429	10,042	145	19	16	M	C	
Bronislaw Lachowicz	1974	10,129	11,632	161	23	21	M	CO	
Ceynowa*	1982	14,056	15,622	157	24	16	M	C	
Czacki	1965	5,576	8,553	146	19	16	M	C	
Dzieci Polskie	1979	6,414	5,657	140	18	22	M	R	
Eugeniusz Kwiatkowski	1975	10,129	11,812	161	23	22	M	CO	
Francesco Nullo	1964	8,620	11,600	153	19	15	M	C	
Franciszek Zubrzycki	1973	10,116	11,683	161	23	21	M	CO	
Fredro*	1979	12,778	16,698	170	23	19	M	C	
Frycz Modrzewski	1968	9,637	14,606	151	21	18	M	C	ex-Wilma 72
Garwolin	1973	5,542	6,380	124	17	15	M	C	
Gdansk II‡	1983	18,466	21,334	200	31	18	M	RO	
Gdynski Kosynier	1978	6,414	5,657	140	18	22	M	R	
General Fr. Kleeberg	1980	17,495	17,243	190	25	24	M	CO	

Above: Phillips Petroleum Co, *Phillips Venezuela.* J. Krayenbosch

Below: Polish Government, *Adam Asnyk.* J. M. Kakebeeke

Name	Year	GRT	DWT	LOA	Bm	Kts	Eng	Type	Former names
General Stanislaw Poplawski	1974	10,112	11,632	161	23	21	M	CO	
Grunwald	1968	10,188	12,027	154	20	15	M	C	
Gwardia Ludowa	1969	8,590	11,871	153	19	15	M	C	
Hel	1970	10,970	14,150	167	23	20	M	C	
Henryk Jendza	1966	5,581	8,745	146	19	17	M	C	
Heweliusz	1962	5,699	8,614	146	19	16	M	C	
Jan Dlugosz*	1984	14,097	15,754	157	25	16	M	C	
Jacek Malczewski**	1979	13,008	17,057	168	24	20	M	C	
Jan Matejko	1959	6,748	10,183	154	19	15	M	C	
Jastarnia-Bor	1971	10,960	14,149	167	23	20	M	C	
Jozef Chelmonski**	1980	13,012	17,093	168	24	20	M	C	
Jozef Conrad Korzeniowksi	1978	17,552	17,245	190	25	25	M	CO	
Jurata	1970	10,950	14,149	167	20	16	M	C	
Karlowicz*	1982	14,097	15,754	157	24	16	M	C	
Katowice II‡	1982	18,466	21,334	200	31	18	M	RO	
Kazimierz Pulaski†	1981	30,080	22,620	200	32	20	M	RO	
K. I. Galczynski	1964	5,584	8,553	146	19	16	M	C	
Konin	1968	10,063	12,250	154	21	15	M	C	
Kraszewski*	1963	10,363	14,402	153	20	16	M	C	
Kuznica	1971	10,946	14,150	167	23	21	M	C	
Leningrad	1965	8,682	11,855	153	19	16	M	C	
Lenino	1964	8,614	11,946	153	19	15	M	C	
Leopold Staff*	1977	9,782	16,220	150	21	16	M	C	
Lucjan Szenwald*	1971	10,122	12,180	154	21	18	M	C	
Major Sucharski	1974	8,756	12,120	153	19	16	M	C	
Marian Buczek	1974	8,722	12,129	153	19	16	M	C	
Mieczyslaw Kalinowski	1973	10,112	11,683	161	23	21	M	CO	
Mieszko I	1967	8,408	10,181	145	19	16	M	C	
Mikolaj Rej	1969	9,637	14,605	151	21	18	M	C	ex-Wirta 73
Nowowiejski*	1962	8,992	12,699	153	19	15	M	C	
Paderewski*	1960	9,267	12,666	153	19	15	M	C	
Parandowski*	1982	14,116	15,754	157	24	16	M	C	
Pawel Szwydkoj	1965	5,403	8,732	146	19	17	M	C	
Phenian	1961	6,923	10,124	154	20	15	M	C	
Piotr Dunin	1966	8,650	11,849	153	20	15	M	C	
Poznan‡	1982	18,496	21,334	200	31	20	M	RO	
Profesor Mierzejewski	1979	16,359	15,389	181	27	21	M	CO	
Profesor Rylke	1979	16,396	15,613	181	27	21	M	CO	
Profesor Szafer	1978	16,424	15,613	181	27	21	M	CO	
Pulkownik Dabek	1970	8,731	12,259	153	19	15	M	C	
Roman Pazinksi	1975	10,130	11,632	161	23	21	M	CO	
Romer	1964	5,587	8,553	146	19	16	M	C	
Siemiatycze	1976	5,545	6,390	124	17	17	M	C	
Sienkiewicz	1959	7,675	10,660	139	18	16	M	C	
Smolny	1968	8,718	11,760	153	19	15	M	C	
Staszic	1963	8,011	8,682	146	19	16	M	C	
Stefan Czarnieckl	1967	10,208	12,045	154	20	16	M	C	
Stefan Starzynski†	1981	30,076	22,619	200	32	22	M	RO	
Swiecie	1971	10,073	12,333	155	21	18	M	C	
Tadeusz Kosciuszko†	1981	30,080	22,709	20	32	22	M	RO	
Tadeusz Ocioszynski	1976	10,229	11,812	161	23	21	M	CO	
Ursus	1972	10,071	12,312	155	21	17	M	C	
Westerplatte	1967	10,189	12,013	154	20	15	M	C	
Wieliczka	1973	5,543	6,380	124	17	15	M	C	
Wladyslaw Jagiello	1971	8,148	11,570	145	19	17	M	C	
Wladyslaw Lokietek	1972	8,160	11,625	145	19	17	M	C	
Wladyslaw Orkan*	1971	10,122	12,181	155	21	18	M	C	
Wladyslaw Sikorski†	1981	30,080	22,639	200	32	22	M	RO	
Wladyslawowo	1971	10,929	14,149	166	23	21	M	C	

Polish Government, *Kazimierz Pulaski*. J. K. Byass

Name	Year	GRT	DWT	LOA	Bm	Kts	Eng	Type	Former names
Wroclaw‡	1983	18,466	21,334	200	31	18	M	RO	
Zabrze	1969	6,581	7,039	135	18	17	M	C	
Zakopane	1968	6,576	7,081	135	18	17	M	C	
Zambrow	1969	6,585	7,011	135	18	17	M	C	
Zawichost	1970	6,588	7,022	135	18	17	M	C	
Zawiercie	1969	6,585	7,055	135	18	17	M	C	
Zeromski	1960	7,687	8,850	139	18	16	M	C	
Zygmunt August	1971	8,160	11,625	145	19	17	M	C	
Zygmunt Stary	1971	8,160	11,638	145	19	17	M	C	
Zygmunt III Waza	1972	8,152	11,638	145	19	17	M	C	
Zyrardow	1980	6,414	5,640	140	18	22	M	R	

* Chinese-Polish Joint Stock Co (Chinsko-Polskie Towarzystwo Okretowe SA)
† French-Polish Shipping Co Inc (Francusko-Polskie Towarzystwo Zeglugowe)
‡ Spanish-Polish Shipping Co Inc (Hiszpansko-Polskie Towarzystwo Zeglugowe)
** Polish Ocean Lines (Polskie Linie Oceaniczne)

Zegluga Polska Spolka Akcyjna

Funnel: Black with red band between two narrow yellow bands, and shield with white letters 'PZM' and trident
Hull: Black or grey

Name	Year	GRT	DWT	LOA	Bm	Kts	Eng	Type	Former names
Belchatow	1976	39,309	71,277	232	32	15	M	B	
Bieszczady	1969	10,847	15,680	156	20	15	M	B	
Budowlany	1976	9,267	14,164	147	21	15	M	B	
Cedynia	1973	20,613	31,910	202	24	15	M	B	
Czantoria	1975	81,197	146,110	293	48	15	M	T	
Dolny Slask	1967	11,004	15,688	156	20	15	M	B	
Feliks Dzierzynski	1978	20,309	33,490	198	24	15	M	B	
General Bem	1974	23,307	37,844	201	28	17	M	B	
General Berling*	1984	22,500	38,000	201	28	15	M	B	
General Dabrowski*	1983	22,772	38,000	201	28	15	M	B	
General Jasinski	1974	23,294	37,763	201	28	17	M	B	
General Madalinski	1975	23,298	37,844	201	28	17	M	B	
General Pradzynski	1977	23,305	37,844	201	28	17	M	B	
General Swierczewski	1973	23,329	37,844	201	28	17	M	B	
Gliwice II	1968	8,384	11,720	142	19	15	M	B	
Gorny Slask	1967	11,014	15,650	156	20	15	M	B	
Huta Katowice	1976	36,229	64,485	224	32	14	M	B	ex-Vigan 76
Huta Lenina	1976	36,232	64,334	224	32	14	M	B	ex-Varamis 76
Huta Zgoda	1974	9,268	14,176	146	21	15	M	B	
Huta Zygmunt	1976	9,263	14,164	147	21	15	M	B	
Januz Kusocinski	1983	19,959	33,390	198	24	16	M	B	
Kopalnia Gottwald†	1980	10,979	16,733	159	22	14	M	B	
Kopalnia Grzybow	1972	9,225	14,036	145	21	16	M	B	
Kopalnia Jastrzebie†	1979	11,004	16,653	159	22	14	M	B	
Kopalnia Jeziorko	1971	9,043	13,665	147	20	15	M	B	
Kopalnia Kleofas	1969	8,406	12,480	142	19	15	M	B	
Kopalnia Machow	1972	9,206	14,036	145	21	16	M	B	
Kopalnia Marcel	1969	8,404	12,480	142	19	15	M	B	
Kopalnia Miechowice†	1980	10,999	16,753	159	22	14	M	B	
Kopalnia Moszczenica	1968	8,391	11,780	142	19	15	M	B	
Kopalnia Myslowice†	1980	10,974	16,693	159	22	14	M	B	
Kopalnia Piaseczno	1971	9,050	13,665	147	20	15	M	B	
Kopalnia Siemianowice†	1979	10,998	16,653	159	22	14	M	B	
Kopalnia Siersza†	1980	10,997	16,753	159	22	14	M	B	
Kopalnia Sosnica	1968	8,383	11,700	142	19	15	M	B	
Kopalnia Sosnowiec	1974	9,268	14,179	146	21	15	M	B	
Kopalnia Szczyglowice	1969	8,407	12,480	142	19	15	M	B	

Name	Year	GRT	DWT	LOA	Bm	Kts	Eng	Type	Former names
Kopalnia Szombierki†	1979	10,974	16,728	159	22	14	M	B	
Kopalnia Walbrzych	1975	9,266	14,176	147	21	15	M	B	
Kopalnia Wirek	1969	8,406	11,700	142	19	15	M	B	
Kopalnia Zofiowka	1975	9,268	14,176	147	21	15	M	B	
Kujawy	1968	11,005	15,626	156	20	15	M	B	
Maciej Rataj*	1985	20,000	32,800	199	25	15	M	B	
Major Hubal*	1985	20,000	32,800	199	25	15	M	B	
Miroslawiec	1975	20,593	32,239	199	24	15	M	B	
Narwik II	1973	20,596	31,920	199	24	15	M	B	
Obroncy Poczty	1971	19,684	32,195	202	20	15	M	B	
Pieniny II	1975	18,249	31,016	171	26	15	M	T	
Podhale	1968	11,013	15,686	157	20	15	M	B	
Pomorze Zachodnie*	1985	16,696	27,000	180	23	14	M	B	
Powstaniec Listopadowy	1985	20,000	32,800	199	25	15	M	B	
Powstaniec Slaski	1970	19,677	32,192	202	20	15	M	B	
Powstaniec Warszawski	1982	20,232	33,460	198	24	16	M	B	
Powstaniec Wielkopolski	1974	20,593	33,450	185	24	15	M	B	
Radlo	1985	20,000	32,800	199	25	15	M	B	
Rolnik	1975	9,267	14,176	146	21	15	M	B	
Siekierki	1972	19,775	32,376	202	20	16	M	B	
Sokolica II	1975	81,197	145,648	293	48	15	M	T	
Studzianki	1975	20,597	33,450	199	24	16	M	B	
Syn Pulku	1974	20,593	31,910	199	24	15	M	B	
Tatry	1975	18,244	31,016	171	26	15	M	T	
Tobruk	1972	19,775	32,376	202	20	15	M	B	
Turoszow*	1977	39,319	71,411	232	32	15	M	B	
Uniwersytet Gdanski	1974	30,242	52,019	219	31	15	M	B	
Uniwersytet Jagiellonski	1971	30,380	52,000	219	31	15	M	B	
Uniwersytet Slaski	1979	20,301	33,485	198	24	16	M	B	
Uniwersytet Warszawski	1974	30,248	52,019	219	31	15	M	B	
Uniwersytet Wroclawski	1974	30,244	52,019	219	31	15	M	B	
Walka Mlodych	1978	20,309	33,485	198	24	15	M	B	
Zaglebie Dabrowskie	1967	11,010	15,688	156	20	15	M	B	
Zaglebie Miedziowe	1971	16,028	23,785	187	23	15	M	B	
Zawrat	1975	81,195	144,892	293	48	15	M	T	
Ziemia Bialostocka	1972	15,643	23,736	185	23	15	M	B	
Ziemia Bydgoska	1967	15,732	25,051	179	23	15	M	B	
Ziemia Cheminska*	1984	16,696	27,000	180	23	14	M	B	
Ziemia Gnieznienska*	1985	16,696	27,000	180	23	14	M	B	
Ziemia Kielecka	1969	15,744	26,499	191	23	15	M	B	
Ziemia Koszalinska	1968	15,718	26,499	190	23	15	M	B	
Ziemia Krakowska	1971	16,028	23,792	187	23	15	M	B	
Ziemia Lubelska	1971	16,028	23,785	187	23	15	M	B	
Ziemia Mazowiecka	1967	15,731	24,490	179	23	15	M	B	
Ziemia Olsztynska	1973	15,668	23,719	185	23	15	M	B	
Ziemia Opolska	1973	15,667	23,720	185	23	15	M	B	
Ziemia Suwalska*	1984	16,696	27,000	180	23	14	M	B	
Ziemia Szczecinska	1966	16,452	24,170	190	23	15	M	B	
Ziemia Tarnowska*	1985	16,696	27,000	180	23	14	M	B	
Zeimia Wielkopolska	1967	16,442	26,362	190	23	15	M	B	
Ziemia Zamojska*	1984	16,696	26,600	180	23	14	M	B	

* owned by Polska Zegluga Morska (Polish Steamship Co)
† owned by Polsko-Brytyjskie Przedsiewziecie Zeglugowe Spolka

Einar Rasmussen

Norway

Funnel: Black with blue 'R' on white diamond on blue band
Hull: Grey, red boot-topping

Name	Year	GRT	DWT	LOA	Bm	Kts	Eng	Type
Falcon	1968	6,586	9,652	129	19	15	M	C
Polyclipper	1975	63,887	118,059	260	40	16	M	B

Above: Polish Government, *Huta Zygmunt. M. D. J. Lennon*

Below: Polish Government, *Kopalnia Machow. J. K. Byass*

Name	Year	GRT	DWT	LOA	Bm	Kts	Eng	Type	Former names
Polycrest	1976	63,887	118,049	260	40	16	M	B	
Polycrusader	1977	63,138	118,500	264	41	16	M	B	
Polynesia	1972	112,445	224,617	324	49	16	M	T	
Polystar	1981	39,609	60,935	213	32	15	M	T	
Polysunrise	1981	39,609	61,438	213	32	15	M	T	
Polytrader	1978	65,164	125,690	264	41	16	M	T	
Polytraveller	1978	65,144	125,690	264	41	16	M	T	
Polyvictoria	1976	114,075	232,700	325	48	16	ST	T	
Polyviking	1983	73,935	123,500	265	48	15	M	T	

Johan Reksten R/A — Norway

Funnel: Black with two blue bands on broad white band
Hull: Grey

Name	Year	GRT	DWT	LOA	Bm	Kts	Eng	Type	Former names
Jorek Combiner	1976	66,373	116,281	245	39	16	M	BO	
Sir Charles Hambro	1973	140,465	285,100	348	52	15	ST	T	

Rickmers-Linie GmbH — FRG

Funnel: Black with houseflag on broad white band
Hull: Black

Name	Year	GRT	DWT	LOA	Bm	Kts	Eng	Type	Former names
Bertram Rickmers	1970	14,442	20,376	171	25	17	M	C	ex-Leverkusen 79
Etha Rickmers*	1958	12,468	16,444	167	22	18	M	C	ex-Etha 75, ex-Munchen 71
Mai Rickmers†	1957	10,492	15,555	157	20	15	M	C	ex-Erik Blumenfeld 65
Peter Rickmers†	1962	9,643	14,670	160	20	17	M	C	
Renee Rickmers	1970	14,441	20,376	171	25	17	M	C	ex-Ludwigshafen 80
Sophie Rickmers†	1957	12,283	17,300	167	22	18	M	C	ex-Dresden 71
Ville de Lumiere	1985	10,756	14,198	162	22	17	M	CC	ex-Patricia Rickmers 85

* Panamanian flag
† Singapore flag

Ropner Management Ltd — UK
Ropner Shipping Co Ltd

Funnel: Green with red and white check square
Hull: Green, some with white line and light green boot-topping

Name	Year	GRT	DWT	LOA	Bm	Kts	Eng	Type	Former names
Appleby	1978	64,641	119,500	262	41	15	M	B	ex-Golden Master 78
Farland	1974	64,043	122,976	272	39	16	M	B	ex-Nawala 79, ex-Fernbay 78
Iron Kestrel	1974	16,819	26,843	180	23	15	M	B	ex-Star Kestrel 75
Iron Kirby	1974	16,819	27,299	180	23	15	M	B	ex-Iron Kerry 83, ex-Star Kerry 75
Iron Somersby	1971	57,250	108,198	261	41	15	M	B	
Lackenby	1977	64,640	119,500	262	41	15	M	B	ex-Otterpool 77
Ravenscraig	1979	64,651	119,500	262	41	15	M	B	
Salmonpool	1982	24,785	43,728	205	27	15	M	B	

Rowbotham Tankships Ltd — UK

Funnel: Blue with two entwined silver circles around silver 'I', black top or blue with red 'R' on white diamond
Hull: Black with red boot-topping

Name	Year	GRT	DWT	LOA	Bm	Kts	Eng	Type	Former names
Ingram Osprey	1982	18,959	29,999	171	27	14	M	T	ex-Osco Ingram Osprey 85, ex-Ingram Osprey 82
Tankerman	1983	5,774	10,716	120	19	11	M	T	

Above: Einar Rasmussen, *Polytrader. M. D. J. Lennon*

Above: Rickmers Linie GmbH, *Bertram Rickmers. J. Krayenbosch*

Below: Rowbotham Tankships Ltd, *Tankerman. M. D. J. Lennon*

Ernst Russ

Funnel: Black, red 'ER' bordered by narrow red bands
Hull: Black

Name	Year	GRT	DWT	LOA	Bm	Kts	Eng	Type	Former names
Carsten Russ*	1971	74,513	139,854	282	43	15	M	B	
Jacob Russ	1971	74,513	139,854	282	43	15	M	B	
Juliana*	1971	35,915	66,499	235	32	15	M	B	ex-E.R. Brabantia 82
Lorenzo†	1969	26,100	45,499	216	28	16	M	BC	ex-Cast Porpoise 82, ex-E.R. Montreal 78, ex-Reinhart Lorenz Russ 75
Paul*	1966	8,140	10,674	151	19	17	M	C	ex-Pampana 81, ex-Paul Lorenz Russ 79
Roberto*	1969	6,558	12,655	139	21	16	M	C	ex-Paula Howaldt Russ 79, ex-Paula Howaldt 74
Tilly*	1967	5,586	9,550	136	19	17	M	C	ex-Tilly Russ 80

* Panamanian flag
see also Ahlers NV

B J Ruud-Pedersen A/S

Funnel: Buff with 'R-P' on blue edged white band
Hull: Grey with red boot-topping

Name	Year	GRT	DWT	LOA	Bm	Kts	Eng	Type	Former names
Essi Anne	1958	6,399	9,870	130	17	12	M	T	ex-Essex 69
Essi Camilla*	1975	63,509	119,500	262	41	15	M	B	
Essi Flora	1959	11,977	15,704	158	20	13	M	T	ex-Essiflora 63
Essi Gina	1979	11,721	16,529	156	21	16	M	T	
Essi Silje	1968	11,023	18,716	153	21	15	M	T	ex-Universe Glory 83, ex-Dimitris E 81, ex-Belblue 75, pt ex-Helene Presthus 72, ex-Sabinia 70
Essi Vibeke	1974	45,591	83,986	254	34	16	M	T	ex-E.R. Limburgia 83

* Singapore flag

Chr Salvesen Shipping Ltd

Funnel: Red with white band and blue top
Hull: Black with red boot-topping

Name	Year	GRT	DWT	LOA	Bm	Kts	Eng	Type
Barra Head	1980	4,694	7,162	111	18	15	M	B
Rora Head	1980	4,694	7,160	111	18	15	M	B
Sumburgh Head	1977	4,694	7,174	111	18	15	M	B

Central Electricity Generating Board

Funnel: Red with white 'e' logo, black top
Hull: Black with red boot-topping

Name	Year	GRT	DWT	LOA	Bm	Kts	Eng	Type	Former names
Beacon Point	1969	4,440	7,063	113	16	12	M	C	ex-Duncansby Head 76
Castle Point	1965	5,628	8,442	113	16	13	M	C	ex-Hudson Light 76
Dolphin Point	1965	4,840	7,651	113	16	12	M	C	ex-Corchester 77
Fort Point	1968	4,396	7,021	110	16	12	M	C	ex-Dunvegan Head 77
Lord Citrine	1985	14,200	22,500	155	25	12	M	B	
Lord Hinton	1985	14,200	22,500	155	25	12	M	B	
Sir Charles Parsons	1985	14,201	22,530	155	25	12	M	B	

Above: B. J. Ruud Pedersen A/S, *Essi Anne. M. D. J. Lennon*

Below: Chr. Salvesen Shipping Ltd, *Rora Head. F. de Vries*

H. Schuldt

Funnel: Blue, red 'S' on white triangle, narrow yellow bands at top and base
Hull: Brown

Name	Year	GRT	DWT	LOA	Bm	Kts	Eng	Type	Former names
Bislig Bay‡	1981	14,136	19,035	176	25	18	M	CO	ex-Medi Sea 85
Costa Rica†	1980	8,722	11,464	146	21	18	M	CO	
Guatemala†	1979	8,722	11,500	146	22	17	M	C	
Honduras†	1979	8,724	11,464	146	22	17	M	C	ex-Hoegh Apapa 81, ex-Honduras 80
Lloyd Sao Paulo‡	1984	16,559	19,035	184	25	19	M	CO	
Mexico 1‡	1974	8,661	11,900	146	22	17	M	CO	ex-Mexico 82, ex-Hasselburg 80, ex-Hoegh Apapa 79, ex-Apapa Palm 77, ex-Hasselburg 76
Sulu Bay‡	1981	14,136	19,406	176	25	18	M	CO	ex-Medi Star 84

* Singapore flag
† Liberian flag
‡ Philippine flag

Scindia Steam Nav Co Ltd

Funnel: Black with broad yellow band
Hull: Black with white line and red boot-topping

Name	Year	GRT	DWT	LOA	Bm	Kts	Eng	Type	Former names
Jalabala	1976	11,377	18,815	148	23	15	M	C	ex-Aristonofos 76
Jalagodavari	1979	13,455	20,916	162	23	16	M	C	
Jalagopal	1980	13,504	20,859	162	23	16	M	C	
Jalagouri	1981	13,504	20,851	162	23	16	M	C	
Jalagovind	1979	13,505	20,867	162	23	16	M	C	
Jalajaya	1966	10,933	16,602	158	21	16	M	C	
Jalajyoti	1966	10,928	16,602	158	21	16	M	C	ex-Apj Ambar 66
Jalakala	1964	9,408	13,418	153	20	16	M	C	
Jalakanta	1965	9,371	13,444	153	20	16	M	C	
Jalakendra	1965	9,379	13,454	153	20	16	M	C	
Jalamani	1970	9,566	13,814	151	20	18	M	C	
Jalamatsya	1970	9,564	13,814	151	20	18	M	C	
Jalamayur	1970	9,564	13,814	151	20	18	M	C	
Jalamohan	1971	9,612	13,780	151	20	18	M	C	
Jalamokambi	1972	9,612	13,819	151	20	18	M	C	
Jalamoti	1971	9,612	13,780	151	20	18	M	C	
Jalamudra	1978	10,092	13,715	157	22	18	M	C	
Jalamuragan	1979	10,094	13,715	157	22	18	M	C	
Jalaputra	1971	9,101	15,195	141	20	14	M	C	ex-Moldova 76
Jalarajan	1966	11,323	16,176	160	22	16	M	C	
Jalarashmi	1966	11,323	16,073	160	22	16	M	C	
Jalaratna	1967	11,323	16,073	160	22	16	M	C	
Jalatapi	1978	14,264	20,514	162	23	15	M	C	
Jalatarang	1963	12,089	17,139	165	21	15	M	C	ex-Bente Brovig 69
Jalavihar	1977	42,141	76,583	245	32	16	M	B	
Jalavijaya	1975	30,280	53,407	207	29	15	M	B	ex-Graiglas 75
Jalayamini	1972	10,936	16,424	158	21	16	M	CO	
Jalayamuna	1972	10,936	16,424	158	21	16	M	CO	
Jalvallabh	1973	31,285	54,436	229	29	15	M	B	
Walchand	1973	57,793	104,750	253	39	16	M	OBO	

Above: H. Schuldt, *Lloyd Sao Paulo.* J. Y. Freeman

Below: Scindia Steam Nav Co Ltd, *Jalabala.* M. D. J. Lennon

Sea-Land Service Inc

USA

Reynolds Leasing Corporation

Funnel: White with red and black 'SL' logo, narrow black top
Hull: Black or grey with red boot-topping

Name	Year	GRT	DWT	LOA	Bm	Kts	Eng	Type	Former names
Boston	1944	11,522	9,466	159	22	16	ST	CC	ex-General M.M. Patrick 68
Charleston	1945	11,389	10,181	159	22	17	ST	CC	ex-Marine Shark 68
Galveston	1945	11,558	9,506	160	22	16	ST	CC	ex-Marine Serpent 68
Long Beach	1945	17,184	17,249	209	24	16	ST	CC	ex-Marine Flasher 66
Newark	1945	11,522	9,494	159	22	17	ST	CC	ex-General H. B. Freeman 68
Oakland	1945	17,184	17,249	209	24	17	ST	CC	ex-Marine Tiger 66
Panama	1945	17,192	14,736	209	24	16	ST	CC	ex-Marine Jumper 66
Philadelphia	1946	10,979	9,507	159	22	17	ST	CC	ex-General A. W. Brewster 68
Pittsburgh	1945	18,024	16,215	209	24	16	ST	CC	ex-Seattle 69, ex-Mobile 64, ex-Dorothy 62, ex-Marine Fox 61
Portland	1945	11,349	9,858	159	22	17	ST	CC	ex-General D. E. Aultman 68
St Louis	1944	18,362	15,943	209	24	11	ST	CC	ex-Pittsburgh 69, ex-General M. L. Hersey 69
San Pedro	1945	18,420	15,943	212	24	16	ST	CC	ex-Baltimore 70, ex-Marine Cardinal 65
Sandys Bay‡	1984	8,654	12,085	137	21	16	M	CC	
Sea-Land Adventurer	1963	17,376	15,417	202	24	16	M	CC	ex-San Francisco 78
Sea-Land Consumer	1973	23,763	25,730	220	29	23	ST	CC	ex-Australia Bear 73
Sea-Land Defender	1980	30,085	30,000	257	31	22	M	CC	
Sea-Land Developer	1980	30,085	30,000	257	31	22	M	CC	
Sea-Land Economy	1971	24,773	25,696	220	29	24	ST	CC	ex-SL 181-73, ex-H. P. Baldwin 71
Sea-Land Endurance	1980	30,085	30,000	257	31	22	M	CC	
Sea-Land Explorer	1980	30,085	30,000	257	31	22	M	CC	
Sea-Land Express	1980	30,085	30,000	257	31	22	M	CC	
Sea-Land Freedom	1980	24,337	23,352	227	31	22	M	CC	
Sea-Land Independence	1980	30,085	30,000	257	31	22	M	CC	
Sea-Land Innovator	1980	30,085	30,000	257	31	22	M	CC	
Sea-Land Leader	1962	17,376	15,417	202	24	16	M	CC	ex-Elizabethport 78
Sea-Land Liberator	1980	24,337	23,676	227	31	22	M	CC	
Sea-Land Mariner	1980	30,085	30,000	257	31	22	M	CC	
Sea-Land Pacer	1962	17,376	15,417	202	24	16	M	CC	ex-San Juan 78
Sea-Land Patriot	1980	30,085	30,000	257	31	22	M	CC	
Sea-Land Pioneer	1963	17,376	15,417	202	24	16	M	CC	ex-Los Angeles 78
Sea-Land Producer	1973	23,763	25,730	220	29	23	ST	CC	ex-New Zealand Bear 73
Sea-Land Venture	1970	24,773	25,937	220	29	24	ST	CC	ex-SL 180-73, ex-S. T. Alexander 71
Sea-Land Voyager	1980	30,085	30,000	257	31	22	M	CC	
Seaward Bay†	1983	8,428	12,060	137	21	16	M	CC	
Shelly Bay†	1983	8,635	12,067	137	21	16	M	CC	
Somers Bay‡	1983	8,654	12,083	137	21	16	M	CC	
World Lion*	1978	10,382	13,101	153	23	15	M	CO	
World Lynx*	1979	10,385	13,562	153	23	15	M	CO	
World Tiger*	1978	10,382	13,101	153	23	15	M	CO	

* owned by World Feederships Inc, Singapore flag

† Panamanian flag

‡ Liberian flag

Above: Sea-Land Service Inc, *Sea-Land Developer. J. Krayenbosch*

Below: Sea-Land Service Inc, *Sea-Land Pioneer. W. D. Harris*

Sea Lanes NV

Funnel: Orange, black 'abc' on blue device on white diamond
Hull: Black with red boot-topping

Antwerp Bulkcarriers NV†

Name	Year	GRT	DWT	LOA	Bm	Kts	Eng	Type	Former names
Antwerpen**	1979	24,888	41,100	199	29	15	M	BC	
Brussel**	1979	24,353	41,100	199	29	15	M	BC	
Cornelis Verolme	1983	26,391	42,077	209	30	15	M	BC	
DeLoris	1978	24,101	42,562	199	29	16	M	BC	
Ellen Hudig	1983	26,351	42,077	209	30	15	M	BC	
General M. Makleft‡	1965	22,226	37,881	197	26	16	M	B	ex-Ocean Valour 80, ex-St Providence 76, ex-Sneholt 73, ex-Tower Bridge 70, ex-Silverhow 65
Helen	1978	23,422	42,566	199	29	16	M	BC	
Martha*	1975	36,785	64,172	224	32	16	M	B	
Ruth*	1974	36,785	64,173	224	32	16	M	B	
Yaffa*	1975	37,743	65,202	224	32	16	M	B	

* owned by Ghent Bulkcarriers NV
** owned by NV Cockerill Yds Hoboken
† jointly owned by Thomas Nationwide Transport q.v.
‡ Israeli flag

Seaco Holdings Ltd

Funnel: Buff with black top
Hull: Grey with red boot-topping

Name	Year	GRT	DWT	LOA	Bm	Kts	Eng	Type	Former names
A. E. S. Express*	1975	3,391	6,477	120	19	16	M	RO	ex-Strider Australia 85, ex-Merzario Ionia 78, ex-Maersk Tempo 76
Boxer Captain Cook	1979	5,654	8,945	134	25	17	M	RO	
Cavara	1981	11,445	18,500	173	30	19	M2	RO	ex-Contender Argent 84
Emma*	1976	3,391	6,383	119	19	16	M	RO	ex-Strider Broadsword 84, ex-Jeddah Crown 79, ex-Strider Broadsword 76
Forum New Zealand	1978	6,266	6,945	127	20	17	M	RO	ex-Strider Iris 80
Nagara	1974	22,270	20,770	209	27	23	M	CO	
Seafreight Freeway†	1981	5,088	6,235	151	20	19	M2	RO	ex-Stena Driver 85, ex-Lucky Rider 84
Seafreight Highway	1981	5,072	6,235	151	20	19	M2	RO	ex-Easy Rider 85
Strider Crystal	1977	3,498	6,800	119	19	16	M	RO	ex-Nedlloyd Crystal 82, ex-Strider Crystal 80, ex-Aqaba Crown 79
Strider Exeter*	1977	5,311	6,583	119	19	16	M	RO	ex-CCNI Austral 85, ex-Strider Exeter 84, ex-CCNI Antartico 82, ex-Opal Bounty 77
Strider Fearless*	1977	5,306	6,596	119	19	16	M	RO	ex-CCNI Andino 82, ex-Turquoise Bounty 77
Strider Juno	1979	6,266	6,943	127	20	17	M	RO	
Tavara	1973	22,270	20,770	209	27	23	M	CO	ex-Tamara 84

* Liberian flag
† Bahamas flag

Above: Sea Lanes NV, *DeLoris. M. D. J. Lennon*

Below: Seaco Holdings Ltd, *Nagara. M. D. J. Lennon*

Shell Group

Funnel: Red with yellow sea-shell (scallop) and narrow black top
Hull: Black or grey with red or blue boot-topping

Shell Tankers (UK) Ltd/UK

Name	Year	GRT	DWT	LOA	Bm	Kts	Eng	Type	Former names
Drupa	1966	39,796	72,008	244	34	16	M	T	
Ebalina	1980	19,763	31,170	170	26	14	M	T	
Eburna	1979	19,763	31,375	170	26	14	M	T	
Entalina*	1978	19,656	31,486	169	26	14	M	T	
Erinna*	1977	19,656	31,487	169	26	15	M	T	
Erodona*	1978	19,656	30,990	169	26	14	M	T	
Ervilia	1979	19,763	31,375	170	26	14	M	T	
Etrema*	1978	19,656	30,990	169	26	14	M	T	
Eulima	1982	17,955	29,951	171	26	14	M	T	ex-Martita 84, ex-Balder Carrara 84
Eulota	1983	17,955	29,951	171	26	14	M	T	ex-Liana 84, ex-Balder Apuania 84
Euplecta	1980	19,763	31,170	170	26	14	M	T	
Gadila	1973	48,662	37,441	257	35	17	ST	LNG	
Gadinia	1972	48,662	37,441	257	35	17	ST	LNG	
Gari	1973	48,662	37,441	257	35	17	ST	LNG	
Gastrana	1974	48,662	37,441	257	35	17	ST	LNG	
Genota	1975	53,128	37,529	258	35	17	ST	LNG	
Geomitra	1975	53,128	37,529	258	35	17	ST	LNG	
Gouldia	1975	48,662	37,441	257	35	17	ST	LNG	
Isocardia	1982	39,932	47,989	210	31	17	M	LPG	
Isomeria	1982	39,932	47,989	210	31	17	M	LPG	
Lampas†	1975	161,632	317,996	351	55	14	ST	T	
Lanistes	1975	159,936	311,896	344	56	15	ST	T	
Leonia†	1976	161,626	318,000	351	55	15	ST	T	
Lepeta†	1976	161,632	317,996	351	55	16	ST	T	
Lima†	1977	161,632	318,013	355	56	15	ST	T	
Naticina‡	1967	60,703	117,455	265	42	15	M	T	
Northia	1971	64,815	133,559	280	41	15	M	T	ex-Oceanic Renown 80, ex-Kronoland 79
Paludina	1968	15,385	25,539	175	23	15	M	T	ex-Urshalim 73
Pomella	1967	15,842	23,542	175	23	15	M	T	ex-Horama 74, ex-Nordvard 67
Rapana	1973	120,698	227,408	333	46	16	ST	T	ex-San Giusto 80, ex-Runa 73
Rimula	1974	121,165	227,400	333	46	16	ST	T	ex-Ambrosiana 80, ex-Rinda 75
Serenia	1961	41,728	72,400	249	34	16	ST	T	
Tectus	1974	65,135	119,500	262	41	15	M	B	ex-Canadian Bridge 78
Tribulus	1981	69,230	127,907	258	41	14	M	B	
Tricula	1981	69,230	127,907	258	41	14	M	B	

* owned by Shell Bermuda (Overseas) Ltd
† owned by Airlease International Nominees (Lombard) Ltd
‡ managed for Tanker Finance Ltd

Soc Maritime Shell/France

Name	Year	GRT	DWT	LOA	Bm	Kts	Eng	Type
Batillus	1976	275,267	550,001	414	63	16	ST2	T
Bellamya	1977	275,267	553,662	414	63	16	ST2	T
Leda	1973	138,482	282,684	343	52	15	ST	T
Lucina	1974	138,482	276,699	343	52	15	ST	T

Shell Tankers BV/Netherlands

Name	Year	GRT	DWT	LOA	Bm	Kts	Eng	Type
Acila	1958	12,221	18,380	170	21	14	M	T
Acmaea	1959	12,222	18,380	170	21	14	M	T
Cardissa	1983	14,605	19,999	170	23	15	M	T
Caurica	1982	14,605	19,999	170	23	15	M	T

Above: Shell Group, *Tricula. F. R. Sherlock*

Below: Shell Group, *Cardissa. J. M. Kakebeeke*

Name	Year	GRT	DWT	LOA	Bm	Kts	Eng	Type	Former names
Cinulia	1955	9,094	13,190	153	19	12	M	T	
Felania†	1975	19,275	32,229	171	26	15	M	T	
Felipes*	1975	19,274	32,229	171	26	15	M	T	
Ficus*	1976	19,278	32,229	171	26	15	M	T	
Flammulina*	1976	19,274	32,400	171	26	15	M	T	
Fossarina*	1976	19,275	32,201	171	26	15	M	T	
Fossarus*	1976	19,275	32,231	171	26	15	M	T	
Fulgar†	1974	19,274	32,229	171	26	15	M	T	
Fusus*	1975	19,274	32,400	171	26	15	M	T	
Niso‡	1966	62,845	121,293	265	42	14	M	T	
Ondina	1961	31,030	53,291	229	31	16	ST	T	
Solaris	1985	50,000	82,000	244	43	15	M	T	
Spectrum	1985	50,000	84,000	244	43	15	M	T	
Stellata	1985	50,000	84,000	244	43	15	M	T	
Tagelus	1972	65,333	120,186	261	41	15	M	B	ex-Stirling Bridge 79
Vitrea	1962	21,873	34,128	203	26	15	ST	T	
Zafra	1966	26,144	40,164	213	29	16	ST	T	

* managed for United States Trust Co of New York, Liberian flag
† managed for Lepton Shipping Corp, Liberian flag
‡ owned by NV Curacaosche Maats, Netherlands Antilles flag

Deutsche Shell AG/FGR

Name	Year	GRT	DWT	LOA	Bm	Kts	Eng	Type	Former names
Diala	1966	39,426	70,895	244	34	16	ST	T	
Elona†	1979	19,240	31,487	169	26	14	M	T	
Ensis†	1979	19,240	31,487	169	26	14	M	T	
Liotina	1974	162,225	317,521	351	55	15	ST	T	
Lottia	1976	162,488	317,209	351	55	15	ST	T	
Nacella	1968	60,275	117,156	265	42	14	M	T	
Narica	1967	59,863	115,305	265	42	14	M	T	
Neverita	1968	57,910	111,470	265	40	14	M	T	

† owned by Lepton Shipping Corp, managed by Deutsche Shell Tanker GmbH, Liberian flag

Shell Co of Australia Ltd/Australia

Name	Year	GRT	DWT	LOA	Bm	Kts	Eng	Type	Former names
Conus	1981	26,324	37,784	178	27	14	M	T	
Nivosa	1984	72,609	115,350	265	46	14	M	T	

managed by Associated Steamships Pty Ltd (TNT Bulkships)

Norske Shell A/S/Norway

Name	Year	GRT	DWT	LOA	Bm	Kts	Eng	Type	Former names
Fjordshell	1973	18,623	32,477	171	26	15	M	T	

Shell Compania Argentina de Petroleo SA/Argentina

Name	Year	GRT	DWT	LOA	Bm	Kts	Eng	Type	Former names
Estrella Antarctica	1962	12,978	20,991	170	22	14	M	T	ex-Fleet Trader 78, ex-Herstein 78, ex-Landvard 69
Estrella Argentina	1960	22,083	35,724	203	26	15	ST	T	ex-Videna 69
Estrella Fueguina	1962	12,780	21,649	171	22	15	M	T	ex-Polystar 78
Estrella Patagonica	1962	24,406	39,113	203	27	16	ST	T	ex-Voluta 70
Harvella	1956	12,224	19,294	169	21	14	ST	T	
Pecten	1955	10,711	16,916	160	21	13	M	T	ex-San Patricio 65

Shell Group, *Conus. J. Y. Freeman*

British Gas Corp/UK

Funnel: Black with three narrow white bands
Hull: Black with red boot-topping

Name	Year	GRT	DWT	LOA	Bm	Kts	Eng	Type	Former names
Methane Princess*	1964	21,876	24,608	189	25	17	ST	LNG	
Methane Progress*	1964	21,876	24,502	189	25	17	ST	LNG	

managed by Shell Tankers (UK) Ltd

Thai Ocean Transportation Co Ltd/Thailand

Mena	1966	40,170	70,147	244	34	14	M	T	ex-Donacilla 77
Siam	1967	39,505	70,273	244	34	15	M	T	ex-Dorcasia 77

associated company managed by Shell Tankers (UK) Ltd

The Shipping Corporation of India

India

Funnel: Black with white edged blue wheel between two red bands
Hull: Black with red or blue boot-topping

Abul Kalam Azad	1974	62,563	114,338	255	39	15	M	OBO	
Ajanta	1968	23,395	42,062	194	28	14	M	B	
Akbar	1971	8,279	9,017	150	19	18	M	CP	
Annapurna	1975	10,921	18,037	142	21	14	M	B	
Anupama	1975	10,526	18,003	142	21	14	M	B	
Aradhana	1973	10,921	18,036	142	21	14	M	B	
Archana	1976	10,526	18,002	142	21	14	M	B	
Arunachal Pradesh	1976	11,832	18,848	147	23	17	M	B	ex-Aristolaos 76
Bailadila	1971	45,752	87,203	257	32	15	M	OBO	
Barauni	1970	45,752	87,203	257	32	15	M	OBO	
Bellary	1970	45,752	86,962	257	32	15	M	OBO	
Bharata	1963	21,282	37,000	191	27	12	M	B	ex-Bharata Jayanti 74
Bharatendu	1980	11,311	15,700	152	23	16	M	C	
Bhava Bhuti	1981	11,311	15,714	153	23	16	M	C	ex-Bhuskan 81
Chandidas	1980	12,913	16,209	152	23	16	M	C	
Devaraya	1964	21,635	37,076	191	27	12	M	B	ex-Devaraya Jayanti 74
Har Rai	1977	23,339	41,420	194	28	15	M	B	
Hargobind	1977	23,340	41,438	194	28	15	M	B	
Harkishin	1978	23,339	41,438	194	28	15	M	B	
Harsha Vardhana	1974	8,871	5,269	133	22	17	M	CP	
Jhansi-ki-Rani	1975	42,141	76,583	245	32	15	M	B	
Kabirdas	1980	12,913	16,217	162	23	16	M	C	
Kalidas	1980	12,914	16,351	162	23	16	M	C	
Kanishka	1964	21,635	37,114	191	27	12	M	B	ex-Kanishka Jayanti 74
Karnataka	1967	13,054	23,386	166	23	15	M	B	ex-Calypso 76, ex-Filipinas 1 73
Kasturba	1975	42,141	76,583	245	32	15	M	B	
Laxmi	1963	21,635	37,056	191	27	12	M	B	ex-Akbar Jayanti 74
Lok Manya	1976	10,525	18,003	145	21	16	M	B	
Lok Nayak	1973	10,921	15,000	145	21	16	M	B	
Lok Palak	1975	10,526	18,037	142	21	16	M	B	
Lok Pragati	1984	16,040	26,928	172	23	15	M	B	
Lok Prakash	1985	15,500	26,450	184	23	15	M	B	
Lok Pratima	1985	16,000	27,000	172	23	15	M	B	
Lok Priti	1981	15,638	27,418	172	23	15	M	B	
Lok Sahayak	1975	10,526	18,003	145	21	15	M	B	
Lok Vihar	1976	10,526	18,003	145	21	14	M	B	
Lok Vikas	1975	12,726	20,878	159	23	16	M	C	
Lok Vinay	1975	12,726	20,878	159	23	16	M	C	
Lok Vivek	1975	12,726	20,878	159	23	16	M	C	

Above: The Shipping Corp of India, *Lok Nayak. J. Krayenbosch*

Below: The Shipping Corp of India, *Vishva Nayak. F. R. Sherlock*

Name	Year	GRT	DWT	LOA	Bm	Kts	Eng	Type	Former names
Maharshi Dayanand..............	1978	66,926	123,465	257	39	15	M	OBO	
Maharshi Karve......................	1978	66,926	123,450	257	39	15	M	OBO	
Mizoram	1976	11,832	18,839	147	23	17	M	B	ex-Aristofon 76
Motilal Nehru.......................	1973	62,857	114,090	255	39	15	M	OBO	
Parvati	1963	21,632	37,082	191	27	12	M	B	ex-Gotama Jayanti 75
Ramdas	1980	12,914	16,209	162	23	16	M	C	
Rani Padmini	1981	42,010	76,600	245	32	15	M	B	
Ravidas	1979	12,914	16,386	162	23	15	M	C	
Samrat Ashok.......................	1974	72,583	129,513	261	41	15	M	B	ex-Gautama Buddha 74
Samudragupta	1964	21,635	37,049	191	27	12	M	B	ex-Samudragupta Jayanti 75
Sanchi	1968	23,372	42,062	194	28	14	M	B	
Shahjehan	1963	21,635	37,063	191	27	12	M	B	ex-Shahjehan Jayanti 75
State of Andhra Pradesh........	1977	14,261	20,628	162	23	15	M	C	
State of Gujarat	1984	11,410	16,800	142	23	15	M	C	
State of Haryana..................	1980	11,493	16,534	142	23	15	M	C	
State of Himachal Pradesh	1971	10,268	14,245	153	20	18	M	C	ex-Jolandia 74
State of Madhya Pradesh.......	1965	9,376	13,409	153	20	16	M	C	
State of Maharashtra............	1959	9,332	14,421	154	19	15	M	C	ex-Oregon Leader 60, ex-Continental Leader 59
State of Manipur...................	1978	14,261	20,628	162	23	15	M	C	
State of Meghalaya	1972	9,484	13,943	153	20	16	M	C	ex-Orphee 72
State of Mysore....................	1966	9,371	13,412	153	20	16	M	C	
State of Nagaland................	1978	14,262	20,574	162	23	15	M	C	
State of Orissa	1985	11,400	16,800	142	23	15	M	C	
State of Punjab	1962	9,191	13,016	154	20	17	M	C	
State of Tripura	1978	14,261	20,587	162	23	15	M	C	
State of West Bengal............	1966	9,373	13,421	155	20	16	M	C	
Tulsidas	1980	12,914	16,351	162	23	16	M	C	
Vallabhbhai Patel	1976	62,563	113,925	254	39	14	M	OBO	
Vallathol	1976	62,563	114,152	254	39	14	M	OBO	
Vishva Abha..........................	1974	9,965	13,635	156	21	16	M	C	
Vishva Aditya........................	1973	11,179	14,578	167	23	18	M	C	
Vishva Ajay	1975	11,179	14,895	166	23	20	M	C	
Vishva Ambar	1975	11,179	14,580	166	23	20	M	C	
Vishva Amitabh	1973	11,179	14,578	167	23	18	M	C	
Vishva Anurag	1974	11,179	14,580	166	23	20	M	CO	
Vishva Apurva.......................	1974	11,179	14,662	166	23	20	M	C	
Vishva Asha	1973	9,965	13,635	156	21	16	M	C	
Vishva Bandhan.....................	1974	9,983	13,764	154	20	17	M	C	
Vishva Bhakti	1968	9,332	13,142	154	20	17	M	C	
Vishva Dharma	1969	9,335	12,852	154	20	17	M	C	
Vishva Jyoti	1959	9,173	12,997	154	20	17	M	C	ex-Jala Vishva Jyoti 61, ex-Vishva-Jyoti 59
Vishva Karuna	1973	10,000	13,967	154	20	17	M	C	
Vishva Kaumudi.....................	1980	10,092	13,671	157	22	18	M	C	
Vishva Madhuri.....................	1974	9,983	13,671	154	20	17	M	C	
Vishva Mamta.......................	1973	9,991	13,986	154	20	17	M	C	
Vishva Maya	1963	9,150	13,016	154	20	17	M	C	
Vishva Mohini	1978	10,092	15,000	157	22	18	M	C	
Vishva Nandini	1978	10,092	13,715	157	22	18	M	C	
Vishva Nayak........................	1971	9,302	12,880	154	20	17	M	C	
Vishva Nidhi	1961	6,209	9,667	155	20	17	M	C	
Vishva Pallav	1980	12,810	16,169	152	23	15	M	C	
Vishva Pankaj.......................	1980	12,810	16,169	152	23	15	M	C	
Vishva Parag........................	1980	12,810	16,146	152	23	15	M	C	
Vishva Parijat.......................	1980	12,810	16,146	152	23	15	M	C	
Vishva Parimal......................	1980	12,810	16,169	152	23	15	M	C	
Vishva Prafulla	1981	12,809	16,146	152	23	15	M	C	
Vishva Prayas	1973	9,135	12,885	149	22	18	M	C	ex-Saint Jacques 73
Vishva Raksha	1966	8,956	12,288	153	19	17	M	C	
Vishva Seva	1968	9,360	13,448	153	20	16	M	C	

The Shipping Corp of India, *Vishva Pankaj. J. K. Byass*

Name	Year	GRT	DWT	LOA	Bm	Kts	Eng	Type	Former names
Vishva Shakti	1969	9,337	12,901	154	20	16	M	C	
Vishva Shobha	1969	9,337	12,931	154	20	16	M	C	
Vishva Siddhi	1968	9,330	12,972	154	20	16	M	C	
Vishva Sudha	1959	10,447	16,050	161	20	15	M	C	ex-Westfalia 62
Vishva Tarang	1973	9,665	13,635	156	21	17	M	C	
Vishva Tej	1967	9,367	13,403	153	20	16	M	C	
Vishva Tirth	1967	9,360	13,391	153	20	16	M	C	
Vishva Umang	1973	9,965	13,635	156	21	17	M	C	
Vishva Vibhuti	1966	8,959	12,282	153	19	16	M	C	
Vishva Vikram	1970	9,262	12,880	154	20	16	M	C	
Vishva Vivek	1959	10,843	15,251	159	20	14	M	C	ex-Figaro 68
Vishva Yash	1973	9,993	13,986	154	20	17	M	C	

In addition there are 25 ocean-going tankers.

Shipping Management SAM

Monaco

Funnel: Yellow with blue 'V'
Hull: Black with green or red boot-topping

Name	Year	GRT	DWT	LOA	Bm	Kts	Eng	Type	Former names
Adelaide Express†	1972	8,352	12,478	144	22	18	M	CO	ex-Marina Sea 85, ex-Rheingold 85, ex-Albion Star 84, ex-Rheingold 82, ex-Bavaria Hongkong 80, ex-Columbus California 79, ex-Rheingold 73
All Star‡	1976	51,200	101,478	258	39	15	M	T	ex-Panstar 1 85
Almalaz*	1965	25,503	50,875	221	31	16	M	T	ex-Serra Trader 78, ex-Osco Surf 75, ex-Saga Surf 75, ex-Brigitta Fernstrom 72
Catalan Bay	1976	9,158	14,900	141	21	13	M	C	ex-Arafura Sea 85, ex-Santa Ines 82
Fremantle Express†	1973	8,351	12,478	144	22	18	M	CO	ex-Marina Sky 85, ex-Walkure 84, ex-Devon 84, ex-Walkure 81, ex-Bavaria Trieste 80, ex-Columbus Canada 79, ex-Walkure 73
Lucayan Trader**	1971	9,411	13,700	147	20	12	M	B	ex-Progreso Argentino 82
Lucerna*	1977	24,132	39,728	183	32	15	M	T	ex-Baraka 83, ex-Alrai 82, ex-Athelmonarch 80
Marina Bay‡	1968	16,611	27,891	172	26	16	M	B	ex-Star Gazer 84, ex-Star Athenian 79, ex-Star Cariboo 78
Marina Breeze‡	1968	16,612	27,891	172	26	16	M	B	ex-Star Delta 84, ex-Star Olympian 79, ex-Star Columbia 77
Ocelot*	1977	33,329	57,372	210	32	16	M	T	ex-Algol 83
Red Sea†	1973	120,734	225,010	332	46	15	M	OBO	ex-Alva Sea 85
Rosiá Bay*	1976	9,158	14,900	141	21	13	M	C	ex-Banda Sea 85, ex-Santa Teresa 82
Salina*	1978	33,329	57,372	210	32	165	M	T	ex-Alkes 83, ex-Alice Redfield 80

* Liberian flag   ** Bahamas flag   † British flag   ‡ Panamanian flag

Silver Navigation Ltd/UK

Name	Year	GRT	DWT	LOA	Bm	Kts	Eng	Type	Former names
Almak	1978	33,329	57,375	210	32	16	M	T	
Altanin	1977	24,132	39,728	183	32	15	M	T	ex-Athelqueen 80
Alvega	1977	33,329	57,372	210	32	16	M	T	
Alvenus	1979	33,329	57,375	210	32	16	M	T	
Bold 1‡	1968	5,211	5,248	117	17	17	M	LPG	ex-Humboldt 84

‡ Panamanian flag

Shipping Management SAM, *Marina Breeze. M. D. J. Lennan*

I. M. Skaugen & Co

Norway

Funnel: Yellow, black top with white diamond, blue and red border and black 'S'.
Hull: White, or black

Name	Year	GRT	DWT	LOA	Bm	Kts	Eng	Type	Former names
Skaubord	1979	31,070	43,343	183	32	14	M	RO	
Skaugran	1979	31,074	43,103	183	32	14	M	RO	
Skauvannt†	1975	76,624	132,415	273	44	15	M	OBO	
Skeena*	1982	33,059	41,668	183	32	14	M	RO	

* owned by Seaboard Shipping Co Ltd, Canada; British flag
† Liberian flag

Ove Skou Rederi A/S

Denmark

Funnel: Black with white 'S' on broad blue band.
Hull: White or grey with blue line.

Name	Year	GRT	DWT	LOA	Bm	Kts	Eng	Type	Former names
Adriatic Skou*	1976	37,784	71,999	230	32	15	M	B	ex-Captain Ioannis 80
Benny Skou	1969	14,332	21,060	166	24	16	M	CO	ex-Ditte Skou 82
Jytte Skou	1968	14,332	21,060	166	24	16	M	CO	ex-Dorte Skou 82
Ove Skou	1982	16,507	23,706	160	25	16	M	CO	

* Liberian flag

Christen Smith Shipping Co

Norway

Belships Co Ltd Skibs A/S

Funnel: Blue with blue 'CS' monogram and anchor on white disc
Hull: Grey with red boot-topping

Name	Year	GRT	DWT	LOA	Bm	Kts	Eng	Type	Former names
Belcargo	1975	59,962	110,440	266	38	14	M	B	
Belforest†	1985	28,400	32,500	199	30	15	M	B	
Belnor	1977	22,960	38,406	193	26	15	M	B	ex-Norbulk 85, ex-Melsomvik 79
Belstar	1972	22,494	38,406	193	26	15	M	B	
Beltimber†	1985	28,400	35,200	199	30	15	M	B	
Belwood†	1985	28,400	35,200	199	30	15	M	B	

† Singapore flag

Stove Shipping

Name	Year	GRT	DWT	LOA	Bm	Kts	Eng	Type	Former names
Aleppo*	1974	22,997	38,406	195	26	14	M	B	
Jessie Stove	1972	60,414	110,342	266	38	15	M	B	
Jorgen J. Lorentzen*	1975	72,614	134,372	282	38	15	M	T	ex-Stove Caledonia 75
Stove Campbell	1973	22,495	38,406	193	26	15	M	B	
Stove Trader*	1976	59,960	110,444	265	38	15	M	B	ex-Horn Crusader 79
Stove Transport*	1974	23,010	38,406	194	26	15	M	B	

* Swedish flag

South African Marine Corp Ltd

South Africa

Funnel: Grey with black top and narrow blue and white and wide orange bands; red with white 'U' (Universal Reefers Ltd)
Hull: Grey or white with red or green boot-topping

Name	Year	GRT	DWT	LOA	Bm	Kts	Eng	Type	Former names
Atlantic Universal‡	1983	13,361	12,271	150	24	20	M	R	
Bora Universal‡	1979	8,429	9,175	154	23	21	M	R	
Caribbean Universal‡	1979	9,996	10,873	155	22	21	M	R	ex-Polar Costa Rica 81
Morgenster‡‡	1969	12,239	15,410	182	23	19	M	C	ex-SA Morgenster 85
Pacific Universal‡	1984	13,361	12,271	150	24	20	M	R	
Constantia	1968	12,239	15,409	182	23	29	M	C	ex-SA Constantia 85

Above: I. M. Skaugen & Co, *Skaugran. J. Krayenbosch*

Above: Ove Skou A/S, *Benny Skou. F. R. Sherlock*

Below: Christen Smith Shipping Co, *Belstar. J. K. Byass*

Name	Year	GRT	DWT	LOA	Bm	Kts	Eng	Type	Former names
SA Helderberg	1977	53,023	48,878	258	32	21	M2	CC	
SA Langeberg	1977	28,259	23,868	208	31	21	ST	CC	
SA Sederberg	1978	53,023	48,878	258	32	21	M2	CC	
SA Vaal	1982	31,225	34,098	210	32	18	M	CC	
SA Waterberg	1979	53,050	49,662	258	32	22	M2	CC	
SA Winterberg	1978	53,050	50,819	258	32	22	M2	CC	
Sabie†	1976	16,211	27,140	177	23	15	M	B	ex-SA Sabie 77
Safocean Nederburg	1967	12,752	16,316	192	23	19	M	C	ex-SA Nederberg 80
Scamper Universal‡	1980	9,074	12,475	156	23	22	M	R	ex-Hilco Scamper 81
Scirocco Universal*	1979	10,763	9,193	154	23	21	M	R	
Sea Merchant*	1983	21,308	35,419	178	30	15	M	B	
Sea Pioneer*	1983	21,308	35,371	177	30	15	M	B	
Sea Transporter*	1983	21,308	35,340	178	30	15	M	B	
Sishen	1977	91,750	169,999	297	48	15	M	O	
Venture	1978	18,575	28,052	173	24	15	M	B	
Vergelegen‡‡	1969	12,337	15,072	182	23	19	M	C	ex-SA Vergelegen 85
Victory	1978	18,297	28,048	173	24	16	M	B	

* British flag   † Panamanian flag   ‡ managed by Gateway Shipping Ltd, Sir Lanka flag   ‡‡ St Vincent and Grenadines flag

Standard Oil Company (Indiana)   USA

Funnel: Blue with red top, white band with torch and oval emblems
Hull: Grey

Name	Year	GRT	DWT	LOA	Bm	Kts	Eng	Type	Former names
Amoco Baltimore†	1969	38,715	79,313	241	36	16	M	T	
Amoco Brisbane†	1968	35,450	73,993	241	36	16	M	T	
Amoco Cairo*†	1975	76,472	155,868	280	54	15	M	T	
Amoco Cremona†	1968	35,450	73,982	241	36	15	M	T	
Amoco Europa†	1975	109,979	232,164	334	51	15	M	T	
Amoco Milford Haven†	1973	109,700	232,162	334	51	15	M	T	
Amoco Savannah†	1970	39,246	78,679	240	36	16	M	T	
Amoco Seafarer†	1974	126,895	271,891	332	56	16	M	T	ex-Polybritannia 79
Amoco Texas City†	1970	39,246	78,696	240	36	16	M	T	
Amoco Trinidad*†	1974	76,484	155,755	280	54	15	M	T	
Amoco Whiting†	1975	76,472	155,703	280	54	16	M	T	ex-Amoco Tehran 80
Amoco Yorktown†	1969	38,714	79,313	241	36	16	M	T	
Ocean Voyager†	1973	35,315	72,346	239	34	16	M	T	ex-Amoco Voyager 85, ex-Navarchos Miaoulis 77

* owned by Mammoth Bulk Carriers (Central Gulf Lines Inc)   † Liberian flag

Stena AB (Sten A. Olsson)   Sweden

Funnel: White, 'S' on wide red band separated from black top and base by narrow white bands
Hull: White, grey or blue with red boot-topping

Name	Year	GRT	DWT	LOA	Bm	Kts	Eng	Type	Former names
Stena Adriatica*	1973	12,806	22,705	159	24	15	M	T	ex-Esso Nagoya 83
Stena Arctica	1978	21,110	31,900	186	27	16	M	BC	ex-Columbialand 85, ex-Seatrain London 79, ex-Columbialand 79
Stena Atlantica†	1977	123,660	269,195	334	55	15	ST	T	ex-Santillana 83
Stena Caribica†	1975	19,460	31,185	184	26	16	M	T	ex-Afran Neptune 84
Stena Carrier*	1978	5,466	8661	151	20	16	M2	RO	ex-Jolly Smeraldo 83, ex-Jolly Bruno 82, ex-Stena Carrier 82, ex-Imparca Miama 81, ex-Stena Carrier 80, ex-Imparca Express I 80
Stena Freighter	1977	5,744	8,672	151	22	17	M2	RO	ex-Jolly Turchese 83, ex-Jolly Giallo 82, ex-Stena Freighter 82, ex-Merzario Ausonia 81

Above: South African Marine Corp Ltd, *Safocean Nederburg. Table Bay Underway Shipping*

Below: Stena AB, *Stena Adriatica. J. Krayenbosch*

Name	Year	GRT	DWT	LOA	Bm	Kts	Eng	Type	Former names
Stena Grecia*	1978	5,466	8,661	151	22	16	M2	RO	ex-Merzario Grecia 83, ex-Tor Felicia 78
Stena Hispania*	1978	5,753	8,672	151	23	17	M2	RO	ex-Kotka Violet 85, ex-Stena Hispania 84, ex-Merzario Hispania 83, ex-Atlantic Project 81
Stena Ionia*	1978	5,753	8,672	151	23	17	M2	RO	ex-Merzario Ionia 82, ex-Stena Ionia 81, ex-Atlantic Prosper 81
Stena Oceanica*	1974	34,230	41,256	216	32	17	M	LPG	ex-Mandrill 80, ex-Malmros Multina 79, ex-Dovertown 74
Stena Pacifica†	1977	66,942	132,478	277	40	15	M	T	ex-Elvira C 84, ex-Beatriz Maria 81
Stena Transporter**	1978	8,596	7,620	151	22	16	M2	RO	ex-Syria 83, ex-Alpha Enterprise 79

* British flag   † Liberian flag   ** Cypriot flag

Stephenson Clarke Shipping Ltd

UK

Funnel: Black with broad silver band
Hull: Black

Name	Year	GRT	DWT	LOA	Bm	Kts	Eng	Type
Aldrington	1978	4,334	6,570	104	16	14	M	B
Ashington	1979	4,334	6,570	104	16	14	M	B
Dallington	1975	7,658	12,140	138	19	14	M	B
Donnington	1975	7,658	12,140	138	19	14	M	B
Durrington	1981	7,673	11,990	138	18	14	M	B
Pulborough	1965	4,995	7,889	113	16	12	M	B
Rogate	1967	4,997	7,810	113	16	12	M	B
Storrington	1982	7,673	11,990	138	19	14	M	B
Washington	1977	6,236	9,008	127	19	14	M	B
Wilmington	1969	5,689	9,119	125	17	13	M	B

Stolt-Nielsens Rederi A/S

Norway

Funnel: White, white 'S' on large red square
Hull: Yellow

Name	Year	GRT	DWT	LOA	Bm	Kts	Eng	Type	Former names
Stolt Aquamarine	1985	24,000	35,076	177	32	15	M	T	
Stolt Avance*	1977	14,418	22,908	171	24	16	M	T	
Stolt Avenir*	1978	14,418	22,908	171	24	16	M	T	
Stolt Boel*	1971	13,831	24,835	171	24	15	M	T	
Stolt Castle*	1970	11,240	18,421	159	22	15	M	T	
Stolt Condor*	1979	20,760	36,613	177	30	16	M	T	ex-Stolt Okpo 79
Stolt Crown*	1970	11,235	18,130	159	22	15	M	T	
Stolt Eagle*	1980	20,760	37,067	177	30	16	M	T	ex-Stolt Ulsan 80
Stolt Emerald	1985	24,000	35,076	177	32	15	M	T	
Stolt Excellence*	1979	18,731	30,992	177	27	16	M	T	
Stolt Falcon*	1978	20,760	36,613	174	30	15	M	T	ex-Stolt Seoul 79
Stolt Hawk*	1978	20,760	36,613	177	30	16	M	T	ex-Stolt Inchon 79
Stolt Heron*	1979	20,760	36,613	177	30	16	M	T	ex-Stolt Yosu 79
Stolt Integrity*	1977	18,731	30,992	177	27	18	M	T	
Stolt Jade	1985	24,000	35,076	177	32	15	M	T	
Stolt Llandafff†	1971	14,116	25,060	171	24	15	M	T	
Stolt Loyalty*	1978	18,566	31,500	177	27	17	M	T	
Stolt Osprey*	1978	20,760	36,498	177	30	15	M	T	ex-Stolt Busan 80
Stolt Pride*	1976	18,570	30,822	177	27	17	M	T	
Stolt Sapphire	1985	24,000	35,600	177	32	15	M	T	
Stolt Sceptre‡	1971	15,427	23,985	170	25	15	M	T	ex-Anco Sceptre 83
Stolt Sea*	1971	15,007	23,127	170	25	16	M	T	ex-Anco Sea 73
Stolt Sheaf*	1972	14,578	25,060	171	24	15	M	T	

Above: Stena AB, *Stena Ionia. M. D. J. Lennon*

Above: Stephenson Clarke Shipping Ltd, *Dallington. J. Krayenbosch*

Below: Stolt-Nielsens Rederi A/S, *Stolt Eagle. J. M. Kakebeeke*

Name	Year	GRT	DWT	LOA	Bm	Kts	Eng	Type	Former names
Stolt Sincerity*	1976	18,566	30,822	177	27	17	M	T	
Stolt Span*	1970	14,977	23,127	170	25	16	M	T	ex-Anco Span 73
Stolt Spirit*	1976	18,567	30,822	177	27	16	M	T	
Stolt Spur*	1969	14,912	23,299	170	25	16	M	T	ex-Anco Spur 73
Stolt Stane‡	1972	15,003	24,223	170	25	15	M	T	ex-Anco Stane 83
Stolt Surf*	1970	15,804	23,299	170	25	16	M	T	ex-Anco Ville 73
Stolt Sydness*	1970	11,065	18,236	159	22	15	M	T	
Stolt Templar‡	1972	15,427	23,985	170	25	15	M	T	ex-Anco Templar 83
Stolt Tenacity*	1978	18,731	30,992	177	27	17	M	T	
Stolt Venture*	1976	18,352	31,543	170	30	14	M	T	ex-Stolt Sagona 83, ex-Osco Sagona 83, ex-Sagona 80

* Liberian flag   † Panamanian flag   ‡ Owned by John Swire and Sons Ltd, British flag q.v. jointly controlled by The British Petroleum Co Ltd q.v.

Sudan Shipping Line Ltd

Sudan

Funnel: White with narrow blue band and red top
Hull: Pale green with 'SUDAN LINE' in white, dark green boot-topping

Name	Year	GRT	DWT	LOA	Bm	Kts	Eng	Type
Blue Nile	1980	9,140	12,905	133	21	16	M	RO
Darfur	1979	9,691	12,111	149	21	16	M	C
Dongola	1979	9,691	12,111	149	21	16	M	C
El Obeid	1979	9,691	12,111	149	21	16	M	C
Gedaref	1979	9,691	12,111	149	22	16	M	C
Khartoum	1980	10,066	14,347	153	22	17	M	C
Merawi	1980	9,691	12,111	149	21	16	M	C
Nyala	1973	5,665	8,563	118	18	15	M	C
Omdurman	1974	8,634	13,714	144	20	16	M	C
White Nile	1979	9,140	12,905	133	21	16	M	RO

Soc D'Arm Mar Suisse-Atlantique SA

Switzerland

Funnel: Grey with yellow and red houseflag interrupting two yellow bands
Hull: Grey with red boot-topping

Name	Year	GRT	DWT	LOA	Bm	Kts	Eng	Type	Former names
Bregaglia	1985	22,342	36,800	183	28	15	M	B	
Celerina	1975	20,879	34,156	175	26	15	M	B	ex-Cruzeiro do Sul 83
El Gaucho†	1969	31,551	59,819	229	32	15	M	B	ex-Atlantic Lady 83, ex-Meilly 82, ex-Asian 80, ex-Daigoh Maru 79
Engiadina†	1985	30,000	60,800	225	32	14	M	B	
General Guisan	1973	33,991	54,202	221	32	15	M	B	
Iguazu†	1980	33,632	64,443	224	32	15	M	B	
Lavaux	1977	16,921	27,860	180	25	15	M	B	
Lucendro	1967	25,168	47,503	203	29	14	M	B	ex-Aquabelle 79
Moleson	1984	22,342	37,489	183	28	15	M	B	
Nordland	1975	20,797	34,168	186	26	17	M	B	ex-Diavolezza 82
Nyon	1978	36,207	59,840	225	32	14	M	B	ex-Itel Polaris 79, ex-Pearl Corona 78
Romandie	1975	20,797	33,629	186	26	17	M	B	
Sils	1976	17,874	27,860	180	25	15	M	B	ex-Los Andes 79
Silvaplana†	1972	18,349	32,413	183	26	15	M	B	ex-Pantokratos 72
Silvretta	1972	18,503	30,235	197	23	15	M	B	ex-Los Andes 73, ex-Iatis 72
Vanil	1978	10,909	15,357	151	21	16	M	C	

† Liberian flag

Above: Stolt-Nielsens Rederi A/S, *Stolt Sceptre. J. Krayenbosch*

Above: Sudan Shipping Line Ltd, *Khartoum. F. R. Sherlock*

Below: Soc D'Arm Mar Suisse-Atlantique SA, *Sils. F. R. Sherlock*

A/S Sigurd Sverdrup

Norway

Funnel: Black with white band
Hull: Grey or black with red boot-topping

Name	Year	GRT	DWT	LOA	Bm	Kts	Eng	Type	Former names
Aura Adventure*	1975	17,795	32,290	191	27	15	M	T	ex-Strait of Canso 82
Aura Bravery*	1973	17,795	32,483	192	27	16	M	T	ex-Simonburn 82, ex-Kurdistan 79, ex-Frank D. Moores 76
Norbella	1982	27,807	45,508	193	29	15	M	B	

* managed by Common Bros plc. Liberian flag

John Swire & Sons Ltd

UK

Funnel: Blue or black with houseflag
Hull: Black with white line, red boot-topping

China Navigation Co Ltd/UK

Name	Year	GRT	DWT	LOA	Bm	Kts	Eng	Type	Former names
Aotea†	1970	24,433	23,069	213	30	23	M	CC	ex-Ariake 77
Chengtu*	1978	6,216	7,727	118	20	14	M	CC	ex-Jeddah Crown 81, ex-Timber Bay 79, ex-Strathkirn 79
Coral Chief	1977	6,373	7,078	118	20	15	M	CO	
Coral Princess	1962	9,369	2,737	146	19	18	M2	CP	ex-Princesa Leopoldina 70
Eriskay‡	1975	117,511	229,936	330	49	16	ST	T	ex-Jagorda 82, ex-Harry Borthen 76
Fengtien	1979	16,430	24,274	177	23	15	M	BC	
Hunan	1981	23,410	40,507	182	29	15	M	B	
Hupeh	1984	26,239	45,260	183	31	14	M	B	
Kweilin	1981	16,289	21,889	178	23	16	M	B	ex-Palapur 82
Nimos	1977	7,354	8,706	132	20	15	M	CC	
Pacific Islander**	1977	8,012	15,532	156	25	16	M	RO	ex-Pacific Princess 82
Papuan Chief	1977	7,354	8,710	132	20	15	M	CC	
Polynesia‡	1979	8,084	12,276	138	22	15	M	CC	

† owned jointly by Overseas Containers Ltd (Crusader Swire Container Services Ltd)

* Singapore flag   ‡ Liberian flag   ** Panamanian flag

see also Nedlloyd Group and Stolt-Nielsens Rederi A/S

Swiss Shipping & Neptun Co Ltd

Switzerland

Funnel: Black with three green bands on broad white band
Hull: Grey with red boot-topping

Alpina Reederei AG

Name	Year	GRT	DWT	LOA	Bm	Kts	Eng	Type	Former names
Alpina	1970	9,600	14,955	140	21	16	M	C	
Calanda	1975	7,698	10,250	144	19	15	M	BC	ex-Safats Continent 83, ex-Calanda 82 ex-Iren 79, ex-Skotland 79
Maloja	1974	7,680	10,220	144	19	15	M	BC	ex-Petra Crown 83, ex-Maloja 79, ex-Ida 79, ex-Vinland 79, ex-Maersk Tempo 78, ex-Vinland 77
Regina	1978	8,562	11,075	136	21	16	M	CO	

Texaco Inc

USA

Funnel: Black, broad green band with 'TEXACO' in black on white disc, outlined in red and white
Hull: Black with red boot-topping

Name	Year	GRT	DWT	LOA	Bm	Kts	Eng	Type	Former names
Texaco Africa*	1974	126,974	274,585	332	56	15	ST	T	
Texaco Brasil*	1972	131,028	290,576	348	52	15	ST	T	ex-Richard Maersk 76
Texaco California	1954	23,460	39,973	220	27	18	ST	T	ex-California 60
Texaco Caribbean†	1977	125,857	274,347	327	55	16	ST	T	
Texaco Connecticut	1953	23,459	39,976	220	27	18	ST	T	ex-Connecticut 59

Above: A/S Sigurd Sverdrup, *Aura Bravery. M. D. J. Lennon*

Below: Swiss Shipping & Neptun Co Ltd/Alpina Reederei AG, *Calanda. M. D. J. Lennon*

Name	Year	GRT	DWT	LOA	Bm	Kts	Eng	Type	Former names
Texaco Darient‡	1967	41,187	79,183	232	37	15	ST	T	ex-Texaco Australia 72
Texaco Florida	1956	23,459	39,733	220	27	16	ST	T	ex-Florida 60
Texaco Georgia	1963	16,515	26,755	184	24	17	ST	T	
Texaco Hannover*	1968	54,497	103,490	271	39	15	M	T	ex-Ernst G. Russ 74
Texaco Ireland*	1972	143,686	290,068	348	52	15	ST	T	ex-Roy Maersk 76
Texaco Japan*	1975	123,648	267,732	337	54	15	ST	T	
Texaco Maine*	1959	28,675	44,907	224	31	16	ST	T	ex-Maine 60
Texaco Maryland	1963	16,514	26,976	184	24	17	ST	T	
Texaco Massachusetts	1963	16,515	26,972	184	24	17	ST	T	
Texaco Minnesota	1943	15,622	26,152	190	23	14	TE	T	ex-Minnesota 60, ex-Churubusco 50
Texaco Mississippi	1944	15,688	27,013	190	23	14	TE	T	ex-Mississippi 59, ex-South Mountain 50
Texaco Montana	1965	16,584	26,972	184	24	17	ST	T	
Texaco Nederland*	1972	131,014	289,154	348	52	15	ST	T	ex-Rosa Maersk 75
Texaco New York	1953	23,460	42,667	220	27	18	ST	T	ex-New York 60
Texaco Rhode Island	1964	16,584	26,972	184	24	17	ST	T	
Texaco South America*	1976	130,959	272,832	344	54	15	ST	T	
Texaco Texas*	1949	17,973	30,257	190	26	16	ST	T	ex-Texas 60
Texaco Veraguast†	1976	125,857	274,165	337	55	16	ST	T	

* Panamanian flag
† owned by D. K. Ludwig Group (National Bulk Carriers Inc), Panamanian flag
‡ owned by Gotaas-Larsen Inc, Panamanian flag

Texaco Overseas Tankship Ltd/UK

Name	Year	GRT	DWT	LOA	Bm	Kts	Eng	Type	Former names
Texaco Melbourne	1945	13,899	23,694	172	24	14	TE	T	ex-Caltex Melbourne 67, ex-Victory Loan 51
Texaco Westminster	1981	54,076	79,999	247	40	14	M	T	
Texaco Windsor	1980	54,110	79,999	242	40	14	M	T	ex-Globtik Windsor 80

Texaco Norway A/S/Norway

Name	Year	GRT	DWT	LOA	Bm	Kts	Eng	Type	Former names
Texaco Baltic	1976	18,380	31,502	169	26	16	M	T	
Texaco Bergen	1977	18,378	31,502	169	26	16	M	T	
Texaco Bogota	1960	13,632	22,455	182	23	14	M	T	
Texaco Norge	1962	13,223	21,502	176	23	15	M	T	
Texaco Oslo	1960	12,884	20,029	175	22	15	M	T	
Texaco Skandinavia	1962	13,222	21,540	176	23	15	M	T	
Texaco Stockholm	1977	18,378	31,502	169	26	16	M	T	

Saudi International Petroleum Carriers Ltd/Saudi Arabia

Name	Year	GRT	DWT	LOA	Bm	Kts	Eng	Type	Former names
Asir	1974	136,718	267,848	337	54	15	ST	T	ex-Texaco Italia 83
Bishah	1976	139,892	272,739	344	54	15	ST	T	ex-Texaco London 83

Getty Oil Co/USA

Funnel: White with orange disc inside orange 'G'
Hull: Black

Name	Year	GRT	DWT	LOA	Bm	Kts	Eng	Type	Former names
Alabama Getty†	1971	63,234	135,235	281	41	15	M	T	ex-Curro 76
California Getty†	1979	71,208	128,320	250	45	15	M	OBO	ex-Norrland 82
George F. Getty II*	1973	101,440	227,440	320	52	15	ST	T	
Houston Getty*	1975	65,287	136,100	280	41	16	M	T	
J. Paul Getty*	1971	101,438	227,355	320	52	15	ST	T	
Kansas Getty†	1976	55,973	81,233	256	44	16	M	T	ex-Malmros Merrimac 79
Los Angeles Getty*	1974	101,417	227,305	320	52	15	ST	T	
Texas Getty†	1975	55,973	81,233	256	44	16	M	T	ex-Malmros Monitor 79
Tulsa Getty*	1971	64,961	133,458	280	41	15	M	T	ex-Markland 77

* Liberian flag
† Bahamas flag

Texaco Inc, *Texaco Norge*. M. D. J. Lennon

Thomas Nationwide Transport   Australia

Funnel: Black, white and orange bands beneath black top
Hull: Orange with red boot-topping

Name	Year	GRT	DWT	LOA	Bm	Kts	Eng	Type	Former names
Timur Carriers (Pte) Ltd/Singapore									
TFL Democracy	1978	13,941	15,270	157	25	18	M	CC	
TFL Enterprise	1979	13,941	15,285	157	25	18	M	CC	ex-Eagle Faith 85,
									ex-TFL Enterprise 85,
									ex-Alltrans Enterprise 82,
									ex-Incotrans Enterprise 82,
									ex-TFL Enterprise 81,
									ex-Alltrans Enterprise 80
TFL Express	1978	13,941	15,271	157	25	18	M	CC	ex-Alltrans Express 80
TFL Freedom	1978	13,977	15,435	157	25	18	M	CC	
TFL Independence	1978	13,977	15,451	157	25	18	M	CC	
TFL Jefferson	1979	15,827	18,964	177	27	22	M	CC	ex-Seatrain Saratoga 80
TFL Liberty	1978	13,941	15,273	157	25	18	M	CC	
TNT Express*	1984	29,223	41,300	209	30	16	M	BC	

* British flag
joint owners of Antwerp Bulkcarriers NV (Sea Lanes NV) q.v.

The Thornhope Shipping Co Ltd   UK

Funnel: Blue with white 'H' on red band (or white with red 'C'*)
Hull: Black or dark grey with red boot-topping

Name	Year	GRT	DWT	LOA	Bm	Kts	Eng	Type	Former names
Crusader Point	1980	5,574	7,805	123	18	15	M	C	ex-Beate 80
Garrison Point	1976	8,014	12,330	127	20	13	M	C	
Landguard Point*	1982	4,968	8,161	108	18	13	M	B	
Sir Alexander Glen	1975	91,178	162,465	294	44	15	M	OBO	
Warden Point	1978	3,894	6,440	106	15	13	M	C	ex-Red Sea 80

* managed for Carless Solvents Ltd

D/S Torm A/S   Denmark

Funnel: Black with blue 'T' on white band between two red bands
Hull: Black or grey with red boot-topping

Name	Year	GRT	DWT	LOA	Bm	Kts	Eng	Type
Torm Alice	1983	26,693	44,969	183	31	15	M	B
Torm Rask	1977	20,036	33,650	171	26	15	M	T
Torm Rotna	1976	20,036	33,650	171	26	15	M	T
Torm Thyra	1985	26,000	45,000	183	32	15	M	T

Total Cie Francaise de Nav   France

Funnel: Yellow narrow black top with red, white and blue comet device
Hull: Black with red boot-topping

Name	Year	GRT	DWT	LOA	Bm	Kts	Eng	Type	Former names
Autan	1975	138,460	278,219	343	52	16	ST	T	ex-Labiosa 81
Boree	1976	132,914	283,861	343	53	15	ST	T	ex-Spio 79, ex-Stran Spio 76
Chamal	1974	68,914	134,473	280	41	13	M	T	ex-Jonny 83
Eole	1980	52,743	82,137	244	42	14	M	T	ex-Ionia 83
Galion	1981	74,298	126,667	280	42	14	M	B	ex-Gallant Lion 82
Iseult	1974	138,222	280,086	344	51	16	ST	T	
Nan Hai Xi Wang*	1976	92,500	174,007	291	46	16	ST	T	ex-Almirante Rotaeche 85
Onyx	1975	138,255	268,951	339	54	15	ST	T	
Opale	1975	138,222	279,999	343	52	15	ST	T	
Rigel	1960	30,801	51,038	225	31	16	M	T	
Stratus*	1979	64,426	132,207	277	40	14	M	T	ex-Astrapesa Uno 80

* Liberian flag see also Ciè Navale Worms.

Above: Thomas Nationwide Transport, *TNT Express.* J. Krayenbosch

Below: D/S Torm A/S, *Torm Rask.* J. Krayenbosch

Transatlantic Rederi A/B

Funnel: Yellow with blue top
Hull: Grey or red with red boot-topping

Sweden

Name	Year	GRT	DWT	LOA	Bm	Kts	Eng	Type	Former names
Barranduna	1972	24,437	24,564	207	30	22	M	RO	
Boogabilla	1978	22,325	31,460	229	32	20	M	RO	
Elgaren	1979	21,722	28,173	217	32	22	M	RO	
Kolsnaren	1978	21,722	28,092	217	32	22	M	RO	ex-Merzario Asia 79, ex-Kolsnaren 79
Paralla	1971	23,196	20,549	199	29	20	M	RO	

see also Atlantic Container line and Australian National Line

Rederiaktiebolaget Transocean

Name	Year	GRT	DWT	LOA	Bm	Kts	Eng	Type	Former names
Atlantic Premier	1972	10,999	9,511	162	19	17	M2	RO	ex-Incotrans Premier 84, ex-Atlantic Premier 84, ex-Mont Royal 78
Barber Nara	1979	22,087	33,300	229	32	22	M	RO	
Nihon	1972	55,241	40,972	291	32	26	M3	CC	
Thebeland	1978	9,374	12,200	165	26	19	M2	RO	
Tyrusland	1978	9,373	12,007	165	26	19	M2	RO	ex-Jolly Ocra 85, ex-Tyrusland 84
Vegaland	1979	9,386	12,200	165	26	21	M2	RO	ex-Tarn 83, ex-Vegaland 81
Vikingland	1979	9,386	12,200	165	26	19	M2	RO	

Transportacion Maritima Mexicana SA

Mexico

Funnel: Yellow with white 'MTM' on red/green diagonally divided square, black top
Hull: Grey with green boot-topping, 'LINEA MEXICANA' in black

Name	Year	GRT	DWT	LOA	Bm	Kts	Eng	Type	Former names
Amparo*	1967	11,893	16,486	156	22	16	M	C	ex-Star Alcyone 74, ex-Herring Lotte 71
Azteca	1969	16,039	26,072	186	23	15	M	B	
Bibi*	1979	16,818	22,378	178	27	18	M	CO	
Bocha‡	1971	5,447	8,814	131	18	18	M	C	ex-Acuario 79
Colima	1985	29,660	46,650	197	32	17	M	BC	
El Mexicano	1964	8,967	13,120	146	20	15	M	C	
Gloria‡	1971	5,447	8,694	131	18	15	M	C	ex-Geminis 79
Guaicuri	1973	68,171	122,431	261	41	15	M	B	ex-Chokai Maru 83
Jalapa	1966	11,453	15,764	156	22	16	M	C	ex-Samia 81, ex-Elena 79, ex-Star Procyon 74, ex-Heering Susan 69
Jalisco	1979	16,087	22,270	178	27	21	M	CO	ex-Barbara Mariana 81
Lacandon†	1970	16,639	26,289	174	26	15	M	B	ex-Victoria City 83
Lerma**	1978	9,247	10,555	180	28	18	M	V	ex-Nissan Silvia 84
Maya	1969	16,066	25,503	186	23	15	M	B	
Mitla	1985	29,660	46,650	197	32	17	M	BC	
Monterrey	1971	12,611	16,392	173	24	21	M	CO	
Olmeca†	1970	16,310	26,289	174	26	15	M	B	ex-Fresco City 82
Puebla	1965	8,948	13,330	146	20	14	M	C	
Sarita‡	1980	16,087	22,229	178	27	21	M	CO	
Silvia Sofia*	1979	16,843	22,229	178	27	21	M	CO	
Sonia M*	1971	11,143	13,300	157	23	19	M	CO	ex-Strathmuit 82, ex-Mulbera 75
Sonora	1979	16,087	22,267	178	27	21	M	CO	ex-Gina Luisa 82
Tepozteco**	1973	8,537	8,870	169	26	17	M	V	
Toluca	1971	12,611	16,130	173	24	21	M	CO	
Yaqui†	1970	16,310	26,289	174	26	15	M	B	ex-Prince Rupert City 82

* British flag   ** Panamanian flag
† Singapore flag   ‡Liberian flag

Above: Transatlantic Rederi A/B, *Tyrusland. J. Krayenbosch*

Below: Transportacion Maritima Mexicana SA, *Toluca. J. Krayenbosch*

Cia Trasatlantica Espanola SA

Spain

Funnel: Black
Hull: Black with red boot-topping and white line

Name	Year	GRT	DWT	LOA	Bm	Kts	Eng	Type	Former names
Almudena	1982	18,209	19,183	184	27	20	M	CC	
Belen	1972	5,270	9,513	156	19	18	M	C	
Galeona	1972	5,270	9,513	156	19	18	M	C	
Pilar	1981	18,209	19,185	184	27	20	M	CC	
Roncesvalles	1972	5,450	9,513	156	19	18	M	C	
Valvanuz	1972	5,450	9,513	156	19	18	M	C	

Tschudi & Eitzen

Norway

Funnel: Black with blue and white shield on red band
Hull: Grey

Name	Year	GRT	DWT	LOA	Bm	Kts	Eng	Type	Former names
Sibig Venture	1972	27,719	44,144	222	42	16	M	HLS	ex-Venture Espana 82, ex-Conoco Espana 78
Sibofem*	1972	44,140	85,397	252	32	13	M	OBO	ex-Transud III 79, ex-Diamantis Pateras 79
Siboseven	1982	44,071	75,395	243	32	15	M	OBO	

* Panamanian flag

C. Y. Tung Group

Hong Kong (UK)

Island Navigation Corp (Ship Management) Ltd

Funnel: Yellow with red and gold flower
Hull: Black, white or grey

Name	Year	GRT	DWT	LOA	Bm	Kts	Eng	Type	Former names
Araguaney*	1982	23,843	45,396	195	32	14	M	T	ex-Intermar Transporter 85
Asian Banner*	1985	21,300	35,600	(178)	28	15	M	B	
Asian Brilliance†	1984	19,522	36,995	190	28	14	M	B	
Asian Express*	1976	17,073	30,744	179	25	17	M	BV	
Asian Progress	1981	36,031	62,132	224	32	15	M	B	ex-Pacific Peace 81
Atlantic Amity	1985	50,700	79,900	(234)	40	15	M	T	
Atlantic Charity*	1970	16,016	28,793	180	23	15	M	B	
Atlantic Charisma	1985	23,300	36,750	(166)	30	15	M	T	
Atlantic Concord*	1985	23,300	36,750	(166)	30	15	M	T	
Atlantic Confidence	1980	23,115	37,560	171	30	14	M	T	ex-Cys Mariner 84
Atlantic Conquest*	1985	23,300	36,750	(166)	30	14	M	T	
Atlantic Dignity*	1975	42,439	89,935	247	40	15	M	T	ex-Cys Dignity 85
Atlantic Peace*	1983	43,943	86,631	249	42	15	M	T	ex-Cys Olympia 84
Atlantic Venturer*	1969	75,268	133,429	291	42	15	ST	OBO	ex-Marcona Venturer 79, ex-San-Juan Venturer 73
Brazilian Friendship*	1977	48,938	9,070	253	37	15	M	OBO	
Brazilian Hope*	1976	177,045	392,809	370	64	16	ST	T	ex-World Giant 76
Brazilian Pride*	1975	176,007	372,201	364	63	16	ST	T	ex-Malmros Mariner 78
Brazilian Splendour*	1974	176,053	372,217	363	63	16	ST	T	ex-Hemland 77
Canadian Explorer	1978	26,051	33,869	219	31	23	M	CC	ex-Dart Canada 81
Cayambe*	1969	11,208	13,817	161	23	19	M	CO	ex-Eidanger 83, ex-Singapore Pride 77
China Container‡	1979	38,124	40,379	251	32	25	M	CC	
China Pride‡	1972	68,176	156,109	305	43	16	M	OBO	ex-Emerald Glory 85, ex-Makikawa Man 82
China Trader‡	1984	36,303	66,732	230	32	15	M	B	
China Victory‡	1970	65,056	115,353	259	41	14	M	OBO	ex-Oceanic Victory 85, ex-Ocean Bridge 78

Above: Cia Trasatlantica Espanola SA, *Almudena*. J. Krayenbosch

Below: Tschudi & Eitzen, *Sibig Venture*. F. R. Sherlock

Name	Year	GRT	DWT	LOA	Bm	Kts	Eng	Type	Former names
Columbia Liberty*	1980	43,570	81,282	243	42	14	M	T	
Cotopaxi††	1969	11,208	12,215	161	23	19	M	CO	ex-Villanger 83, ex-Singapore Triumph 76
Cys Brilliance*	1974	43,441	89,961	247	40	15	M	T	
Cys Crown*	1974	114,585	258,336	340	54	16	ST	T	
Cys Excellence*	1975	43,429	89,943	247	40	15	M	T	
Cys Integrity*	1977	17,286	30,244	171	25	15	M	T	
Cys Justice*	1980	28,825	55,275	216	36	15	M	T	
Dart Atlantica	1979	15,584	17,100	177	27	22	M	CC	ex-Seapac Chesapeake 81, ex-Seatrain Chesapeake 81
Dart Britain	1979	15,584	18,643	177	27	22	M	CC	ex-Seapac Oriskany 81, ex-Seatrain Oriskany 81
Energy Courage*	1975	105,902	231,490	319	54	16	ST	T	ex-Pan Asia Courage 80
Energy Explorer*	1976	187,887	390,038	374	64	16	ST	T	ex-Titus 80
Energy Growth*	1974	105,662	233,949	320	53	16	ST	T	
Energy Mobility*	1972	103,163	223,911	327	48	16	ST	T	
Energy Progress*	1974	130,969	231,052	340	54	15	ST	T	
Energy Renown*	1975	121,542	240,830	326	49	15	ST	T	ex-Schleswig Holstein 83
Hongkong Container	1974	38,864	35,518	265	32	26	M2	CC	
Knight*	1980	20,273	36,827	175	30	15	M	T	ex-Cys Knight 84
Manchester Challenge	1970	30,817	28,488	232	31	22	M	CC	ex-Dart America 81
Manhatten Baron*	1975	44,061	87,076	246	38	15	M	T	
Neptune Concord‡‡	1981	31,071	30,714	222	32	23	M	CC	ex-Kawana 84, ex-Ace Concord 82
Ocean Commander 1*	1972	22,648	27,109	234	26	21	M	CC	ex-Ocean Commander 85, ex-Oriental Commander 82, ex-Pacific Phoenix 75, ex-Oriental Commander 72
Ocean Legend*	1971	18,936	27,091	235	26	21	M	CC	ex-Oriental Leader 82
Omex Pioneer‡‡	1972	25,514	27,672	235	26	21	M	CC	ex-Oriental Scholar 81, ex-Oriental Educator 80, ex-Atlantic Phoenix 75, ex-Oriental Educator 72
Oriental Ambassador	1977	17,385	17,607	169	25	20	M	CC	ex-Oriental Venture 84, ex-Rhein Express 83, ex-Oriental Venture 81, ex-Manchester Venture 80, ex-Marseille 80, ex-Manchester Venture 79, ex-Seatrain Bennington 79, ex-Manchester Venture 77
Oriental Bravery*	1979	52,340	105,684	252	42	14	M	T	
Oriental Champion†	1966	15,002	17,444	195	24	21	M	CC	ex-Priam 79
Oriental Chief	1976	39,505	41,587	271	31	22	M	CC	
Oriental Diplomat*	1972	30,495	31,830	243	31	21	M2	CC	ex-Seapac Concord 81, ex-Asiafreighter 81
Oriental Educator	1977	36,170	38,743	252	31	23	M	CC	ex-Seapac Lexington 83, ex-Oriental Researcher 81, ex-Oriental Chevalier 78
Oriental Executive*	1977	35,599	38,743	252	31	23	M	CC	
Oriental Expert‡	1977	16,544	16,955	169	25	20	M	CC	ex-Ibn Majid 83, ex-Manchester Vanguard 82, ex-Oriental-Vanguard 81, ex-Manchester Vanguard 80, ex-Keelung 80, ex-Manchester Vanguard 79, ex-Seatrain Trenton 79, ex-Manchester Vanguard 77
Oriental Explorer‡	1976	35,536	39,365	252	31	23	M	CC	ex-Seapac Princeton 83, ex-Oriental Statesman 81
Oriental Exporter†	1967	14,954	16,310	195	24	21	M	CC	ex-Main Express 84, ex-Oriental Exporter 81, ex-Peisander 78
Oriental Freedom	1985	40,978	40,500	(227)	32	21	M	CC	
Oriental Governor*	1971	30,495	31,830	243	31	21	M2	CC	ex-Seapac Trenton 81, ex-Euroliner 81

C. Y. Tung, *Oriental Chief. F. R. Sherlock*

Name	Year	GRT	DWT	LOA	Bm	Kts	Eng	Type	Former names
Oriental Knight‡	1971	29,870	31,830	243	31	21	M2	CC	ex-Seapac Valley Forge 81, ex-Euro-freighter 81
Oriental Majesty*	1972	64,149	138,291	267	44	15	M	T	
Oriental Merchant†	1967	14,863	16,565	195	24	21	M	CC	ex-Oriental Merchant No 1 79, ex-Oriental Merchant 79, ex-Prometheus 79
Oriental Minister*	1972	30,495	31,830	243	31	21	M2	CC	ex-Seapac Bunker Hill 81, ex-Asia-liner 81
Oriental Patriot‡	1981	32,238	30,804	222	32	25	M	CC	
Oriental Phoenix*	1971	65,746	140,606	275	43	16	M	T	
Oriental Premier‡	1978	27,297	33,621	228	28	19	M	CC	ex-Oriental Expert 83
Oriental Prince	1978	27,297	24,035	186	28	19	M	CC	ex-Oriental Ambassador 84
Oriental Sovereign*	1975	41,029	47,150	210	32	15	M	B	
Oriental Star†	1957	9,160	13,778	138	19	14	M	C	
Oriental Taio*	1974	36,952	46,623	206	31	14	M	B	
Pacific Challenge	1981	69,281	127,774	264	41	14	M	B	
Pacific Courage	1982	69,282	123,000	264	41	14	M	B	
Pacific Defender*	1984	17,054	27,300	(167)	23	14	M	B	ex-Santa Lucia 84
Pacific Exporter*	1973	14,362	26,379	172	25	15	M	B	
Pacific Faith*	1973	17,918	28,782	181	25	16	M	B	ex-Union Harvest 83
Pacific Fortune*	1973	12,132	20,813	157	23	15	M	B	ex-Union Brilliancy 83
Pacific Freedom*	1977	16,731	27,544	178	23	16	M	B	ex-Union Beauty 83
Pacific Friendship*	1970	13,867	24,591	175	23	15	M	B	ex-Union Progress 83
Pacific Gallantry*	1985	26,200	41,890	186	30	14	M	B	
Pacific Grace*	1985	26,087	41,890	186	30	14	M	B	
Pacific Greeting	1985	26,200	41,890	186	30	14	M	B	
Pacific Guardian	1985	26,200	41,890	186	30	14	M	B	
Pacific Importer*	1973	16,106	26,454	172	25	15	M	B	
Pacific Insurer*	1973	16,107	26,453	172	25	15	M	B	
Pacific Patriot	1982	28,408	68,980	228	32	15	M	B	
Pacific Peace	1981	38,409	66,844	228	32	15	M	B	
Pacific Prestige	1981	35,840	65,015	225	32	15	M	B	
Pacific Pride	1981	37,562	61,322	228	32	15	M	B	
Pacific Progress	1981	36,032	62,105	224	32	16	M	B	
Pacific Prominence	1982	35,627	64,916	225	32	16	M	B	
Pacific Prosperity	1982	32,229	64,976	228	32	15	M	B	
Paramount Act†	1981	13,730	13,834	186	32	19	M	V	
Pride*	1980	23,290	36,834	175	30	15	M	T	ex-Cys Pride 85, ex-Mototama Maru 84
R. R. Ratna‡	1974	12,102	13,867	161	19	20	M	CC	ex-Manchester Reward 82, ex-TFL Reward 80, ex-Seatrain Norfolk 79, Manchester Reward 79, ex-Asian Reward 78, ex-Manchester Reward 74
Ratih**	1974	12,577	12,126	161	19	20	M	CC	ex-Manchester Renown 82, ex-Asian Renown 78, ex-Manchester Renown 74
Sarda*	1985	50,272	79,900	(234)	40	14	M	T	
Seawise Giant	1976	238,558	564,739	458	69	16	ST	T	ex-Oppama 79
Sentis	1985	50,272	89,570	(234)	40	14	M	T	
Sidelia	1985	50,200	79,900	(234)	40	14	M	T	
South Victor*	1973	54,900	119,500	262	41	15	M	B	ex-Mount Newman 82
Stellaris	1985	50,272	88,186	(234)	40	15	M	T	
Toyota No 23*	1976	10,491	11,457	169	26	19	M	V	
Weser Ore*	1974	139,410	274,326	335	52	12	M2	OBO	ex-Brazilian Wealth 81, ex-Tarfala 78

* Liberian flag

†† Ecuador flag

** Indonesia flag

‡ Taiwan flag

†Panamanian flag

‡‡ Singapore flag

C. Y. Tung, *Oriental Knight. J. Krayenbosch*

UBEM SA
Belgium

Funnel: Yellow with 'U' on white diamond on broad green band
Hull: Grey with red boot-topping

Name	Year	GRT	DWT	LOA	Bm	Kts	Eng	Type	Former names
Kyoto	1973	36,914	64,085	224	32	15	M	B	
Leon & Pierre C	1976	39,240	75,453	242	32	15	M	B	
Zeebrugge	1974	36,914	65,085	224	32	15	M	B	

see also Fednav Ltd

A/S Uglands Rederi
Norway

Funnel: Yellow, red band with white 'U', black top
Hull: Grey with green or red boot-topping

Name	Year	GRT	DWT	LOA	Bm	Kts	Eng	Type	Former names
Akarita‡	1978	109,880	230,683	330	49	16	S	ST	ex-Schelderix 82
Bonita‡	1968	13,767	23,700	160	23	15	M	B	ex-Kristin Brovig 77
Cagayan†	1970	12,636	20,722	159	23	15	M	B	ex-Norita 84, ex-Ingeren 78
Evita	1975	68,977	130,080	268	41	16	M	T	
Favorita	1975	35,512	66,091	219	32	16	M	B	ex-Moldanger 77
Fermita	1976	17,945	29,168	170	26	15	M	B	ex-Moslake 82
Gleneagles†	1984	26,257	43,381	186	30	14	M	BC	
Hera‡	1963	10,097	29,465	185	24	13	M	O	ex-Angelita 78
Hual Angelita	1981	14,165	11,977	180	29	17	M	V	ex-Angelita 82
Hual Carmencita	1983	17,610	15,500	180	31	17	M	V	
Hual Ingrita†	1980	12,369	12,165	180	29	17	M	V	ex-Ingrita 82
Hual Karinita	1980	12,553	15,603	194	32	18	M	Y	ex-Karinita 82
Hual Lisita	1980	14,155	12,003	180	32	17	M	V	ex-Lisita 82
Hual Rolita†	1980	12,369	12,169	180	29	17	M	V	ex-Rolita 82
Hual Torinita	1970	6,535	7,706	159	26	20	M	V	ex-Torinita 82
Iberita††	1981	77,226	144,348	263	43	15	M	B	ex-Tiberius 85
Laurita‡	1970	6,533	7,794	159	26	20	M	V	
Mahinda**	1960	10,950	16,226	157	21	13	M	O	ex-Iron Barque 70
Miranda‡	1968	25,906	51,714	219	31	15	M	B	ex-Lisita 78
Philippine Obo 2†	1984	32,607	55,000	207	32	15	M	OBO	
Philippine Obo 3†	1984	32,607	54,500	207	32	15	M	OBO	
Philippine Obo 4†	1984	32,607	54,500	207	32	15	M	OBO	
Rosyth**	1961	17,444	26,610	184	24	13	M	O	ex-Norita 77, ex-Filefjell 67
Samu‡	1970	11,083	19,024	150	23	15	M	B	ex-Samuel S 85
Savonita†	1971	6,535	7,730	159	26	20	M	V	
Tamarita‡	1976	17,945	29,168	170	26	15	M	B	ex-Mosriver 82
Ugland Obo-One	1983	31,769	54,500	207	32	15	M	OBO	
Ugland Obo 5*	1984	31,758	54,500	207	32	15	M	OBO	
Ugland Obo-Six†	1976	45,330	84,141	253	32	15	M	OBO	ex-Pericles Halcoussis 84
Vivita	1981	30,754	54,626	207	32	15	M	T	ex-Morning Light 84, ex-Viking Lady 83

* Panamanian flag   ** Singapore flag   ‡ Liberian flag   †Philippine flag   †† British flag

Union Industrielle et Maritime SA
France

Funnel: Black, 'UIM' emblem on band between two white rings
Hull: Black

Name	Year	GRT	DWT	LOA	Bm	Kts	Eng	Type	Former names
Amandine	1977	23,627	38,931	185	28	14	M	B	
Eglantine	1968	18,737	31,065	197	23	17	M	B	
Laurentine	1974	15,499	26,638	183	24	15	M	B	

UBEM SA, *Zeebrugge. J. Krayenbosch*

229

Union Navale SA

Funnel: Black, white bordered broad blue band with red diamond containing black interlinked 'un'
Hull: Black

Name	Year	GRT	DWT	LOA	Bm	Kts	Eng	Type	Former names
Cetra Vela†	1974	93,894	169,317	295	47	15	M	OO	

† managed for Consortium Europeen de Transport Maritime

United Arab Shipping Co (SAG)

Funnel: Black, broad white band with green and red bands towards top and bottom, overlaid with black 'A'
Hull: Grey with green boot-topping

Name	Year	GRT	DWT	LOA	Bm	Kts	Eng	Type	Former names
Addiriyah†	1979	20,526	24,272	183	27	17	M	CC	
Ahmad Al-Fateh	1978	15,446	23,618	175	24	16	M	C	
Al Ahmadiah†	1969	14,049	15,763	194	22	18	M	CC	
Al Fujairah	1978	15,446	23,618	175	23	16	M	C	
Al Ihsa'a†	1983	32,534	35,653	211	32	19	M	CC	
Al Manakh	1983	32,534	35,627	211	32	19	M	CC	
Al Mariyah	1983	32,534	35,642	211	32	19	M	CC	
Al Mirqab	1983	32,534	35,615	211	32	19	M	CC	
Al Mubarakiah	1974	15,920	23,841	175	23	16	M	C	
Al Muharraq	1978	15,387	23,740	175	23	16	M	C	
Al Rayyan**	1978	15,043	23,740	175	23	16	M	C	
Al Rumaithiah	1970	14,405	16,850	194	22	18	M	CC	
Al Sabahiah	1968	10,355	13,656	156	21	17	M	C	
Al Salimiah	1974	15,920	23,841	175	23	16	M	C	
Al Shamiah	1968	14,405	17,120	194	22	18	M	CC	
Al Shidadiah	1972	9,859	13,655	156	21	17	M	C	
Al Solaibiah†	1972	9,482	13,717	156	21	17	M	C	
Al Wajba**	1983	33,762	35,596	211	32	19	M	CC	
Al-Wattyah	1979	20,526	24,302	183	27	17	M	CC	
Al Yamamah†	1977	15,041	23,741	175	23	16	M	C	
Arafat†	1978	15,040	23,740	175	23	16	M	C	
Bar'zan**	1979	20,658	24,302	183	27	17	M	CC	ex-Barazan 79
Danah*	1978	15,446	23,618	175	23	16	M	C	
Dubai	1982	32,534	35,615	211	32	19	M	CC	
Fathulkhair**	1978	15,125	23,995	175	23	16	M	C	
Hammurabi	1983	32,534	35,616	211	32	19	M	CC	
Hijaz**	1978	15,043	23,740	175	23	16	M	C	
Ibn Abdoun	1976	15,516	23,890	175	23	16	M	C	
Ibn Al Abbar**	1977	15,125	23,618	175	24	16	M	C	
Ibn Al-Atheer†	1976	15,122	23,800	175	23	16	M	C	
Ibn Al Beitar	1977	15,122	23,618	175	24	16	M	C	
Ibn Al-Haitham	1976	15,516	23,890	175	24	16	M	C	
Ibn Al Moataz†	1977	15,122	23,618	175	24	16	M	C	
Ibn Al-Nafees**	1976	15,122	23,618	175	23	16	M	C	
Ibn Al Roomi†	1976	15,122	23,612	175	23	16	M	C	
Ibn Asakir	1976	15,122	23,618	175	23	16	M	C	
Ibn Bajjah**	1977	15,043	23,830	175	24	16	M	C	
Ibn Bassam**	1977	15,125	23,618	175	24	16	M	C	
Ibn Battotah	1974	15,920	23,891	175	23	16	M	C	
Ibn Duraid‡	1976	15,122	23,618	175	23	16	M	C	
Ibn Hayyan	1975	15,919	23,891	175	23	16	M	C	
Ibn Hazm	1977	15,041	23,890	175	23	16	M	C	
Ibn Jubayr	1977	15,387	23,830	175	24	16	M	C	
Ibn Khaldoon	1976	15,446	23,618	175	23	16	M	C	
Ibn Khallikan	1977	15,122	23,618	175	24	16	M	C	

United Arab Shipping Co (SAG), *Al Ihsa'a. J. M. Kakebeeke*

Name	Year	GRT	DWT	LOA	Bm	Kts	Eng	Type	Former names
Ibn Malik	1977	15,446	23,618	175	24	16	M	C	
Ibn Qutaibah†	1976	15,122	23,618	175	23	16	M	C	
Ibn Rushd	1975	15,919	23,841	175	23	16	M	C	
Ibn Shuhaid	1977	15,446	23,618	175	24	16	M	C	
Ibn Sina**	1977	15,043	23,829	175	24	16	M	C	
Ibn Tufail	1975	15,919	23,841	175	23	16	M	C	
Ibn Younus‡	1977	15,122	23,800	175	24	16	M	C	
Ibn Zuhr†	1977	15,041	23,983	175	24	16	M	C	
Jebel Ali	1979	20,526	24,349	183	27	17	M	CC	
Jilfar	1977	15,446	23,800	175	24	16	M	C	
Khaled Ibn Al Waleed	1983	32,534	35,615	211	32	19	M	CC	
Kubbar*	1978	15,446	23,618	175	23	16	M	C	
Qarouh*	1978	15,446	23,618	175	23	16	M	C	
Qatari Ibn Al Fuja'a**	1983	33,761	35,625	211	32	19	M	CC	
Salah Aldeen	1978	15,041	23,740	175	23	16	M	C	
Tabuk†	1978	15,122	23,618	175	23	16	M	C	
Theekar	1978	15,122	23,618	175	24	16	M	C	

* owned by Kuwait Maritime Transport Co
** Qatar flag
† Saudi Arabian flag
‡ Iraqi flag

United Fruit Company

USA

Fyffes Group Ltd/UK

Funnel: Yellow with white diamond on red band beneath black top
Hull: White with red boot-topping

Name	Year	GRT	DWT	LOA	Bm	Kts	Eng	Type	Former names
Barrydale	1973	6,513	5,818	145	20	20	M	R	ex-Manzanares 84
Bluestream	1973	6,513	6,118	145	20	20	M	R	ex-Magdalena 84
Fleet Wave	1972	6,513	6,127	145	20	20	M	R	ex-Manistee 84
Sky Clipper	1973	6,513	5,911	145	20	20	M	R	ex-Mazatec 84

Empresa Hondurena de Vapores SA/Honduras

Name	Year	GRT	DWT	LOA	Bm	Kts	Eng	Type	Former names
Condata	1968	8,135	10,023	148	20	20	M	R	ex-Tangerinecore 76
Rio Cuyamel	1978	6,405	5,656	133	18	21	M	R	
Rio Sixaola†	1980	6,317	5,656	140	18	22	M	R	ex-Rio Ulua 80
Rio Sulaco*	1978	6,417	5,656	140	18	21	M	R	

† Panamian flag

United States Lines

USA

Funnel: Dark red with white band and blue top
Hull: Black or grey with red boot-topping

Name	Year	GRT	DWT	LOA	Bm	Kts	Eng	Type	Former names
American Accord	1954	15,827	15,452	202	23	18	ST	CC	ex-Pioneer Mart 71, ex-Sunflower Mariner 56
American Ace	1953	15,827	15,452	202	23	18	ST	CC	ex-Pioneer Moor 70, ex-Mountain Mariner 56
American Alabama	1984	57,075	58,500	290	32	18	M	CC	
American Alliance	1954	15,827	15,772	202	23	18	ST	CC	ex-Pioneer Mill 71, ex-Show Me Mariner 56
American Altair	1965	14,001	16,443	203	23	21	ST	CO	ex-Mormacaltair 83
American Apollo	1970	19,127	20,336	215	27	22	ST	CC	
American Aquarius	1971	19,454	20,428	215	27	22	ST	CC	
American Archer	1954	15,827	15,692	202	23	18	ST	CC	ex-Pioneer Mist 71, ex-Peninsular Mariner 56

United States Lines, *American Altair. Table Bay Underway Shipping*

233

Name	Year	GRT	DWT	LOA	Bm	Kts	Eng	Type	Former names
American Argo	1964	14,081	15,244	203	23	21	ST	CO	ex-Mormacargo 83
American Argosy	1953	15,827	15,066	202	23	18	ST	CC	ex-Pioneer Main 70, ex-Cotton Mariner 56
American Astronaut	1969	19,283	20,904	214	27	23	ST	CC	
American Banker	1962	16,518	19,581	204	23	20	ST	CC	ex-Santa Paula 85, ex-President Eisenhower 83, ex-Philippine Mail 75
American Builder	1961	16,518	20,190	204	23	20	ST	CC	ex-Santa Rosa 85, ex-President Roosevelt 83, ex-Washington Mail 75
American California	1985	57,000	58,500	290	32	18	M	CC	
American Draco	1965	14,001	16,443	203	23	21	ST	CO	ex-Mormacdraco 83
American Entente	1973	28,492	31,495	248	27	23	ST	CC	ex-Austral Entente 83
American Envoy	1972	28,492	28,200	248	27	23	ST	CC	ex-Austral Envoy 83
American Illinois	1985	57,000	58,500	290	32	18	M	CC	
American Kentucky	1985	57,000	58,500	290	32	18	M	CC	
American Lancer	1968	19,046	22,582	214	27	23	ST	CC	
American Lark	1969	19,203	20,904	214	27	23	ST	CC	
American Leader	1953	15,864	15,772	202	23	18	ST	CC	ex-Pioneer Minx 70, ex-Gopher Mariner 56
American Legacy	1954	15,854	15,786	202	23	18	ST	CC	ex-Pioneer Ming 71, ex-Silver Mariner 56
American Legend	1954	15,864	15,694	202	23	18	ST	CC	ex-Pioneer Myth 71, ex-Pelican Mariner 56
American Legion	1968	19,157	22,493	214	27	23	ST	CC	
American Liberty	1968	18,894	22,013	214	27	23	ST	CC	
American Lynx	1968	19,203	20,904	214	27	23	ST	CC	
American Maine	1984	57,075	58,620	290	32	18	M	CC	
American Marketer	1972	21,687	19,842	204	27	23	ST	CC	ex-Austral Ensign 81
American Merchant	1972	21,687	19,842	204	27	23	ST	CC	ex-Austral Endurance 81
American Michigan	1985	32,781	24,100	199	32	18	M	RO	ex-Sea Witch 85
American Monarch	1969	13,053	13,285	176	25	23	ST	CO	ex-Wyoming 81
American Moon	1965	11,202	13,477	166	23	21	ST	CO	ex-Mormacmoon 83, ex-Austral Pilot 80, ex-American Rover 69
American Nebraska	1985	57,000	58,500	290	32	18	M	CC	
American New Jersey	1984	57,075	58,620	290	32	18	M	CC	
American New York	1984	57,075	58,870	290	32	18	M	CC	
American Oklahoma	1985	57,000	58,500	290	32	18	M	CC	
American Pioneer	1979	28,222	30,903	248	27	22	ST	CC	ex-Austral Pioneer 83
American Puritan	1980	28,222	30,976	248	27	22	ST	CC	ex-Austral Puritan 83
American Reservist	1964	14,081	15,244	203	23	21	ST	CO	ex-Mormaclynx 83
American Rigel	1965	14,081	15,244	203	23	21	ST	CO	ex-Mormacrigel 83
American Saga	1962	12,724	14,699	172	23	20	ST	C	ex-Mormacsaga 83, ex-M.M. Dant 77
American Sea	1962	12,691	14,554	172	23	20	ST	C	ex-Mormacsea 83, ex-Hawaii 77
American Spitfire	1969	13,053	13,285	176	25	23	ST	CO	ex-Idaho 81
American Tide	1962	12,691	14,620	172	23	20	ST	C	ex-Mormactide 84, ex-Oregon 77
American Titan	1968	13,053	13,285	176	25	23	ST	CO	ex-Colorado 81
American Trader	1971	28,162	30,226	250	31	22	ST	CC	ex-Pacific Bear 79
American Utah	1985	57,000	58,500	290	32	18	M	CC	
American Vega	1964	14,081	12,968	203	23	21	ST	CO	ex-Mormacvega 83
American Veteran	1973	26,456	30,298	250	31	22	ST	LC	ex-Austral Moon 84, ex-Australia Bear 76, ex-Philippine Bear 75
American Virginia	1985	57,000	58,500	290	32	18	M	CC	
American Washington	1985	57,000	58,500	290	32	18	M	CC	
Mormacdawn	1965	11,202	13,477	166	23	21	ST	CO	ex-Austral Patriot 80, ex-American Resolute 69
Mormacglen	1961	9,258	12,590	147	21	19	ST	C	
Mormacwave	1962	12,691	14,591	172	23	20	ST	C	ex-Washington 77

United States Lines, *American Pioneer*. F. R. Sherlock

Delta Steamship Lines Inc

Name	Year	GRT	DWT	LOA	Bm	Kts	Eng	Type	Former names
American Hawaii	1985	32,781	24,100	199	32	18	M	RO	ex-Sea Fox 85
American North Carolina	1984	32,781	24,100	199	32	18	M	RO	ex-Sea Wolf 85
Delta Caribe	1971	26,406	39,564	250	30	22	ST	LC	ex-LASH Turkiye 78
Delta Mar	1973	29,508	41,363	272	31	22	ST	LC	
Delta Norte	1973	29,508	41,363	272	31	22	ST	LC	
Delta Sud	1973	29,508	41,363	272	31	22	ST	LC	

USSR

Funnel: White or black with yellow hammer and sickle on red band
Hull: White, black or red with red boot-topping

Name	Year	GRT	DWT	LOA	Bm	Kts	Eng	Type	Former names
Adler	1973	16,406	27,145	177	23	15	M	B	ex-Ajax 84
Admiral Ushakov	1979	13,572	19,590	162	23	14	M	B	
Agostinho Neto	1980	12,843	17,665	181	28	20	M	RO	ex-Boris Limanov 80
Aitodor	1973	16,406	27,143	177	23	15	M	B	ex-Anchises 83
Akademik Bakulev	1984	31,661	52,450	215	32	14	M	B	
Akademik Davitaya	1983	16,541	24,150	184	23	14	M	B	
Akademik Sechenov	1979	63,146	108,890	258	40	15	M	OBO	
Aleksey Danchenko	1985	31,661	52,450	215	32	14	M	B	
Aleksey Kosygin	1984	37,464	40,881	263	32	20	M	LC	
Alexsandr Matrosov	1974	30,070	52,699	213	32	15	M	B	
Alexsandr Nevskiy	1978	13,572	19,590	162	23	14	M	B	
Aleksandr Saveliev	1978	26,712	44,750	182	30	15	M	B	ex-Torm Hilde 85
Alexsandr Suvorov	1979	13,572	19,590	162	23	14	M	B	
Anatoliy Kolesnichenko	1985	18,574	20,000	174	25	17	M	RO	
Anatoliy Lyapidevskiy	1984	14,009	19,240	162	23	15	M	B	
Anatoliy Vasilyev	1981	15,639	22,447	204	31	22	M	RO	
Anatoliy Zheleznyakov	1984	19,394	8,420	154	29	12	M2	LC	
Aram Khachaturyan	1983	12,030	14,900	162	22	16	M	C	
Arkhangelsk	1983	18,627	19,943	174	25	17	M	RO	
Belgrad	1964	31,817	50,599	231	31	17	ST	T	
Boris Babochkin	1984	12,030	14,930	162	23	16	M	C	
Boris Butoma*	1978	63,180	109,640	259	40	15	M	OBO	
Borodino	1969	31,524	50,569	231	31	17	ST	T	
Bratislava	1964	31,817	50,770	231	31	16	ST	T	
Bratsk	1983	18,627	19,943	174	25	17	M	RO	
Brest	1985	12,000	18,020	172	23	17	M	RO	
Budapesht	1985	15,893	17,850	172	23	17	M	RO	
Burgas	1966	31,524	50,599	235	31	17	ST	T	
Chernovtsy	1983	23,836	38,003	201	27	15	M	B	ex-Natica 85
Chusovoy	1981	23,608	38,498	201	27	15	M	B	ex-Sabinia 85, ex-Doceorion 81
Dmitriy Donskoy	1977	13,567	19,590	162	23	14	M	B	
Dmitriy Pozharskiy	1978	13,481	19,590	162	23	14	M	B	
Dobrush	1982	17,266	28,160	196	23	15	M	B	ex-World Goodwill 85
Dresden	1965	31,817	50,770	230	31	17	ST	T	ex-Gyda 74
Fedor Poletaev	1964	31,294	48,800	227	31	15	M	T	
Filipp Makharadze	1972	20,317	32,404	202	24	15	M	B	
Galileo Galilei	1964	30,269	50,840	227	31	17	M	B	
Gamel Abdel Naser	1980	63,146	108,890	259	40	15	M	OBO	
Gdansk	1965	31,817	50,809	231	31	17	ST	T	
Gdynia	1964	31,817	50,770	231	31	17	ST	T	
General Leselidze	1973	20,512	31,923	202	24	15	M	B	
George Georgiu-Dezh	1966	31,817	50,770	232	31	17	ST	T	
Georgiy Leonidze	1973	20,513	31,923	199	24	16	M	B	
Georgiy Pyasetskiy	1982	12,843	17,773	182	28	20	M	RO	
Geroi Bresta	1966	31,524	50,669	232	31	17	ST	T	
Geroi Monkadly	1984	17,845	16,030	175	24	21	M	CC	
Geroi Stalingrada	1983	31,661	52,450	215	32	14	M	B	

USSR, *Kapitan Kudlay. W. D. Harris*

Name	Year	GRT	DWT	LOA	Bm	Kts	Eng	Type	Former names
Giordano Bruno	1964	31,294	50,720	227	31	15	M	T	
Giuseppe Verdi	1964	30,269	50,840	227	31	16	M	T	
Gorlovka	1976	19,999	34,996	196	24	15	M	B	ex-Pampero 85
Grigoriy Alekseev	1974	18,398	23,606	169	25	15	M	B	
Havana	1964	31,817	50,770	231	31	17	ST	T	
Igarka	1983	18,627	19,943	174	25	17	M	RO	
Inzhener Yermoshkin	1980	14,345	20,075	217	30	25	GT2	RO	
Inzhenier Parkhonyuk	1978	26,712	44,750	183	30	15	M	B	ex-Torm Helene 83
Ion Soltys	1976	30,072	52,699	214	32	15	M	B	
Ivan Bogun	1981	13,511	19,590	162	23	14	M	B	
Ivan Kotiyarevskiy	1970	12,280	15,203	176	21	17	M	CC	
Ivan Makarin	1981	13,520	19,252	162	23	14	M	B	
Ivan Pereverzev	1980	12,030	14,930	162	23	16	M	C	
Ivan Susanin	1981	13,511	19,655	162	23	14	M	B	
Ivan Tevosyan	1982	62,860	108,480	259	40	15	M	OBO	
Izgutty Aytykov	1975	30,072	52,699	214	32	15	M	B	
Julio Antonio Mella	1966	31,524	50,669	232	31	17	ST	T	
Kapitan A. Polkovskiy	1978	15,563	26,016	173	23	15	M	B	ex-Kopelia 83
Kapitan Bochek	1982	13,520	19,240	162	23	14	M	B	
Kapitan Chukhchin	1981	13,520	19,240	162	23	14	M	B	
Kapitan Fomenko	1982	20,699	34,700	186	29	15	M	BC	ex-Bah Kim 83
Kapitan Fomin	1977	18,965	34,318	179	27	15	M	B	ex-Gunver Cord 83
Kapitan Gavrilov	1982	17,720	15,950	174	26	21	M	CC	
Kapitan Kanevskiy	1982	17,720	15,950	174	26	21	M	CC	
Kapitan Kozlovskiy	1982	17,720	15,950	174	26	20	M	CC	
Kapitan Kudlay	1983	14,009	19,240	162	23	15	M	B	
Kapitan Medvedev	1978	15,950	27,536	178	23	15	M	B	ex-Felicia V 83
Kapitan Mezentsyev	1979	14,345	20,075	217	30	25	GT2	RO	
Kapitan Nazarev	1984	14,009	19,240	162	23	15	M	B	
Kapitan Smirnov	1979	14,345	20,075	217	30	25	GT2	RO	
Kapitan Soroka	1981	20,755	34,170	187	29	15	M	C	ex-Sah Kim 83
Kapitan Sviridov	1982	17,757	19,252	162	23	14	M	B	
Kapitan Trubkin	1981	14,441	27,082	171	25	14	M	B	ex-Manila Spirit 83, ex-Jaylock 81
Kapitan Tsirul	1981	13,520	19,252	162	23	14	M	B	
Kapitan V. Trush	1983	17,845	16,030	174	26	20	M	CC	
Kapitan V. Ushakov	1983	17,845	16,030	174	26	20	M	CC	
Kapitan Vakula	1983	14,009	19,240	162	23	15	M	B	
Kapitan Vodenko	1982	13,520	19,240	162	23	15	M	B	
Kavkaz	1977	88,692	150,498	295	45	15	ST	T	
Khudozhnik A. Gerasimov	1977	15,643	24,254	185	23	16	M	B	
Khudozhnik Fedorovskiy	1978	15,643	24,354	185	23	16	M	B	
Khudozhnik Gabashvili	1979	15,643	24,285	185	23	16	M	B	
Khudozhnik Ioganson	1976	15,306	14,490	170	25	20	M	CC	
Khudozhnik Kasyan	1978	15,643	24,354	185	23	16	M	B	
Khudozhnik Kustodiyev	1978	15,643	24,285	185	23	16	M	B	
Khudozhnik Moor	1983	16,502	24,110	185	23	14	M	B	
Khudozhnik Pakhomov	1977	15,306	14,520	170	25	20	M	CC	
Khudozhnik Prorokov	1978	15,306	14,519	170	25	20	M	CC	
Khudozhnik Repin	1978	15,306	14,520	170	25	20	M	CC	
Khudozhnik Romas	1978	15,306	14,520	170	25	20	M	CC	
Khudozhnik Saryan	1975	15,306	14,490	170	25	20	M	CC	
Khudozhnik Toidze	1976	15,662	24,354	185	23	16	M	B	
Khudozhnik Vladimir Serov	1977	15,643	24,354	185	23	16	M	B	
Khudozhnik Zhukov	1976	15,306	14,490	170	25	20	M	CC	
Komsomolets Kubani	1966	31,817	50,770	231	31	17	ST	T	
Komsomolets Leningrada	1968	31,524	50,569	232	31	17	ST	T	
Komsomolsk	1976	15,709	21,002	206	31	22	M	RO	
Konstantin Paustovskiy	1970	12,880	14,300	176	21	17	M	CC	
Kostroma	1985	15,893	17,850	172	23	17	M	RO	
Kremenchug	1985	15,893	17,850	172	23	17	M	RO	

USSR, *Kapitan Smirnov. F. R. Sherlock*

Name	Year	GRT	DWT	LOA	Bm	Kts	Eng	Type	Former names
Krivbass	1979	88,692	150,500	295	45	15	ST	T	
Krym	1975	88,692	150,500	295	45	15	ST	T	
Kuban	1976	88,692	150,500	295	45	15	ST	T	
Kuzbass	1978	88,692	150,500	294	45	15	ST	T	
Kuzma Minin	1980	13,572	19,590	162	23	14	M	B	
Leninsk	1975	19,999	34,995	196	24	15	M	B	ex-Lita 84
Lensovet	1980	49,817	55,729	232	36	16	M	LPG	
Leonid Sobolyev	1985	16,502	25,000	(172)	23	14	M	B	
Magnitogorsk	1976	15,709	21,002	206	31	22	M	RO	
Makeevka	1982	17,265	21,836	196	23	16	M	B	ex-World Shanghai 85
Maksim Mikhaylov	1979	17,834	14,520	170	25	20	M	CC	
Marshal Bagramyan	1984	37,409	67,980	243	32	15	M	T	
Marshal Budyonnyy	1975	59,581	101,877	245	39	14	M	OBO	
Marshal Chukov	1984	38,792	67,980	243	32	15	M	T	
Marshal Govorov	1979	65,763	116,283	246	39	14	M	OBO	
Marshal Grechko	1978	65,763	116,283	246	39	14	M	OBO	
Marshal Konev	1975	59,581	102,538	246	39	15	M	OBO	
Marshal Rokossovskiy	1975	59,581	102,140	246	39	15	M	OBO	
Marshal Vasilyeuskiy	1982	37,409	67,980	243	32	15	M	T	
Marshal Zakharov	1979	65,763	116,283	246	39	14	M	OBO	
Marshal Zhukov	1978	59,638	103,307	244	39	15	M	OBO	
Mikhail Stelmakh	1978	18,639	35,246	177	28	15	M	B	ex-General Mascardo 85, ex-Brisknes 85
Maurice Thorez	1965	31,817	50,770	231	31	17	ST	T	
Mekhanik Afanasyev	1968	31,524	50,600	232	31	17	ST	T	
Mekhanik Dren	1977	15,950	27,536	178	23	15	M	B	ex-Patricia V 83
Mekhanik P. Kilimenchuk	1979	23,080	38,510	202	28	16	M	B	ex-Kamar 83
Mikha Tskhakaya	1972	20,317	32,404	202	24	15	M	B	
Mikhail Kutuzov	1979	13,572	19,590	162	23	14	M	B	
Mikhail Strekalovskiy	1981	13,520	19,547	162	23	14	M	B	
Mossovet	1979	49,817	55,000	233	36	16	M	LPG	
Nadezhda Obukhova	1979	17,834	14,520	170	25	20	M	CC	
Nikel	1984	18,627	19,943	174	25	17	M	RO	
Niko Nikoladze	1972	20,317	32,404	202	24	15	M	B	
Nikolay Cherkasov	1979	12,843	17,665	181	28	20	M	RO	
Nikolay Golovanov	1979	17,834	14,520	170	25	19	M	CC	
Nikolay Kuznetsov	1984	31,661	53,450	215	32	14	M	B	
Nikolay Markin	1984	17,394	8,727	154	29	12	M2	LC	
Nikolay Tikhonov	1983	17,845	16,030	174	25	20	M	CC	
Nikolay Voznesenskiy	1978	22,566	38,250	200	28	15	M	B	
Nizhneyansk	1983	18,627	19,943	174	25	17	M	RO	
Otto Grotevohl	1965	31,817	50,770	230	31	17	ST	T	
Palmiro Togliatti	1965	31,817	50,770	231	31	17	ST	T	
Parfentiy Grechanyy	1975	30,070	52,699	214	32	15	M	B	
Pavel Rybin	1975	18,397	23,625	169	25	15	M	B	
Pavel Vavilov	1981	13,520	19,252	162	23	15	M	B	
Petr Masherov	1982	12,843	18,000	182	28	20	M	RO	
Petr Smorodin	1978	20,164	35,164	177	28	15	M	B	ex-Becknes 83
Petr Velikiy	1978	13,481	19,590	162	23	14	M	B	
Pobyeda	1981	37,409	67,980	243	32	15	M	T	
Professor Kostiukov	1978	26,712	44,750	183	30	15	M	B	ex-Torm Helvig 83
Professor Tovstykh	1985	17,757	16,030	174	25	20	M	CC	
Pyatidesyatiletiye Oktyabrya	1967	31,524	50,600	232	31	17	ST	T	
Raphael	1965	30,269	48,919	228	31	17	M	T	
Richard Sorge	1966	31,524	50,600	232	31	17	ST	T	
Rostov	1984	15,893	18,020	182	28	20	M	RO	
Skulptor Golubkina	1978	12,843	18,459	181	28	20	M	RO	
Skulptor Konenkov	1976	12,718	18,462	181	28	20	M	RO	
Skulptor Vuchetich	1976	12,718	18,462	181	28	20	M	RO	
Skulptor Zalkalns	1978	12,843	18,462	181	28	20	M	RO	

USSR, *Nikolay Golovanov. F. R. Sherlock*

241

Name	Year	GRT	DWT	LOA	Bm	Kts	Eng	Type	Former names
Smolensk	1981	15,639	22,447	204	31	22	M	RO	
Sofia	1963	31,817	50,757	231	31	16	ST	T	
Sovetskaya Neft	1980	88,692	150,000	295	45	17	ST	T	
Sovfracht	1967	26,031	44,470	211	28	16	M	B	ex-Magdi 73, ex-Saara Aarnio 73
Sovietskiy Khudozhnik	1976	15,663	23,454	185	23	16	M	B	
Sovinflot	1969	25,999	44,633	212	28	16	M	B	ex-Olga 73, ex-Annukka Aarnio 73
Stepan Artemenko	1977	15,949	26,200	178	23	15	M	B	ex-Lavinia V 83
Stepan Razin	1980	13,572	19,590	162	22	15	M	B	
Tibor Szamueli	1979	35,877	37,850	266	35	19	M2	LC	
Tikhon Kiselyev	1984	17,845	16,030	174	26	20	M	CC	
Tiksi	1983	18,627	19,943	174	25	17	M	RO	
Unan Avetisyan	1976	30,072	52,699	214	32	15	M	B	
Varna	1964	31,817	50,770	230	31	17	ST	T	
Vasiliy Azhaev	1977	19,169	34,544	180	28	15	M	B	ex-General Roxas 85, ex-Binsnes 82
Vasiliy Koval	1978	26,712	44,750	183	30	15	M	B	ex-Torm Herdis 85
Vasiliy Matuzenko	1982	21,500	38,793	189	28	15	M	B	ex-Maritime Pride 85
Vasiliy Solovyev Sedoy	1984	16,502	24,105	184	23	14	M	B	
Vinnitsa	1984	15,893	17,850	172	23	17	M	RO	
Vladimir Gavrilov	1977	20,384	35,271	177	28	15	M	B	ex-Borgnes 83
Yasnoye	1967	15,810	25,450	180	23	15	M	B	ex-Cornas 79, ex-Torm Gyda 77, ex-Gyda 74
Yemelyan Pugachev	1980	13,572	19,590	162	22	15	M	B	
Yevgeniy Vakhtangov	1984	16,451	24,150	184	23	14	M	B	
Yulius Fuchik	1978	35,817	37,850	266	35	20	M2	LC	
Yuriy Dolorukiy	1980	13,511	19,590	162	22	15	M	B	
Zadonsk	1970	16,331	22,686	187	23	15	M	B	
Zakarpatye	1969	16,015	22,884	187	23	15	M	B	
Zaporozhye	1968	16,015	22,884	187	23	15	M	B	
Zarechensk	1968	16,043	22,884	187	23	15	M	B	
Zlatoust	1969	16,015	22,884	187	23	15	M	B	
Zolotye Dyuny	1983	12,383	9,360	153	22	17	M	R	
Zorinsk	1970	16,063	22,686	187	23	15	M	B	
Zoya Kosmodemyanskaya	1973	30,070	49,999	214	32	15	M	B	
Zvenigorod	1967	16,043	22,895	187	23	15	M	B	

this fleet list only includes tankers over 30,000grt and dry cargo vessels over 12,000grt. In addition, there are over 100 tankers between 10,000-29,999grt, nearly 200 cargo vessels between 10,000-11,999grt and a large number of smaller vessels.

Phs Van Ommeren NV

Netherlands

Funnel: Black with white 'V' inside white 'O'
Hull: Grey with red boot-topping

Name	Year	GRT	DWT	LOA	Bm	Kts	Eng	Type	Former names
Kieldrecht	1977	16,281	28,363	178	23	15	M	B	
Loosdrecht	1978	21,816	36,071	175	28	15	M	B	ex-Amax Mariner 80
Meerdrecht	1978	26,680	44,600	191	32	16	M	BC	ex-Seatrain Rotterdam 79, ex-Meerdrecht 78
Menhir†	1971	15,553	25,651	180	23	16	M	B	ex-Penhir 79
Mijdrecht	1978	26,844	44,602	191	32	16	M	BC	ex-Seatrain Amsterdam 79, ex-Mijdrecht 78
Moordrecht	1979	26,845	44,600	191	32	16	M	BC	
Rio Plata†	1970	13,836	24,594	175	23	14	M	B	ex-Ocean Navigator 79, ex-Cosmos Fomalhaut 78
Wieldrecht	1982	26,171	41,219	187	30	16	M	BC	
Willine Tokyo	1982	26,171	41,800	187	30	16	M	BC	ex-Waardrecht 84, ex-Ibn Al Kadi 83, ex-Waardrecht 82
Woensdrecht	1982	26,171	41,820	187	30	16	M	BC	

† Liberian flag

242

Above: USSR, *Sofia. M. D. J. Lennon*

Below: Phs Van Ommeren NV, *Mijdrecht. J. K. Byass*

Phs Van Ommeren (France) SA/France

Funnel: Black with two narrow white bands on broad green band
Hull: Black with red boot-topping

Name	Year	GRT	DWT	LOA	Bm	Kts	Eng	Type	Former names
Port Bara	1982	18,999	29,992	173	28	15	M	T	
Port Blanc	1975	21,267	37,797	186	26	15	M	T	ex-Finnanger 85
Port Joinville	1972	15,026	25,228	175	25	14	M	T	ex-Elissa 80, ex-Harmaliyah 79, ex-Wilke 77
Port Vendres	1973	15,285	25,253	175	25	16	M	T	ex-Mont-Agel 81, ex-Wiiri 78

Dock Express BV/Netherlands

Funnel: Blue, broad white band with two red rings, and red diamond outline with blue 'DES'
Hull: Orange with blue 'DOCK EXPRESS', with red boot-topping

Name	Year	GRT	DWT	LOA	Bm	Kts	Eng	Type
Dock Express 10	1979	5,496	7,071	154	27	16	M2	HLS
Dock Express 11	1979	5,496	7,071	154	27	16	M2	HLS
Dock Express 12	1979	5,496	7,071	154	27	16	M2	HLS
Dock Express 20	1983	14,319	14,591	164	26	15	M2	HLS

Cia Naviera Vascongada SA   Spain

Funnel: Black with interlinking red 'V' and blue 'N' on broad white band
Hull: Black with red boot-topping

Name	Year	GRT	DWT	LOA	Bm	Kts	Eng	Type
Banderas	1970	15,528	27,179	183	22	14	M	B
Cobetas	1973	15,525	27,400	183	22	14	M	B
Serantes	1969	15,494	27,062	183	22	14	M	B
Valentina Frias	1960	8,691	13,614	144	19	13	M	C

F. A. Vinnen & Co   FRG

Funnel: Black with black 'M' on broad white band
Hull: Black with red boot-topping

Name	Year	GRT	DWT	LOA	Bm	Kts	Eng	Type	Former names
Merkur Bay*	1981	8,832	12,720	150	21	17	M	C	
Merkur Beach*	1984	10,383	12,680	150	21	17	M	C	
Merkur Delta*	1984	10,383	12,680	150	21	17	M	C	
Merkur Island*	1985	15,000	24,400	166	27	19	M	C	
Merkur Lake*	1982	8,719	12,720	150	21	17	M	C	
Merkur River*	1980	8,842	12,720	150	21	17	M	C	ex-Lloyd Hudson 82, ex-Merkur River 81
Merkur Sea	1984	16,500	20,000	166	27	18	M	CC	

* Liberian flag

Wallenius Rederierna   Sweden

Funnel: Yellow with yellow 'OW' on broad green band
Hull: Green with red boot-topping

Name	Year	GRT	DWT	LOA	Bm	Kts	Eng	Type	Former names
Aida	1973	23,767	28,565	221	32	15	M	V	
Aniara	1978	16,886	12,178	196	32	20	M	V	ex-Avesta 83
Atlantic Prelude	1972	11,017	9,663	162	19	15	M2	RO	ex-Incotrans Prelude 85, ex-Atlantic Prelude 83, ex-Montmorency 78
Carmen	1982	18,661	28,100	200	32	19	M	V	
Don Carlos	1976	14,479	15,000	201	27	19	M	V	
Don Juan	1975	14,480	15,000	201	27	19	M	V	
Falstaff	1985	52,800	16,800	200	32	20	M	V	
Faust	1985	52,800	16,800	200	32	20	M	V	

Above: Phs Van Ommeren NV/Dock Express BV, *Dock Express 20. J. Krayenbosch*

Above: F. A. Vinnen & Co, *Merkur Bay. F. R. Sherlock*

Below: Wallenius Rederierna, *Carmen. F. R. Sherlock*

Name	Year	GRT	DWT	LOA	Bm	Kts	Eng	Type	Former names
Figaro	1981	18,661	28,210	200	32	19	M	V	
Isolda	1985	23,850	17,000	200	32	19	M	V	
Madame Butterfly	1981	18,728	28,223	200	32	19	M	V	
Medea	1982	18,661	28,100	200	32	19	M	V	
Oberon†	1974	12,138	15,249	197	28	20	M	V	ex-Univenture No 1 83
Otello	1974	23,761	28,283	221	32	15	M	V	
Rigoletto	1977	17,502	13,438	192	32	21	M	V	
Tosca	1978	16,883	12,197	196	32	20	M	V	
Traviata	1977	17,511	13,446	192	32	21	M	V	
Tristan	1985	51,071	28,070	200	32	19	M	V	

see also Atlantic Container Line
† Singapore flag

Waterman Steamship Corp

USA

Funnel: Yellow with black 'W' on white diamond on broad blue band
Hull: Black with red boot-topping

Name	Year	GRT	DWT	LOA	Bm	Kts	Eng	Type	Former names
Robert E. Lee	1974	28,580	41,578	272	31	22	ST	LC	
Sam Houston	1974	28,580	41,578	272	31	22	ST	LC	
Stonewall Jackson	1974	28,580	41,578	272	31	22	ST	LC	

Reederi Jonny Wesch

FRG

Funnel: Yellow, white 'W' on blue diamond on blue-edged broad white band
Hull: Black or grey with red boot-topping

Name	Year	GRT	DWT	LOA	Bm	Kts	Eng	Type	Former names
Bold Eagle	1985	5,950	12,500	146	23	18	M	CC	
Christian Wesch	1980	8,191	10,800	142	22	15	M	C	
Jonny Wesch	1980	8,187	10,800	142	22	15	M	C	ex-Bretagne 83, ex-Jonny Wesch 83
Kirsten Wesch*	1976	4,612	8,182	118	18	15	M	C	
Magdalena Wesch	1980	8,187	10,800	142	22	15	M	C	
Norasia Gabrielle	1983	18,540	25,085	169	26	16	M	BC	ex-Victoria Bay 83, ex-Gabrielle Wesch 83
Norasia Karsten	1983	18,553	25,855	169	26	16	M	BC	ex-Karsten Wesch 83
Norasia Rebecca	1982	18,535	25,085	169	26	16	M	BC	ex-Rebecca Wesch 83
Norasia Samantha	1985	19,400	27,150	172	28	17	M	CC	
Norasia Susan	1985	19,400	27,150	172	28	17	M	CC	
Proud Eagle	1985	9,700	12,500	146	23	18	M	CC	
Sandra Wesch	1979	8,193	10,800	142	22	15	M	C	ex-Ville de Sandra 82, ex-Sandra Wesch 81, ex-Tynebank 80, ex-Sandra Wesch 79
Wild Eagle	1985	10,300	13,300	146	23	18	M	CC	
Wilhelm Wesch*	1971	8,223	11,000	146	19	17	M	C	ex-Isla Pinzon 84, ex-Wilhelm Wesch 83, ex-Lloyd Maryland 81, ex-Wilhelm Wesch 80, ex-Ilri 79, ex-Newfoundland 75, ex-Ana Luisa 74, ex-Ilri 72

* Singapore flag

Westfal-Larsen & Co A/S

Norway

Funnel: Yellow with narrow black top and two narrow black bands
Hull: Grey with green boot-topping

Name	Year	GRT	DWT	LOA	Bm	Kts	Eng	Type	Former names
Austanger*	1982	13,331	23,077	159	23	14	M	T	
Berganger	1980	19,882	35,000	174	32	15	M	T	

Above: Reederi Jonny Wesch, *Norasia Rebecca. F. R. Sherlock*

Below: Westfal-Larsen & Co A/S, *Torvanger. J. Y. Freeman*

Name	Year	GRT	DWT	LOA	Bm	Kts	Eng	Type	Former names
Brimanger	1977	17,057	28,088	171	25	17	M	T	
Dalanger†	1982	16,949	29,912	174	25	15	M	T	
Grenanger*	1982	13,331	23,077	159	23	16	M	T	
Hardanger	1972	6,823	8,700	125	19	17	M	LPG	
Mauranger	1981	18,715	33,695	183	30	15	M	T	ex-Kaupanger 81
Nordanger	1976	17,056	28,060	171	25	17	M	T	
Orkanger	1970	13,003	21,718	171	22	15	M	T	
Porsanger	1976	17,056	28,060	171	25	17	M	T	
Risanger	1976	16,890	28,025	171	25	17	M	T	
Spinanger	1977	17,057	28,053	171	25	17	M	T	
Torvanger	1976	17,057	28,025	171	25	17	M	T	

* Panamanian flag   † owned by Naess Shipping (Holland) BV, Liberian flag
operated by Odfjell Westfal-Larsen Tankers A/S formed jointly with A/S Rederiet Odfjell q.v.

Wijsmuller BV   Netherlands

Funnel: Blue with white band beneath black top
Hull: Grey

Name	Year	GRT	DWT	LOA	Bm	Kts	Eng	Type	Former names
Mighty Servant 1	1983	19,954	23,760	160	40	14	ME2	HLS	
Mighty Servant 2	1983	21,162	25,743	170	40	14	ME2	HLS	
Mighty Servant 3	1984	22,391	27,720	181	40	14	ME2	HLS	
Super Servant 1	1979	10,184	14,449	139	32	13	M2	HLS	
Super Servant 3	1982	10,135	14,138	140	32	13	M2	HLS	
Super Servant 4	1982	10,135	14,138	140	32	13	M2	HLS	
Super Servant 5	1982	10,282	13,282	139	32	13	M2	HLS	ex-Dan Lifter 85
Super Servant 6	1982	10,282	13,310	139	32	13	M2	HLS	ex-Dan Mover 85

Anders Wilhelmsen & Co A/S   Norway

Funnel: Black with white 'W' on red/black divided diamond on broad white band with two red rings
Hull: Grey with red boot-topping

Name	Year	GRT	DWT	LOA	Bm	Kts	Eng	Type	Former names
Wilanna	1985	44,000	76,000	229	32	15	M	T	
Wilmona	1978	40,392	63,787	225	32	15	M	B	
Wilnina	1977	40,392	61,840	225	32	15	M	B	
Wilnora	1977	80,751	125,457	285	44	16	M	T	ex-Thalassini Niki 79

Wilh. Wilhelmsen   Norway

Funnel: Black with two light blue bands close together
Hull: Black with white line and red boot-topping

Name	Year	GRT	DWT	LOA	Bm	Kts	Eng	Type	Former names
Barber Taif	1979	21,976	31,931	229	32	22	M	RO	
Barber Tampa	1984	28,287	44,013	262	32	21	M	RO	
Barber Texas	1984	28,287	44,080	262	32	21	M	RO	
Barber Toba	1979	22,008	32,015	229	32	22	M	RO	
Barber Tonsberg	1979	22,070	31,800	229	32	22	M	RO	
Hoegh Carrier	1977	18,994	27,937	171	26	17	M	C	ex-Terrier 85, ex-Barber Terrier 84, ex-Terrier 81
Rosa Tucano	1985	31,050	17,930	185	32	17	M	RO	
Tachibana‡	1974	36,243	64,567	224	32	15	M	B	

Above: Wijsmuller BV, *Mighty Servant 1. F. de Vries*

Below: Wilh. Wilhelmsen, *Rosa Tucano. J. Krayenbosch*

Name	Year	GRT	DWT	LOA	Bm	Kts	Eng	Type	Former names
Tacna II**	1977	18,834	27,750	171	26	17	M	C	ex-Thermopylae 85, ex-Als Confidence 84, ex-Barber Thermopylae 84, ex-Thermopylae 81
Takasago†	1972	36,354	63,416	224	32	15	M	B	ex-Tambo River 79, ex-Takasago 75
Takayama**	1983	9,959	10,599	165	28	18	M	V	
Talabot†	1977	39,562	70,610	234	32	15	M	B	ex-Tamesis 84
Tarcoola	1977	64,692	121,200	268	39	15	M	B	
Tatra†	1977	39,562	69,600	234	32	15	M	B	ex-Tagus 84
Taurus	1984	29,919	55,289	207	32	14	M	T	ex-Taurus Horten 85
Tennessee	1977	18,998	27,807	171	26	17	M	C	ex-Barber Tennessee 85, ex-Tennesse 81
Thalatta	1973	65,329	120,143	261	41	15	M	B	ex-Yu Sing 83, ex-Erskine Bridge 83
Theben**	1977	17,880	31,600	171	26	16	M	T	ex-Crown Inland 83, ex-Inland 82
Themis	1976	64,076	122,976	272	39	16	M	B	ex-You're My Sunshine 84, ex-Fernsea 81
Toluma	1985	44,000	72,000	229	32	15	M	T	
Tongala	1977	64,718	121,300	268	39	15	M	B	
Toro Horten	1983	30,050	55,337	207	32	15	M	T	
Tourcoing	1978	22,435	31,460	229	32	20	M	RO	
Toyama	1972	57,123	39,949	289	32	26	M3	CC	
Troll Lake†	1971	22,160	33,932	183	27	16	M	B	
Troll Maple**	1970	24,102	41,300	192	30	15	M	B	ex-Kelkheim 82, ex-Roland Kelkheim 71, ex-Kelkheim 70
Troll Viking**	1971	24,102	41,270	192	30	15	M	B	ex-Mannheim 82, ex-Roland Bremen 74
Willine Taro*	1970	20,222	22,150	187	26	15	M	CC	ex-Troll Forest 80
Willine Toyo	1969	17,631	26,100	175	27	15	M	CC	ex-Havrais 80, ex-Conon Forest 80
Willine Tysla*	1977	12,755	21,981	171	26	17	M	C	ex-Tysla 82

* Singapore flag   ** Liberian flag
‡ managed on behalf of Morten Werring's Rederi, British flag
† British flag
joint owner of 'NOSAC', see under O. Lorentzen A/S

Idwal Williams & Co Ltd

UK

Funnel: Red 'G' on white over green bands separating white from black top
Hull: Green with dark green boot-topping

Name	Year	GRT	DWT	LOA	Bm	Kts	Eng	Type	Former names
OT Garth	1974	18,309	31,241	171	26	15	M	T	ex-Sofie 85
Graiglas	1974	57,255	108,144	254	41	15	M	B	ex-Benwyvis 83, ex-Alnwick Castle 81
Green Rock	1966	5,392	7,975	113	16	14	M	B	ex-Cymbeline 84, ex-Dalewood 74
Nassau Pride*	1968	56,871	108,649	261	41	15	M	B	ex-Graigffion 85, ex-Energy Pioneer 83, ex-Mount Pelion 83, ex-Skaufast 78

* Bahamas flag

World-Wide Shipping

Hong Kong (UK)

Funnel: Blue, white 'W' on red band bordered by white bands
Hull: Black

Name	Year	GRT	DWT	LOA	Bm	Kts	Eng	Type	Former names
Asia Culture*	1971	48,868	104,942	253	39	15	M	OBO	
Asia Heron*	1974	20,513	33,092	185	26	14	M	B	
Asia Industry*	1974	20,513	33,034	185	26	14	M	B	
Beau Fortune*	1981	33,539	64,120	225	32	15	M	B	ex-Danelock 85
Beau Success‡	1981	36,202	64,120	225	32	15	M	B	ex-Manila Honour 85, ex-Hydrolock 84

Above: Wilh. Wilhelmsen, *Theben. J. Krayenbosch*

Below: World-Wide Shipping, *Star World. J. Krayenbosch*

Name	Year	GRT	DWT	LOA	Bm	Kts	Eng	Type	Former names
Crown Bridge†	1982	24,655	48,531	177	32	14	M	T	ex-World Bridge 82
Donau Ore*	1971	113,173	218,957	328	50	15	ST	OBO	ex-World Era 81, ex-Jarl Malmros 79
Eastern Hazel	1972	41,164	76,370	238	36	16	M	OBO	
Eastern Spirit*	1972	85,565	164,742	295	47	16	ST	OBO	
Golden Bliss*	1976	19,633	34,320	186	26	17	M	B	
Golden Canary*	1977	19,471	31,030	184	26	15	M	T	ex-Golden Crane 78
Golden Cape*	1976	19,459	30,907	184	26	15	M	T	ex-Sweet Briar 76
Golden Clover*	1971	89,138	164,639	295	47	16	ST	BO	
Golden Lotus*	1971	15,922	26,635	171	23	15	M	B	
Golden Rio*	1979	20,331	38,186	194	28	16	M	B	ex-Weinheim 79
Golden Tulip*	1971	89,137	164,516	295	47	16	ST	BO	
Philippine Sampagulta‡	1981	31,006	65,535	224	32	14	M	B	ex-Kuniang 84
Star Hong Kong	1978	26,925	43,052	183	31	15	M	B	
Star Magnate	1978	26,925	43,051	183	31	15	M	B	
Star Mercury	1983	22,148	37,497	186	28	15	M	B	ex-Star Teresa 85
Star Orient†	1982	19,653	37,599	186	28	15	M	B	
Star World	1978	26,925	43,051	183	31	15	M	B	
United Approach	1983	34,446	61,539	223	32	14	M	B	
United Drive	1982	9,282	15,175	144	20	15	M	C	
United Effort	1982	9,282	15,000	144	20	15	M	C	
United Enterprise	1982	9,282	15,191	144	20	15	M	C	
United Faith†	1982	29,787	61,569	223	32	14	M	B	
United Hope†	1983	37,995	69,011	229	32	14	M	B	
United Peace†	1984	28,822	37,000	168	32	15	M	T	
United Spirit	1982	9,282	15,175	144	20	15	M	C	
World Admiral*	1974	106,673	237,311	324	53	15	ST	T	
World Ambassador*	1975	106,799	237,474	324	53	15	ST	T	
World Amber*	1980	28,448	55,245	216	36	15	M	T	
World Bermuda*	1974	117,775	275,937	337	55	16	ST	T	ex-World Monarch 74
World Brasilia*	1976	133,894	283,761	343	51	15	ST	T	
World Brigadier†	1974	105,179	233,348	319	53	16	ST	T	
World Canada*	1974	122,193	276,574	341	54	16	ST	T	
World Castle†	1982	24,655	48,532	177	32	14	M	T	ex-World Cosmos 83
World Challenger*	1973	85,737	164,338	314	44	15	M	OBO	
World Cheer†	1980	14,441	27,148	183	25	15	M	B	
World Cliff†	1981	41,893	88,272	244	42	15	M	T	ex-Cliff 84, ex-World Cliff 83
World Creation*	1976	39,411	56,786	224	33	16	M	LPG	
World Crown*	1974	107,955	23,082	324	53	16	ST	T	
World Crystal†	1982	13,275	23,791	160	25	17	M	B	
World Dawn†	1981	41,893	88,260	244	42	15	M	T	
World Diamond†	1982	13,275	23,415	160	25	17	M	B	
World Dove†	1982	32,231	67,670	235	32	14	M	B	
World Duke†	1975	111,406	241,297	324	54	16	ST	T	
World Dulce	1981	63,076	133,361	271	43	14	M	B	
World Eden	1981	72,940	138,102	270	43	14	M	B	
World Eminence*	1975	115,323	261,729	338	52	15	ST	T	
World Encouragement*	1978	40,894	81,282	236	41	15	M	T	
World Fame†	1980	41,912	81,561	249	42	15	M	T	
World Finance*	1975	20,513	33,034	185	26	14	M	B	
World Fortress†	1982	13,281	23,794	168	25	17	M	B	
World Flora*	1980	32,342	67,958	220	35	15	M	B	
World Freeport*	1980	25,728	51,248	209	32	15	M	T	
World Gala*	1973	133,748	286,981	338	55	15	M	OBO	ex-Svealand 78
World Hitachi Zosen*	1975	124,879	268,904	331	51	16	ST	T	
World Jade†	1982	29,781	61,349	223	32	14	M	B	
World Light	1981	72,910	134,060	270	43	14	M	B	
World Nancy†	1981	32,231	67,485	235	32	14	M	B	
World Nisseki*	1974	124,871	268,467	331	51	15	ST	T	
World NKK*	1973	115,354	266,169	338	52	15	ST	T	
World Oak	1983	22,148	36,701	186	28	15	M	B	

Above: World-Wide Shipping, *United Drive.* F. R. Sherlock

Below: World-Wide Shipping, *World Spring.* J. M. Kakebeeke

Name	Year	GRT	DWT	LOA	Bm	Kts	Eng	Type	Former names
World Pearl†	1982	23,436	37,415	190	28	14	M	B	
World Petrobras*	1977	193,779	411,508	362	70	15	ST	T	
World President†	1984	37,955	69,041	229	32	14	M	B	
World Progress*	1972	105,787	237,285	231	52	15	ST	T	
World Radiance*	1974	64,820	141,671	267	44	15	M	T	
World Rainbow†	1971	36,917	49,724	224	35	15	M	LPG	
World Ranger*	1978	40,894	81,282	236	41	15	M	T	
World Renown*	1974	118,475	262,267	333	55	15	ST	T	
World Sky†	1971	36,556	49,486	211	33	15	M	LPG	ex-World Bridgestone 85
World Spear	1983	37,955	69,001	229	32	14	M	B	
World Splendour*	1972	89,138	164,190	295	47	16	ST	OBO	
World Spring†	1985	30,230	37,000	168	32	15	M	T	
World Sun*	1974	122,348	260,064	341	52	15	ST	T	ex-Pacific Sun 79
World Symphony*	1975	164,717	356,324	363	60	15	ST	T	ex-Sea Symphony 80
World Texas*	1980	25,727	51,248	209	32	15	M	T	
World Trophy*	1975	114,574	258,488	339	54	15	ST	T	
World Truth*	1972	113,950	249,223	326	52	15	ST	OBO	ex-La Loma 78
World Vale*	1982	87,133	194,941	300	50	14	M	B	
World Zeal†	1981	41,911	81,162	244	42	15	M	T	

* Liberian flag   † Panamian flag   ‡ Philippine flag

Yangming Marine Transport Corp

Taiwan

Funnel: Black with red over yellow bands
Hull: Grey with 'YANG MING LINE' in red, red boot-topping

Name	Year	GRT	DWT	LOA	Bm	Kts	Eng	Type	Former names
Ming Autumn	1978	18,555	29,112	172	28	15	M	B	
Ming Belle	1974	17,573	28,787	181	25	16	M	B	
Ming Cheer	1970	14,199	14,299	187	23	19	M	CC	ex-Chii Ming 77, ex-Hai Yeh 73
Ming Comfort	1982	30,779	30,637	210	32	23	M	CC	
Ming Courage	1984	36,303	66,754	230	32	15	M	B	
Ming Energy	1983	30,779	30,800	210	32	23	M	CC	
Ming Fortune	1983	30,779	30,800	210	32	23	M	CC	
Ming Galaxy	1980	30,730	31,264	210	32	20	M	CC	
Ming Glory	1980	30,730	31,208	210	32	21	M	CC	
Ming Hope	1970	14,366	14,393	187	23	19	M	CC	ex-Ho Ming 77, ex-Hai Mou 73
Ming Joy	1972	16,056	26,447	166	25	14	M	B	ex-Ji Ming 77, ex-Hai Jung 73
Ming Leader	1971	16,056	26,477	165	25	14	M	B	ex-Li Ming 77, ex-Hai Lo 73
Ming Longevity	1983	30,779	30,800	210	32	23	M	CC	
Ming Mercy	1984	36,303	66,799	230	32	15	M	B	
Ming Moon	1980	30,730	31,246	210	32	22	M	CC	
Ming Ocean	1980	30,730	31,208	210	32	23	M	CC	
Ming Shine	1971	16,061	26,459	166	25	14	M	B	ex-Shin Ming 77, ex-Hai Chuan 73
Ming Spring	1978	18,555	29,129	172	28	15	M	B	
Ming Star	1980	30,731	31,251	210	32	21	M	CC	
Ming Summer	1978	18,554	29,121	172	28	15	M	B	
Ming Sun	1980	30,731	30,752	210	32	22	M	CC	
Ming Universe	1980	30,731	31,206	210	32	23	M	CC	
Ming Winter	1978	18,555	29,111	172	28	15	M	B	
Ming Wisdom	1984	36,303	66,786	230	32	15	M	B	

Cie Maritime Zairoise

Zaire

Funnel: Green, with yellow 'CMZ' on red disc
Hull: Grey, with red boot-topping

Name	Year	GRT	DWT	LOA	Bm	Kts	Eng	Type	Former names
Bandundu	1974	9,441	15,322	140	22	16	M	C	
Bukavu	1975	9,438	15,079	140	22	16	M	C	
Kananga	1973	13,481	15,350	161	23	19	M	CO	
Kisangani	1975	9,440	15,079	140	22	16	M	C	

Above: Yangming Marine Transport Corp, *Ming Energy.* J. Krayenbosch

Below: Cie Maritime Zairoise, *Kananga.* J. M. Kakebeeke

Name	Year	GRT	DWT	LOA	Bm	Kts	Eng	Type	Former names
Lumumba	1974	9,448	15,082	140	22	16	M	C	
Mbandaka	1975	9,440	15,082	140	22	16	M	C	
Mbuji Mayi	1975	9,438	15,079	140	22	16	M	C	

Zim Israel Navigation Co Ltd   Israel

Funnel: White with seven gold stars between two blue bands
Hull: White or grey with green boot-topping, or Black with red boot-topping

Name	Year	GRT	DWT	LOA	Bm	Kts	Eng	Type	Former names
Aquila*	1974	112,825	225,668	330	49	15	ST	T	
Atara‡	1984	93,052	166,013	290	47	15	M	B	
Beer Sheva*	1973	25,647	51,913	219	31	15	M	B	ex-Thorunn 83
Besor*	1976	32,567	60,740	224	32	15	M	B	ex-Bonnieway 82
Gold Leaf*	1964	7,070	9,382	139	18	16	M	C	ex-Qeshet 73
Gold Mountain*	1963	7,076	9,725	138	18	16	M	C	ex-Tsedek 74
Gold Stream*	1963	7,062	9,555	138	18	16	M	C	ex-Sahar 74
Hadera*	1983	93,052	166,000	290	47	15	M	B	
Iris	1973	8,243	4,174	128	21	16	M2	RO	
Kedma	1978	9,189	16,436	145	22	16	M	B	ex-Montalto 79, ex-Moncey 79
Moran	1978	11,872	18,043	152	23	14	M	B	ex-Timur Star 81
Narcis	1973	8,224	4,174	128	21	16	M2	RO	
Negba	1977	10,604	17,527	148	22	14	M	B	ex-Tengco 79
Palmah II	1978	6,066	8,732	128	20	17	M	CC	ex-Zim Sydney 83, ex-Palmah II 79
Raqefet	1979	6,066	8,570	128	20	17	M	CC	
Sigal	1976	6,066	8,570	130	20	17	M	CC	
Vered	1978	6,066	8,570	128	20	17	M	CC	ex-Zim Melbourne 80, ex-Vered 78
Virgo*	1974	112,835	225,668	330	49	15	ST	T	
Yama 1†	1978	9,189	16,422	145	22	16	M	B	ex-Hellespont 80, ex-Montechristo 79, ex-L'Acropole 78
Zim Buenos Aires	1977	12,236	16,997	154	23	16	M	RO	ex-Zim Livorno 85, ex-Wilri 79
Zim California	1971	23,367	25,121	208	31	25	ST	CC	ex-Taeho 76, ex-Ariel 71
Zim Eilat	1983	11,860	14,920	153	23	15	M	CC	
Zim Genova	1972	26,024	25,199	208	31	23	ST	CC	
Zim Haifa	1972	26,024	25,199	208	31	23	ST	CC	
Zim Hong Kong	1973	24,575	31,846	219	29	23	ST	CC	
Zim Houston	1978	14,939	19,800	169	23	16	M	C	ex-Lagos Star 80
Zim Iberia	1982	29,373	29,547	210	32	22	M	CC	
Zim Keelung	1981	29,373	29,082	210	32	22	M	CC	
Zim Marseilles	1979	14,938	19,800	145	22	16	M	C	ex-Kobe Star 80
Zim Miami	1978	14,938	19,787	165	22	16	M	C	ex-Abidjan Star 80
Zim Montreal	1973	24,575	31,846	219	29	23	ST	CC	
Zim New Orleans	1979	14,938	19,800	145	22	16	M	C	ex-Tema Star 80
Zim New York	1972	25,830	24,815	208	31	23	ST	CC	ex-Thermopylae 72
Zim Savannah	1981	29,373	23,969	210	32	22	M	CC	
Zim Singapore	1982	11,859	14,921	153	23	15	M	CC	
Zim Tokyo	1972	25,830	25,212	208	31	23	ST	CC	ex-Serica 72

* Liberian flag   ‡ British flag
† Panamanian flag

Haverton Shipping Ltd/UK

Name	Year	GRT	DWT	LOA	Bm	Kts	Eng	Type	Former names
Gold Alisa	1973	11,897	18,863	147	23	16	M	C	ex-Alisa 80
Gold Hilla	1973	11,897	18,863	147	23	16	M	C	ex-Hilla 79
Gold Orli	1973	11,897	18,863	147	23	16	M	C	ex-Orli 79
Gold Varda	1973	11,895	18,863	147	23	16	M	C	ex-Varda 79

Zim Israel Navigation Co Ltd, *Zim New Orleans. Table Bay Underway Shipping*

Above: The British Petroleum Co Ltd, *British Skill.* British Petroleum Co Ltd

Addenda

Details of latest new deliveries/launches, name changes, sales, demolitions and fleet changes up to the end of January 1986.

PART ONE

Chandris SA
Regina Prima broken up

CTM-Cia Portuguesa de Transportes Maritimos
Funchal sold to Epirotiki Lines

Cunard Line Ltd
Queen Elizabeth 2 to be re-engined between 10/1986 and 4/1987

VEB Deutfracht/Seereederei
Volkerfreundschaft sold and renamed *Volker* (Panamanian flag)

Epirotiki Steamship Nav Co SA
Funchal acquired from CTM

Home Lines Inc
Oceanic reported sold to Premier Cruises

P & O Steam Nav Co Ltd
Oriana to be withdrawn 3/1986

USSR
Mikhail Lermontov sunk off New Zealand on 16 February 1986

PART TWO

Ahlers NV
Isla Payana renamed *Potomac*

Christian F. Ahrenkiel
Aquitania renamed *Lanka Amitha*
Fuerte Venture reported sold

Genova	1981	20,096	28,042	177	27	18	M2	RO	ex-Conti Bavaria 85, ex-Costa Ligure 84

Lanka Amila renamed *Eschenbach*
Lanka Amitha renamed *Brabant*

Manhattan	1981	20,096	28,082	177	27	18	M2	RO	ex-Conti Hammonia 85, ex-Costa Arabica 84

Anglo Nordic Shipping Ltd
Chemical Explorer sold and renamed *Brilliant* (Cypriot)
Chemical Venturer sold and renamed *Venturer* (Cypriot)

Australian National Line
Allunga broken up

The Ben Line Steamers Ltd
Bencruachan reported sold to Japanese owners and chartered back

Sig Bergesen d.y. & Co
Subsidiary companies merged to form A/S Bergesen
Berge Emperor sold, renamed *Emperor* and broken up
Berge Empress sold, renamed *Empress* and broken up
Berge Prince, *Berge Princess* and *Berge Septimus* reported sold, chartered back with repurchase option

Langfonn†	1977	33,746	59,250	211	32	17	M	T

Blue Star Line Ltd
Canterbury Star completed 2/1986

British & Commonwealth Shipping Co Ltd
Bridgeworth sold and renamed *St Cergue* (Suisse-Atlantique)
Caspian Universal reported sold
Scottish Lion sold and renamed *Leon*

The British Petroleum Co Ltd
British Avon sold and renamed *Mare di Kara* (Italian)
British Spey sold and renamed *Tank Progress* (Panamanian)

Bugsier Reederei AG
Hodeidah Crown renamed *Ostfriesland*

Burmah Oil Tanker Co Ltd
Burmah Bahamas charter ended, renamed *Miramar* (Panamanian)

Canadian Pacific Steamships Ltd
CP Ambassador renamed *CanMar Ambassador*
W. C. Van Horne sold and renamed *Pratincole*

Cenargo Navigation Ltd

Merchant Patriot	1979	5,802	8,327	127	18	15	M	C	ex-Saronic 85

Chevron Corp
Gulf Oil Corp vessels now merged into main fleet
Chevron Freeport broken up
George M. Keller reported sold for breaking up
Howard W. Bell reported sold for breaking up
J. R. Grey broken up
L. W. Funkhouser broken up
Rudolph Peterson reported sold for breaking up

China Ocean Shipping Co
Hong Qi 123 sold and renamed *Silver Song* (Liberian)

Ji Di	1971	7,890	10,160	147	20	17	M	C	ex-Rhea 85
Qui He amend to Qiu He									
Su Lin	1972	6,616	8,253	129	19	17	M	C	ex-Castor 85, ex-Finntrader 82
Yu He	1986	24,040	31,000	(191)	28	16	M	CC	

Cho Yang Shipping Co Ltd

Orion Star	1969	10,236	19,103	154	23	14	M	B	ex-Agelos Seraphim 81, ex-Silver Light 74, Ex-Ganges Maru 71

NV CMB SA
CMB Europe renamed *CanMar Europe*
Mercator being re-engined from ST to M

Mineral Alegria	1973	36,330	66,510	235	32	16	M	B
Mineral Dampier	1986	75,000	168,500	282	45	13	M	B
Mineral Europe	1986	75,000	168,500	282	45	13	M	B

CTM-Cia Portuguesa de Transportes Maritimos
Alcoutim renamed *Rui de Pina*
Bernardino Correa broken up
Lobito renamed *Independencia*
Porto broken up
Rio Zambeze renamed *Garcia de Resende*

The Cunard Steam-Ship Co plc
Carinthia sold and renamed *Pegusus* (Greek flag)
Carmania sold and renamed *Perseus* (Greek)
Samaria sold and renamed *Capricorn* (Greek)
Saxonia sold and renamed *Carina* (Greek)
Scythia sold and renamed *Centaurus* (Greek)
Servia sold and renamed *Castor* (Greek)

J & J Denholm Ltd

Polhymnia†	1976	13,193	22,312	165	23	14	M	B	ex-Transocean Transport II 85, ex-Tradewind West 77
Riviera*	1974	18,498	34,710	196	24	15	M	B	ex-Fadura 79
Terpsichore†	1974	13,198	22,623	164	23	14	M	B	ex-Oromonte 85, ex-Everray 80

† Panamanian flag

VEB Deutfracht/Seereederei

Eisenhuttenstadt reported broken up
John Schehr sold and renamed *John S* (Maltese)
Lubbenau broken up

Neustadt	1986	6,520	7,960	(113)	20	14	M	CC
Mukran	1986	22,404	11,700	190	26	16	M	RO
Ruhland	1985	13,769	18,000				M	CC
Ruebeland	1985	13,769	18,000				M	CC

H. Ditlev-Simonsen & Co

Scandia Team sold and renamed *Abant* (Turkish)
Vanja transferred to Swedish Govt, renamed *Zenit Kraka*
Velma transferred to Swedish Govt, renamed *Zenit Juno*

The East Asiatic Co Ltd

Mixteco renamed *Samoa*, then sold and renamed *Primorje* (Panamanian)

Ellerman City Liners

City of York reported sold

John T. Essberger

Woermann Wadai renamed *Wadai* (Togo flag)

The Ethiopian Shipping Lines

Netsanet	1985	11,691	14,896	(126)	23	15	M	C

Ras Dedgen transferred to Ethiopian Navy

Evergreen Marine Corp (Taiwan) Ltd

Ever Guest	1986	40,300	43,800	231	32	21	M	CC

Exxon Corp

Esso Danica renamed *Esso Puerto Rico* (Bahamas flag)
Esso Indonesia reported sold for breaking up
Esso Kagoshima reported sold for breaking up
Esso Okinawa reported sold for breaking up

Fearnley & Eger A/S

Ferncourt sold and renamed *Antonio J. Dovali* (Mexican)
Ferncraig sold and renamed *Antonio J. Bermudes* (Mexican)
Mirafiori renamed *Rafio*
Nahoda Biru reported sold

Fednav Ltd

Federal Hunter lengthened, now 83,784grt, 164,500dwt, 289m loa
Federal Skeena lengthened, now 83,784grt, 164,500dwt, 289m loa

Laurentian Forest	1972	15,036	20,545	208	23	19	M2	RO	ex-Grand Encounter 85, ex-Laurentian Forest 80

(to be renamed *Federal Seaway*)

O/Y Finnlines

Finn Falcon renamed *Finnfalcon*
Finn Whale renamed *Finnwhale*

Finska Ang. A/B

Atalaya renamed *Star Atalaya*
Castor sold and renamed *Su Lin* (China)
Rhea sold and renamed *Ji Di* (China)

James Fisher & Sons plc

Sir John Fisher reported sold
Thamesfield reported sold

Furness Withy & Co Ltd

Clerk-Maxwell reported sold for breaking up
Oswestry Grange sold, renamed *Stenjohan* (Swedish) and converted for static storage

Cie Generale Maritime

Champlain sold and renamed *Akoe* (US flag)
Eiffel renamed *Elma Diez*
Pascal sold and renamed *Kepler* (FRG)

Globtik Management Ltd
Globtik London broken up
Globtik Tokyo reported sold for breaking up

Great Eastern Shipping Co Ltd
Jag Jyoti sold and renamed *Fal XV* (United Arab Emirates)

Christian Haaland
Concordia Star renamed *Noble Star* (Liberian)

Hapag-Lloyd AG
Dusseldorf Express lengthened, now 38,930grt, 40,900dwt, 241m loa
Koln Express lengthened, now 38,930grt, 40,900dwt, 241m loa
Melbourne Express sold and renamed *Melbourne* (FRG)

A/S Havtor Management
Athene reported sold to Norwegian owners
Havlyn sold and renamed *Skaugan* (Norwegian)

Probo Hawk	1986	20,000	37,000	183	32	14	M	OBO	(Singapore flag)

Headlam & Son
Egton broken up

Per Henriksen
Diplomat renamed *Mercandian Diplomat*

Mercandian Arrow	1986	13,500	9,200	160	21	16	M	RO
Mercandian Continent	1986	13,500	9,250	160	21	16	M	RO

Leif Hoegh & Co A/S
Trigger sold and renamed *Nosac Trigger* (O. Lorentzen A/S)

Islamic Rep. of Iran Shipping Lines

Iran Abozar	1986	25,768	40,000	190	30	14	M	B

Iran Emdad sold for breaking up

Iran Godousi	1986	25,768	40,000	190	30	14	M	B
Iran Hamzem	1986	25,768	40,000	190	30	14	M	B

Iran Saoughi amend to *Iran Sadoughi*

Iran Saeidi	1986	25,768	40,000	190	30	14	M	B

Iran Seeyan reported sold

Anders Jahre
Janega renamed *Euro Trident* (British)
Jarmada sold, renamed *FSU Covenas* and converted to barge

A/S Kristian Jebsens Rederi
Bedouin Brunes sold and renamed *Dneproges* (USSR)
Bergnes renamed *General Lacunda* (Philippine flag)
Brooknes renamed *General Estrella* (Philippine)

*General Cabal**	1976	7,952	12,100	146	20	15	M	B	ex-Bruni 85

General Lim sold and renamed *Veli Varos* (Yogoslav)

*General Mata**	1985	18,977	29,446	170	28	14	M	B	ex-Saltnes 85
*General Vargas**	1977	7,952	12,100	146	20	15	M	B	ex-Brunto 85

Johnson Line A/B
Annie Johnson reported sold
Axel Johnson reported sold
Bahia Blanca sold and renamed *Bahia*
Johnson Chemstar reported sold
Johnson Chemstream reported sold to Indian owners
Margaret Johnson reported sold
San Francisco sold and renamed *Diego* (Mediterranean Shipping)

Jugolinija
Kragujevac broken up
Plitvice broken up

M. A. Karaageorgis SA
Aristagelos renamed *Victor* (Papua New Guinea flag)
Aristogenis renamed *Vulcan*
Messiniaki Anagennisis renamed *Welcomer*
Messiniaki Doxa renamed *Wonderous*

Kawasaki Kisen KK

Forest Duke††	1975	33,702	41,962	195	30	15	M	B	ex-Honshu Gloria 85
Gemini Pioneer††	1977	16,736	28,218	177	23	15	M	B	
Kazukawa Maru broken up									
Macassar Maru sold and renamed Kota Maju (Singapore flag)									
Oriebtal Highway†	1980	10,975	12,434	175	27	17	M	V	
Shinanogawa Maru re-engined from ST to M									
Shokawa Maru renamed Australian Searoader 2									
Sunny Glorious	1983	32,649	65,029	228	32	15	M	B	ex-Sunrise Glory 85, ex-Ocean Prosper 84
Tatekawa Maru	1985	93,479	168,700	280	40	14	M	B	
Yonekawa Maru renamed Trans Pacific									

Torvald Klaveness & Co A/S

Bark††	1971	16,035	27,258	163	26	15	M	B	ex-Bahia Portete 85, ex-Havbjorn 82

†† Panamanian flag

Korea Shipping Corp Ltd

One West No 7, One West No 8 and One West No 9 all broken up									
Crystal Reed	1973	12,074	17,918	155	23	14	M	B	

Kuwait Oil Tanker Co SAK

Umm Al Madafaa	1977	144,688	300,078	348	54	15	ST	T	ex-Yucatan Valley 85, ex-Ocean Cloud 84, ex-Mundaca 84
Umm Al Qurah	1974	109,752	236,807	326	49	15	ST	T	ex-Caribbean Breeze 85, ex-Katarina Sea 84, ex-Pogeez 84, ex-St Benedict 83, ex-Minerva 82

F. Laeisz Schiff GmbH & Co
Norasia Dagmar renamed Dagmar Reeckmann

J. Lauritzen A/S
Dana Futura lengthened, now 6,513grt, 10,150dwt, 163m loa

Leonhardt & Blumberg Reederei

Fine Eagle	1986	10,282	13,500	137	22	17	M	CC

Livanos Group
Atlantic Hawk reported sold

Cia. de Nav. Lloyd Brasileiro

Lloyd Altamira reported sold								
Rio Acre	1986	25,000	39,000	175	29	14	M	B
Rio Coari	1986	25,200	51,000	191	32	14	M	B

London & Overseas Freighters Ltd
Overseas Argonaut sold and renamed Anastasis (Greek)

Oivind Lorentzen A/S

Nosac Trigger*	1976	6,923	9,835	188	23	18	M	V	ex-Trigger 85, ex-Hoegh Trigger 84

SA Louis Dreyfus & Cie/Buries Markes Ltd

Dominique LD renamed La Chesnair									
Florence Virginia‡	1973	32,510	66,491	219	32	16	M	B	ex-Maro 85
Gerald LD sold and renamed Summerfield (British)									
Gretchen Anne‡	1970	18,634	32,268	183	26	15	M	B	ex-Georgios Xylas 85
Jody Lynn‡	1977	19,253	37,519	196	27	15	M	B	ex-Joanna 85
Melissa Mary‡	1977	19,253	37,519	196	27	15	M	B	ex-Fotini 85

‡ Liberian flag

Lykes Bros Steamship Co Inc

Almeria Lykes, Charles Lykes, Doctor Lykes, Tillie Lykes and Velma Lykes all transferred to US reserve fleet								
Doctor Lykes	1986	39,700	33,360	245	32	21	M	CC

Mavroleon Bros Ltd
Kasos reported sold

Mediterranean Shipping Co SA

Diego reported sold for breaking up

Diego	1970	15,769	14,936	174	26	21	M2	CO	ex-San Francisco 86

Mitsui-OSK Lines KK

*Alps Maru**	1985	15, 350	20,700	154	27	15	M	HL	

Amazon Maru sold and renamed *Al-Swamruz* (Bahaman flag)
Izumisan Maru broken up

Lambert Maru	1986	99,100	196,000	288	50	13	M	B	

Kokisan Maru amend to *Kohkisan Maru*
Mitsui Maru sold and renamed *Flag Mersindi* (Panamanian)
Mitsui Maru No 2 sold and renamed *Yih Sen* (Taiwan)
Ocean Cavalier sold and renamed *Galaxy Star* (Panamanian)

Orion Trader†	1976	106,109	236,767	322	52	15	ST	T	ex-Al Riyadh 85
Pacific Lady†	1971	15,590	26,480	169	25	15	M	O	ex-Kyushu Maru 85
Southern Cosmos†	1985	14,031	23,846	(150)	24	14	M	B	ex-Soarer Bellona 85

Tama Maru sold and renamed *Fortune 1* (Panamanian)
Wakaume Maru sold and renamed *Pipod Samut* (Thai)
Wendy sold and renamed *Larkspur* (Japanese)

Mobil Oil Corp

Mobil Hawk renamed *Al Saqr Al Arabi* (Saudi Arabian)
Mobil Brilliant sold and renamed *Glory* (Cypriot)

A. P. Moller

Challenger converted from M2 to M, renamed *Dragor Maersk*, lengthened, now 40,391grt

McKinney Maersk	1985	43,431	52,000	270	32	24	M	CC

Cia. Nacional de Nav Sarl

Amarante sold and renamed *Spyvag II* (Cypriot)
Cunene sold and renamed *Spyvag I* (Cypriot)
Cabo Bojador broken up
Manica broken up
Quelimane sold and renamed *Luso Ana* (Portuguese)

Cie. Nationale de Navigation

Prairial	1978	198,764	409,404	382	63	16	ST	T	ex-Zenit Iduna 85, ex-Nai Genova 85

Prairial (above) now reported sold to Greek owners

Soc. Navale Chargeurs Delmas Vieljeux

Adeline Delmas	1986	23,100	33,000	176	30	14	M	B
Blandine Delmas	1986	23,000	33,000	176	30	14	M	B
Caroline Delmas	1986	23,000	33,000	176	30	14	M	B
Delphine Delmas	1986	23,000	33,000	176	30	14	M	B

Lucie Delmas renamed *Lucie* (Bahamas flag)
Marie Delmas renamed *Marie* (Bahamas flag)

Monique Delmas	1985	26,298	39273	183	29	13	M	B

Cie Navale Worms

Artois transferred to Mauritius flag
Obernai renamed *Ace One* (St Vincent flag)

Nedlloyd Lijnen BV

Amsteldiep sold and renamed *Novsun* (Cypriot)

Avanti	1985	25,365	41,150	178	32	14	M	T

Flevoland sold and renamed *Sindbad Mariner* (Panamanian)
Maaskade, Maaskant, Maaskerk and *Maaskroon* all sold to Mercury Shipping (British flag) and respectively renamed *Seaville, Capeville, Bayville* and *Riverville*
Nedlloyd Gooiland reported sold to Egyptian owners
Nile renamed *Nedlloyd Nile*, then renamed *Seas Brazil*
Salland sold and renamed *Marego K* (Panamanian flag)

Neptune Orient Lines Ltd

Neptune Jade	1986	40,177	41,000	244	32	21	M	CC

Neptune Sapphire renamed *Neptune Ivory*

Niarchos Group

Northern Naiad broken up

Nippon Yusen Kaisha (NYK)

Belle Undine**	1976	31,156	56,233	200	32	15	M	B	ex-Torrent 85, ex-Giannini 77
Century Leader No 3	1986	45,900	10,000	170	32	18	M	V	

Chikura Maru reported sold to Taiwanese owners
Fujikawa Maru re-engined from ST to M
Fushimi Maru broken up
Fuso Maru broken up
Futami Maru broken up
Hakozaki Maru reported sold and to be renamed *Crescent* (Panamanian)
Mino Maru sold and renamed *Bertha* (Philippine flag)

Tagawa Maru	1985	133,940	235,994	307	54	14	M	T	

Tokitsu Maru to be re-engined from ST to M
** Philippine flag

Ocean Transport & Trading plc

Barber Priam reported sold to US reserve fleet
Bello Folawiyo to be renamed *Sekondi*
Clytoneus sold and renamed *Affinity* (Singapore flag)
Lloyd San Francisco to be renamed *Memnon*
Maron reported sold and to be renamed *Yinka Folawiyo* (Nigerian)

Rudolf A. Oetker

Bahia reported sold to East Germany
Columbus Australia being re-engined from ST to M
Columbus America and *Columbus New Zealand* to be re-engined from ST to M
Danisa renamed *St Petri* (FRG)
Monte Sarmiento lengthened to 200m loa, now 24,080grt; 60% owned by NV CMB SA

Egon Oldendorff

Western Glory broken up

Fred Olsen & Co

Star Denver	1978	25,077	43,793	183	31	15	M	B	ex-Star Enterprise 85

Olympic Maritime SA

Olympic Bond renamed *Bond* and subsequently broken up

Overseas Containers Ltd

Main Express renamed *Strathconan*
Mosel Express to be renamed *Falmouth Bay*

P & O Steam Nav Co Ltd

Newforest sold but not renamed

Pakistan National Shipping Corp

Bagh-e-Dacca broken up
Nawabshah sank on voyage from Karachi to Yokohama

Palm Line Ltd

Company renamed UAC Ltd after trading name sold to Ocean Transport & Trading plc
Badagry Palm renamed *Badagry*
Lloyd Texas renamed *Bamenda Palm*, then sold and renamed *Arko Glory* (Cypriot)
Matadi Palm renamed *Matadi*

Petrofina SA

Fina Norvege reported sold for breaking up

Polish Shipping Association

Praca*	1977	18,998	27,807	171	26	17	M	CO	ex-Tennessee 85, ex-Barber Tennessee 85, ex-Tennessee 81
Warszawa	1986	11,200	14,000	150	22	16	M	CO	

Zegluga Polska SA

Bronislaw Czech	1986	20,000	32,800	198	25	15	M	B
General Grot-Rowecki	1985	22,500	38,000	201	28	14	M	B
Ossolineum	1986	35,000	61,000	215	32	14	M	B
Powstaniec Styczniowy	1986	20,000	32,800	199	25	15	M	B

Ernst Russ
Jacob Russ renamed *Caroline J* (Panamanian)

H. Schuldt

Lamon Bay‡	1985	16,910	19,400	176	25	18	M	CC

Scindia Steam Nav Co Ltd
Jalakendra broken up

Sea-Land Service Inc
Sea-Land Freedom lengthened to 257m loa; now 30,085grt, 29,764dwt
Sea-Land Liberator lengthened to 257m loa; now 30,085grt, 29,764dwt

Seaco Holdings Ltd
Strider Exeter renamed *A. E. S. Challenger*

Shell Group
Acila reported sold for breaking up
Batillus broken up
Bellamya broken up
Leda broken up
Lottia broken up
Lucina broken up
Vitrea broken up

The Shipping Corp of India
Karnataka broken up
Nalanda broken up

Shipping Management SAM
Management company name amended to **V Ships**

Asia Marine*	1976	34,104	60,814	207	32	15	M	T	ex-Avon Maru 85
Marina Bay sold breakers									
Marina Star	1975	8,489	12,470	144	22	18	M	CO	ex-Muscat Bay 85, ex-Monte Pascoal 81, ex-Senta 81, ex-Columbus Coromandel 80, ex-Senta 75

Ocelot renamed *Daogli* (Philippine flag)

I. M. Skaugen & Co

Skaubo	1974	66,767	132,409	273	44	15	M	OBO	ex-Ocean Maritime 85, ex-Skaubo 83
Skaugran	1982	8,311	11,772	128	21	16	M	LPG	ex-Havlyn 85

Standard Oil Company (Indiana)
Amoco Milford Haven sold and renamed *Haven* (Cypriot)
Amoco Seafarer renamed *Ocean Seafarer*

Stena AB
Stena Ionia renamed *Stena Gothica*
Stena Pacifica sold and renamed *Eleonora M* (Greek)

Stolt-Nielsens Rederi A/S

Stolt Topaz	1986	24,000	35,076	177	32	15	M	T

Soc D'Arm Mar Suisse-Atlantique SA
Bregaglia renamed *Lausanne*

St Cergue	1983	35,749	64,310	225	32	15	M	B	ex-Bridgeworth 85

A/S Sigurd Sverdrup
Aura Adventure sold and renamed *Seaborn* (Cypriot)
Aura Bravery sold and renamed *Sea Bravery* (Cypriot)

Swiss Shipping & Neptun Co Ltd
Alpina sold and renamed *Her Chang* (Panamanian)

Texaco Inc
Getty Oil vessels now merged into main fleet
George F. Getty II, *J. Paul Getty* and *Los Angeles Getty* reported sold to NYK
Texaco Melbourne broken up
Texaco Ohio broken up

Thomas Nationwide Transport

Port of Chioggia	1969	12,836	14,279	157	22	17	M	CC	ex-Cavadonga 85, ex-CP Hunter 80, ex-Seatrain Galveston 80, ex-Trans Europe 79, ex-Cheshire Venture 79, ex-Trans Europe 79, ex-Kanimbla 76
Port of Savannah	1969	9,162	12,590	157	22	17	M	CC	ex-Gundalupe 1 85, ex-Seatrain Texas 80, ex-Trans America 79, ex-Cheshire Endeavour 79, ex-Trans America 78, ex-Manoora 76

Total Cie Francaise de Nav
Nan Hai Wang to be converted to floating production storage vessel
Onyx renamed *Faroship L* (Greek)

Transatlantic Rederi A/B
Atlantic Premier sold and renamed *Atlantic Star*, then renamed *Canada Maritime* (Singapore flag)
Barranduna and *Paralla* sold to US reserve fleet

Transportacion Maritima Mexicana SA
Azteca renamed *Explorer III* (Panamanian)
Maya renamed *Voyager 1* (Panamanian)

C. Y. Tung Group
Some vessels now managed by **Orient Overseas Management Ltd**

*Asian Bonanza**	1986	21,300	35,600	186	28	15	M	B	
Asian Brilliance sold and renamed *Noble* (Panamanian)									
Atlantic Assurance	1986	50,700	79,990	234	40	14	M	T	
Brazilian Hope reported sold to Iranian owners									
Brazilian Splendour sold and renamed *Hawaii* (Panamanian)									
Columbia Liberty sold and renamed *Canadian Liberty* (Liberian)									
Manhattan Baron sold and renamed *Cloudesdale*									
Oriental Faith	1986	42,000	40,560	241	32	21	M	CC	
Oriental Prince renamed *Tokyo Bridge*									
Sunset Peak	1973	43,867	78,228	233	32	14	M	OBO	ex-Carcape 84

UBEM SA

Belval	1986	75,000	168,500	202	45	13	M	B	
Kyoto sold to Liberian flag owners									

A/S Uglands Rederi

Danita‡‡	1985	43,733	84,000	228	32	14	M	T	
Jorita	1985	23,981	35,000	180	31	14	M	B	
Norita‡‡	1986	35,000	84,000	228	32	14	M	T	
Oden	1972	8,929	10,079	142	21	16	M	BV	ex-Modena 85, ex-Weyroc 82
Tinita	1985	23,981	35,000	180	31	14	M	B	
Rosita	1986	23,981	35,000	180	31	14	M	B	

Ugland Obo-Six reported sold and to be renamed *Aghia Eleni* (Cypriot)
Miranda sold and renamed *Amaldi* (Cypriot)
Evita renamed *Vida 1* (Norwegian)
Favorita renamed *Sirena 1* (Philippine)
‡‡ owned by Dansk Invest, Danish flag

Union Navale SA
Cetra Vela reported sold to Norwegian owners

United Fruit Co

Irma M	1985	12,659	13,584	169	24	20	M	R	

United States Lines

American Accord, *American Ace*, *American Alliance*, *American Archer*, *American Argosy*, *American Leader*, *American Legacy* and *American Legend* all sold for breaking up

Delta Caribe, *Delta Mar*, *Delta Norte*, *Delta Sun*, *American Moon*, *Mormacglen* and *Mormacwave* all transferred to US reserve fleet

American Georgia	1985	23,850	35,900	174	25	21	M	CC	
American Ohio	1985	23,850	35,900	174	25	21	M	CC	

USSR

Dneproges	1977	19,158	34,488	180	28	15	M	B	ex-Bedouin Brunes 85
Kapitan Man	1985	17,910	19,684	174	24	17	M	RO	
Petr Vasev	1981	18,604	32,961	187	27	15	M	B	ex-Sea Orchid 85, ex-Carrianna Orchid 84
Petr Tomasevich	1983	21,500	38,747	189	28	15	M	B	ex-Maritime Queen 85
Roman Karmen	1981	21,464	38,625	189	28	17	M	B	ex-Maritime Victor 85
Yuriy Maksayev	1986	12,800	18,000	181	28	20	M	RO	

Zolotye Dyuny — non-commercial fish carrier

Phs Van Ommeren NV

Willine Tokyo renamed Waardrecht, then renamed *Westwood Magellan*

Wallenius Rederierna

Atlantic Prelude reported sold

Reederei Jonny Wesch

Brave Eagle	1985	10,282	12,500	146	23	18	M	CC	

Wild Eagle sold to Rendsburg Schiff GmbH — not renamed

Westfal-Larsen & Co A/S

Star Derby	1979	25,078	43,700	183	31	15	M	B	ex-Star Carrier 85

Wilh Wilhelmsen

Barber Taif and *Barber Tonsberg* reported sold to US reserve fleet

Docefjord‡‡	1986	120,000	305,675	332	57	13	M	BO	

Takasago sold and renamed *Gesalina* (Cypriot)

Talabot renamed *Wuwurry*

Tennessee sold and renamed *Praca* (Polish)

Tijuca‡‡	1987	120,000	305,675	332	57	13	M	BO	
Toranus	1981	21,384	38,960	175	32	15	M	T	ex-Oranus 85

Troll Lake sold and renamed *Cielo di Amalfi* (Italian)

‡‡ Jointly owned by Liberian flag subsidiary of Docenave, Brazil

World-Wide Shipping

World Cheer, *World Diamond*, *World Dove*, *World Fortress*, *World Nancy* and *World Pearl* all sold to Panamanian owners and renamed respectively *Great Cheer*, *Great Diamond*, *Great Dove*, *Great Fortress*, *Great Nancy* and *Great Pearl*

Golden Lotus sold and renamed *Welkin* (Maltese)

World Canada renamed *World Xanadu*

World Crown broken up

World Duke sold and renamed *Bright Duke* (Panamanian)

World Fame sold and renamed *Sepia* (FRG)

World Jade sold and renamed *Captain George Tsangaris* (Greek)

World Finance renamed *Wordl Finch* then sold and renamed *Flag Malina* (Panamanian)

World Resolve broken up

World Sun renamed *World Summit*

World Truth broken up

Zim Israel Nav Co Ltd

Iris sold and renamed *Zea* (Maltese)

Narcis sold and renamed *Alkyon* (Maltese)

Index

A.E.S. Express 194
A.M. Carrier 70
A.M. Trader 70
A.P. Moller 144
Abbay Wonz 78
Abbey 92
Abul Kalan Azad 200
Abyot 78
Acadia Forest 48
Acadia 86
Achille Lauro 16
Acila 196
Acmaea 196
Acquila Trader 76
ACT 1 30
ACT 2 30
ACT 3 30
ACT 4 30
ACT 5 30
ACT 6 30
ACT 7 30
ACT 8 72
Actuaria 72
Ada Gorthon 96
Adabelle Lykes 132
Adam Asnyk 178
Adam Mickiewicz 178
Addiriyah 230
Adelaide Express 204
Adler 236
Admiral Ushakov 236
Admiral Zmajevik 116
Adolf Leonhardt 128
Adria 88
Adrian Maersk 144
Adriano 24
Adriatic Skou 206
Aegis Athenic 24
Aegis Baltic 24
Aegis Bravery 24
Aegis Harvest 24
Aegis Ionic 24
Aegis Logic 24
Aegis Progress 24
Aegis Stoic 24
Aegis Topic 24
Afovos 28
Afran Energy 52
Afran Equator 52
Afran Horizon 52
Afran Meteor 52
Afran Ocean 52
Afran Sky 52
Afran Star 52
Afran Stream 52
Afran Sun 52

Afran Zenith 52
Afran Zodiac 52
Afric Star 38
Africa Maru 138
Africa 88
African Reefer 126
Agapi 28
Agboville 110
Agostinho Neto 236
Ahmad Al-Fateh 230
Aida 244
Aitodor 236
Ajanta 200
Akademik Bakulev 236
Akademik Davitaya 236
Akademik Sechenov 236
Akarita 228
Akbar 200
Aken 66
Akikawa Maru 118
Al Ahmadiah 230
Al Berry 30
Al Bida 30
Al-Faiha 124
Al Fujairah 230
Al Funtas 124
Al Haramain 142
Al Ihsa'a 230
Al Manakh 230
Al Maqwa 124
Al Mariyah 230
Al Mirqab 230
Al Mubarakiah 230
Al Muharraq 230
Al Nisr Al Arabi 142
Al Rawdatain 124
Al Rayyan 230
Al Rekkah 124
Al Rumaithiah 230
Al Sabahiah 230
Al Salimiah 230
Al Shamiah 230
Al Shidadiah 230
Al Solaibiah 230
Al Wajba 230
Al Yamamah 230
Al-Wattyah 230
Alabama Getty 216
Alain LD 132
Alaska Maru 138
Alaska 26
Albert Maersk 144
Albin Kobis 66
Albright Explorer 90
Albright Pioneer 90
Alcoutim 148

Alcyon 74
Aldabi 160
Aldebaran 88
Alden W. Clausen 50
Aldrington 210
Aleksander Zawadski 178
Aleksandr Matrosov 236
Aleksandr Nevskiy 236
Aleksandr Pushkin 22
Aleksandre Saveliev 236
Aleksandr Suvorov 236
Aleksey Danchenko 236
Aleksey Kosygin 236
Alemania Express 98
Aleppo 206
Alessandra 74
Alexa II 136
Alexander S. Onassis 172
Alexandra 136
Alhena 160
Aliakmon 128
Alida Gorthon 96
Alkisma Alarabia 142
Alkuds 138
All Star 204
Allunga 32
Almak 204
Almalaz 204
Almaris 74
Almeria Lykes 132
Almirante Jose Padilla 90
Almirante Stewart 74
Almirante Storni 74
Almudena 222
Alnati 160
Alnave 74
Alpha Challenge 28
Alpha Faith 28
Alpha Jupiter 28
Alphacca 160
Alpina 214
Alpine Rose 138
Alps Highway 118
Alsama Alarabia 142
Altai Maru 138
Altanin 204
Altenburg 66
Alva Maersk 144
Alvega 204
Alvenus 204
Alybella 170
Amagi Maru 162
Amagisan Maru 138
Amandine 228
Amarante 148
Amazon Maru 138

Amazon Pioneer 128
Amazon Prosperity 128
Amazon 86
Ambasador 14
Ambia Fair 104
Ambia Finjo 104
America Express 98
America Maru 138
American Accord 232
American Ace 232
American Alabama 232
American Alliance 232
American Altair 232
American Apollo 232
American Aquarius 232
American Archer 232
American Argo 234
American Argosy 234
American Astronaut 234
American Banker 234
American Builder 234
American California 234
American Draco 234
American Entente 234
American Envoy 234
American Hawaii 236
American Illinois 234
American Kentucky 234
American Lancer 234
American Lark 234
American Leader 234
American Legacy 234
American Legend 234
American Liberty 234
American Lynx 234
American Maine 234
American Marketer 234
American Merchant 234
American Michigan 234
American Monarch 234
American Moon 234
American Nebraska 234
American New Jersey 234
American New York 234
American North Carolina 236
American Oklahoma 234
American Pioneer 234
American Puritan 234
American Reefer 126
American Reservist 234
American Resolute 84
American Rigel 234
American Saga 234
American Sea 234
American Spitfire 234
American Tide 234

American Titan 234
American Trader 234
American Utah 234
American Vega 234
American Veteran 234
American Virgina 234
American Washington 234
Americana 86
Amerikanis 8
Amilla 28
Amoco Baltimore 208
Amoco Brisbane 208
Amoco Cairo 208
Amoco Cremona 208
Amoco Europa 208
Amoco Milford Haven 208
Amoco Savannah 208
Amoco Seafarer 208
Amoco Texas City 208
Amoco Trinidad 208
Amoco Whiting 208
Amoco Yorktown 208
Amparo 220
Amsteldiep 154
Amsteldreef 154
Amstelmeer 154
Amstelmolen 154
Amstelvaart 154
Amstelvliet 154
Amstelvroon 154
Amstelwal 154
An Da Hai 52
An Dong Jiang 52
An Fu Jiang 52
An Hua 52
An Ji Hai 52
An Lu Jiang 52
An Sai Jiang 52
An Shan 52
An Ting 52
Ana Luisa 74
Anangel Apollo 28
Anangel Ares 28
Anangel Argonaut 28
Anangel Atlas 28
Anangel Champion 28
Anangel Diligence 28
Anangel Endeavour 28
Anangel Fidelity 28
Anangel Fortune 28
Anangel Glory 28
Anangel Happiness 28
Anangel Harmony 28
Anangel Honour 28
Anangel Hope 28
Anangel Horizon 28
Anangel Leader 28
Anangel Liberty 28
Anangel Luck 28
Anangel Might 28
Anangel Peace 28
Anangel Prosperity 28

Anangel Sky 28
Anangel Spirit 28
Anangel Sun 28
Anangel Triumph 28
Anangel Victory 28
Anangel Widsom 28
Anatoliy Kolesnichenko 236
Anatoliy Lyapidevskiy 236
Anatoliy Vasilyev 236
Anatoliy Zheleznyakov 236
Anders Maersk 144
Andes Maru 138
Andes Trader 44
Andes 92
Andinet 78
Andre Delmas 150
Andrea Merzario 138
Ango 48
Aniara 244
Aniello 136
Anita Dan 126
Anja Leonhardt 128
Anjou 92
Anna I. Angelicoussi 28
Anna Leonhardt 128
Anna Maersk 144
Annapurna 200
Annie Johnson 114
Anniversary Thistle 122
Annoula 28
Anona 26
Anro Australia 32
Anro Temasek 158
Antarctic 26
Antares 88
Antilla Bay 154
Anton Saefkow 66
Antwerpen 194
Anupama 200
Aotea 214
Appleby 186
Apulia 88
Aquarius 14
Aquila 256
Aquitania 24
Arabian Sea 142
Aradhana 200
Arafat 230
Arafura 174
Araguaney 222
Aram Khachaturyan 236
Archana 200
Archangelos 128
Arctic Tokyo 178
Arcturus 90
Areti 28
Argonaut (Am) 84
Argonaut (Gk) 12
Ariake 174
Ariel 90
Arild Maersk 144
Arimasan Maru 138

Arion 162
Aristagelos 118
Aristogenis 118
Aristotle S. Onassis 72
Arkhangelsk 236
Arkona (DDR) 12
Arkona (FGR) 72
Armagnac 150
Armand Hammer 30
Armeniya 22
Arnold Maersk 144
Arnstadt 66
Artemis Garofalidis 172
Arthur Maersk 144
Artois 150
Artur Grottger 178
Arturo Gomez J. 90
Arunachal Pradesh 200
Asama Maru 162
Ashington 210
Ashley Lykes 132
Asia Culture 250
Asia Heron 250
Asia Industry 250
Asia Maru 138
Asian Banner 222
Asian Brilliance 222
Asian Express 222
Asian Jade 156
Asian Pearl 156
Asian Progress 222
Asian Reefer 126
Asir 216
Astra Peak 138
Astral Mariner 162
Astral Neptune 162
Astral Ocean 162
Astrea 90
Atalaya 90
Atara 256
Athene 102
Athos 144
Atlantic 14
Atlantic Amity 222
Atlantic Cartier 30
Atlantic Causeway 30
Atlantic Charisma 222
Atlantic Charity 222
Atlantic Companion 32
Atlantic Compass 32
Atlantic Concert 32
Atlantic Concord (Lib) 222
Atlantic Concord (Pan) 162
Atlantic Confidence 222
Atlantic Conquest 222
Atlantic Conveyor 32
Atlantic Dignity 222
Atlantic Emperor 128
Atlantic Forest 48
Atlantic Hawk 128
Atlantic Helmsman 128
Atlantic Heritage 128

Atlantic Hero 128
Atlantic Highway 118
Atlantic Horizon 128
Atlantic Marquess 128
Atlantic Maru 138
Atlantic Patriot 138
Atlantic Peace 222
Atlantic Prelude 244
Atlantic Premier 220
Atlantic Saga 32
Atlantic Seaman 128
Atlantic Service 32
Atlantic Song 32
Atlantic Star 32
Atlantic Superior 86
Atlantic Universal 206
Atlantic Venturer 222
Atlas Maru 138
Atlas 12
Auckland Star 38
Aue 66
August Cesareo 114
Aura Adventure 214
Aura Bravery 214
Auriga 76
Aurora Ace 138
Aurora 174
Ausonia 12
Austanger 246
Australia Maru 138
Australia Star 38
Australia 66
Australian Emblem 32
Australian Enterprise 32
Australian Escort 32
Australian Explorer 32
Australian Exporter 32
Australian Highway 118
Australian Progress 32
Australian Prospector 32
Australian Purpose 32
Australian Reefer 126
Australian Venture 32
Autan 218
Author 100
Autoestrada 130
Autovia 130
Ava 44
Avon 168
Axel Johnson 114
Axel Maersk 144
Ayubia 176
Ayvazoskiy 22
Azerbaydzhan 22
Aziz Bhatti 176
Azteca 220
Azur 8
Azure Seas 12

Baarn 156
Badagry Palm 176
Bagh-e-Dacca 176

Bahia Blanca 114
Bahia 168
Bahrah 124
Bai Yu Hai 52
Baikal 22
Bailadila 200
Bailundo 64
Bajka 122
Bakar (Lib) 122
Bakar (Yug) 114
Balao 122
Balduin 172
Balkan Reefer 126
Baltic Mermaid 170
Baltik 114
Baltika 22
Banat 116
Banderas 224
Bandundu 254
Banglar Asha 32
Banglar Baani 32
Banglar Gourab 32
Banglar Kakoli 32
Banglar Kallol 32
Banglar Kiron 32
Banglar Mamata 32
Banglar Maya 32
Banglar Mita 32
Banglar Moni 32
Banglar Progoti 32
Banglar Robi 32
Banglar Sampad 32
Banglar Swapna 32
Banglar Tarani 32
Banglar Upohar 32
Banija 118
Banja Luka 118
Banshu Maru 162
Banta 122
Bao Qing Hai 52
Bao Ting 52
Bao Xing 52
Baranja 118
Barauni 200
Barbara Brovig 42
Barbara Leonhardt 128
Barber Hector 166
Barber Nara 220
Barber Perseus 166
Barber Priam 166
Barber Taif 248
Barber Tampa 248
Barber Texas 248
Barber Toba 248
Barber Tonsberg 248
Bardu 122
Barnworth 40
Baron Belhaven 134
Baron Kinnaird 134
Baron Murray 134
Barra Head 188
Barranduna 220

Barry 122
Barrydale 232
Barwa 122
Bar'zan 230
Bashkiria 22
Baska 114
Bassein 44
Batillus 196
Bauchi 122
Baumare 122
Bavang 122
Bavaria 98
Bay Bridge 118
Bayard 172
Beacon Point 188
Beate Leonhardt 128
Beau Fortune 250
Beau Success 250
Beaver 112
Bedouin Birknes 112
Bedouin Brunes 112
Beer Sheva 256
Belcargo 206
Belchatow 182
Belen 222
Belforest 206
Belgian Reefer 126
Belgrad 236
Bellamya 196
Bellary 200
Bello Folawiyo 166
Belnor 206
Belorussiya 22
Belstar 206
Beltimber 206
Belwood 206
Benalder 34
Benavon 34
Bencruachan 34
Benedict 38
Benhope 34
Benny Skou 206
Benvalla 34
Berganger 246
Bergc Adria 34
Berge Arrow 34
Berge Big 34
Berge Bragd 34
Berge Brioni 34
Berge Charlotte 34
Berge Chief 34
Berge Duke 34
Berge Eagle 34
Berge Emperor 36
Berge Empress 36
Berge Enterprise 36
Berge Fister 36
Berge Gdansk 36
Berge Gdynia 36
Berge Helene 36
Berge King 36
Berge Lord 36

Berge Master 36
Berge Odel 36
Berge Pioneer 36
Berge Prince 36
Berge Princess 36
Berge Rachel 36
Berge Racine 36
Berge Ragnhild 36
Berge Saga 36
Berge Septimus 36
Berge Sisar 36
Berge Sisu 36
Berge Strand 36
Berge Sund 36
Bergebonde 36
Bergen 66
Bergnes 114
Berlin (FGR) 10
Berlin (Lib) 100
Berlin-Hauptstadt der DDR 66
Bermuda Star 20
Bernardino Correa 64
Bernburg 66
Bernhard Bastlein 66
Bernhard Oldendorff 170
Bertram Rickmers 186
Besor 256
Betula 168
Bharata 200
Bharatendu 200
Bhava Bhuti 200
Bi Sheng 52
Bia River 38
Bianca 74
Bibi 220
Bieszczady 182
Bilderdyk 48
Bing He 52
Binsnes 112
Bow Sun 168
Boxer Captain Cook 194
BP Achiever 40
BP Endeavour 40
BP Energy 40
BP Enterprisc 40
BP Humber 40
BP Tweed 40
BP Vigour 40
BP Vision 40
Braemar 18
Bratislava 236
Bratsk 236
Brazil Glory 94
Brazil Pride 94
Brazilian Friendship 222
Brazilian Hope 222
Brazilian Pride 222
Brazilian Reefer 126
Brazilian Splendour 222
Breda 156
Bregaglia 212
Bremen Express 98

Bremerhaven 110
Brest 236
Bribir 114
Bridgeworth 40
Brierfield 132
Brigitte Jacob 110
Brimanger 248
Brinton Lykes 134
Brissac 42
Britanis 8
British Avon 40
British Beech 40
British Dart 40
British Esk 42
British Fidelity 40
British Forth 42
British Kennet 42
British Norness 40
British Ranger 40
British Reliance 40
British Renown 42
British Resolution 42
British Resource 40
British Respect 40
British Security 42
British Skill 42
British Spey 42
British Spirit 42
British Steel 92
British Success 42
British Tamar 42
British Tay 40
British Tenacity 42
Biscay 98
Biscaya 70
Bishah 216
Bishu Maru 162
Bislig Bay 190
Bissaruni 122
Black Prince 16/18
Black Watch 16/18
Blankensee 66
Blankenburg 66
Blue Nile 212
Bluestream 232
Blumenthal 110
Bo Johnson 114
Bocha 220
Boheme 10
Bohemund 172
Boizenburg 66
Bolan 176
Bold Challenger 170
Bold Eagle 246
Bold 1 204
Boleslaw Chrobry 178
Boleslaw Krzywousty 178
Boleslaw Ruminski 178
Boleslaw Smialy 178
Bolnes 112
Bondoukou 110
Boniface 38

Bonita 228
Bonoua 110
Boogabilla 220
Bora Universal 206
Boree 218
Boringia 72
Boris Babochkin 236
Boris Butoma 236
Borodino 236
Borussia 98
Bosanka 118
Bosna 114
Boston 192
Botany Bay 174
Bouaka 110
Bow Cedar 168
Bow Fagus 168
Bow Fighter 168
Bow Flower 168
Bow Fortune 168
Bow Hunter 168
Bow Pioneer 168
Bow Saphir 168
Bow Sea 168
Bow Sky 168
Bow Spring 168
Bow Star 168
British Test 40
British Trent 40
British Trident 40
British Wye 40
Bronislaw Lachowicz 178
Brooknes 114
Broompark 66
Brussel 194
Bubiyan 30
Budapesht 236
Budowlany 182
Budva 116
Bukavu 254
Bulk H 86
Bulk I 86
Bunga Angsana 134
Bunga Chempaka 134
Bunga Kantan 134
Bunga Kemboja 134
Bunga Kenanga 136
Bunga Kesidang 136
Bunga Kesumba 136
Bunga Mawar 136
Bunga Melati 136
Bunga Melawis 136
Bunga Melor 136
Bunga Orkid 136
Bunga Permai 136
Bunga Raya 136
Bunga Selasih 136
Bunga Sepang 136
Bunga Seroja 136
Bunga Srigading 136
Bunga Sripagi 136
Bunga Suria 136

Bunga Tanjong 136
Bunga Tembusu 136
Bunga Teratai 136
Burg 66
Burgas 236
Burmah Bahamas 44
Burmah Endeavour 44
Burmah Enterprise 44
Bussewitz 66
Buzet 114

C. R. Libreville 48
C. R. Paris 48
C. R. Tokyo 48
C. W. Kitto 50
Cabo Bojador 148
Cabo Verde 148
Cagayan 228
Cala Atlantica 24
Cala Mediterranea 24
Calanda 214
Calandrini 130
California Getty 216
California Star 38
Cam Bilinga 44
Cam Bubinga 44
Cam Doussie 44
Cam Ebene 44
Cam Ilomba 44
Cam Iroko 44
Camargue 152
Canadian Ace 140
Canadian Explorer 222
Canadian Reefer 126
Canberra Maru 140
Canberra 18
Candia 24
Cang Zhou 52
Canopus 90
Cantal 150
Canterbury Star 38
Cantuaria 130
Cap Ferrato 148
Cap Frio 148
Cape Arnhem 134
Cape Finisterre 134
Cape Hawke 134
Cape Otway 134
Cape Race 134
Capriolo 126
Caraibe 92
Cardigan Bay 174
Cardissa 196
Caribbean Universal 206
Caribe 1 10
Caribia Express 98
Carinthia 64
Carla A. Hills 50
Carla C 10
Carmania 64
Carmen 244
Carnivale 8

Carolina 72
Caroline Oldendorff 170
Carsten Russ 188
Cartagena de Indias 90
Carvalho Araujo 64
Caspian Universal 40
Cassinga 148
Cast Caribou 118
Cast Husky 46
Cast Muskox 46
Cast Otter 46
Cast Polarbear 118
Castle Point 188
Castor (Fin) 90
Castor (FRG) 24
Catalan Bay 204
Catamarca II 74
Caurica 196
Cavara 194
Cavelier de la Salle 92
Cavendish 92
Cayambe 222
Cecilie Maersk 146
Cedar Voyageur 44
Cedynia 182
Ceekay 172
Celchem Catalyst 140
Celebration 8
Celerina 212
Celsius 102
Celtic Link 34
Centum 102
Century 102
Century Highway No 1 118
Century Highway No 2 118
Century Hope 140
Century Leader No 1 162
Century Leader No 2 162
Century Progress 140
Cervo 126
Cetra Cassiopea 48
Cetra Corona 48
Cetra Sagitta 132
Cetra Vela 230
Ceynowa 178
CGM Bretagne 92
CGM Languedoc 24
CGM Lorraine 98
CGM Provence 100
CGM Var 92
CGM Velay 92
Chaco 74
Challenger 146
Chamal 218
Chambord 42
Champlain 92
Chanakya 146
Chandidas 200
Chang De 52
Chang Ming 52
Chang Shu 52
Chang Ting 52

Chang Xing 52
Chao He 52
Chao Yang 52
Charles LD 132
Charles Lykes 134
Charles Pigott 50
Charleston 192
Charlotta 72
Charlotte Lykes 134
Charlotte Maersk 146
Chastine Maersk 146
Chaumont 42
Chelsfield 132
Chemical Explorer 30
Chemical Venturer 30
Chengtu 214
Chenonceaux 42
Chernovtsy 236
Chevalier Paul 48
Chevalier Roze 48
Chevalier Valbelle 48
Chevron Antwerp 50
Chevron Arizona 50
Chevron Brussels 50
Chevron Burnaby 50
Chevron California 50
Chevron Colorado 50
Chevron Copenhagen 50
Chevron Edinburgh 50
Chevron Feluy 50
Chevron Frankfurt 50
Chevron Freeport 50
Chevron London 50
Chevron Louisiana 50
Chevron Mississippi 50
Chevron Nagasaki 50
Chevron North America 50
Chevron Oregon 50
Chevron Pacific 50
Chevron Perth 50
Chevron South America 50
Chevron Washington 50
Chiaki Maru 162
Chiara S 138
Chidorisan Maru 140
Chihirosan Maru 140
Chikubu Maru 162
Chikuho Maru 162
Chikumagawa Maru 120
Chikumasan Maru 140
Chikura Maru 162
China Container 222
China Pride 222
China Trader 222
China Victory 222
Chios 128
Chishirokawa Maru 120
Chita Maru 162
Chitral 176
Christian Maersk 146
Christian Wesch 246
Christina 64

Chubut 74
Chun He 52
Chun Lin 52
Chusovoy 236
Cinulia 198
City of Edinburgh 34
City of Liverpool 24
City of Mikanos 10
City of Rhodos 10
City of York 72
Ciudad de Armenia 90
Ciudad de Barrancabermeja 90
Ciudad de Bogota 90
Ciudad de Bucaramanga 90
Ciudad de Buenaventura 90
Ciudad de Cucuta 90
Ciudad de Manizales 90
Ciudad de Medellin 90
Ciudad de Neiva 90
Ciudad de Pasto 90
Ciudad de Popayan 90
Ciudad de Santa Marta 90
Clean River 120
Clerk-Maxwell 92
Clifford Maersk 146
Clio 90
Clover Ace 140
Clydebank 34
Clymene 92
Clytoneus 166
CMB Europe 60
Cobetas 244
Colditz 66
Colima 220
Coltair 42
Columbia Highway 120
Columbia Liberty 224
Columbia Star 38
Columbus America 168
Columbus Australia 168
Columbus Louisiana 168
Columbus New Zealand 168
Columbus Queensland 168
Columbus Victoria 168
Columbus Virginia 168
Columbus Wellington 168
Comandante Revello 138
Common Venture 28
Conastoga 144
Concordia Fjord 98
Concordia Star 98
Concordia Sun 98
Condata 232
Congo 64
Conscience 24
Constantia 206
Constellation 14
Constitution 22
Conus 198
Co-op Sunshine 140
Copacabana 74
Coral Chief 214

Coral Princess 214
Coral 60
Corato 92
Cordoba 74
Cornelia Maersk 146
Cornelis Verolme 194
Corona Star 76
Corrientes II 74
Corsicana 144
Costa Rica 190
Costa Riviera 10
Costas Konialidis 172
Cotopaxi 224
Cottbus 66
CP Ambassador 44
Cranach 24
Crestbank 34
Creuse 150
Crikvenica 114
Crimmitschau 66
Crown Bridge 252
Crown Broland 42
Crusader Point 218
Crystal Ace 140
Cumana 102
Cunard Countess 10
Cunard Princess 10
Cunene 148
Cunewalde 66
Cvijeta Zuzoric 118
Cypress 42
Cys Brilliance 224
Cys Crown 224
Cys Excellence 224
Cys Integrity 224
Cys Justice 224
Czacki 178
Czantoria 182

D. L. Bower 50
D'Albertis 88
D'Artagnan 144
Da Chang Zhen 52
Da Cheng 52
Da De 52
Da Jin Chuan 52
Da Long Tian 52
Du Muslu 80
Da Ning 52
Da Pu 52
Da Qing Shan 52
Da Sha Ping 52
Da Shi Qiao 52
Da Tian 52
Da Ye 52
Dacebank 34
Dagmar Maersk 146
Dai Hai 54
Dalanger 248
Dallington 210
Dalmacija 14
Dana Futura 126

Dana Hafnia 126
Danae 10
Danah 230
Daniela 74
Danisa 168
Daphne 10
Darfur 212
Dart Americana 46
Dart Atlantica 224
Dart Britain 224
Dart Continent 60
David Gas 62
David Packard 50
Dawn 48
De Du 54
DeLoris 194
De Rong Hai 54
De Xing 54
Delta Caribe 236
Delta Mar 236
Delta Norte 236
Delta Sud 236
Deng Long Hai 54
Devaraya 200
Devonshire 36
Dewa Maru 162
Diala 198
Diego 138
Dilkara 30
Diplomat 102
Dirch Maersk 146
Dirk Jacob 110
Discovery Bay 174
Dmitriy Donskoy 236
Dmitriy Pozharskiy 236
Dmitriy Shostakovich 22
Dobra 114
Dobrush 236
Dock Express 10 244
Dock Express 11 244
Dock Express 12 244
Dock Express 20 244
Doctor Lykes 134
Dolny Slask 182
Dolphin IV 22
Dolphin Point 188
Dominique L.D. 132
Don Carlos 244
Don Juan 244
Donau Ore 252
Dong Ming 54
Dongola 212
Donnington 210
Dora Oldendorff 170
Dorthe Maersk 146
Dorthe Oldendorff 170
Dr Atilio Malvagni 74
Dragonja 114
Drava 114
Dresden (DDR) 66
Dresden (Ru) 236
Drupa 196

Drvar 114
Dubai 230
Dubrovnik 118
Duchess 60
Dumont d'Urville 92
Dun Hua 54
Dunedin 92
Durmitor 116
Durrington 210
Dusseldorf Express 98
Dzieci Polskie 178

E.W. Beatty 46
E.R. Brugge 24
Eastern Alliance 120
Eastern Enterprise 30
Eastern Hazel 252
Eastern Lily 140
Eastern Spirit 252
Ebalina 196
Eburna 196
Echigo Maru 162
Eckert Oldendorff 170
Ecuadorian Reefer 126
Edco 112
Edgar Andre 66
Edouard L.D. 132
Eeklo 62
Efthitis 28
Egda 148
Eglantine 228
Egton 102
Eichsfeld 66
Eichwalde 66
Eiffel 92
Eilenburg 66
Eisenhuttenstadt 66
El Gaucho 212
El Mexicano 220
El Obeid 212
Elbe Maru 140
Elbe Ore 152
Elbia 76
Elgaren 220
Elgin 30
Elisabeth Maersk 146
Elisabeth Oldendorff 170
Elizabeth Lykes 134
Ellen Hudig 194
Ellinis 8
Elona 198
Elpis 28
Emerald Seas 12
Emilia S 138
Emma Maersk 146
Emma 194
Encounter Bay 174
Energy Courage 224
Energy Explorer 224
Energy Growth 224
Energy Mobility 224
Energy Progress 224

273

Energy Renown 224
Engladina 212
English Star 38
Enrico C 10
Ensis 198
Ensor 62
Entalina 196
Entre Rios II 74
Eole 218
Epimelia 28
Erfurt 66
Erika Jacob 110
Erinna 196
Eriskay 214
Erlangen Express 98
Ernst Moritz Arndt 66
Ernst Schneller 68
Erodona 196
Ervilia 196
Espenhain 68
Essi Anne 188
Essi Camilla 188
Essi Flora 188
Essi Gina 188
Essi Silje 188
Essi Vibeke 188
Esso Aberdeen 80
Esso Africa 82
Esso Albany 82
Esso Atlantic 82
Esso Bahamas 191
Esso Bangkok 82
Esso Bayonne 82
Esso Bayway 82
Esso Bilbao 82
Esso Bombay 82
Esso Callunda 84
Esso Caribbean 82
Esso Castellon 82
Esso Clyde 80
Esso Coral Gables 82
Esso Danica 84
Esso Demetia 80
Esso Deutschland 84
Esso Fawley 80
Esso Forth 82
Esso Fuji 82
Esso Geneva B2 82
Esso Genova 82
Esso Gippsland 82
Esso Hafnia 84
Esso Hamburg 84
Esso Hawaii 82
Esso Honolulu 82
Esso Humber 82
Esso Indonesia 82
Esso Japan 82
Esso Kagoshima 82
Esso Kaohsiung 82
Esso Kawasaki 82
Esso Languedoc 82
Esso Le Havre 82

Esso Madrid 82
Esso Mediterranean 82
Esso Melbourne 82
Esso Mersey 82
Esso Mexico 82
Esso Milford Haven 82
Esso Nassau 82
Esso Normandie 82
Esso Okinawa 82
Esso Orient 84
Esso Osaka 82
Esso Pacific 82
Esso Palm Beach 82
Esso Parentis 82
Esso Picardie 82
Esso Port Dickson 84
Esso Port Jerome 82
Esso Portland 84
Esso Saba 84
Esso Severn 82
Esso Shimizu 84
Esso Slagen 84
Esso Tampa 84
Esso Tees 82
Esso Venezia 82
Esso Warwickshire 82
Esso Westernport 84
Esso Yokohama 84
Esso Zurich 84
Estonia 22
Estrella Antarctica 198
Estrella Argentina 198
Estrella Fueguina 198
Estrella Patagonica 198
Etha Rickmers 186
Ethnic 126
Etienne Denis 150
Etrema 196
Eugenio C 10
Eugeniusz Kwiatkowski 178
Eulima 196
Eulota 196
Euplecta 196
Europa (FRG) 12
Europa (Italian) 88
European Highway 120
Evelyn Maersk 146
Ever Better 78
Ever Breeze 78
Ever Bridge 78
Ever Garden 78
Ever Gather 78
Ever Genius 78
Ever Gentle 78
Ever Gentry 78
Ever Giant 78
Ever Gifted 78
Ever Gleamy 78
Ever Globe 78
Ever Glory 78
Ever Going 78
Ever Golden 78

Ever Goods 78
Ever Govern 78
Ever Grace 78
Ever Grade 78
Ever Grand 78
Ever Greet 78
Ever Growth 78
Ever Guard 78
Ever Guide 78
Ever Laurel 78
Ever Level 78
Ever Linking 78
Ever Living 78
Ever Loading 78
Ever Lyric 78
Ever Oasis 78
Ever Obtain 78
Ever Ocean 78
Ever Onward 78
Ever Order 78
Ever Orient 78
Ever Shine 78
Ever Spring 78
Ever Summit 78
Ever Superb 78
Ever Trust 78
Ever Valor 78
Ever Value 78
Ever Vigor 78
Ever Vital 78
Evimeria 28
Evita 228
Evros 128
Export Challenger 84
Export Champion 84
Export Freedom 84
Export Patriot 84
Exxon Baltimore 80
Exxon Baton Rouge 80
Exxon Baytown 80
Exxon Benicia 80
Exxon Boston 80
Exxon Charleston 80
Exxon Galveston 80
Exxon Gettysburg 80
Exxon Houston 80
Exxon Jamestown 80
Exxon Lexington 80
Exxon New Orleans 80
Exxon North Slope 80
Exxon Philadelphia 80
Exxon Princeton 80
Exxon San Francisco 80
Exxon Washington 80
Exxon Wilmington 80
Exxon Yorktown 80

Fabiolaville 60
Fair Spitit 170
Fairsea 20
Fairsky 20
Fairstar 20

Fairwind 20
Fairwinds 140
Falcon 184
Falknes 112
Falstaff 244
Falstria 72
Faraday 92
Farland 186
Farnes 112
Fathulkhair 230
Faust 244
Favorita 228
Federal Calumet 86
Federal Danube 86
Federal Elbe 86
Federal Fraser 86
Federal Hudson 86
Federal Hunter 86
Federal Huron 86
Federal Lakes 86
Federal Maas 86
Federal Ottawa 86
Federal Rhine 86
Federal Saguenay 86
Federal Schelde 86
Federal Skeena 86
Federal St Laurent 86
Federal Thames 86
Fedor Poletaev 236
Fedor Shalyapin 22
Fei Cui Hai 54
Felania 198
Feliks Dzerjinsky 22
Feliks Dzierzynski 182
Felipes 198
Fen He 54
Feng Chi 54
Feng Hang 54
Feng Sheng 54
Feng Xiang 54
Feng Yan 54
Fengtien 214
Ferdinand Freiligrath 68
Fermita 228
Ferncarrier 84
Ferncourt 84
Ferncraig 84
Ferncroft 84
Ferngolf 84
Fernpassat 84
Fernteam 86
Festivale 8
Fichtelberg 68
Ficus 198
Figaro 246
Filipp Makharadze 236
Fina America 178
Fina Belgica 178
Fina Italie 178
Fina Norvege 178
Finn Falcon 88
Finn Timber 88

Finn Whale 88	Fort Toronto 46	Gamal Abdel Naser 236	Georgiy Leonidze 236
Finnarctis 68	Fort Victoria 46	Gambada 174	Georgiy Pyasetskiy 236
Finnbeaver 88	Fort Yale 46	Gambhira 174	Gerald L. D. 132
Finneagle 88	Forthbank 34	Gan Jiang 54	Gerd Maersk 146
Finnfighter 88	Forum New Zealand 194	Gandara 174	Gerdt Oldendorff 170
Finnfury 88	Fosna 148	Garala 174	Gerhart Hauptmann 68
Finnhawk 88	Fossarina 198	Garbeta 174	Geringswalde 68
Finnmerchant 88	Fossarus 198	Gari 196	Geroi Bresta 236
Finnoak 88	Fossnes 112	Garinda 174	Geroi Monkadiy 236
Finnoceanis 88	FP Carrier 72	Garrison Point 218	Geroi Stalingrada 236
Finnpine 88	FP Clipper 72	Garwolin 178	Gertrud Jacob 110
Finnpolaris 88	FP Conveyor 72	Gas Al-Ahmadi 124	Getaldic 118
Finnrose 88	Francesca 138	Gas Al-Burgan 124	Gimi 96
Finnsnes 112	Francesco Nullo 178	Gas Al-Kuwait 124	Gioacchino Lauro 126
Finntrader 88	Franciszek Zubrzycki 178	Gas Al-Minagish 124	Giordano Bruno 238
Fionia 72	Francois LD 132	Gas Enterprise 40	Giovanna S. 138
Firmnes 112	Frangiskos C. K. 28	Gas Rising Sun 140	Giuseppe Verdi 238
Fjellnes 112	Franina 118	Gastor 154	Gjertrud Maersk 146
Fjord Bridge 110	Frank Delmas 150	Gastrana 196	Glaciar Ameghino 74
Fjord Land 110	Frankfurt Express 98	Gauguin 94	Glaciar Perito Moreno 74
Fjord Mariner 110	Frankfurt/Oder 68	Gazana 174	Glaciar Viedma 74
Fjord Ranger 110	Franz Stenzer 68	Gazzella 126	Glauchau 68
Fjord Thistle 148	Frederic Joliot Curie 68	Gdansk II 178	Gleichberg 68
Fjord Trader 110	Fredro 178	Gdansk 236	Gleneagles 228
Fjord Wind 110	Freeport Chief 110	Gdynia 236	Gliwice II 182
Fjordnes 112	Freezer Leopard 64	Gdynski Kosynier 178	Global Highway 120
Fjordshell 198	Freital 68	Gedaref 212	Globe Trader 170
Flamengo 74	Fremantle Express 204	Geestbay 92	Globtik Britain 94
Flaming 68	Freyburg 68	Geestland 92	Globtik London 94
Flammulina 198	Friedrich Engels 68	Geestport 92	Globtik Tokyo 94
Fleesensee 68	Frines 112	Geeststar 92	Gloria 220
Fleet Wave 232	Fritz Reuter 68	General Aguinaldo 112	Glorious Ace 140
Flevoland 156	Fronisis 28	General Bem 182	Godwit 140
Fliegerkosmonaut der DDR	Frycz Modrzewski 178	General Berling 182	Goho Maru 120
Sigmund Jahn 68	Fuerte Ventura 26	General Capinpin 112	Golar Freeze 96
Flinders Bay 174	Fuji Maru 162	General Cruz 112	Golar Frost 96
Floreal 150	Fujikawa Maru 162	General Dabrowski 182	Golar Kansai 96
Folga 148	Fujisan Maru 120	General Fr. Kleeberg 178	Golar Kanto 96
Formosa 74	Fulgar 198	General Guisan 212	Golar Petrosea 96
Fort Assiniboine 146	Full Moon 140	General Hizon 112	Golar Petrosun 96
Fort Calgary 46	Funchal 10	General Jasinski 182	Golar Petrotrade 96
Fort Carleton 46	Furstenwalde 68	General Leselidze 236	Golar Robin 96
Fort Coulonge 46	Furstenberg 68	General Lim 112	Golar Spirit 96
Fort Desaix 94	Fushimi Maru 162	General M. Makleff 194	Gold Alisa 256
Fort Dufferin 46	Fuso Maru 162	General Madalinski 182	Gold Hilla 256
Fort Edmonton 46	Fusus 198	General Manuel Belgrano 74	Gold Leaf 256
Fort Fleur d'Epee 94	Futami Maru 162	General Pradzynski 182	Gold Mountain 256
Fort Frontenac 46	Future Hope 170	General Santos 112	Gold Orli 256
Fort Garry 46		General Segundo 112	Gold Stream 256
Fort Hamilton 46	G. A. Walker 46	General Stanislaw Poplawski 180	Gold Varda 256
Fort Kamloops 46	Ga Chau 66	General Swierczewski 182	Goldean Pioneer 60
Fort Kipp 46	Gacka 144	General Tinio 112	Golden Ace 140
Fort Macleod 46	Gadila 196	Genevieve Lykes 134	Golden Bliss 252
Fort Nanaimo 46	Gadinia 196	Genota 196	Golden Canary 252
Fort Nelson 46	Galaxia 14	Geomitra 196	Golden Cape 252
Fort Point 188	Galconda 174	Georg Handke 68	Golden Clover 252
Fort Providence 46	Galeona 222	Georg Schumann 68	Golden Gate Bridge 120
Fort Resolution 46	Galileo Galilei 236	Georg Weerth 68	Golden Lotus 252
Fort Rouge 46	Galileo 8	George F. Getty II 216	Golden Odyssey 18
Fort Royal 94	Galion 218	George Georgiu-Dezh 236	Golden Orchid 172
Fort Saint Charles 94	Galpara 174	George H. Weyerhaeuser 50	Golden Rio 252
Fort Steele 46	Galveston 192	George M. Keller 50	Golden Tulip 252

Golfo de Chiriqui 90
Good Faith 170
Goran Kavacic 114
Gorlitz 68
Gorlovka 238
Gorny Slask 182
Gotha 68
Gouldia 196
Graiglas 250
Great Marine 120
Green Harbour 48
Green Island 48
Green Rock 250
Green Saikai 140
Green Valley 48
Green Wave 48
Grena 148
Grenanger 248
Gretke Oldendorff 170
Grey Fighter 34
Grey Hunter 34
Grigoriy Alekseev 238
Grigory Ordzhonikidze 22
Grobnik 114
Groditz 68
Grunwald 180
Gruziya 22
Guaicuri 220
Guang He 54
Guatemala 190
Gudrun Maersk 146
Gui Hai 54
Gui Yang 54
Gulf Glory 162
Gulf Harvest 162
Gulf Ideal 162
Gundulic 118
Gwardia Ludowa 180

H. Capelo 64
H. J. Haynes 50
Hachinohe Maru 162
Hadera 256
Hai Feng 54
Hai Men 54
Hai Zhou 54
Haisbon 122
Hakata Maru 162
Hakone Maru 162
Hakuba Maru 162
Hakusan Maru 162
Halberstadt 68
Halle 68
Halul 30
Hamburg Express 98
Hammonia 98
Hammurabi 230
Hampshire 36
Han Chuan 54
Hans Leonhardt 128
Hanse 24
Hao Long 8

Hapag Lloyd Brasil 152
Happy Buccaneer 156
Happy Chance 170
Happy Mammoth 156
Har Kishin 200
Har Rai 200
Hardanger 248
Harefield 132
Hargobind 200
Harriet Maru 140
Harsha Vardhana 200
Harvella 198
Havana 238
Havfalk 102
Havis 102
Havjo 102
Havkatt 102
Havlyn 102
Havorn 102
Havtroll 102
Hayakawa Maru 162
Hei Long Jiang 54
Heide Leonhardt 128
Heina 148
Heinrich Heine 68
Heinz Kapelle 68
Heiwa Maru 162
Hektos 90
Hel 180
Helen 194
Helene Delmas 150
Helvetia 76
Henriette Maersk 146
Henryk Jendza 180
Hera 228
Herceg Novi 116
Hercegovina 118
Hermes Ace 162
Herta Maersk 146
Hesperus 90
Hettstedt 68
Heweliusz 180
Hijaz 230
Hikawa Maru 162
Hille Oldendorff 170
Hilli 96
Himalaya Maru 140
Hinglaj 176
Hira Maru 162
Hodeidah Crown 44
Hoegh Banniere 104
Hoegh Cairn 104
Hoegh Cape 104
Hoegh Carrier 248
Hoegh Clipper 104
Hoegh Dene 104
Hoegh Drake 104
Hoegh Duke 104
Hoegh Dyke 104
Hoegh Falcon 104
Hoegh Favour 104
Hoegh Foam 104

Hoegh Fortuna 104
Hoegh Forum 104
Hoegh Fountain 104
Hoegh Fulmar 104
Hoegh Gandria 104
Hoegh Hill 104
Hoegh Hood 104
Hoegh Mallard 104
Hoegh Marlin 104
Hoegh Mascot 104
Hoegh Minerva 104
Hoegh Miranda 104
Hoegh Skean 104
Hoegh Sword 104
Holiday 8
Homeric 14
Honam Ruby 96
Honduras 190
Hongkong Container 224
Hongkong Express 98
Hong Men 54
Hong Qi 123 54
Hong Shou Shan 54
Honolulu 66
Horda 148
Hornbay 94
Horncap 94
Hornfels 94
Hotaka Maru 162
Houston Getty 216
Howard W. Bell 50
Hreljin 114
Hrvatska 114
Hu Lin 54
Hu Po Hai 54
Hua Chun 54
Hua Shan 54
Hua Ting 54
Hua Tuo 54
Hua Xing 54
Huai Yang 54
Hual Angelita 228
Hual Carmencita 228
Hual Ingrita 228
Hual Karinita 228
Hual Lisita 228
Hual Rolita 228
Hual Torinita 228
Hual Tracer 104
Hual Trader 104
Hual Transporter 104
Hual Trapper 104
Hual Traveller 104
Hual Trotter 104
Huang Shan 54
Hugo Oldendorff 170
Hulda Maersk 146
Humboldt Express 98
Hun Jiang 54
Hunan 214
Hunza 176
Hupeh 214

Huta Katowice 182
Huta Lenina 182
Huta Zgoda 182
Huta Zygmunt 182
Hyderabad 176
Hyogo Maru 162
Hyuga Maru 162

I. D. Sinclair 46
Ibaraki Maru 140
Iberita 228
Ibn Abdoun 230
Ibn Al Abbar 230
Ibn Al Beitar 230
Ibn Al Moataz 230
Ibn Al Roomi 230
Ibn Al-Atheer 230
Ibn Al-Haitham 230
Ibn Al-Nafees 230
Ibn Asakir 230
Ibn Bajjah 230
Ibn Bassam 230
Ibn Battotah 230
Ibn Duraid 230
Ibn Hayyan 230
Ibn Hazm 230
Ibn Jubayr 230
Ibn Khaldoon 230
Ibn Khallikan 230
Ibn Malik 232
Ibn Qutaibah 232
Ibn Rushd 232
Ibn Shuhaid 232
Ibn Sina 232
Ibn Tufail 232
Ibn Younus 232
Ibn Zuhr 232
Igarka 238
Igloo Finn 102
Igloo Moss 102
Igloo Norse 102
Igloo Polar 102
Iguazu 212
Ile de la Reunion 152
Ile Maurice 152
Imme Oldendorff 170
Incotrans Pacific 98
Incotrans Speed 42
Incotrans Spirit 42
Independence 22
Indian Courier 106
Indian Endurance 106
Indian Explorer 106
Indian Faith 106
Indian Fame 106
Indian Fortune 106
Indian Fraternity 106
Indian Freedom 106
Indian Glory 106
Indian Goodwill 106
Indian Grace 106
Indian Prestige 106

Indian Progress 106
Indian Prosperity 106
Indian Security 106
Indian Trust 106
Indian Valour 106
Indian Venture 106
Inge Maersk 146
Ingram Osprey 186
Ingrid Gorthon 96
Ingrid Leonhardt 128
Invicta 76
Inzhener Parkhonyuk 238
Inzhener Yermoshkin 238
Ioannis Zafirakis 128
Ion Soltys 238
Iran Abad 106
Iran Adalat 106
Iran Adi 106
Iran Afzal 106
Iran Akhavan 106
Iran Amanat 106
Iran Ashrafi 106
Iran Azadi 106
Iran Bahonar 106
Iran Bayan106
Iran Beheshti 106
Iran Besat 106
Iran Borhan106
Iran Chamran 106
Iran Dahr 106
Iran Dastghayb 106
Iran Deyanat 106
Iran Ehsan 106
Iran Ejtahad 106
Iran Ekram 106
Iran Elham 106
Iran Emdad 108
Iran Enghelab 108
Iran Entekhab 108
Iran Ershad 108
Iran Eshraghi 108
Iran Eslami 108
Iran Esteghlal 108
Iran Fakori 108
Iran Fallahi 108
Iran Fateh 108
Iran Ghafari 108
Iran Ghazi 108
Iran Gheyam 108
Iran Gheyamat 108
Iran Hojjat 108
Iran Jahad 108
Iran Jamal 108
Iran Javad 108
Iran Jenan 108
Iran Jomhuri 108
Iran Kalam 108
Iran Kashani 108
Iran Madani 108
Iran Meead 108
Iran Meelad 108
Iran Meezan 108

Iran Meysam 108
Iran Modares 108
Iran Mofateh 108
Iran Motahari 108
Iran Nabuvat 108
Iran Nahad 108
Iran Namjoo 108
Iran Nasr 108
Iran Nehzat 108
Iran Rajai 108
Iran Reshadat 108
Iran Sabr 108
Iran Sadoughi 108
Iran Sadr 108
Iran Salam 108
Iran Sarbaz 108
Iran Seeyam 108
Iran Sepah 108
Iran Shahadat 108
Iran Shahamat 108
Iran Shariat 108
Iran Shariati 108
Iran Shojaat 108
Iran Sokan 108
Iran Takhti 108
Iran Taleghani 108
Iran Teyfouri 110
Iran Torab 110
Iran Vahdat 110
Iran Vojdan 110
Irene Greenwood 124
Iris Leonhardt 128
Iris 256
Irish Spruce 106
Iron Kestrel 186
Iron Kirby 186
Iron Somersby 186
Isar Express 98
Iseult 218
Isla de la Plata 98
Isla Payana 24
Isla Plaza 60
Isla Pongal 24
Island Princess 18
Isocardia 196
Isolde 246
Isomeria 196
Istra 14
Istranka 118
Itabera 130
Itagiba 130
Itaimbe 130
Itaite 130
Italica 88
Itanage 130
Itapage 130
Itape 130
Itapuca 130
Itapui 130
Itapura 130
Itaquatia 130
Itassuce 130

Ivan Bogun 238
Ivan Franko 22
Ivan Kotiyarevskiy 238
Ivan Makarin 238
Ivan Perevervez 238
Ivan Susanin 238
Ivan Tevosyan 238
Ivo Vojnovic 118
Ivybank 34
Izgutty Aytykov 238
Izumisan Maru 140

J. Paul Getty 216
J. R. Grey 50
J. T. Higgins 50
Jacek Malczewski 180
Jacob Russ 188
Jacqueville 110
Jade Bounty 60
Jadran Express 114
Jadran 118
Jag Deesh 96
Jag Dharma 96
Jag Dhir 96
Jag Doot 96
Jag Jiwan 96
Jag Jyoti 96
Jag Krishi 96
Jag Laadki 96
Jag Laxmi 96
Jag Leela 96
Jag Manek 96
Jag Palak 96
Jag Pari 96
Jag Prabhat 96
Jag Pragati 96
Jag Prakash 96
Jag Preeti 96
Jag Priya 96
Jag Rakshak 98
Jag Shakti 98
Jag Shanti 98
Jaguar 110
Jahre Lion 62
Jahre Tiger 62
Jakob Maersk 146
Jalabala 190
Jalagodavari 190
Jalagopal 190
Jalagouri 190
Jalagovind 190
Jalajaya 190
Jalajyoti 190
Jalakala 190
Jalakanta 190
Jalakendra 190
Jalamani 190
Jalamatsya 190
Jalamayur 190
Jalamohan 190
Jalamokambi 190
Jalamoti 190

Jalamudra 190
Jalamuragan 190
Jalapa 220
Jalaputra 190
Jalarajan 190
Jalaratna 190
Jalrashmi 190
Jalatapi 190
Jalatarang 190
Jalavlhar 190
Jalavijaya 190
Jalayamini 190
Jalayamuna 190
Jalinga 110
Jalisco 220
Jalvallabh 190
James Lykes 134
Jamunda 110
Jan Dlugosz 180
Jan Matejko 180
Janega 110
Janus 110
Janusz Kusocinski 182
Japana 110
Jarabella 110
Jaraconda 110
Jarama 110
Jarena 110
Jarilla 112
Jarmada 112
Jarmina 112
Jason 12
Jastarnia-Bor 180
Jean Lykes 134
Jebel Ali 232
Jebsen Napier 112
Jebsen Tauranga 112
Jebsen Timaru 112
Jedforest 174
Jena 68
Jeppeson Maeesk 146
Jesbon 122
Jesenice 114
Jesper Maersk 146
Jessie Stove 206
Jhansi-ki Rani 200
Jia Xing 54
Jiang Chuan 54
Jiang Ting 54
Jiao Cheng 54
Jiao Zhou Hai 54
Jilfar 232
Jin Cheng Jiang 54
Jin Cheng 54
Jin Hai 54
Jin Jiang 54
Jin Shan Hai 54
Jin Tian Hai 54
Jin Zhou Hai 54
Jin Zhou 54
Jindai Maru 162
Jinei Maru 162

Jing Hai 54
Jingu Maru 162
Jinmei Maru 162
Jinryu Maru 164
Jinsbon 122
Jinsen Maru 164
Jinto Maru 164
Jinyo Maru 164
Jinyu Maru 164
Jo Birk 168
Jo Clipper 168
Jo Cypress 168
Jo Lind 168
Jo Lonn 168
Jo Oak 168
Joh Gorthon 96
Johanngeorgenstadt 68
Johar 176
John A. McCone 50
John Brinckman 68
John Lykes 134
John Schehr 68
Johnson Chemspan 114
Johnson Chemstar 114
Johnson Chemstream 114
Johnson Chemsun 114
Jonna Dan 126
Jonny Wesch 246
Jorek Combiner 186
Jorgen J. Lorentzen 206
Joseph Lykes 134
Jozef Chelmonski 180
Jozef Conrad Korzeniowski 180
Ju Hai 54
Jubilee 8
Jujuy II 74
Julia 88
Juliana 188
Julio Antonio Mella 238
Jun Liang Cheng 54
Jupiter (Greek) 12
Jupiter No 1 120
Jupiter (Norwegian) 16/18
Jurata 180
Jurina 118
Jutlandia 72
Juventia 76
Jytte Skou 206

K. I. Galczynski 180
Kabirdas 200
Kaga Maru 164
Kaghan 176
Kai Maru 164
Kalidas 200
Kamakura Maru 164
Kananga 254
Kang Hai 54
Kang Su Hai 54
Kangourou 94
Kanishka 200
Kansas Getty 216

Kapetan Martinovic 116
Kapitan A. Polkovskiy 238
Kapitan Bochek 238
Kapitan Chukhchin 238
Kapitan Fomin 238
Kapitan Fomenko 238
Kapitan Gavrilov 238
Kapitan Kanevskiy 238
Kapitan Koziovskiy 238
Kapitan Kudlay 238
Kapitan Medvedev 238
Kapitan Mezentsev 238
Kapitan Nazarev 238
Kapitan Smirnov 238
Kapitan Soroka 238
Kapitan Sviridov 238
Kapitan Trubkin 238
Kapitan Tsirul 238
Kapitan V. Trush 238
Kapitan V. Ushakov 238
Kapitan Vakula 238
Kapitan Vodenko 238
Kaptai 176
Karama Maersk 146
Karen Maersk 146
Karl Leonhardt 128
Karl Marx Stadt 68
Karl Marx 68
Karlowicz 180
Karnataka 200
Karoline Maersk 146
Kasos 1316
Kastav 114
Kasturba 200
Kasuga Maru 164
Kasugai Maru 164
Kate Maersk 146
Katorisan Maru 140
Katowice II 180
Katrine Maersk 146
Kavkaz 238
Kazimah 124
Kazimierz Pulaski 180
Kazakhstan 22
Kazukawa Maru 120
Kedma 256
Kenneth E. Hill 50
Kenneth T. Derr 50
Kentavros 14
Kenyo Maru 164
Keta Lagoon 38
Khabarovsk 22
Khairpur 176
Khaled Ibn Al Waleed 232
Khannur 96
Khartoum 212
Khudozhnik A. Gerasimov 238
Khudozhnik Federovskiy 238
Khudozhnik Gabashvili 238
Khudozhnik Ioganson 238
Khudozhnik Kasyan 238
Khudozhnik Kustodiyev 238

Khudozhnik Moor 238
Khudozhnik Pakhomov 238
Khudozhnik Prorokov 238
Khudozhnik Repin 238
Khudozhnik Romas 238
Khudozhnik Saryan 238
Khudozhnik Toidze 238
Khudozhnik Vladimir Serov 238
Khudozhnik Zhukov 238
Kieldrecht 242
Kiho Maru (K) 120
Kiho Maru (NYK) 164
Kii Maru 164
Kildare 174
Kim Hae 122
Kinokawa Maru 120
Kirsten Maersk 146
Kirsten Wesch 246
Kisangani 254
Kiso Maru 164
Kitano Maru 164
Klaus Leonhardt 128
Klorte Lagoon 38
Knight 224
Kohjusan Maru 140
Kohzan Maru 140
Koiteli 88
Kohkisan Maru 140
Kollbjorg 34
Koln Express 98
Kolpinsee 68
Kolsnaren 220
Komsomolets Kubani 238
Komsomolets Leningrada 238
Komsomolsk 238
Konavie 118
Konin 180
Konstantin Paustovskiy 238
Kopalnia Gottwald 182
Kopalnia Grzybow 182
Kopalnia Jastrzebia 182
Kopalnia Jeziorko 182
Kopalnia Kleofas 182
Kopalnia Machow 182
Kopalnia Marcel 182
Kopalnia Miechowice 182
Kopalnia Moszczenica 182
Kopalnia Myslowice 182
Kopalnia Piaseczno 182
Kopalnia Siemianwice 182
Kopalnia Siersza 182
Kopalnia Sosnica 182
Kopalnia Sosnowiec 182
Kopalnia Szczyglowice 182
Kopalnia Szombierki 184
Kopalnia Walbrzych 184
Kopalnia Wirek 184
Kopalnia Zofiowka 184
Korana 114
Kordun 116
Korea Pacific 122
Korea Rainbow 122

Korean Chance 60
Korean Jacejin 122
Korean Jacewon 122
Korean Loader 60
Korean Peace 60
Korean Pigeon 60
Korean Pioneer 60
Korean Wonis Jin 122
Korean Wonis One 122
Korean Wonis Seven 122
Korean Wonis Sun 122
Korrigan 94
Kosmaj 116
Kostrena 114
Kostroma 238
Kothen 68
Kotkaniemi 88
Kotor 116
Kotowaka Maru 164
Kowloon Bay 174
Kozara 116
Kragujevac 118
Kraljevica 114
Kranjcevic 114
Krasica 114
Kraszewski 180
Kremenchug 238
Kristine Maersk 146
Krivbass 240
Krk 114
Krusevac 116
Krym 240
Kuang Hai 54
Kuban 240
Kubbar 232
Kujawy 184
Kumanovo 116
Kumrovec 116
Kun Ming 54
Kunimisan Maru 140
Kupa 116
Kurama Maru 164
Kurobe Maru 164
Kurotakisun Maru 140
Kuzbass 240
Kuzma Minin 240
Kuznica 180
Kwellin 214
Kyoei Maru 164
Kyoto 228

L. W. Funkhouser 50
La Chacra 132
La Fayette 94
La Palma 14
La Pampa (Br) 132
La Pampa (Arg) 74
La Richardais 132
La Rioja 74
Lacandon 220
Lackenby 186
Lago Lacar 74

Lakenes 112
Lalazar 176
Lamma Forest 66
Lampas 196
Lanai 66
Landguard Point 218
Lanistes 196
Lanka Abhaya 26
Lanka Ajitha 48
Lanka Amila 26
Lanka Amitha 26
Lanka Athula 48
Lanka Mahapola 48
Lanka Rani 48
Lanka Ratna 48
Lanka Shanthi 48
Lanka Srimani 48
Lanka Srimathi 48
Lantana 164
Lantau Trader 66
Larina 36
Lars Maersk 146
Latvia 22
Laura Maersk 146
Laurel Wreath 120
Laurentine 228
Laurita 228
Laust Maersk 146
Lavaux 212
Laxmi 200
Le Ting 54
Leadbon 122
Leda Maersk 146
Leda 196
Ledenice 116
Leeward 98
Legia 60
Lei Zhou Hai 54
Leila 138
Leipzig 68
Leiria 64
Leise Maersk 146
Leningrad 180
Lenino 180
Leninsk 240
Lensovet 240
Leon & Pierre C 228
Leonia 196
Leonid Brezhnev 22
Leonid Sobinov 22
Leonid Sobolyev 240
Leopold Staff 180
Lepeta 196
Lerma 220
Leslie Lykes 134
Letitia Lykes 134
Lev Tolstoy 22
Lexa Maersk 146
Li Ming 54
Li Yang 54
Lian Yun Shan 56
Liao Hai 65

Liao Yang 56
Libertador General Jose de
    San Martin 74
Liberte 20
Lica Maersk 146
Licorne Atlantique 94
Licorne Oceane 94
Licorne Pacique 94
Liebenwalde 68
Lieselotte Herrmann 68
Lika 116
Lily 74
Lima 196
Lincolnshire 36
Lindnes 112
Ling Quan He 56
Linngsbon 122
Lion of Ethiopia 78
Lions Gate Bridge 120
Liotina 198
Lista 148
Litva 22
Liu Lin Hai 56
Liverpool Bay 174
Lloyd Alegrete 130
Lloyd Altamira 130
Lloyd Argentina 130
Lloyd Atlantico 130
Lloyd Australia 176
Lloyd Bage 130
Lloyd Bahia 130
Lloyd California 44
Lloyd Cuiaba 130
Lloyd Genova 130
Lloyd Hamburgo 130
Lloyd Houston 130
Lloyd Liverpool 130
Lloyd Londres 44
Lloyd Mandu 130
Lloyd Marselha 130
Lloyd Mexico 130
Lloyd Pacifico 130
Lloyd Rio 176
Lloyd Santarem 130
Lloyd Santos 130
Lloyd San Francisco 166
Lloyd Sao Paulo 190
Lloyd Texas 176
Lloyd Tupiara 130
Lloyd Venezuela 130
Lloydbras 130
Lloydiana 88
Lobito 64
Loftnes 112
Lok Manya 200
Lok Nayak 200
Lok Palak 200
Lok Pragati 200
Lok Prakash 200
Lok Pratima 200
Lok Priti 200
Lok Sahayak 200

Lok Vihar 200
Lok Vikas 200
Lok Vinay 200
Lok Vivek 200
London Spirit 130
London Team 70
London Victory 130
Long Beach 192
Long Hua 56
Long Lin 56
Loosdrecht 242
Lord Citrine 188
Lord Hinton 188
Lord Kelvin 92
Lorenzo 188
Los Angeles Getty 216
Losinj 116
Lotila 88
Lottia 198
Louis Maersk 146
Louise Lykes 134
Lovcen 116
Lovisa Gorthon 96
Lu Ban 56
Lu Cheng 56
Lu Feng 56
Lu Shan 56
Luan He 56
Lubbenau 68
Lucayan Trader 204
Lucendro 212
Lucerna 204
Lucie Delmas 150
Lucien Delmas 150
Lucina 196
Lucjan Szenwald 180
Luckenwalde 68
Ludolf Oldendorff 170
Ludwigshafen Express 98
Luise Leonhardt 128
Lumber State 140
Lumiere 64
Luminetta 64
Lumumba 256
Luna Maersk 146
Luo Fu Shan 56
Luo He 56
Luo Shan Hai 56

Maaskade 154
Maaskant 154
Maaskerk 156
Maaskroon 156
Maasslot 156
Maassluis 156
Maasstad 156
Maasstroom 156
Macassar Maru 120
Maciej Rataj 184
Madame Butterfly 246
Maersk Angus 148
Maersk Ascension 148

Maersk Buchan 148
Maersk Clementine 124
Maersk Harrier 148
Maersk Mango 148
Maersk Neptun 146
Maersk Sebarok 148
Maersk Seletar 148
Maersk Sembawang 148
Maersk Sentosa 148
Maersk Serangoon 148
Maersk Tempo 148
Maersk Triton 146
Maersk Wave 146
Maersk Wind 146
Maeterlinck 60
Magdalena Wesch 246
Magdeburg 68
Magwe 44
Magnitogorsk 240
Magritte 60
Maharshi Dayanand 202
Maharshi Karve 202
Mahinda 228
Mai Rickmers 186
Main Express 174
Mairangi Bay 174
Maizuru Maru 164
Major Hubal 184
Major Sucharski 180
Makeevka 240
Makran 176
Maksim Gorkiy 22
Maksim Mikhaylov 240
Malacca 72
Malakand 176
Malange 64
Malayan Reefer 66
Mallory Lykes 134
Maloja 214
Manaka 122
Manchester Challenge 224
Mandalay (Bm) 44
Mandalay (Li) 42
Manhattan Baron 224
Manhattan Prince 86
Manica 148
Mansfeld 68
Marathon 104
Mardi Gras 8
Margaret Johnson 114
Margaret Lykes 134
Margit Gorthon 96
Maria Angelicoussi 28
Maria Gorthon 96
Maria I.A. 28
Maria Oldendorff 170
Marian Buczekl 180
Marie Delmas 150
Marina Bay 204
Marina Breeze 204
Marine Ranger 170
Marina 128

Maringa (BZ) 74
Maringa (FRG) 76
Maripasoula 94
Maris Otter 150
Maris Sportsman 150
Marita Leonhardt 128
Marjorie Lykes 134
Maron 166
Marshal Bagramyan 240
Marshal Budyonnyy 240
Marshal Chukov 240
Marshal Govorov 240
Marshal Grechko 240
Marshal Konev 240
Marshal Rokossovskiy 240
Marshal Vasilyevskiy 240
Marshal Zakharov 240
Marshal Zhukov 240
Marshall Clark 36
Martha 194
Matadi Palm 176
Matco Avon 142
Matco Clyde 142
Matco Thames 142
Mathias Thesen 68
Mauranger 248
Maurice Thorez 240
Mavro Vetranic 118
Maw-La-Myaing 44
Max Reichpietsche 68
Maya 220
Mbandaka 256
Mbuji Mayi 256
Meadowbank 34
Meandros 128
Medea 246
Mediteranea 88
Meerdrecht 242
Mei Jiang 56
Meisho Maru 140
Meissen 68
Meistersinger 26
Meitai Maru 140
Mekhanik Afanasyev 240
Mekhanik P. Kilimenchek 240
Mekhanik Dren 240
Mela 132
Melampus 166
Melbourne Express 98
Melbourne Highway 120
Mena 200
Mendoza 74
Menelaus 166
Menhir 242
Menina Daniela 140
Meonia 72
Merawi 212
Mercandian Admiral II 102
Mercandian Ambassador 102
Mercandian Duke 102
Mercandian Governor 102
Mercandian Ocean 102

Mercandian President 102
Mercandian Prince II 102
Mercandian Queen II 102
Mercandian Senator 102
Mercator 60
Merchant Pilot 46
Merchant Pioneer 46
Merchant Prelude 46
Merchant Principal 46
Merchant Providence 46
Mercury Ace 140
Mergui 44
Merkur Bay 244
Merkur Beach 244
Merkur Delta 244
Merkur Island 244
Merkur Lake 244
Merkur River 244
Merkur Sea 244
Mermoz 8
Merzario Arabia 138
Merzario Arcadia 138
Merzario Britannia 138
Merzario Fenicia 138
Merzario Italia 138
Merzario Persia 138
Messiniaki Anagennisis 118
Messiniaki Doxa 118
Methane Princess 200
Methane Progress 200
Methania 60
Metohija 116
Mexican Reefer 66
Mexico 1 190
Meyenburg 68
Mi Yun Hai 56
Michael Delmas 150
Michele 138
Mieszko I 180
Miezyslaw Kalinowski 180
Mifunesan Maru 140
Mighty Servant 1 248
Mighty Servant 2 248
Mighty Servant 3 248
Mijdrecht 242
Mikha Tskhakaya 240
Mikhail Kalinin 22
Mikhail Kutzov 240
Mikhail Lermontov 22
Mikhail Stelmakh 240
Mikhail Strekalovskiy 240
Mikhail Suslov 240
Mikolaj Rej 180
Mineral Antwerpen 60
Mineral Hoboken 60
Mineral Luxembourg 60
Mineral Marchienne 60
Mineral Samitri 60
Ming Autumn 254
Ming Belle 254
Ming Cheer 254
Ming Comfort 254

Ming Courage 254
Ming Energy 254
Ming Fortune 254
Ming Galaxy 254
Ming Glory 254
Ming Hope 254
Ming Hua 8
Ming Joy 254
Ming Leader 254
Ming Longevity 254
Ming Mercy 254
Ming Moon 254
Ming Ocean 254
Ming Shine 254
Ming Spring 254
Ming Star 254
Ming Summer 254
Ming Sun 254
Ming Universe 254
Ming Winter 254
Ming Wisdom 254
Ming Xi Hai 56
Mino Maru 164
Mirafiori 86
Miranda 288
Miroslawiec 184
Misiones II 74
Mississippi 46
Mitla 220
Mitsui Maru No 2 140
Mitsui Maru 140
Mittenwalde 68
Mixteco 72
Mizoram 202
Mizukawa Maru 120
Mljet 118
Mobil Acme 142
Mobil Aladdin 142
Mobil Arctic 142
Mobil Astral 142
Mobil Australis 144
Mobil Brilliant 144
Mobil Challenge 142
Mobil Courage 142
Mobil Endeavour 142
Mobil Endurance 142
Mobil Engineer 144
Mobil Enterprise 144
Mobil Falcon 144
Mobil Flinders 144
Mobil Hawk 144
Mobil Kestrel 144
Mobil Marketer 144
Mobil Meridian 142
Mobil Navigator 144
Mobil Petrel 144
Mobil Producer 144
Mobil Refiner 144
Mobil Swift 144
Mobil Valiant 144
Mobil Vanguard 144
Moenjodaro 176

Molda 148
Moleson 212
Monet 94
Monge 94
Monique L.D. 132
Monisbon 122
Mont Blanc Maru 140
Montcalm 94
Monte Alto 74
Monte Cervantes 168
Monte Cristo 74
Monte Pascoal 74
Monte Rosa 168
Monte Sarmiento 168
Montenaken 62
Monterrey 220
Montsalva 62
Moordrecht 242
Moran 256
Morelia 72
Moreton Bay 174
Morgenster 206
Mormacdawn 234
Mormacglen 234
Mormacwave 234
Moscenice 116
Mosel Express 174
Moslavina 116
Mossovet 240
Mostbon 122
Motilal Nehru 202
Motovun 116
Mreznica 116
Muggelsee 68
Mulhausen Thomas-Muntzer
     Stadt 68
Multan 176
Mungo 136
Murree 176
Musashi Maru 164
Muse 140
Mutsu Maru 164
Muxima 64
Myoma Ywa 44
Myrmidon 166

Nacala 150
Nacella 198
Nacional Braganca 150
Nacional Faro 150
Nacional Figueira 150
Nacional Monchique 150
Nacional Sagres 150
Nacional Setubal 150
Nacional Sines 150
Nada III 164
Nada V 164
Nadezhda Obukhova 240
Naess Leopard 62
Naess Panther 62
Nagara 194
Nahoda Biru 86

Nalanda 146
Nan Hai Xi Wang 218
Nan Jiang 56
Nan Ping Shan 56
Nan Ping 56
Nancy Lykes 134
Nara 48
Narcis 256
Narica 198
Narnian Sea 94
Narval 48
Narwik II 184
Nasbon 122
Nassau Pride 250
Nathalie Delmas 150
Naticina 196
Naumburg 68
Nausicaa 48
Nautic Pioneer 170
Nawabshah 176
Nectarine 26
Nedlloyd Alkmaar 156
Nedlloyd Amersfoort 156
Nedlloyd Bahrain 152
Nedlloyd Baltimore 152
Nedlloyd Bangkok 152
Nedlloyd Barcelona 152
Nedlloyd Brussel 24
Nedlloyd Clarence 152
Nedlloyd Clement 152
Nedlloyd Colombo 152
Nedlloyd Dejima 154
Nedlloyd Delft 154
Nedlloyd Gooiland 156
Nedlloyd Hollandia 156
Nedlloyd Hoorn 154
Nedlloyd Houtman 154
Nedlloyd Katwijk 154
Nedlloyd Kembla 154
Nedlloyd Kimberley 154
Nedlloyd Kingston 154
Nedlloyd Kyoto 154
Nedlloyd Leuve 154
Nedlloyd Linge 154
Nedlloyd Loire 154
Nedlloyd Madras 154
Nedlloyd Manila 154
Nedlloyd Marseilles 154
Nedlloyd Moji 154
Nedlloyd Nagasaki 154
Nedlloyd Nagoya 154
Nedlloyd Napier 154
Nedlloyd Nassau 154
Nedlloyd Oranjestad 154
Nedlloyd Rochester 154
Nedlloyd Rosario 154
Nedlloyd Rotterdam 154
Nedlloyd Rouen 154
Nedlloyd San Juan 154
Nedlloyd Santos 154
Nedlloyd Seoul 154
Nedlloyd Singapore 154

Nedlloyd van Diemen 154
Nedlloyd van Neck 154
Nedlloyd van Noort 154
Nedlloyd Willemstad 154
Negba 256
Nehaj 116
Nei Jiang 56
Nele Maersk 146
Nelly Maersk 146
Nelson Maru 164
Neptune Ace 140
Neptune Agate 158
Neptune Aldebaran 158
Neptune Altair 158
Neptune Amber 158
Neptune Aries 158
Neptune Beryl 158
Neptune Canopus 158
Neptune Concord 224
Neptune Coral 158
Neptune Crystal 158
Neptune Cyprine 158
Neptune Diamond 158
Neptune Emerald 158
Neptune Iolite 158
Neptune Iris 158
Neptune Jasper 158
Neptune Kiku 158
Neptune Leo 158
Neptune Orion 158
Neptune Pavo 158
Neptune Pearl 158
Neptune Pegasus 158
Neptune Peridot 158
Neptune Ruby 158
Neptune Sapphire 158
Neptune Sardonyx 158
Neptune Schedar 158
Neptune Seginus 158
Neptune Sheratan 158
Neptune Sirius 158
Neptune Spinel 158
Neptune Tourmaline 158
Neptune Turquoise 158
Neptune 12
Nestor 166
Neubrandenburg 68
Neuquen II 74
Neverita 198
New Jersey Maru 140
New League 164
New Progress 140
New Promotion 140
New York Maru 140
New Zealand Caribbean 158
New Zealand Mariner 158
New Zealand Pacific 158
New Zealand Star 38
New Zealand Trader 158
Newark 192
Newforest 174
Nichigoh Maru 164

Nichirin Maru 164
Nicholas G. Papalios 24
Nicolai Maersk 146
Nicoline Maersk 146
Niels Maersk 146
Nienburg 68
Nieuw Amsterdam 14
Nihon 220
Nikel 240
Niko Nikoladze 240
Nikola Tesla 116
Nikolay Cherkasov 240
Nikolay Golovanov 240
Nikolay Kuznetsov 240
Nikolay Markin 240
Nikolay Tikhonov 240
Nikolay Voznesenskiy 240
Nile 154
Nimos 214
Ning Hai 56
Nippon Highway 120
Nippon Maru 16
Nipponica 88
Niso 198
Nisshu Maru 120
Nivi Ittuk 126
Nivosa 198
Nizhneyansk 240
Noble Supporter 170
Noordam 14
Nora Maersk 146
Norasia Caria 26
Norasia Carthago 26
Norasia Dagmar 124
Norasia Gabriele 246
Norasia Karsten 246
Norasia Rebecca 246
Norasia Samantha 246
Norasia Susan 246
Norbella 214
Nordanger 248
Nordhausen 68
Nordic Louisiana 30
Nordic Prince 18
Nordic Stream 114
Nordland 212
Norlandia 72
Norman Amstel 86
Norman King 48
Norman Lady 104
Norman Maas 86
Norman Prince 48
Norman Queen 48
Normannia 26
Norse Falcon 100
North Star 12
Northern Naiad 158
Northia 196
Norway 16
Nosac Barbro 132
Nosac Branco 132
Nosac Express 132

Nosac Mascot 132
Nosac Sel 132
Nosac Tasco 132
Nosac Verde 132
Nosira Lin 38
Nosira Madeleine 38
Nosira Sharon 38
Novi Vinodolski 116
Nowowiejski 180
Nurnberg Express 98
Nyala (Gr) 24
Nyala (Sud) 212
Nyhammer 98
Nyhavn 98
Nyholt 98
Nyhorn 98
Nyon 212

Oakland 192
Obernai 152
Oberon 246
Obo Baron 102
Obo Empress 102
Obo King 104
Obo Princess 104
Obo Queen 104
Obroncy Poczty 184
Ocean Cavalier 140
Ocean Commander 1 224
Ocean Envoy 176
Ocean Hawk 164
Ocean Highway 120
Ocean Islander 16
Ocean Legend 224
Ocean Pearl 60
Ocean Princess 16
Ocean Trader 60
Ocean Traveller 170
Ocean Voyager 208
Oceania Maru 140
Oceanic 14
Ocelot 204
Odessa 22
Ohminesan Maru 140
Ohrmazd 176
Ohtsu Maru 164
Oihonna 90
Olga Maersk 146
Olinda (BZ) 74
Olinda (Lib) 170
Olmeca 220
Oluf Maersk 146
Olympic Armour II 172
Olympic Aspiration 172
Olympic Avenger 172
Olympic Banner 172
Olympic Bond 172
Olympic Breeze 172
Olympic Brilliance 172
Olympic Dignity 172
Olympic Dream 172
Olympic Harmony 172

Olympic History 172
Olympic Hope 172
Olympic Leader 172
Olympic Liberty 172
Olympic Melody 172
Olympic Merit 172
Olympic Miracle 172
Olympic Peace 172
Olympic Phoenix 172
Olympic Progress 172
Olympic Promise 172
Olympic Rainbow 172
Olympic Splendour 172
Olympic Star 172
Olympic Sun II 172
Omdurman 212
Omex Pioneer 224
Ondina 198
Ondo Maru 164
One West No 7 122
One West No 8 122
One West No 9 122
Onga Maru 164
Ono 110
Onoe Maru No 2 164
Onyx 218
Opale 218
Opatija 116
Orange Ace 140
Oranjenburg 70
Orchid Ace 140
Oriana 18
Orient Maru 140
Oriental Ambassador 224
Oriental Bravery 224
Oriental Champion 224
Oriental Chief 224
Oriental Diplomat 224
Oriental Educator 224
Oriental Executive 224
Oriental Expert 224
Oriental Explorer 224
Oriental Exporter 224
Oriental Freedom 224
Oriental Govenor 224
Oriental Knight 226
Oriental Majesty 226
Oriental Merchant 226
Oriental Minister 226
Oriental Patriot 226
Oriental Phoenix (Li) 226
Oriental Phoenix (Pan) 164
Oriental Pine 140
Oriental Premier 226
Oriental Prince 226
Oriental Road 120
Oriental Sovereign 226
Oriental Star 226
Oriental Taio 226
Orinoco 86
Orion Diamond 164
Orion Highway 120

Orion 14
Orjen 116
Orkanger 248
Oroya 92
Orpheus 12
Orque 48
Ortelius 62
Osaka Bay 174
Oscar Ace 140
Oswestry Grange 92
OT Garth 250
Otello 246
Otto Grotevohl 240
Otto Leonhardt 128
Otto N. Miller 50
Ove Skou 206
Overseas Argonaut 130
Owari Maru 164

Pacific Aries 164
Pacific Challenge 228
Pacific Courage 226
Pacific Defender 226
Pacific Exporter 226
Pacific Express 66
Pacific Faith 226
Pacific Fortune 226
Pacific Freedom 226
Pacific Friendship 226
Pacific Gallantry 226
Pacific Grace 226
Pacific Greeting 226
Pacific Guardian 226
Pacific Highway 120
Pacific Importer 226
Pacific Insurer 226
Pacific Islander 214
Pacific Patriot 226
Pacific Peace 226
Pacific Prestige 226
Pacific Pride 226
Pacific Princess 18
Pacific Progress 226
Pacific Prominence 226
Pacific Prosperity 226
Pacific Road 120
Pacific Trader 164
Pacific Universal 206
Padang 76
Paderewski 180
Pag 116
Pago 44
Palizzi 126
Pallas 90
Palmah II 256
Palmiro Togliatti 240
Paludina 196
Panama (Dmk) 72
Panama Maru 140
Panama (US) 192
Pancaldo 88
Papuan Chief 214

Papyrus Maru 164
Paralla 220
Paramount Ace 226
Paranagua 72
Parandowski 180
Parfentiy Grechanyy 240
Parnassos 26
Parvati 202
Pasadena 72
Pascal 94
Pasewalk 70
Passero 100
Patagonia 72
Patria 90
Patricia Delmas 150
Patricia R. 172
Patricia VI 140
Patriotic 126
Pattaya 72
Paul L. Fahrney 50
Paul 188
Paula Maersk 146
Pavel Rybin 240
Pavel Vavilov 240
Pawel Szwydkoj 180
Pazin 116
Pearl of Scandinavia 16
Pecten 198
Pegasus 12
Peggy Dow 66
Peljesac 118
Pelleas 28
Penavel 152
Penbreizh 152
Penchateau 152
Pengall 152
Penthievre 152
Pereira d'Eca 64
Permeke 62
Peter Maersk 146
Peter Rickmers 186
Petersfield 132
Petr Masherov 240
Petr Smorodin 240
Petr Velikiy 240
Petrogas II 62
Pharos 124
Phenian 180
Philadephia 192
Philippine Obo 2 228
Philippine Obo 3 228
Philippine Obo 4 228
Philippine Sampaguita 252
Phillips America 178
Phillips Arkansas 178
Phillips Enterprise 178
Phillips Mexico 178
Phillips Oklahoma 178
Phillips Venezuela 178
Philmac Venturer 178
Pieniny II 184
Pierre LD 132

Pikebank 34
Pilar 222
Ping Ding Shan 56
Ping Jiang 56
Pinya 44
Piotr Dunin 180
Pisces Pioneer 100
Pisces Planter 100
Pistis 30
Pittsburgh 192
Planeta 124
Plantin 62
Plata 124
Plitvice 118
Pobeda 240
Podhale 184
Pointe la Rose 94
Pointe Madame 94
Pointe Sans Souci 94
Poitou 152
Pokkinen 88
Polar Alaska 178
Pollenger 174
Pollux 90
Polyclipper 184
Polycrest 186
Polycrusader 186
Polynesia (Li) 214
Polynesia (No) 186
Polystar 186
Polysunrise 186
Polytrader 186
Polytraveller 186
Polyvictoria 186
Polyviking 186
Pomella 196
Pomorze Zachodnie ???
Porer 118
Porsanger 248
Port Bara 244
Port Blanc 244
Port Hawkesbury 46
Port Joinville 244
Port Latta Maru 140
Port Quebec 46
Port Royal 134
Port Vancouver 46
Port Vendres 244
Portland 192
Porto 54
Potsdam 70
Powstaniec Listopadowy 184
Powstaniec Slaski 184
Powstaniec Warszawski 184
Powstaniec Wielkpolski 184
Poznan 180
Premnitz 70
President Cleveland 26
President Eisenhower 26
President F. D. Roosevelt 26
President Fillmore 26
President Grant 26

President Hoover 26
President Jackson 26
President Jefferson 26
President Johnson 26
President Kennedy 26
President Lincoln 26
President Madison 26
President McKinley 26
President Monroe 26
President Pierce 26
President Taft 26
President Taylor 26
President Truman 26
President Tyler 26
President Van Buren 28
President Washington 28
President Wilson 28
Presidente Ramon S. Castillo 74
Priamurye 22
Pride 226
Prignitz 70
Prima Maersk 146
Pritzwalk 70
Probo Bani 122
Profesor Mierzejewski 180
Profesor Rylke 180
Profesor Szafer 180
Professor Kostiukov 240
Professor Tovstykh 240
Prosperity 128
Protektor 124
Proud Eagle 246
Providence Bay 174
Prvi Februar 116
Puebla 220
Puhos 88
Pulborough 210
Pulkownik Dabek 180
Puritan 124
Pyatidesyatiletiye Obtyabrye 240

Qarouh 232
Qatari Ibn Al Fuja'a 232
Qi Lian Shan 56
Qi Men 56
Qian Shan 56
Qing He Cheng 56
Qing He 56
Qing Jiang 56
Qing Shui 56
Qiu He 56
Quan Zhou Hai 56
Quedlinburg 70
Queen Elizabeth 2 10
Queen of Sheeba 78
Queen's Way Bridge 120
Quelimane 150
Quellin 62

R. A. Emerson 46
R. R. Ratna 226
Rab 116

Rabenau 70
Radebeul 70
Rafaela (Bz) 74
Rafaela (Pan) 138
Raffaele Cafiero 126
Ragna Gorthon 96
Ragnhild Brovig 42
Rainbow Ace 140
Ralph B. Johnson 50
Ramdas 202
Randi Brovig 42
Rangamati 176
Rani Padmini 202
Rapana 196
Raphael 240
Rapid 48
Raqefet 256
Ras Al Barshah 124
Ras Al Jlay'Ah 124
Ras Al Zour 124
Ras Dedgen 78
Ratih 226
Rautaruukki 88
Ravenscraig 186
Ravidas 202
Red Sea 204
Regent Sea 18
Regina D. 138
Regina Maersk 146
Regina Prima 8
Regina 214
Rehab 124
Remuera Bay 174
Renata 74
Renate Leonhardt 128
Renee Delmas 150
Renee Rickmers 186
Renoir 94
Republica de Colombia 90
Resolution Bay 174
Reynolds 38
Rhapsody 8
Rhea 90
Rhein Express 62
Rhenania 26
Rhine Maru 140
Rhinsee 70
Richard Sorge 240
Richmond Bridge 120
Rigel 218
Rigoletto 246
Rijeka 116
Rimba Balau 136
Rimba Keruing 136
Rimba Meranti 136
Rimba Merbau 136
Rimba Ramin 136
Rimba Sepetir 136
Rimula 196
Rio Abaucan 74
Rio Branco 130
Rio Calchaqui 74

Rio Calingasta 74
Rio Cincel 74
Rio Corrientes 76
Rio Cuanza 64
Rio Cuyamel 232
Rio de la Plata 76
Rio Deseado 76
Rio Esquel 76
Rio Frio 66
Rio Grande 130
Rio Gualeguay 76
Rio Iguazu 76
Rio Limay 76
Rio Los Sauces 76
Rio Magdalena 76
Rio Marapa 76
Rio Negro (Bz) 130
Rio Negro II (Arg) 76
Rio Neuquen 76
Rio Olivia 76
Rio Parana 76
Rio Pilcomayo 76
Rio Plata 242
Rio Purus 130
Rio Salado 76
Rio Sixaola 232
Rio Sulaco 232
Rio Tefe 130
Rio Teuco 76
Rio Trombetas 130
Rio Verde 130
Rio Zambeze 64
Risan 116
Risanger 248
River Aboine 162
River Adada 160
River Andoni 160
River Asab 160
River Guma 160
River Gurara 160
River Hadejia 160
River Ikpan 160
River Jimini 160
River Kerawa 160
River Mada 160
River Maje 162
River Majidun 162
River Ngada 162
River Ogbese 162
River Oji 162
River Oli 162
River Oshun 162
River Osse 162
River Princess 120
River Rima 162
Rjecina 116
Roachbank 34
Robert E. Lee 246
Roberto 188
Rocadas 64
Rodin 94
Rodlo 184

Rogate 210
Rokkahsan Maru 140
Rolnik 184
Roman Pazinski 180
Romandie 212
Romanza 8
Romer 180
Romney 38
Roncesvalles 222
Rong Jiang 56
Ronneburg 70
Ronsard 48
Rora Head 188
Ro-Ro Genova 94
Ro-Ro Manhattan 94
Rosa Blanca 114
Rosa S 138
Rosa Tucano 248
Rosandra 150
Rosia Bay 204
Rostand 94
Rostock 70
Rostov 240
Rosyth 228
Rotterdam 14
Rousseau 94
Rover 48
Royal Odyssey 18
Royal Princess 18
Royal Viking Sea 16
Royal Viking Sky 16
Royal Viking Star 16
Rubens 38
Ruder Boskovic 118
Rudolf Breitscheid 70
Rudolf Diesel 70
Rudolph Peterson 50
Rudolstadt 70
Ruth Lykes 134
Ruth 194

SA Helderberg 208
SA Langeberg 208
SA Sederberg 208
SA Vaal 208
SA Waterberg 208
SA Winterberg 208
Sabie 208
Sable 24
Sachem 142
Sachikawa Maru 120
Sacramento Highway 120
Safocean Mildura 154
Safocean Nederburg 208
Sagafjord 10
Sagaing 44
Sagami Maru 164
Saikai Maru 164
Saint Roch 104
Saint Roland 104
Saint Romain 104
Salah Aldeen 232

Salina 204
Salla 90
Salland 156
Sally Maersk 146
Sally Ocean 120
Salmonpool 186
Salta 76
Sam Houston 246
Samaria 64
Samoan Reefer 126
Samrat Ashok 202
Samu 228
Samudragupta 202
Samuel H. Armacost 50
San Andres y Providencia 90
San Francisco 114
San Juan 76
San Luis 76
San Pedro 192
Sanchi 202
Sandra Wesch 246
Sandys Bay 192
Sangerhausen 70
Santa Cruz II 76
Santa Fe II 76
Santa Marta 60
Santiago del Estero 76
Sanyo Maru 164
Sapele 166
Sapporo Maru 164
Sarda 226
Sarfaraz Rafiqi 176
Sargodha 176
Sarita 220
Sarnia 76
Satsuma 26
Satucket 142
Saudi Glory 144
Sava 116
Savonita 228
Saxon Star 170
Saxonia 64
Scamper Universal 208
Scandia Team 70
Scandinavian Highway 120
Schonwalde 70
Schwarzburg 70
Schwedt 70
Schwerin 70
Schwielowsee 70
Scirocco Universal 208
Scottish Eagle 40
Scottish Lion 40
Scottish Star 38
Scythia 64
Sea Goddess I 20
Sea Goddess II 20
Sea Merchant 208
Sea Pioneer 208
Sea Princess 18
Sea Scout 170
Sea Taian 134

Sea Transporter 208
Sea-Land Adventurer 192
Sea-Land Consumer 192
Sea-Land Defender 192
Sea-Land Developer 192
Sea-Land Economy 192
Sea-Land Endurance 192
Sea-Land Explorer 192
Sea-Land Express 192
Sea-Land Freedom 192
Sea-Land Independence 192
Sea-Land Innovator 192
Sea-Land Leader 192
Sea-Land Liberator 192
Sea-Land Mariner 192
Sea-Land Pacer 192
Sea-Land Patriot 192
Sea-Land Pioneer 192
Sea-Land Producer 192
Sea-Land Venture 192
Sea-Land Voyager 192
Seaward Bay 192
Seafreight Freeway 194
Seafreight Highway 194
Seawise Giant 226
Selandia 72
Senftenberg 70
Senj 116
Senshu Maru 164
Sentis 226
Serantes 244
Serena 88
Serenia 196
Serpa Pinto 64
Servia 64
Setsuyo Maru 164
Seven Ocean 120
Seven Seas Bridge 120
Sha He 56
Shahjehan 202
Shalamar 176
Shams 176
Shan Yin 56
Shao Xing 56
Sheldon Gas 62
Sheldon Lykes 134
Shelly Bay 192
Shen Zhou 56
Shi Tang Hai 56
Shigeo Nagano 36
Shin Ohgishima Maru 164
Shin Sakura Maru 16
Shinano Maru 164
Shinanogawa Maru 120
Shiraishi Maru 164
Shirley Lykes 134
Shiromine Maru 164
Shirotae Maru 164
Shoho Maru No 2 120
Shoho Maru 120
Shokawa Maru 120
Shota Rustaveli 22

Shuho Maru 120
Shun-ei Maru 120
Siam 200
Sibelius 94
Sibi 176
Sibig Venture 222
Sibofem 222
Siboseven 222
Sidelia 226
Siekierki 184
Siemiatycze 180
Sienkiewicz 180
Sierra Express 100
Sigal 256
Sils 212
Silvaplana 212
Silver Ace 142
Silverland 42
Silvia Sofia 220
Silvretta 212
Simon Bolivar 90
Simon Gas 62
Simona 1 138
Sine Maersk 146
Sir Alexander Glen 218
Sir Charles Hambro 186
Sir Charles Parsons 188
Sir John Fisher 90
Sirius Highway 120
Sishen 208
Sissili River 38
Sit-Tway 44
Skaubord 206
Skaugran 206
Skauvann 206
Skeena 206
Skulptor Golubkina 240
Skulptor Konenkov 240
Skulptor Vuchetich 240
Skulptor Zalkalns 240
Sky Clipper 232
Skyward 16
Slavonija 116
Slovenija 116
Smolensk 242
Smolny 180
Snimos Ace 164
Snimos King 164
Sofia 242
Sofie Maersk 146
Sokolica II 184
Sokoto 166
Solaris 198
Sologne 152
Solon Turman 134
Somers Bay 192
Sonderhausen 70
Song Lin 56
Song of America 18
Song of Norway 18
Sonia M 220
Sonisbon 122

Sonneberg 70
Sonora 220
Sophie B. 132
Sophie Rickmers 186
Soufflot 94
South County 26
South Faith 26
South Victor 226
Southern Cross Trader 142
Southern Pacific 60
Southern Progress 60
Southland Star 38
Southward 16
Sovereign Accord 164
Sovetskaya Neft 242
Sovfracht 242
Sovetskiy Khudozhnik 242
Sovinflot 242
Spectrum 198
Speedster Universal 40
Spinanger 248
Splendid Fortune 170
Spring Bear 66
Spring Bob 66
Spring Delight 62
Spring Panda 66
St Helena 20
St Louis 192
St Michaelis 170
St Nikolai 170
St Petri 170
Staffordshire 36
Star Dieppe 36
Star Dover 36
Star Eagle 36
Star Evviva 36
Star Florida 36
Star Fraser 36
Star Fuji 36
Star Hong Kong 252
Star Lanao 172
Star Magnate 252
Star Mercury 252
Star Orient 252
Star Sulu 172
Star World 252
Stardancer 20
Starward 16
Staszic 180
State of Andhra Pradesh 202
State of Gujarat 202
State of Haryana 202
State of Himachal Pradesh 202
State of Madhya Pradesh 202
State of Maharashtra 202
State of Manipur 202
State of Meghalaya 202
State of Mysore 202
State of Nagaland 202
State of Orissa 202
State of Punjab 202
State of Tripura 202

State of West Bengal 202
Stavros G. L. 128
Stefan Batory 18
Stefan Czarniecki 180
Stefan Starzynski 180
Stella Lykes 134
Stella Maris II 20
Stella Oceanis 20
Stella Solaris 20
Stellaris 226
Stellata 198
Stena Adriatica 208
Stena Arctica 208
Stena Atlantica 208
Stena Caribica 208
Stena Carrier 208
Stena Freighter 208
Stena Grecia 210
Stena Hispania 210
Stena Ionia 210
Stena Oceanica 210
Stena Pacifica 210
Stena Transporter 210
Stepan Artemenko 242
Stepan Razin 242
Stig Gorthon 96
Stollberg 70
Stolt Aquamarine 210
Stolt Avance 210
Stolt Avenir 210
Stolt Boel 210
Stolt Castle 210
Stolt Condor 210
Stolt Crown 210
Stolt Eagle 210
Stolt Emerald 210
Stolt Energie 152
Stolt Entente 152
Stolt Excellence 210
Stolt Falcon 210
Stolt Hawk 210
Stolt Heron 210
Stolt Integrity 210
Stolt Llandaff 210
Stolt Loyalty 210
Stolt Osprey 210
Stolt Pride 210
Stolt Sapphire 210
Stolt Sceptre 210
Stolt Sea 210
Stolt Sheaf 210
Stolt Sincerity 212
Stolt Span 212
Stolt Spirit 212
Stolt Spur 212
Stolt Stane 212
Stolt Surf 212
Stolt Sydness 212
Stolt Templar 212
Stolt Tenacity 212
Stolt Ventura 70
Stolt Venture n212

Stolt Vincita 70
Stonewall Jackson 246
Stolt Venture 212
Stolt Vincita 70
Stonewall Jackson 246
Storrington 210
Stove Campbell 206
Stove Trader 206
Storrington 210
Stove Campbell 206
Stove Trader 206
Stove Transport 206
Stratus 218
Stream Balabac 148
Stream Bantayan 148
Stream Biliran 148
Stream Busuanga 148
Strider Crystal 194
Strider Exeter 194
Strider Fearless 194
Strider Juno 194
Strymon 128
Studzianki 184
Stuttgart Express 100
Subin River 38
Sudan Crown 44
Suhl 70
Sulu Bay 190
Sumadija 116
Sumburgh Head 188
Sun Hope 164
Sun Kobe 120
Sun Maya 120
Sun Princess 18
Sun River 120
Sun Viking 18
Sunda Sea 76
Sunderbans 176
Sunny Wisteria 142
Sunward II 16
Super Servant 1 248
Super Servant 3 248
Super Servant 4 248
Super Servant 5 248
Super Servant 6 248
Susak 116
Susan B. 122
Susan Maersk 148
Sutjeska 116
Suzanne Delmas 150
Suzukasan Maru 142
Svend Maersk 148
Svendborg Maersk 148
Swibon 122
Swiecie 180
Sydney Express 100
Syn Pulku 184

Tabuk 232
Tachibana 248
Tacna II 250
Tactic 126

Tadeusz Kosciuszko 180
Tadeusz Ocioszynski 180
Tagama 76
Tagasan Maru 142
Tagelus 198
Tai Bai Shan 56
Tai Xing 56
Tai Zhou Hai 56
Taibit 70
Taichu 134
Taiei Maru 164
Taikai Maru 142
Tajima Maru 164
Takasago 250
Takasaka Maru 164
Takatorisan Maru 142
Takayama Maru 166
Takayama 250
Talabot 250
Tama Maru 142
Tamaitai Samoa 170
Tamarita 228
Tamba Maru 166
Tang He 56
Tango Maru 166
Tanja Jacob 110
Tankerman 186
Tano River 38
Tao Lin 56
Taras Schevchenko 22
Tarbela 176
Tarcoola 250
Target 104
Tasman 154
Tatra 250
Tatry 184
Taurus (Fi) 90
Taurus (No) 250
Tausala Samoa 170
Tavara 194
Taxila 176
Team Borga 148
Team Frosta 148
Team Troma 148
Tectus 196
Tellier 94
Tellus 90
Telnes 112
Temse 62
Tenaga Dua 136
Tenaga Empat 136
Tenaga Lima 136
Tenaga Satu 136
Tenaga Tiga 136
Tenchbank 34
Tennessee 250
Tenryu Maru 166
Tenryusan Maru 142
Tepozteco 220
Tertnes 112
Testarosa 60
Texaco Africa 214

Texaco Baltic 216
Texaco Bergen 216
Texaco Bogota 216
Texaco Brasil 214
Texaco California 214
Texaco Caribbean 214
Texaco Connecticut 214
Texaco Darien 216
Texaco Florida 216
Texaco Georgia 216
Texaco Hannover 216
Texaco Ireland 216
Texaco Japan 216
Texaco Maine 216
Texaco Maryland 216
Texaco Massachusetts 216
Texaco Melbourne 216
Texaco Minnesota 216
Texaco Mississippi 216
Texaco Montana 216
Texaco Nederland 216
Texaco New York 216
Texaco Norge 216
Texaco Ohio 216
Texaco Oslo 216
Texaco Rhode Island 216
Texaco Skandinavia 216
Texaco South America 216
Texaco Stockholm 216
Texaco Texas 216
Texaco Veraguas 216
Texaco Westminster 216
Texaco Windsor 216
Texas Getty 216
TFL Adams 148
TFL Democracy 218
TFL Enterprise 218
TFL Express 218
TFL Franklin 26
TFL Freedom 218
TFL Independence 218
TFL Jefferson 218
TFL Liberty 218
Thalatta 250
Thale 70
Thames Maru 142
Thamesfield 90
The Victoria 8
Thebeland 220
Theben 250
Theekar 232
Themis 250
Theodor Fontane 70
Theodor Korner 70
Theodor Storm 70
Theofano Livanos 128
Therese Delmas 150
Thermidor 150
Thompson Lykes 134
Thor I 64
Thorsaga 64
Thorscape 64

Thorseggen 64
Thorsholm 64
Thuleland 42
Tian Men 56
Tian Tai Shan 56
Tibor Szamueli 242
Tielrode 62
Tierra del Fuego II 76
Tigre 126
Tikhon Kiselev 242
Tiksi 242
Tilia Gorthon 96
Tilia 176
Tillie Lykes 134
Tilly 188
Tina 128
Tineke 66
Tinnes 112
Titan 120
Tivat 116
TNT Express 218
Toana Papua 34
Tobruk 184
Tohoku Maru 120
Tokio Express 100
Tokitsu Maru 166
Tokiwa Maru 166
Tokurasan Maru 142
Tokyo Bay 174
Tokyo Highway 120
Tokyo Maru 142
Tolaga Bay 174
Toluca 218
Toluma 250
Tong Cheng 56
Tong Chuan 56
Tong Hai 58
Tongala 250
Topusko 116
Tor Bay 174
Torgnes 112
Torm Alice 218
Torm Rask 218
Torm Rotna 218
Torm Thyra 218
Tornes 112
Toro Horten 250
Torre del Greco 88
Torvanger 248
Tosca 246
Tottori Maru 166
Toulon 94
Touraine 152
Tourcoing 250
Toyama 250
Toyoshima Maru 120
Toyota Maru No 15 120
Toyota Maru No 16 120
Toyota Maru No 18 166
Toyota Maru No 19 166
Toyota Maru No 20 166
Toyota No 23 226

Trade Winds 142
Transvaal 76
Transworld Bridge 120
Trattendorf 70
Traviata 246
Treci Maj 116
Trenntsee 70
Trepca 116
Tribulus 196
Tricula 196
Trieste 88
Trigger 104
Triglav 116
Trinaesti Juli 118
Tristan 246
Troll Lake 250
Troll Maple 250
Troll Viking 250
Trollnes 112
Tropicale 8
Troutbank 34
Trsat 116
Tsukubasan Maru 142
Tsushima Maru 166
Tu Men Jiang 58
Tucuman 76
Tuhobic 116
Tuira 88
Tulsa Getty 216
Tulsidas 200
Tunisian Reefer 126
Tuo He 58
Turkmeniya 22
Turoszow 184
Tyrusland 220
Tyson Lykes 134

Ubena 76
Ucka 118
Uganda 18
Ugland Obo 5 228
Ugland Obo-One 228
Ugland Obo-Six 228
Ujigawa Maru 120
Ukraina 22
Umm Al Aish 124
Umm Al Jathathel 124
Umm Al Maradem 124
Umm Al Negah 124
Umm Al Roos 124
Umm Casbah 124
Umm Matrabh 124
Umm Ruwaisat 124
Umm Shaif 30
Unan Avetisyan 242
Uni-Forever 80
Uni-Fortune 80
Uni-Forward 80
Uni-Handsome 80
Uni-Humanity 80
Uni-Master 80
Uni-Mercy 80

Uni-Modest 80
Uni-Moral 80
Uni-Pioneer 80
Uni-Promoter 80
United Approach 252
United Drive 252
United Effort 252
United Enterprise 252
United Faith 252
United Hope 252
United Peace 252
United Spirit 252
United Venture 170
Unity 30
Universe 20
Uniwersytet Gdanski 184
Uniwersytet Jagiellonski 184
Uniwersytet Slaski 184
Uniwersytet Warszawski 184
Uniwersytet Wroclawski 184
Ursaula Leonhardt 128
Ursus 180
Usaramo 76
Utrillo 94

Vacationer 22
Valdivia 100
Valencia 102
Valentina Frias 244
Valeria 138
Valetta Trader 42
Vallabhai Patel 202
Vallathol 202
Valvanuz 222
Van Dyck 62
Vanil 212
Vanja 70
Varjakka 88
Varna 242
Vasilis 136
Vasiliy Azhaev 242
Vasiliy Koval 242
Vasiliy Matuzenko 242
Vasiliy Solovyev Sedoy 242
Vegaland 220
Velebit 116
Velma Lykes 134
Velma 70
Vendee 174
Vendemiaire 150
Venture Europe 62
Venture Independence 62
Venture 208
Venus Venturer 10
Venus 16 18
Veracruz 1 8
Vered 256
Vergelegen 208
Vermilion Highway 120
Veronique Delmas 150
Verrazano Bridge 120
Vesalius 62

Vesna 72
Vesta 166
Victoria Bay 76
Victory 208
Vida 72
Vigan 70
Viking Chief 112
Vikingland 220
Ville d'Anvers 152
Ville de Bordeaux 152
Ville de Dunkerque 152
Ville de Genes 152
Ville de Lumiere 186
Ville de Marseille 152
Ville de Nantes 152
Ville de Strasbourg 152
Ville du Havre 152
Ville du Ponant III 72
Ville du Sahara 72
Vinga 148
Vinnitsa 242
Violet Ocean 120
Violetta 136
Virgo 256
Vishva Abha 202
Vishva Aditya 202
Vishva Ajay 202
Vishva Ambar 202
Vishva Amitabh 202
Vishva Anurag 202
Vishva Apurva 202
Vishva Asha 202
Vishva Bandham 202
Vishva Bhakti 202
Vishva Dharma 202
Vishva Jyoti 202
Vishva Karuna 202
Vishva Kaumudi 202
Vishva Madhuri 202
Vishva Mamta 202
Vishva Maya 202
Vishva Mohini 202
Vishva Nandini 202
Vishva Nayak 202
Vishva Nidhi 202
Vishva Pallav 202
Vishva Pankaj 202
Vishva Parag 202
Vishva Parijat 202
Vishva Parimal 202
Vishva Prafulla 202
Vishva Prayas 202
Vishva Raksha 202
Vishva Seva 202
Vishva Shakti 204
Vishva Shobha 204
Vishva Siddhi 204
Vishva Sudha 204
Vishva Tarang 204
Vishva Tej 204
Vishva Tirth 204
Vishva Umang 204

Vishva Vibhuti 204
Vishva Vikram 204
Vishva Vivek 204
Vishva Yash 204
Vistafjord 10
Vitina 136
Vitrea 198
Vivita 228
Vladimir Gavrilov 242
Vockerode 70
Vojvodina 116
Volans 76
Volere 126
Volkerfreundschaft 12
Volosko 116
Volta River 38
Vosges 174

W. A. Mather 46
W. C. Van Horne 46
W. M. Neal 46
Waalekerk 156
Wakaba Maru 166
Wakagiku Maru 166
Wakakusa Maru 166
Wakamizu Maru 166
Wakanami Maru 166
Wakatake Maru 166
Wakaume Maru 166
Walchand 190
Walka Mlodych 184
Walter Leonhardt 128
Wanderer 100
Wang Jiang 58
Wang Ting 58
Warden Point 218
Warrior 100
Warsak 176
Washington 210
Wayfarer 100
Wei He 58
Weimar 70
Wellington Star 38
Wen Deng Hai 58
Wen Zhou Hai 58
Wendy 142
Werbellinsee 70
Werner Seelenbinder 70
Weser Ore 226
West Daori 122
West Jinoriwon 122
West Junori 122
West Mannori 122
West Sunori 124
West Wonori 124
Westbon 124
Westerkerk 156
Western Glory 170
Western Highway 120
Westerplatte 180
Westfield 132
Westin Won 124

Westin 124
White Nile 212
Wieldrecht 242
Wieliczka 180
Wilanna 248
Wild Eagle 246
Wilhelm Florin 70
Wilhelm Wesch 246
Willemskerk 156
William E. Mussman 50
Willine Taro 250
Willine Tokyo 242
Willine Toyo 250
Willine Tysla 250
Willowbank 34
Wilmington 210
Wilmona 248
Wilnina 248
Wilnora 248
Wiltshire 36
Windward 100
Wismar 70
Wissekerk 156
Wittenberg 70
Wladyslaw Jagiello 180
Wladyslaw Lokietek 180
Wladyslaw Orkan 180
Wladyslaw Sikorski 180
Wladyslawowo 180
Woensdrecht 242
Woermann Wadai 76
Woermann Wakamba 76
Wonsbon 124
World Achilles II 158
World Admiral 252
World Aegeus 160
World Agamemnon 160
World Ajax 160
World Ambassador 252
World Amber 252
World Amphion 160
World Apollo 160
World Ares 160
World Aretus 160
World Argonaut 160
World Argus 160
World Bormuda 252
World Brasilia 252
World Brigadier 252
World Canada 252
World Castle 252
World Challenger 252
World Cheer 252
World Cliff 252
World Creation 252
World Crown 252
World Crystal 252
World Dawn 252
World Diamond 252
World Dove 252
World Duality 160
World Duet 160

World Duke 252
World Dulce 252
World Eden 252
World Eminence 252
World Encouragement 252
World Fame 252
World Finance 252
World Flora 252
World Fortress 252
World Freeport 252
World Gala 252
World Hitachi Zosen 252
World Jade 252
World Kinship 160
World Kudos 160
World Light 252
World Lion 192
World Lynx 192
World Marine 160
World Nancy 252
World Nature 160
World Nautilus 160
World Navigator 160
World Negotiator 160
World News 160
World Nisseki 252
World NKK 252
World Nobility 160
World Nomad 160
World Oak 252
World Pearl 254
World Petrobras 254
World President 254
World Process 160
World Produce 160
World Progress 254
World Prologue 160
World Prophet 160
World Protector 160
World Radiance 254
World Rainbow 254
World Ranger 254
World Recovery 160
World Renaissance 12
World Renown 254
World Resolve 160
World Scholar 160
World Score 160
World Sky 254
World Spear 254
World Splendour 254
World Spring 254
World Sun 254
World Symphony 254
World Texas 254
World Tiger 192
World Trophy 254
World Truth 254
World Umpire 160
World Utility 160
World Vale 254
World Zeal 254

Wroclaw 182
Wu Jiang 58
Wu Tai Shan 58

Xi Feng Kou 58
Xia Hai 58
Xia Men 58
Xiang Cheng 58
Xiang He 58
Xin Feng 58
Xing Cheng 58
Xing He 58
Xing Hua 58

Ya Lu Jiang 58
Yaffa 194
Yakasse 110
Yama 1 256
Yamatogawa 120
Yamoussoukro 110
Yan Shan 58
Yan Ting 58
Yanbu Pride 144
Yanbu Progress 144
Yang Ming Shan 58
Yao Hua 8
Yaqui 220
Yasnoye 242
Yemelyan Pugachev 242
Yevgeniy Vakhtangov 242
Yi Men 58
Yolande Delmas 150
Yonekawa Maru 120
Yong Chun 58
Yong Ding 58
Yong Feng Hai 58
Yong Jiang 58
Yong Ning 58
Yong Xing 58
Yopougon 110
Yorkshiro 36
You Hao 58
Yu Jiang 58
Yu Lin 58
Yu Men 58
Yuan Jiang 58
Yujin 166
Yulius Fuchik 242
Yuriy Dolgorukiy 242
Yun Cheng 58
Yun Tai Shan 58

Zabrze 182
Zadonsk 242
Zafra 198
Zaglebie Dabrowskie 184
Zaglebie Miedziowe 184
Zagreb 182
Zakarpatye 242
Zakopane 182
Zambesi 76
Zambeze 94

Zambrow 182
Zaporozhye 242
Zarechensk 242
Zawichost 182
Zawiercie 182
Zawrat 184
Zeebrugge (Be) 228
Zeebrugge (Fr) 94
Zeelandia 156
Zeromski 182
Zeta 118
Zhang Heng 58
Zhang Jia Kou 58
Zhang Yang Hai 58
Zhen Jiang 58
Zheng Rong Hai 58
Zhi Hai 58

Zhong Shan 58
Zhu Hai 58
Zi Jin Shan 58
Ziemia Bialostocka 184
Ziemia Bydgoska 184
Ziemia Chelminska 184
Ziemia Gnieznienska 184
Ziemia Kielecka 184
Ziemia Koszalinska 184
Ziemia Krakowska 184
Ziemia Lubuska 184
Ziemia Mazowiecka 184
Ziemia Olsztynska 184
Ziemia Opolska 184
Ziemia Suwalska 184
Ziemia Szczecinska 184
Ziemia Tarnowska 184

Ziemia Wielkopolska 184
Ziemia Zamojska 184
Zim Brisbane 72
Zim Buenos Aires 256
Zim California 256
Zim Eilat 256
Zim Genova 256
Zim Haifa 256
Zim Hong Kong 256
Zim Houston 256
Zim Iberia 256
Zim Keelung 256
Zim Marseille 256
Zim Miami 256
Zim Montreal 256
Zim New Orleans 256
Zim New York 256

Zim Savannah 256
Zim Singapore 256
Zim Tokyo 256
Zlatoust 242
Zoella Lykes 134
Zolotye Dyuny 242
Zorinsk 242
Zoya Kosmodemysanskaya 242
Zvenigorod 242
Zwickau 70
Zygmunt August 182
Zygmunt III Waza 182
Zygmunt Stary 182
Zyrardow 182